THIS MUST BE THE PLACE

JESSE RIFKIN

THIS MUST BE THE PLACE

MUSIC, COMMUNITY AND
VANISHED SPACES IN NEW YORK CITY

HANOVER
SQUARE
PRESS

HANOVER
SQUARE
PRESS™

ISBN-13: 978-1-335-44932-0

This Must Be the Place

Hanover Square Press
22 Adelaide St. West, 41st Floor
Toronto, Ontario M5H 4E3, Canada
HanoverSqPress.com
BookClubbish.com

Printed in U.S.A.

In memory of my brother
Brady Ian Rifkin
6/10/66–1/1/21

TABLE OF CONTENTS

INTRODUCTION

NEW YORK IS OVER!
(IF YOU WANT IT)

On May 1, 2010, Patti Smith—the groundbreaking musician and poet who helped birth New York City's punk scene in the 1970s—appeared with author Jonathan Lethem at Cooper Union's Great Hall in a promotional event for her memoir *Just Kids*, released earlier that year. During the Q and A, one attendee asked Smith if she thought it was still possible for young artists and musicians to come to New York and have the kind of freewheeling bohemian experiences she'd vividly chronicled in her book. Smith replied in the negative: "New York has closed itself off to the young and the struggling. But there are other cities. Detroit. Poughkeepsie. New York City has been taken away from you. So my advice is: Find a new city."[1]

Though she surely meant well, Smith's declaration felt frustrating and a little patronizing. Of course, it was also one of the most stereotypically "New York" things she could say, as there are few things that New Yorkers seem to relish more than declaring the city "over." A beloved diner closes: "New York is over." A dog park opens: "New York is over." A Republican sets foot below 23rd Street: "New York is over."

But what do people mean, exactly, when they declare New York City over? In Smith's case, perhaps one could have fairly declared the slice of the East Village where she and her peers made their careers in the '70s—an area now overrun with fancy boutiques, luxury apartments, and twenty-four-year-old marketing managers who have big plans to go to the *Friends* Experience on 23rd Street this weekend—as not currently in its creative prime. But what about, for example, Death By Audio, the all-ages DIY venue in Williamsburg, Brooklyn? In 2010, when Smith was reading the city's death notice, Death By Audio was at the peak of its powers, incubating a scene every bit as vibrant (if less profitable) as the one she had participated in back in the day.

In my work as a music historian in the city, I frequently encounter NYC residents eager to declare that the city's best days are behind it, that it could never again incubate the kind of creative culture it once did. I've noticed that depending on who I'm speaking to, the sentiment remains the same, but the timeline changes. There is no universally accepted endpoint for New York City's musical relevance. Rather, many people feel strongly that New York's final golden era occurred when they personally just so happened to be in their twenties, and that the city's decline roughly coincided with them entering their mid or late thirties and tapping out of the cutting edge of youth culture. What are the odds?

For some people, believing that New York City is in decline can be an act of empathy with the next generation—an acknowledgement that they're dealing with a new set of problems that previous generations didn't have to grapple with. But it can also just be a form of tunnel vision that comes with age. As people become burdened with kids, jobs, declining horniness, and bodily decay, nightlife and subcultural identification become deprioritized, and despite their best intentions, their tastes begin to calcify. All the new music they encounter is judged against the enormous backlog of songs that they already know and love. (Why bother checking out the new L'Rain album when you could just listen to

Paul's Boutique again?) They feel a sharp sting every time a business they patronized when they were young closes—even if they haven't spent any time or money at said business in decades. They look back at the world of their twenties as the best possible world, because it was one in which they were allowed to be both culturally dominant and relatively free of concern. (No judgment; it's happening to me, too.)

These supposed golden ages were not fruitful because their chronological circumstances were spectacularly conducive to art and music-making. Amazing stuff happened because a quorum of hardworking, ambitious, and creative people saw the opportunities that their specific circumstances created, and chose to exploit them.

So much groundbreaking music (and art, and film, and everything else under the sun) has come out of New York City (rather than, say, Poughkeepsie) because, by its very nature, it is a cornucopia of possible circumstances. A port city, an international transit hub, dense and chaotic but easily traversed, operating at all hours, diverse in every sense of the word, home to high concentrations of both unimaginable wealth and unimaginable poverty. There are an infinite number of opportunities you can plug yourself into at any given moment, and you can fall ass-backward into the history books just by leaving your house at the right time. The aim of this book is to demystify some of these circumstances and opportunities, and to pinpoint the specifics that allowed these communities to thrive.

To that end, each chapter examines two overlapping ecosystems. The first is that of the music scenes themselves, and the relationships and choices that allowed them to flourish. The musician, producer, visual artist, and all-around idea man Brian Eno calls this ecosystem "scenius." According to Eno, great works of art are never the expression of a singular genius, but rather a product of "very fertile scenes involving lots and lots of people," including artists, collectors, curators, theorists, thinkers, and "people who were fashionable and knew what the hip things were." The end result was "a kind of ecology of talent...that [gave] rise to good new thoughts and good new work."[2]

The second ecosystem is that of the neighborhoods in which these scenes existed, which were mostly working-class or industrial. It's practically a cliché at this point to say that bohemians are the shock troops of gentrification. Nevertheless, fans and storytellers often shift the blame away from their beloved artists and instead frame them as mere pawns or victims in the story of a neighborhood's gentrification. In reality, these artists were neither totally naïve, nor villains plotting to pave paradise and put up a Duane Reade. They are individuals who made a wide range of decisions about where they lived and why, what aspects of their neighborhoods they chose to embrace or ignore, how they behaved there, and how they processed the results of their behavior. Their impacts need to be discussed openly and honestly, without recrimination or apologia.

This is far from the first book to look at the incredible range of music that New York City has produced over the last sixty years. But the wise, experienced writers who came before me likely understood that they had to narrow their focus to specific eras or genres in the interest of their own sanity. I, a novice and fool, had no such realization. If I had, I might not have proposed to cover sixty years' worth of music scenes. But two and a half years and over a hundred interviews later, I recognize that there's no other way I could have told this story. For this project, arbitrarily isolating and elevating specific eras risks feeding into the fallacy of the long-gone golden age, and focusing on specific genres overlooks the cross-pollination that was so crucial to their developments. This book aims to present New York's music history as the continuum it is.

Of course, the paradox is that, in attempting to convey the full range of sounds that were nourished in New York City over a sixty-year time period, I had to exclude several of them. So, this book does not aim to be a comprehensive survey of all the music made in the city over the course of the last six decades. Because I've concentrated on scenes and venues rather than specific artists, some of the most significant acts to emerge from the city only appear peripherally (Simon and Garfunkel, Run–DMC, Yeah Yeah

Yeahs, Lady Gaga), while others are excluded entirely (Dion and the Belmonts, Anthrax, Jay-Z, LCD Soundsystem). There is minimal discussion of recording studios, record labels, or any of the things artists did after they became famous and transcended their immediate communities, because those communities are the focus.

As long as this book currently is, the first draft was considerably longer, and significant cuts were made out of necessity. Ultimately, the difficult decision was made to narrow the book's focus from all of New York City to Lower Manhattan specifically (the final chapter shifts the focus to Williamsburg, Brooklyn, which, being one subway stop away from the East Village, essentially functioned as an extension of Downtown). Other parts of the city—especially Harlem and the South Bronx—have their own rich musical heritages, the majority of which emerged from their Black and Latinx communities. The musical legacies of those neighborhoods merit their own books, and though I adore so much of that music, I'm not an expert. For those interested, I give my highest possible recommendation to Joseph C. Ewoodzie's *Break Beats in the Bronx: Rediscovering Hip-Hop's Early Years* (University of North Carolina Press, 2017), which looks at the socioeconomic and geographic factors that helped birth that genre in a way that heavily influenced my work.

When people romanticize the past, the unromantic present inevitably pales in comparison. But that sentimentality obscures the ways in which similar experiences are currently obtainable. My hope is that the stories in this book can serve as inspiration and instruction for building and nurturing vibrant music scenes in the future, in New York and everywhere else. New York is never over, so long as we don't want it to be.

WHAT WE TALK ABOUT WHEN WE TALK ABOUT $100

When telling stories about New York's past, there is an understandable tendency to wax nostalgic for the low cost of living back in the city's musical glory days. Though it's true that the cost of city living has ballooned to an absurd degree, it is important to note that many of these storytellers neglect to account for inflation.

It is one thing for me to tell you that three founding members of Talking Heads paid a combined $289 for a full floor of a mostly vacant industrial building at 195 Chrystie Street in 1975. But the story changes a little when you consider that $289 in 1975 is equivalent in purchasing power to approximately $1,552 in 2022—for which they received a space without heat, plumbing, partitioning walls of any kind, or a readily available superintendent. A great deal to be sure, but not quite the bargain of the century that it initially appears to be.

As I write this, a tiny one-bedroom apartment in Sunset Park,

Brooklyn, is listed on Craigslist for a mere $850, and while it might be difficult to hold a band practice there, that price does include heat, plumbing, and walls. Three people—especially one couple and one single person, as Talking Heads were—could conceivably make do within those confines. Within this context, Talking Heads were still irrefutably living on the cheap, but not absurdly so.

Throughout this book, I'll be going into detail regarding the prices of commercial and residential rents, food and drink, band payouts, etc. I want to encourage you to consult the following chart as you go, which will help approximate and contextualize the actual financial burdens.

$100 in	2022 equivalency
1960	$1,006.80
1965	$946.07
1970	$768.07
1975	$553.93
1980	$361.67
1985	$276.96
1990	$228.01
1995	$195.55
2000	$173.06
2005	$152.59
2010	$136.67
2015	$125.73

1

ALL THE NEWS THAT'S FIT TO SING: FOLK MUSIC IN GREENWICH VILLAGE

Judy Collins (singer-songwriter): After I moved here, I immediately ran into everybody in town who wrote songs. I'd walk down the street and there would be Tom Paxton, and he'd say, "You want to record this song?" and then he'd sing me "Bottle of Wine."

It all started innocently enough: In the 1940s, Greenwich Village, a heavily Italian-American neighborhood that doubled as a bohemian enclave, became home to a small, nascent community of folk musicians who mostly staged performances in their homes and jammed in public parks.

It didn't feel like anything out of the ordinary, at first—bohemians had peacefully coexisted alongside Greenwich Village's Italian and Irish immigrant communities since the late nineteenth century, when all three groups began to settle in the previously upper-crust neighborhood. Artsy types like Mark Twain, Edgar

Allan Poe, Isadora Duncan, Salvador Dalí, and Anaïs Nin arrived, and with them, a network of theaters, businesses, and community spaces for artists opened, which coexisted alongside Italian- and Irish-owned restaurants and coffeehouses. By the early twentieth century, the Irish community was largely moving elsewhere, but the Italian and bohemian communities grew and, if not quite became friends, lived side by side for decades, largely keeping to themselves.

But by the mid-sixties, the neighborhood had become folk music's own Universal CityWalk, overstuffed with guitar-toting hopefuls searching for their big break, and home to enough tourist-trap venues to exploit them all. Most Italian families were long gone by that point, as were many folk musicians who felt the scene had grown too commercial.

It was shocking, and not just because it had turned a relatively quiet neighborhood into ground zero for the nascent youth culture. It was shocking because it had never happened before. The Greenwich Village folk scene marked the first time that the mainstream success of an ostensibly countercultural musical community played such a pivotal role in the gentrification of the neighborhood that birthed it.

It also created the playbook for how many of the successive music communities that flourished in Lower Manhattan over the second half of the twentieth century would live and die: 1) A small, tight-knit community of mostly white musicians making oppositional, marginal art settle in a neighborhood primarily inhabited by a longstanding ethnic community. 2) The music is promoted through a network of small, shabby venues. 3) Increasing attention on the scene draws in entrepreneurs looking to exploit the music and the neighborhood for their own gain. 4) The scene itself collapses, with a handful of artists elevated to fame, and many more fleeing the city because they can no longer afford their neighborhood, which has been taken over by wealthy Johnny-come-latelies who displace all the people responsible for the things that made it appealing to them in the first place.

THE ALMANAC SINGERS

In the decade before the emergence of folk, Greenwich Village had already established itself as a hotspot for jazz thanks to venues like the Village Vanguard (178 7th Avenue South), which opened in 1935, and Arthur's Tavern (57 Grove Street), in 1937. Café Society, which opened at 1 Sheridan Square in 1938, was America's first racially integrated nightclub, drawing the likes of Billie Holiday, Miles Davis, Charlie Parker, Burl Ives, and Sarah Vaughn. But for the most part, the performers at these clubs lived in even poorer neighborhoods that were traditionally home to people of color, like the Lower East Side and Harlem. Greenwich Village was in the 1930s a hub for music, but not yet the hub for musicians that it would become.

Those seeds were arguably planted in March of 1940, when a mutual friend introduced folk singers Pete Seeger and Woody Guthrie.

The Manhattan-raised Seeger had a decidedly well-heeled upbringing that included boarding schools in Connecticut and a scholarship to Harvard, but he was uniquely pedigreed for the folk scene: his father, Charles Seeger, was a prominent musicologist and composer. The elder Seeger introduced his son to acclaimed musicologist Alan Lomax;[i] Pete briefly worked as Lomax's assistant in 1939, combing through Library of Congress archives of what was then called "race" and "hillbilly" music.[ii]

Unlike Seeger, Guthrie had been raised in poverty in Oklahoma. Seeger and others in the scene exoticized and fetishized Guthrie as a link to the "real" American folk tradition; Guthrie hardly minded the attention, and embellished his biography for maximum effect.

By 1941, Guthrie and Seeger—along with fellow folk singers Millard Lampell, Lee Hays, Agnes "Sis" Cunningham, Pete Hawes, and Bess Lomax (Alan's sister)—formed a collective they dubbed

---

i   Full disclosure: I have been employed by Lomax's foundation, the Association for Cultural Equity.

ii   Music made by poor Black people and poor white people, respectively.

130 West 10th Street.

the Almanac Singers, and except for Lomax, moved into a shared townhouse at 130 West 10th Street. There, the group lived communally in the truest sense of the word, sharing meals, chores, and credit for any songs written in the building. The rent, which totaled $95 a month, was largely subsidized with informal Sunday performances in the building's basement, which they referred to as "hootenannies" (a term that Seeger and Guthrie had picked up in their travels, and eagerly introduced into the city's lexicon).

For the price of thirty-five cents, you could watch the city's best and brightest folk singers in a low-key setting; Burl Ives and Lead Belly were among the regular guest performers. Though New York City had a handful of folk musicians and dedicated fans, and some nightclubs (including the Village Vanguard and Café Society) were hosting occasional folk performances, there were no dedicated folk venues—the Almanac hootenannies were the closest thing going.

The Almanac Singers' career was short-lived—when World War II broke out in 1942, the band's anti-war material became unfashionable.[iii] That same year, Seeger was drafted and left New York to serve in the army, putting any hopes of an Almanac Singers comeback to rest.

Upon his return in 1946, Seeger and his new bride, Toshi Ota, moved into her parents' house at 129 MacDougal Street. The Otas were encouraging of Seeger's musical pursuits, and loved when Pete brought his friends over to jam; their house became an even less formal version of the Almanac Singers' hootenannies. Pete and Toshi moved to Beacon, New York, in 1949, but Seeger remained a regular presence in town; the following year, Seeger, Lomax, and Irwin Silber launched *Sing Out!*, a zine that reported on folk music and also included lyrics and chord charts for traditional songs, which they published out of an office at 106 East 14th Street.

In the early 1940s, folk singers and aficionados from around the city began congregating in Washington Square Park on Sundays, taking full advantage of the fact that, for a genre that required no amplification, a public park offered free unlimited practice space with a built-in audience.

By 1947, these Sunday afternoon jams had attracted enough attention (both positive and negative) from Village residents that NYPD started requiring musicians to get permits from the Parks Department in order to play. These permitting regulations only

---

iii First Lady Eleanor Roosevelt, a noted folk music aficionado, reportedly considered the Almanac Singers' pacifist songs to be in poor taste.

allowed for singing and playing stringed instruments, banning any percussion—the ruling, in effect, took the side of the folkies, banishing the growing cadre of bongo-bashing beatniks who competed with them for sonic and physical space in the park. Though music was initially only permitted for two hours each Sunday, in 1952 string bassist Lionel Kilberg convinced the authorities to expand the permit to four hours—2:00 p.m. to 6:00 p.m.—with the stipulation that the musicians not ask the crowd for money.

For many of the young musicians congregating in the park, Sunday jams were not only a musical education, but a social one. The performances didn't have a typical performer/audience dynamic; most attendees brought their own instruments, and sang and played along. Every imaginable iteration of folk music found a corner of the park in which to commune: there were political progressives playing union songs, bluegrass aficionados and jug bands playing old-time standards, Zionists playing traditional Hebrew songs. It was a universe of subgenres that was open to all, at no cost—having the confidence to show up was the only admission fee.

Happy Traum (singer-songwriter): While I was in high school, other kids were telling me about going to Washington Square on Sunday. I started going in '54 or '55, and I continued going into the early '60s. Not every single week, but enough so that I knew the scene.

Nobody at that point had the idea that it would be anything you could do professionally—it was just pure fun. A lot of those great pickers became lawyers or accountants or whatever, but there were some really good musicians there: Mike Seeger, Tom Paley, Eric Weissberg, Dave Van Ronk. John Herald, who later joined the Greenbrier Boys. Marshall Brickman, a banjo player who later went on to write Annie Hall *with Woody Allen.*

According to Alan Lomax, who lived two blocks away from the park at 121 West 3rd Street, "Some of the young folkniks... asserted that there was more folk music in Washington Square on Sunday afternoon than there was in all rural America... The idea that these nice young people, who were only just beginning to learn how to play and sing in good style, might replace the glories of the real thing, frankly horrified me."[3]

Lomax was all too aware of the scene's absurd underlying paradox: though oriented around traditional rural music, often played by and for segregated communities, it was now blossoming in a decidedly progressive and urban environment. As the community began to gain wider notice, that subtext turned into an unresolvable tension.

Beyond the park, the neighborhood was also becoming more and more of a beacon for both folk musicians and small folk-oriented record labels: Vanguard Records, at 80 East 11th Street, debuted in 1950 as a classical label, but began pivoting to folk four years later. Elektra began as a folk label in 1950, operating for the first four years out of owner Jac Holzman's apartment at 40 Grove Street, and then an office at 361 Bleecker. The Irish group the Clancy Brothers founded Tradition Records with an office at 132 Christopher Street, which they operated with funding from heiress Dianne Guggenheim Hamilton. Initially devoted to traditional Irish music, Tradition soon expanded to include all forms of folk music (Odetta's first album was an early release).

At the same time, some longtime Italian-American residents were leaving the Village in droves. Many utilized the recently passed G.I. Bill, which allowed veterans to receive generous home loans, and fled to tonier parts of the Outer Boroughs, Long Island, and New Jersey. White flight—a citywide mass exodus of white residents to ethnically homogenous suburbs where people of color were less welcome—had begun. As a result, empty apartments in the Village were plentiful and often cheap—inevitably, bait for bohemian types.

THE FOLKLORE CENTER

In 1957, thirty-year-old Israel "Izzy" Young opened a shop called the Folklore Center at 110 MacDougal Street. Young was a Bronx-raised Jew with an almost comically prototypical "Nu Yawk" ac-

PHOTO BY THE AUTHOR, 2023.

110 MacDougal Street.

cent, but his passion for rural American music was intense. Young's Folklore Center stocked everything a folk aficionado could want, like instruments, records, sheet music, and folk-centric zines, including *Sing Out!*, for which Young wrote a regular column entitled "Frets and Frails."

> *Traum: I can remember getting off the subway, and the first thing I'd do was go over to the Folklore Center to see who was hanging out. Izzy was a total character: He was a curmudgeon, but really a sweethearted person who encouraged everybody. And he would let you get away with stuff—you could pick up a magazine, and if you didn't have enough money, he'd say, "Pay me next time."*

In a short time, Young also began hosting performances in the store, primarily for artists who couldn't get booked at legitimate clubs.

Tom Paxton (singer-songwriter): If you finished a song in a different key from the one you started in, you were Izzy's guy. There was one singer he favored; I can't remember the guy's name. Which is just as well, because I remember asking Van Ronk if he'd heard this guy, and he said, "He's so pure, he's got surface noise in his voice."

Young's store wasn't the only folk game in town—Allan Block, an amateur fiddler and professional sandal maker, held Saturday afternoon jam sessions in his sandal shop at 171 West 4th Street. If a visiting musician didn't have an instrument on hand, one could be borrowed from the Music Inn, an instrument and record shop located next door at 169 West 4th Street. But Young's became the social epicenter of the growing scene. Photos of Village folk singers adorned the walls, providing newcomers with an informal who's who of the scene. Those looking to expand their repertoire came to the Folklore Center to find new material, musicians advertised upcoming gigs, and some of the more itinerant members of the scene even picked up their mail there.

Even as the neighborhood began to fill up with folk venues, Young's remained a performer favorite. This may be, in part, because as Young later recalled, "It turned out that I was paying people more than folk singers were getting paid at the famous basket houses."[4]

Peter K. Siegel (folk musician; staff producer, Elektra Records): Izzy Young was one of the worst businessmen I ever met. He's not alive anymore; if he were, he would tell you he was not a great hustler. But that's a good thing: If he'd been guided solely by the desire to make money, he wouldn't have done any of the things he did, which turned out to be great things.

CAFE BIZARRE AND THE FOLKSINGERS GUILD

Around the same time that Izzy Young was preparing to open the Folklore Center, academic Roger Abrahams was holding informal after-hours folk jam sessions in his loft at 190 Spring Street. These caught the attention of Abrahams's landlord, Rick Allmen, who realized that the folk scene was becoming significant enough to be financially exploited. In 1957, Allmen opened Cafe Bizarre, a coffee shop at 106 West 3rd Street. Though several coffeehouses already existed in the area—typically owned by members of the local Italian-American community, with a handful catering to the tastes of the neighborhood's growing bohemian contingent—

The Cafe Bizarre banner, photographed in the late 1950s or early '60s.

Allmen's was the first in the Village to regularly feature folk singers as live entertainment.

Allmen rightly recognized that bohemian subcultures can be simultaneously repellant and compelling to mainstream audiences. But he made the (ahem) bizarre decision to express that by giving the cafe a monsters-and-witches theme. The dark, candlelit cafe's interior could have doubled as a Spirit Halloween store: fake cobwebs, skulls, shrunken heads, paintings of monsters on the walls, and waitresses in cheap-looking Morticia Addams getups. Gilding the proverbial lily, the cafe's menu warned visitors to "be prepared 4 the unexpected," and advertised, among other things, the "Suffering Bastard Sundae" ("don't ask, just eat!") and a "Voodoo Do-It-Yourself Sundae" which served "2 and their aggressions" and included a "voodoo fruit doll with toothpicks," recommended for "landlords, bosses, mothers-in-law."[5]

The Cafe Bizarre officially opened on August 18, 1957, with an inaugural performance by Odetta. It was an immediate success—so much so, in fact, that Allmen decided to maximize profits with a move that would be replicated by venues of all stripes for decades to come: demanding that musicians who played there perform for "exposure," rather than cash. Dave Van Ronk, writing in the folk-oriented zine *Caravan*, railed that "businessmen who have no cash have absolutely no right to employ singers, and entrepreneurs who cop the poverty plea would have their faces laughed in if there weren't so many militant victim-types around this field."[6]

In reaction, Van Ronk and several others on the scene launched the Folksingers Guild, operating out of a loft at 13 W. 17th Street belonging to guitarist Dave Greenhaus and his wife, Kiki. The Guild attempted to serve as a union for musicians, and representatives communicated with club owners about pay standards, and booked some of their own shows. Unfortunately, the Folksingers Guild only lasted for about a year, disintegrating because in trying to wear many hats, it successfully wore none—a major win for venue owners looking to exploit the scene for profit.

THE GASLIGHT

The Gaslight Café opened in the basement of 116 MacDougal Street in 1958. The venue had formerly been a speakeasy in the '20s and '30s, serving a largely gay clientele; in the intervening decades, it had been an antique shop, plumbing warehouse, and coal cellar. When Gaslight owner John Mitchell acquired the space, it was dirty and decrepit, with a ceiling too low to accommodate much of anything. Mitchell opted to lower the floor, digging it out himself late at night due to his lack of permits.

Even after Mitchell got the place set up, it remained far from comfortable—there was no air-conditioning, it was only lit by a few dim Tiffany lamps, and its legal capacity of 110 audience members was routinely exceeded. Like the Cafe Bizarre before it, and many of the Village venues that sprang up in its wake, the Gaslight did not serve alcohol—liquor licenses were near impossible to obtain in the Village without going through the Mafia, but the lack of booze also allowed these venues to stay open well past last call, with shows often running as late as 10:00 a.m.

PHOTO BY THE AUTHOR, 2023.

116 MacDougal Street.

While all of the folk clubs and coffeehouses were subject to scorn from the neighborhood's Italian-American community, the Gaslight was especially distressing to the people who lived in the apartments above it. To be fair, their primary complaint was legitimate: the building's air shafts carried sound from the basement up to residents' apartments. After multiple noise complaints were received, Mitchell came up with a bizarre but effective compromise: he banned clapping. Enthusiastic audiences were instead encouraged to show their appreciation by softly snapping their fingers, a move that was soon imitated without context by bohemian-minded audiences across the country.

The headaches didn't end there: in June 1960, the fire department closed the Gaslight, ostensibly for violating health codes. The likelier motivation seems to have been that Mitchell had recently stopped paying the customary bribes to said fire department, and instead decided to whistle-blow on the whole operation.[iv] For his troubles, Mitchell was arrested and charged with disorderly conduct and assault. It took him three months to reopen the Gaslight, during which he opened the Commons, another coffeehouse located across the street at 105 MacDougal.

Still, the Gaslight quickly became one of the most popular venues in the Village, and one of the most artistically credible. Initially, the club leaned heavily on stand-up comedy and Beat poets, and was even briefly called the Gaslight Poetry Cafe, with folk singer Len Chandler the only musician performing there. Poet-comedians Hugh Romney[v] and John Brent were the main emcees and "entertainment directors," although others followed, including a recent Michigan transplant named Noel Paul Stookey.

Better known as "Paul" from the folk trio Peter, Paul and Mary, Stookey began his New York City performance career as a stand-up comedian at the Gaslight, starting in 1960.

---

iv Mitchell's legal representation in the case was future NYC mayor Ed Koch.

v Romney would later go on to reinvent himself as Hog Farm commune leader Wavy Gravy, and famously deployed his Gaslight-honed emcee skills at the 1969 Woodstock Festival.

Stookey: Part of what got me in the door there is that I was comfortable being a Master of Ceremonies, which few musicians were—they were proud enough of their work that their music spoke for them. But I had fun being Master of Ceremonies, because it was bridge-building between an audience and people that they maybe hadn't seen before, or weren't used to seeing, and in the process I made a few clams. I made some mistakes on stage, but as any comedian knows, if you're willing to capitalize on your mistakes, you become a [better] comedian. I would [imitate] the flushing of a toilet, which I introduced as "an American Standard"—that had a double meaning, because there was a toilet manufacturer called American Standard.[vi]

As folk music gained traction in the neighborhood, the Gaslight wisely pivoted away from poets and toward folk singers. Dave Van Ronk hosted Tuesday night hootenannies, but most nights involved a handful of performers playing very short sets repeatedly, throughout the night.

Though the Gaslight became *the* hip venue in the Village, its lack of air-conditioning meant that few performers hung out there when they weren't on stage.

Stookey: When you finished your set, one of two things happened. You either went upstairs to play poker in a room that was laughingly referred to as "the dressing room," because nobody ever changed clothes there—you just wore your street clothes. Or, you went out and caught other acts at other coffeehouses—and there were a lot of coffeehouses! I would say there were at least five active places, and there were probably more that we didn't even know about. You'd go hear someone like Odetta or Peter Yarrow, and then occasionally, if you were in the audience, you got spotted by somebody who knew

---

vi   Other routines that Stookey deployed included impressions of Charlie
     Chaplin and Little Richard, and a falsetto Hitler at Nuremberg. Brief but
     compelling footage of Stookey emceeing at the Gaslight can be seen in the
     1963 film *Greenwich Village Story.*

your work from the Gaslight, and you might get called up to do a tune or a guest set.

The crowning piece of music every night at the Gaslight was "Lloyd George." The entire cast of the Gaslight—that was everybody from Dylan, Len Chandler, Dave Van Ronk, maybe Adam Keefe and his comedy partner Murray Roman—we would all assemble on stage. We would not be so corny as to join hands or put our arms around each other, but we'd all sing [to the tune of "Onward Christian Soldiers"] "Lloyd George knew my father; my father knew Lloyd George." That was the end of it, and then we'd stumble out to the bar or whatever. The Gaslight was strictly cider and lemonade, so the bar was either across the street at Minetta's [113 MacDougal] or upstairs at the Kettle of Fish [114 MacDougal].

By 1960, the Gaslight had gained so much notoriety that Mitchell released a live LP of Romney, Brent, and Chandler on his own Gaslight Records label, under the title *The Beat Generation.* Two years later, Gaslight Records issued its only other release, singer Tom Paxton's debut LP *I'm the Man That Built the Bridges.* Paxton had first made his way to the Village while an active member of the armed services.

Paxton: I was stationed first at Fort Slocum up by New Rochelle, and then I was transferred to Fort Dix in New Jersey. The first weekend that I got off, in early 1960, I was wandering around the Village, and I stumbled across MacDougal Street and the Gaslight. They had two poets and one folk singer, a guy named Jimmy Gavin. By the end of December, the poets were all gone, and it was all folk singers. I started meeting the other folk singers, and they would invite me to get up and do a guest set. I did that whenever I could, and then I started getting hired on weekends.

Dave Van Ronk was [booking performers] at the Commons and we became great friends. He would hire me on Friday and Saturday nights, and I think I made about $10 a night. I had all that tremendous money in my pocket from the weekend—I was clearing $20, *for god's sake! The chief value of that was that back at Fort Dix, I could skip lunch in the mess hall and go eat a cheeseburger.*

Upon Paxton's honorable discharge from the army, he and Noel Stookey became roommates, sharing an apartment at 629 E. 5th Street, between Avenue B and Avenue C.

Stookey: Tom Paxton and I lived together in a five-flight walk-up that smelled like the urinal at Grand Central. The rent for the whole place was $47.63. Richie Havens lived down the hall; he wasn't a musician at that point—he was a painter, and he was living with a white girl, which was pretty audacious for that time. The apartments on the Lower East Side were close to being lofts—not that they were intended to be, but the conditions were so bad that you couldn't help yourself from tearing out the walls, just to make it a little bigger and a little nicer. We had a toilet where you didn't go in unless you knew for sure that nobody else was going to the toilet on another floor above you at the same time, because if they flush, you'd have to have an umbrella.

Stookey left comedy behind when Albert Grossman, then managing singer Joan Baez, reached out to him. Grossman was working on assembling a group around folk singer Peter Yarrow and sought out both Stookey and Greenwich Village native Mary Travers.

Stookey: Albert came to a show at the Gaslight and called me over after one of my sets. Everybody knew who Albert was—he had run a club called the Gate of Horn in Chicago and was really well connected—so I was excited about being called over to his table—which he deflated immediately by saying, "Have you ever thought of being in a group?" I said, "No, I haven't, because there's some things I need to do by myself." Which was a really grown-up answer, now that I think of it. But two or three weeks later, I'm at [my apartment] and I get a phone call from Mary, saying, "This guy's come by; he's brought his guitar and we're singing a little bit. We wondered if we could come over and sing with you?" That was a casual enough introduction that when they came over and I found out that Peter was working with Albert, it was cool.

Then the challenge was in front of us: Okay, what are we going to sing? We started off trying to sing "The Golden Vanity,"[vii] but in folk music, everybody knows a slightly different version, so we couldn't agree on the lyrics. We ended up singing "Mary Had A Little Lamb," which was wonderful. It was a very simple tune, we could easily do harmonies to it and it sounded good.

Then Peter said, "I'm putting together a group with Albert; why don't we have some rehearsals?" The logical place to rehearse was at Mary's apartment on MacDougal,[viii] because she had a small child. We made our premiere across the street from Mary's apartment at the Gaslight; Dylan says he was there that night.

GERDE'S FOLK CITY

The first venue in the Village to dedicate itself solely to folk music was a flailing Italian restaurant called Gerde's, located just off the park's northeastern edge in a former spray gun factory at 11 West 4th Street. Though only a handful of blocks away from the bustle around Bleecker and MacDougal, that corner for the Village was comparatively dead, consisting largely of empty factories. With little in the way of foot traffic, owner Mike Porco suspected that music might be the key to luring in customers.

By 1960, the folk scene had grown to a point that Izzy Young recognized the community's need for a larger folk music venue with a valid cabaret license (which is to say, booze). In his words, "All the folkniks were running around the schmucky coffeehouses, and the nightclub owners were giving people folk music and booze and a place to meet other people so they could get laid, instead of

---

vii A traditional folk song, also known as "The Golden Willow Tree" and "The Sweet Trinity."

viii Stookey remembers it being 102 MacDougal, but couldn't say for sure.

sitting there in the afternoon sipping espresso. But they weren't doing it right, because they didn't give a shit about the music."[7]

Young's friend Tom Prendergast alerted him to Gerde's existence, and the two walked over from the Folklore Center and approached Mike Porco with an offer: they would bring in lights and a small PA system, book the musicians, and charge $1.50 at the door; they would keep 100 percent, with which they'd pay musicians; Porco would sell food and drinks and keep 100 percent of those profits.

The venue, which Young and Prendergast dubbed "The Fifth Peg" (as in, the fifth tuning peg on a banjo), officially opened on January 26, 1960. Young's reputation and connections worked in the club's favor, and he booked a phenomenal cross section of local talent—including the Clancy Brothers, Cynthia Gooding, Cisco Houston, Sonny Terry and Brownie McGhee, and Theodore Bikel—who drew substantial crowds, to Porco's delight.

The club was a success by any measure—except for one: In a typical move, Izzy Young had neglected to account for his own fiscal needs when negotiating the financial breakdown. When Young realized the deal was bad and attempted to renegotiate, asking Porco for a cut of the bar, he and Prendergast were forced out.

Four months after its grand opening, the Fifth Peg was no more. But lo and behold, in June 1960, Mike Porco reopened as Gerde's Folk City—a reboot of the Fifth Peg, with Young and Prendergast replaced by booking agent Charlie Rothschild and folk singer Logan English. Rothschild was close with *New York Times* music critic Robert Shelton, the first journalist to write about the Village's folk scene in a major publication. Shelton frequently recommended up-and-coming acts for the club with the unspoken implication that, once booked, he would show up to review them. Rothschild, in turn, would encourage Porco to book them.

Carolyn Hester (folk singer): I saw there was a place called Gerde's Folk City, and I thought, "Wow, Folk City! Amazing, right?!" That sounded like what I wanted, because most places in the Village had poetry. I went in there and I showed them my LP; they dropped everything and had me sing. Mike said, "I think the kids from across the street at NYU would like you."[ix]

Gerde's remained an Italian restaurant during the day, with music starting at 9:00 p.m. or 9:30 p.m., for which customers paid a small admission fee with a two-drink minimum. In stark contrast to the Gaslight and Cafe Bizarre, Folk City was slick, professional, and clean.[x]

On the other hand, because of its liquor license, it was also subject to some of the frustrations that the coffeehouses had scrupulously avoided: performers were required to have musicians' union cards and cabaret performance licenses, the shows couldn't last all night, and the inebriated audiences could be less mannered.

Much like the Gaslight, shows were presented by a singing emcee; regulars included singers Gil Turner and Logan English, and actor/singer Dominic Chianese, now best known for his portrayal of Corrado "Uncle Junior" Soprano on *The Sopranos*.

Collins: I first played in New York in 1961 at Gerde's Folk City. I was the headliner, and my opening act was a 13-year-old kid named Arlo Guthrie. Everybody that I knew in the music business was there: Peter, Paul and Mary before they were Peter, Paul and Mary, Dave Van Ronk, Cisco Houston. Bob Dylan was there.

The club's focus was on professional, signed performers, but Porco still gave a lot of upstarts (including Dylan) their first major gig—at least in part, because he knew he could pay them less than established acts. Although unsigned artists were hard-pressed to get a gig at Gerde's Folk City, they were more than welcome to

---

ix   NYU students made up a significant chunk of Porco's customer base, for both food and music; tourists seemed to make up a slightly smaller portion of the audience than they did at other Village venues, probably due to the club's distance from the MacDougal-centric scene.

x   Mostly clean, anyway: Alix Dobkin recalled that "Gerde's had dressing rooms in the basement with the biggest cockroaches I've ever seen."

come on Monday night for the weekly open mic. These shows, for which admission was free and the drink minimum was lowered to one, were promoted by Porco as hootenannies, although his understanding of the term was somewhat flimsy:

> **Traum:** *"Hootenanny"—that term used to mean something very different. When it was first used by Pete Seeger, they would have concerts with a whole variety of people and call them hootenannies. At Gerde's Folk City, it was more like an open mic night, but it was an open mic for professionals. So on any given Monday night, for the price of a beer, you could go in and hear anybody who was on the scene trying out new stuff: Odetta, the Clancy Brothers, Ian and Sylvia, Judy Collins, any number of people that you could think of would show up and do their two or three songs. By '63, it became a packed meat market, with managers, record company executives, booking agents, even people from other venues around town or from other cities coming to see who the hottest young person was. Somebody like Ian and Sylvia would do their three songs, and then get a record deal out of that.*

THE WASHINGTON SQUARE PARK PROTESTS

As the '50s turned into the '60s, Washington Square Park's Sunday afternoon folk scene blossomed into one of the city's most popular gay cruising spots, and also gained a reputation as a welcoming environment among Black teenagers. Like the Village jazz scene that existed alongside it, folk music was racially integrated for both fans and performers, with Black musicians like Len Chandler, Odetta, Richie Havens, Herb Metoyer, Josh White Jr, Terry Callier, Casey Anderson, and Major Willey, and comedians Flip Wilson, Bill Cosby, and Dick Gregory, all performing for major crowds. A number of white Village residents attacked this diversity, sometimes literally—there were so many racially-motivated physical assaults on Black people in the Village that it was the subject of a *Village Voice* article in 1959.

The Park scene's combination of diversity and noise was especially offensive to the Village's entrenched conservative elements. Wealthy residents who lived around 5th Avenue on the northern edge of the park regularly complained to local authorities, as did NYU officials. University president Carroll Newsom, in a letter to parks commissioner Newbold Morris, wrote "There was a time when a folk singer was a person who sang folk songs... Now a folk singer may or may not be able to sing. Sometimes he is a hoodlum; many believe he indulges in abnormal sexual behavior. Judging by his conduct in Washington Square Park, he dislikes little children, and likes to disrupt life in the community."[8] Longtime Italian-American residents complained as well, with one Bleecker Street resident telling the Community Planning Board that the noise coming from the park every Sunday was "degrading to my mother and father."[9]

As a result, on March 3, 1961, Morris announced that he would stop giving permits for live musical performance in the park, writing, "I want to emphasize that I am not opposed to the wonderful symphony concerts, bands, quartets, or chamber music [in Washington Square Park]. What I am against is these fellows that come from miles away to display the most terrible costumes, haircuts, etc. and who play bongo drums and other weird instruments attracting a weird public."[10]

And so, when Izzy Young requested a permit for "folk singing with stringed instruments" every Sunday in April, he was summarily denied. The issue came to a head on April 9, 1961, when a group of approximately two thousand folk singers and supporters, led by Young, clashed with police in the park for several hours. Ten people were arrested and twenty were injured,[xi] including three police officers. In a display of total ignorance toward subcultural

---

xi   Filmmaker Dan Drasin captured the riot in his short documentary *Sunday*. The film's most striking moment shows two policemen dragging away eighteen-year-old Robert Easton as he placidly strums his autoharp. As Easton is thrown into a cop car and driven away, autoharp in hand, a disembodied voice is heard yelling, "Take him down to the Tombs and beat him up, boys!"

nuances, the following day's *New York Mirror* headline read, "3000 Beatniks Riot in Village."

Morris was unmoved. The following day, he doubled down on his commitment to banning folk singers, claiming they were trampling over the park's greenery. He encouraged folk singers to instead apply for permits in East River Park in the Lower East Side, a less prosperous community. Young responded by cofounding the Right to Sing Committee, which staged several protests throughout April 1961.

In the end, Mayor Robert Wagner caved to the folk singers' demands. They would now be allowed to perform in the park between 3:00 p.m. and 6:00 p.m. on Sundays, exclusively in the area between the arch and the fountain (hilariously, the portion of the park located closest to the wealthy 5th Avenue residents). In July, the Appellate Division of the State Supreme Court ordered the parks commissioner to "receive and reconsider" all applications for singing in the park. Commissioner Morris, tail wedged between his legs, claimed, "I never had the slightest hostility toward...folk singers. I'm a singer myself."[11]

THE COFFEEHOUSE BOOM

Though some coffeehouses, like Cafe Bizarre and the Gaslight, had already started hosting folk musicians, those numbers swelled in the wake of the Washington Square protests—the hubbub brought media attention to the neighborhood, and established its identity in the public imagination as a folk music enclave. At the scene's peak in the early '60s, there was upward of twenty folk music venues within a five-block area, including the Bitter End, the Gaslight, Kettle of Fish, Cafe Wha?, Cafe Feenjon, the Commons, Izzy Young's Folklore Center, the Night Owl, Cafe Bizarre, and Cafe Au Go Go.

Initially, all entertainment establishments were required to have a cabaret license if they wanted to host a performance; many of the Village coffeehouses didn't, which resulted in regular fines. In 1961, the cabaret laws were slightly altered, with *Local Laws, 1961,*

No. 95 of City of New York explicitly allowing venues that did not
serve alcohol to have "incidental" music—performed either by
mechanical devices, or by up to three people playing piano, organ,
accordion, guitar, or any other string instrument—without a cabaret license. As had been the case in the Washington Square Park
permit situation, Beat Generation hallmarks like bongos, poetry
readings, and jazz ensembles were excluded, giving legal heft to
a shift in tastes that had already started to transform the Village.

Coffeehouses didn't just have a legal advantage over bars: musicians often preferred them as well. The sober audiences were generally quieter, more attentive, and better behaved—which, for a
solo acoustic performer, can make all the difference. This seems to
have been especially true for female performers, who could find
themselves bearing the brunt of a drunk audience's aggressions.
Contrasting the Gaslight (a coffeehouse) with Gerde's Folk City
(a bar), Alix Dobkin observed that "the Gaslight was very serious.
People really paid attention, they came to hear the music. Gerde's
was much rowdier. People would drink and carry on." Singer Buffy
Sainte-Marie also preferred coffeehouses because, as she explained,
"I didn't drink and was afraid of men in bars."

THE GASLIGHT, TAKE TWO

In the spring of 1961, just as the Washington Square Park controversy was exploding, John Mitchell sold the Gaslight and moved
to Spain. "Mitchell didn't tell anybody he was selling the club or
that it would change ownership," Bob Dylan later recalled. "He
just sold the place and left the country."[12]

It's unclear exactly who bought the Gaslight from Mitchell, as
accounts vary, but by the end of the year it was in the possession
of a married couple, John Moyant and Lynn Hood. Lynn recruited
her father Clarence and brother Sam to oversee the operation, with
both relocating to the city from Mississippi.

*Paxton: Sam Hood was an ex–All American high school football
player. He never went to college, but he was a great, great business*

Buffy Sainte-Marie performing at the Gaslight, 1964.

*guy. He always reminded me of this Southern expression about some-
one who could talk a dog down off a meat truck. He had some legendary back and forth with Phil Ochs. There was one time when
somebody failed to show up and Sam needed Phil to fill in. Phil
quoted him a price that was twice what it should have been, and he
wouldn't budge. Finally, Sam said, "I'll see you on the way down,
Phil."*

Under Clarence and Sam Hood's direction, the Gaslight thrived.
Neither of them knew much about the folk scene or had any
industry experience prior to their arrival, but they were quick
studies—especially Sam, who became the Gaslight's primary
booker. Even with scores of competing venues in their immediate
vicinity, the Gaslight maintained a degree of integrity, authenticity, and quality that set it above the rest.

Some of this was likely due to aesthetics: regardless of what was
taking place, a dirty, dark, cramped basement felt more "authentic" than the scores of well-lit, professional-looking clubs nearby—
especially for tourists coming to the Village in search of an under-

ground atmosphere (and nothing says "underground" quite like a club that is literally under the ground). But Sam Hood's bookings, which tended to prioritize rougher-edged acts over the scene's slicker options, were especially well served by that environment.

Paxton: After Clarence Hood took over, I started working steady there; I think I worked nine straight months at the Gaslight. You never knew who would drop by: Joan Baez, when she was in town, would come in and sing a few songs. Johnny Cash, for Christ's sake! It was at the low point in his life, he was very skinny and he was doing a lot of pills, but none of us knew that—we just knew that this was Johnny Cash, and he could sing like Johnny Cash. Bill Cosby had his first job as a comedian there, he started July 4th weekend, 1962. Fred Willard had a [comedy] partner named Vic Greco at that point; they were hysterically funny to us, but the audience would sit there with their mouths open trying to figure out what the hell was going on.

Beyond the bookings, the Hoods took great pains to integrate themselves into the community, going so far as to open the club on Thanksgiving to provide free food to anyone who needed it. They regularly socialized with folk singers outside of the Gaslight, and Sam Hood even married singer Alix Dobkin in 1965.

While the Hoods were glad to have inherited the club's atmosphere and credibility from John Mitchell, they were less pleased to have inherited the near-constant aggravation from law enforcement. In 1964, Clarence Hood told the *New York Times* that the Gaslight had made seventy-four appearances in court in the last few years. "This has to be harassment," Hood explained. "We're wondering how many judges have to dismiss this before the city departments begin to realize that the law is rather silly."[13]

THE BITTER END

By 1961, folk music was trendy enough that outside entrepreneurs started sniffing around the Village. One such man was thirty-four-year-old Fred Weintraub, who had inherited a successful baby carriage business. After a transformative viewing of Federico Fellini's *La Strada*, Weintraub decided to leave the square life behind and sought out a bohemian existence (legend has him playing piano in a bordello and/or operating a fishing boat in Cuba before ending up in the Village). Or, according to others, he was just looking for an entrée into the entertainment industry.

Either way, he found what he was looking for in folk music, a genre he knew little about and didn't especially care for. When Weintraub learned that a bar called the Cock and Bull at 147 Bleecker Street was going out of business, he took it over and changed the name to the Bitter End, a reference to the fact that of all the coffeehouses and bars lining Bleecker Street, this one was the farthest east.

Weintraub brought a few novel innovations to the tried-and-true folk coffeehouse model. Where other venues positioned patrons at round tables, the Bitter End audience sat in church pews that had been fitted with cup holders—meaning that everyone in

147 Bleecker Street.

the room was looking forward to the stage at all times. As with the other Village coffeehouses, the Bitter End did not serve alcohol, instead offering coffees and ice creams with hacky "bohemian" names like the "Frosty Freud" and "Zen Sundae." But unlike other venues, food and drink service at the Bitter End would only occur between acts. That meant that while performers were on stage, the Bitter End's audience was noticeably quieter and more attentive than its competitors'—a very attractive proposition for a wide range of performers.

> *Stookey: Our primary place to perform in the Village turned out to be the Bitter End. The Gaslight was more intimate and well suited for poetry, flamenco guitar, and individual performers. The Bitter End was better suited for a group—it was a big, wide open place.*[xii]

The quiet nature of the room also made it a natural venue for live recordings. To wit: Fred Neil, Tom Paxton, Pete Seeger, Curtis Mayfield, Arlo Guthrie, Donny Hathaway, the Chad Mitchell Trio, Bill Haley and the Comets, Biff Rose, Len Chandler, the Isley Brothers, Randy Newman, and Biff Rose all recorded albums there. A nationally syndicated radio show hosted by the actor and folk singer Theodore Bikel (who also hosted Tuesday night hootenannies at the club), entitled *Theodore Bikel at Home*, was also taped live at the Bitter End. This ensured that the Bitter End was the number one Greenwich Village folk venue that someone outside the scene might have heard of, making it seem like the center of the scene and not the Johnny-come-lately venue it was.

THE SECOND WAVE

With folk music's popularity growing both in and beyond the Village, new performers were regularly arriving in town. The

---

xii   Peter, Paul and Mary became so closely associated with the club that they took the cover photo for their self-titled 1962 debut album on the Bitter End's stage, with its signature brick wall in the background.

Village scene offered new transplants a clear roadmap to success: The Washington Square Park jams and open mic hootenannies offered a point of entry. Any information they needed about the community was readily available at the Folklore Center. The sheer number of coffeehouses meant that paying gigs were plentiful, and since all the clubs were within a two-block radius of one another, it was easy to spend every night hopping from coffeehouse to coffeehouse until the wee hours. Greenwich Village was no longer just a place where local bohemians might move for cheap rent or to be near their friends—it was now a national magnet for alternative culture, worth moving across the country for.

By 1962, the Village folk scene was being documented by a significant number of homemade zines, the most significant of which was *Broadside*. The mimeographed, hand-stapled publication was founded by the husband-and-wife team of Agnes "Sis" Cunningham (a former member of the Almanac Singers) and Gordon Feirsen, who had brainstormed the idea with Pete Seeger and songwriter Malvina Reynolds.[xiii]

Where *Sing Out!* contained a mix of articles, reviews, and songs, *Broadside* was primarily devoted to publishing sheet music for new topical songs coming out of the local folk scene. In stark contrast to the myth that pre-Dylan folkies were obsessed with traditionalism, Cunningham and Feirsen gave their mission statement about promoting new songs on the first page of the first issue, published in February 1962, writing, "[L]et us remember that many of our best folk songs were topical songs at their inception."[14]

Broadside's reigning champion was Phil Ochs, who published seventy-three songs in the magazine, more than any other songwriter. Bob Dylan was also a regular contributor, as both a songwriter and essayist, and several of his early songs appeared in *Broadside* before they were recorded—most significantly "Blowin' in the Wind," which appeared in *Broadside* a full year before its 1963 release on *The Freewheelin' Bob Dylan*.

---

xiii Reynolds is best remembered for writing the song "Little Boxes."

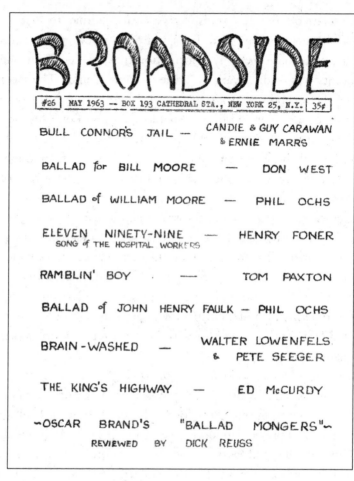

Broadside #26, May 1963.

As *Broadside*'s policy reflected, an increasing number of folk singers in the Village were focused on writing their own material with a decidedly contemporary slant. Though the newer crop of folk singers resembled their predecessors in love for and knowledge of folk tradition, they hadn't gotten there by listening to Woody Guthrie or Lead Belly exclusively—they'd come to folk via early rock 'n' roll, especially doo-wop.

A largely a cappella genre, doo-wop was in essence a DIY movement, built by groups of teenagers who congregated in parks and on street corners. Any group of teenagers that could sing reasonably well could do it; no amplification, or even instruments, were necessary. And like folk music, doo-wop was a multicultural genre, and was popular among (but hardly limited to) both Black and Italian-American teenagers.

For the younger crop of folkies, a shift from doo-wop into folk music wasn't much of a shift at all. As Richie Havens pointed out, "All of us who grew up on doo-wop music and straight rock 'n' roll know that most songs can be built on simple three-and four-chord progressions. Most folk music was also played that way."[15] Several of the scene's biggest names had made their initial forays into music through doo-wop and rock 'n' roll: Fred Neil had been a Brill Building songwriter who wrote for Buddy Holly and Roy Orbison. Noel Paul Stookey had played electric guitar as a teenager in an R & B group called the Birds of Paradise. Bob Dylan's high school yearbook from 1959 states his ambition as being "to follow 'Little Richard,'" and that same year, he had two gigs playing piano for rock 'n' roll heartthrob Bobby Vee under the name "Elston Gunn." Paul Simon and Art Garfunkel made their first records as a doo-wop duo called Tom & Jerry. Carolyn Hester had collaborated with Buddy Holly in their shared home state of Texas, and the two remained friends after they both separately relocated to New York.[xiv]

Hester: One night I was playing at Folk City. It was late at night, like the third set, when Bob Dylan came in. I said, "Here's a song I don't do much in public, because it's written by Buddy Holly and maybe a folk audience wouldn't like it," or something like that. And then this guy in a little cap pulls his chair up beside me up on the little stage, and he said, "Buddy Holly taught you that song?! You really knew Buddy Holly?!"

---

xiv Hester even attended Holly's final recording session at the Pythian Temple, located at 135 West 70th Street.

Most of the breakout stars of the Village folk scene came from this newer crop, not just because they were more motivated, but because after a certain point they were the only people around. Many of the scene's early adopters—who gravitated toward folk music mostly to gain peer approval and foster relationships, without any grander ambitions—had left for college or moved on to new neighborhoods and new endeavors, unable or unwilling to compete for gigs with the newer, more careerist musicians. To that end, many of these younger folk singers were less inclined to hang out in Washington Square Park on Sundays—Buffy Sainte-Marie and Judy Collins both claimed to have spent little time there, as they were already focused on their careers. Dave Van Ronk noticed that "by about 1962, two-thirds of my close associates were people who had blown into town in the last year or so."[16]

It was inevitable that not all of the scene's predecessors would be on board with this new crop. Alan Lomax, for one, harbored serious reservations, noting that "When songs are ripped out of their stylistic contexts and sung 'well,' they are, at best, changed. It would be an extreme form of cultural snobbery to assert...that they have been 'improved.' In my view they have lost something, and that something is important."[17]

Though the Village was a bohemian paradise for the young people now flocking to it, its growing profile also raised some neighborhood tensions between the new folkies and the remaining Italian-American community. The proliferation of folk venues raised Village storefront rents, forcing out several long-standing Italian restaurants and coffee shops that had refused to rebrand for the new trend. The simultaneous expansion of NYU's Greenwich Village campus was also leading to residential rent increases. This kind of urban transformation didn't even have a name until 1964, when British sociologist Ruth Glass coined one: gentrification.

Some white artists felt that the Italian-American community was, if not exactly welcoming, not hostile. But Black folk singers frequently found themselves targeted in the Village. Singer Len Chandler was attacked outside the Gaslight by locals looking to "clean up the neighborhood." Recalling the event, Chandler acknowledged that "the Negro just coming onto the street—he's such an easy symbol to the neighborhood of this wave of outsiders."[18]

The Village folk scene is typically remembered as largely white and middle- or upper-class, because that's what most of its breakout stars were, and that's what much of its national and international audience was. Buffy Sainte-Marie remembered the scene as being "very white," noting that "the white stars did show up for the big photo ops of the civil rights movement." Though a conscious effort was made by many white members of the folk scene to embrace Black musicians and the Black community, it yielded predictably mixed results.

In encompassing Black blues and gospel under the larger "folk" banner, a degree of appropriation was inevitable. Several of the era's white folk singers have at least one cringe-inducing blues or gospel song in their discography, where lyrical references to the brutality of the Black American experience are sung in an almost cheery tone (Dave Van Ronk's 1962 recording of "Whoa, Back, Buck" is a sterling example). And when it came to the scene's activist wing, many white performers embraced "white savior" mentalities, alienating Black activists and performers by presuming to speak for them, rather than ceding the spotlight.

But the Village folk scene was among the more diverse music scenes in the city's history—which says less about the diversity of the folk scene itself than it does about the shameful lack thereof in many of the scenes that appeared in its wake.

There was a significant Native American presence within the Village folk scene as well. Most prominently, Buffy Sainte-Marie, from the Cree Nation, used her music to address the systemic oppression of Native American people. She explained, "I wasn't the Woody Guthrie type (This land USED to be my land, if you catch my drift.) Years later I explained this to Pete Seeger, who finally understood why I didn't want to be part of the finale for a TV show he was on where they all sang that song together." Karen Dalton, who was of Cherokee descent, Patrick Sky, who was of Muscogee Creek descent, and Richie Havens, who was of Blackfoot descent, were also prominent members of the scene.

The folk scene's progressive (for the time) attitude toward racial politics did not extend to gender. As with the rest of the music industry at the time, women were generally considered second-class citizens by men in the scene. They were often excluded from much of the male folk singers' "boys' club" fraternization, notably the Gaslight's backstage poker games. Many venues' bookers were tokenizing at best, rarely booking multiple women on the same night. "No one, including me, ever questioned the conventional wisdom of the time that said, 'two chick singers back-to-back is bad programming,'" Alix Dobkin later recalled.[19]

While male folk singers were often prized for perceived "authenticity" in their scraggly appearances and gravelly voices, female performers needed to be considered attractive to men, leading many to sing in a traditional *bel canto* voice, rather than anything rough or raw. Folk's fixation with "authenticity" did not extend to female performers being their full, authentic selves.

BOB

I'm not going to give you a Dylan biography—there are hundreds, if not thousands, of those out there. If you're reading this book, you either already know the story, or you don't care. For our purposes, Dylan is significant in that he was the first Greenwich Village folkie to find success beyond a folk music audience. Not that he was even around for all that long: Dylan arrived in New York in January 1961, and by November, he was signed to Columbia Records and recording his self-titled debut album.

> **Traum:** *There were many times that I thought Bob Dylan was going to have lasting significance, but I always thought of it in terms of the folk scene, not in terms of world culture.*
>
> *I remember when we played at Gerde's Folk City, he would come and do the late show at like 12:30, 1:00. He'd get on stage with us and do a couple of songs. Sometimes we'd play with him, sometimes*

we'd get off the stage and just listen. The first time I ever heard "A Hard Rain's A-Gonna Fall" was there, when he played it for maybe a dozen people at 1:00 in the morning. I almost fell off my chair listening to that for the first time.

This was one of those light bulb moments just thinking, he is going to be really, really famous. But to me, "really famous" was like Woody Guthrie or Pete Seeger. It wouldn't ever have occurred to me that you could go to Timbuktu and people there would be listening to him, or that he'd win a Nobel Prize.

Depending on who you ask, when Dylan first showed up on the scene he was either a sweet, sensitive kid with a profound knowledge of folk traditions, and/or a phony, manipulative, careerist prick who threw the entire folk scene under the bus in service of his own fame. Either way, it's likely that few would remember or care about the Village folk scene were it not for his success, and most of what's to come in this book might not have occurred at all without him.

The folk scene, already in full swing before Dylan's arrival, went into overdrive after 1963's *The Freewheelin' Bob Dylan* catapulted him beyond what any of the scene's denizens thought possible. The neighborhood—especially Bleecker and MacDougal Streets, with their concentration of venues—became overstuffed with Dylan fans and imitators.

As the scene reached its apex, the legend goes, Bob Dylan got a backing band, plugged in an electric guitar at the 1965 Newport Folk Festival, and that was that: RIP folk music. Never mind that, as previously noted, most of Dylan's peers also revered the rock 'n' roll of their youth.

An uncharitable interpretation of Dylan's Newport stunt would be that he deliberately chose to unveil his new direction for a dogmatic out-of-town audience rather than a supportive hometown crowd of artistic peers to stir up controversy and publicity. Regardless, he dealt a death blow to the genre (if not the specific scene) that had given him his start.

Traum: The Lovin' Spoonful was starting up, people like Jimi Hendrix were coming on the scene, Dylan was going electric, so it was kind of a progression. The Village was certainly not immune to that rock 'n' roll aesthetic. But it was something that for whatever reason was not in my DNA. I've played with electric backup many times, but I'm still an acoustic guy.

Surprisingly, authenticity-obsessed Izzy Young was totally cool with the shift toward rock 'n' roll, preferring it to the sanitized, commercialized folk that had become dominant. Writing in *Sing Out!* in 1964, he explained, "I'd rather hear the Beatles sing 'I Want to Hold Your Hand' than hear the Kingston Trio sing 'Tom Dooley'... If American folk music can be eclipsed by the Beatles, then it deserves to be eclipsed."[20]

With demand for electric guitars and drum kits outpacing acoustic instruments, the Folklore Center fell on hard times. The writing was on the wall in '64, when the Folklore Center, now priced out of MacDougal Street, relocated to 321 6th Avenue. It finally closed in 1973 when the IRS caught up with Izzy Young, who, surprise, surprise, wasn't great about paying his taxes. Young, who had developed a fixation on Swedish folk music, took the opportunity to relocate to Stockholm, where he opened a new Folklore Center. He remained there until his death in 2019 at the age of ninety.

By 1967, tourists flooded the streets, NYU continued expanding, and Village rents were becoming prohibitive to all but the most successful musicians. Dylan, already a spectral presence in the neighborhood thanks to his punishing tour schedule, had fled the city for more bucolic scenery upstate, writing the song "Positively 4th Street" as a bratty kiss-off to the scene and neighborhood he'd once called home. Many of his Village peers similarly evacuated the neighborhood; as *Saturday Review* critic Ellen Sander wrote, "Folk had become too commercial to be comfortable, tourists jamming every coffeehouse were degenerating the scene, cover charges and minimums every place we used to hang out for free was a drag, the stars of the folk world were off the streets and on the road or in secluded, exclusive enclaves."[21]

Like the Folklore Center before it, the Gaslight was priced out of its MacDougal Street home in 1967 and forced to close. For a time, Sam Hood and Alix Dobkin relocated to Miami and attempted to operate a satellite Gaslight there; little came of it. The Gaslight briefly reopened as the Village Gaslight under a new owner, Ed Simon, who wisely brought Hood back from Miami to book the club. Hood again proved himself to be an ingenious booker with his finger on the pulse, bringing in Van Morrison, the Blues Project, Bonnie Raitt, Link Wray, and James Taylor.

Still, the club struggled. According to Dobkin, singer Janis Ian waived her fee one night when the club was particularly cash-strapped. Hood eventually muscled Simon out of the Gaslight, but closed it for good in 1971. An attempt to reopen in the former Cafe Au Go Go space at 152 Bleecker Street didn't amount to much.

THE AFTERLIFE OF THE GREENWICH VILLAGE FOLK SCENE

Despite the embarrassing aging-hippie nostalgia that too often obfuscates it, the Village folk scene was, in its prime, a progressive, egalitarian, experimental, artistically vital community. It's a damn shame that younger audiences are frequently told to dismiss it as a cabal of uptight fuddy-duddies who were scared of electric guitars. Because the music could be made almost anywhere, by almost anybody—three or four chords, mostly in all-ages spaces, no amplification or licensing necessary—it anticipated or invented much of the DIY culture that continues to fuel underground music scenes to this day. And in the specifics of its rise and fall, it mapped the ways almost all the Manhattan music scenes that followed would develop, only to implode under the weight of attention and gentrification.

That magnetic block of MacDougal Street between West 3rd and Bleecker went on to host many future musical developments— disco deejay Francis Grasso opened his flagship club Cafe Francis in the former (and current) Cafe Wha?; 99 Records, a post-punk record store and label that released groundbreaking records by Liquid Liquid, Bush Tetras, and ESG, operated out of 99 MacDougal; a sleaze-metal hangout called Scrap Bar took over the former Gaslight, drawing in members of Guns 'n' Roses, Metallica, Alice in Chains, and Black Crowes. Despite all of that, the Village never shook off the folk era, and all of those spaces were noted for their conspicuous presence in a largely dormant "folk territory."

In the late 1970s, under financial duress, NYU abandoned its longtime Bronx campus and moved all operations to its West Village campus. As the university regained financial solvency in the 1980s, under the direction of President John Brademas, the West Village campus was converted from a largely commuter campus to a residential one. Several major construction projects commenced to accommodate the change, with numerous decrepit apartment complexes and hotels converted into unspectacular dormitories. By the 1990s, the campus extended well into portions of Union Square and the East Village, even evicting two major music venues, the Bottom Line and the Palladium.

The basement at 130 West 10th Street that once housed the Almanac Singers' hootenannies is now home to the Abingdon Square Veterinary Clinic. Pete Seeger and Toshi Ota's residence at 129 MacDougal Street has been transformed into an Italian restaurant, La Lanterna di Vittorio.

The space that once housed Izzy Young's Folklore Center (110 MacDougal Street) has hosted a variety of retail outlets in the years since; it is currently the Village Hemp & Smoke Shop. Up the block, the Gaslight (116 MacDougal) became a series of bars, most recently a fancy-pants cocktail bar called the Up & Up.

Gerde's Folk City (11 West 4th Street) was demolished in the 1970s and replaced by a hideous-looking facility for Hebrew Union College. The Cafe Bizarre (106 West 3rd Street) was similarly demolished in the mid-eighties by NYU, with D'Agostino Hall, a law school dormitory, constructed in its place in 1986.

Allan Block's Sandal Shop is now the Coppola Cafe, which calls itself "a small corner of Sicily in the West Village." Improbably, the Music Inn is still alive and kicking.

Cafe Wha? continues to survive in the Village—kinda. Owner

Manny Roth closed the original in 1968, but a new, spruced-up version opened in 1987, featuring an in-house cover band playing classic rock hits. It is even more touristy and embarrassing than its original incarnation.

The Bitter End was granted landmark status in 1992, the same year landlords unsuccessfully attempted to evict it. It continues to host live music to this day (footage of a prefame Lady Gaga butchering Led Zeppelin's "D'yer Mak'er" there can be found on You-Tube), but it's no longer the artist-friendly venue it once was. In Tom Paxton's words, "I was appalled to hear that the Bitter End had become pay-to-play. It's not enough to perform for nothing, now you have to pay. I'm sorry, that just breaks my rules."

In 2020, as Covid-19 drew many of Manhattan's wealthy residents to wait things out in their Hamptons houses, Washington Square Park once more became a hub for local musicians and artists. By the summer of 2021, nearby residents were once again regularly calling in noise complaints, leading to increased police presence and the institution of a 10:00 p.m. curfew in July of that year. Several documented tussles took place between park revelers and the NYPD—who have been accused of specifically targeting Black and Latinx musicians—some of which have turned violent.

And yet, as I write this in 2022, the park remains a gathering place for students, artists, and weirdos of every stripe. Rock and jazz bands regularly stage impromptu concerts, spontaneous poems and dubious fortunes can be had for a small fee, activists stage protests and circulate petitions, and a smattering of entrepreneurial types hawk newly legal marijuana in all its permutations. Against all odds, Washington Square Park's spirit of free expression, for which Izzy Young and co. fought, endures.

Suggested Listening

The Almanac Singers—*Songs for John Doe* (1941)

Carolyn Hester—*Carolyn Hester* (1960)

Bob Dylan—*Gaslight Tapes* (rec. 1962)

Tom Paxton—*I'm the Man That Built the Bridges* (1962)

Dave Van Ronk—*Dave Van Ronk, Folksinger* (1962)

Peter, Paul and Mary—*In the Wind* (1963)

Phil Ochs—*All the News That's Fit to Sing* (1964)

Buffy Sainte-Marie—*It's My Way!* (1964)

Len Chandler—*To Be a Man* (1967)

Richie Havens—*Mixed Bag* (1967)

2

FRIENDS AND NEIGHBORS, THAT'S WHERE IT'S AT: MINIMALISM, LOFT JAZZ, AND THE INVENTION OF SOHO AND TRIBECA

Charlemagne Palestine (musician; artist): Many of the posters for projects that went on in SoHo and Tribeca in the late '60s and early '70s have a date, but no year. That obviously means in a certain point of view: local, tribal, with no sense of the long-term. It was like fresh bread, not like a fantastic bottle of wine.

William Parker (bassist): It was like, okay, the major jazz venues aren't hiring us, so we're gonna have our own festival, we're gonna have to put out our own records. It was all about self-determination.

Even if Yoko Ono had never become an internationally acclaimed conceptual artist, smuggled avant-garde musical ideas into the global mainstream via her work with a certain Beatle, and influenced everyone from the B-52s to Lady Gaga, her role in music history would still be pivotal for one reason: she arguably operated New York City's first DIY house show venue.

Ono, the daughter of a wealthy Tokyo banker who himself was secretly a frustrated concert pianist, had been classically trained as a singer and pianist. In 1952, she moved from Tokyo to the New York City suburb of Bronxville to attend Sarah Lawrence College, where she was first introduced to the work of the acclaimed avant-garde composers Henry Cowell and John Cage. After three years, Ono dropped out and married a fellow Japanese expat, composer Toshi Ichiyanagi, and the two dove headfirst into New York's avant-garde, frequently attending lectures that Cage gave in the city. They were often accompanied by two of their friends, artist George Maciunas and musician La Monte Young.

By 1960, Ono—already a multidisciplinary artist, composer, and performer—was struggling to find spaces in which to present her and her friends' work. She had also been financially cut off by her parents, who disapproved of her marriage to the proletarian Ichiyanagi. A solution to both problems presented itself in a cheap, unheated fifth-floor walk-up apartment at 112 Chambers Street. "When I first thought of renting a loft, my friends in classical music…advised me not to do it downtown," Ono later recalled. "They said, 'You're crazy, you're wasting your money, nobody's going to go there. Anybody who's interested in "serious" music goes to midtown.'"[22]

Despite her friends' warnings, she and Ichiyanagi moved in, and between December 1960 and June 1961, the apartment hosted a series of intimate concerts, which she and Young co-organized (both have since claimed to be the primary organizer). Programs for the performances uniformly included the all-caps statement "THE PURPOSE OF THIS SERIES IS NOT FOR ENTERTAINMENT," and in addition to Ono and Young, performers included composers Henry Flynt, Terry Riley, Richard Maxfield, and Joseph Byrd, poet Jackson Mac Low, and dancer Simone Forti.

This was hardly the first time that live music had been presented in someone's home in the city: jazz bands had been a core feature of Harlem rent parties going back to the 1920s, and the Almanac

112 Chambers Street.

Singers were hosting their weekly hootenannies at 130 West 10th Street in the early 1940s. At the same time Ono was putting on these house shows, Alan Lomax was bringing a wide variety of folk musicians to perform at soirees in his apartment at 121 West 3rd Street. But Ono and Young's loft shows differed in a ground-breaking way: despite the informality of the venue, these were decidedly formal concerts, *not* parties; attendees were to approach the concerts the same way they would one at a traditional venue. The concert series may have been short-lived, but it kicked off an enormous wave of similar live-in venues, located in decommissioned industrial spaces all over Lower Manhattan—a trend that had great ramifications on both avant-garde music and the development of two major Manhattan neighborhoods.

SOHO

Today, SoHo is the third most expensive neighborhood in Manhattan, with the median sale price for an apartment at $2,850,000.[23] It's synonymous with luxury apartments, luxury dining, and luxury tourists who can't wait to see if the Chanel store in New York is different from the one in Houston/Antwerp/wherever. While this can be frustrating to any nonluxury New Yorkers who find themselves in the neighborhood's vicinity, it's in keeping with the area's early history. In the 1820s, the area now known as SoHo—the quadrant of Lower Manhattan bordered by Houston Street, Canal Street, Crosby Street, and West Broadway—was the most densely populated area in Manhattan, and an expensive one at that. It was also a high-end shopping district, with stores including Tiffany and Co. and Lord & Taylor, as well as ritzy hotels, casinos, and dance halls (as well as numerous brothels, which one assumes were also ritzy).

But by the nineteenth century's end, all that luxury had moved further uptown, and the area became overrun with what we might generously refer to as "factories." The factories—really sweatshops—were largely located in newly erected buildings. Ornate-looking on the outside, with a mishmash of classical and Greco-Roman architectural flourishes, these buildings were in fact some of the cheapest money could buy: prefabricated out of cast iron, they were ordered out of a catalog, and simply bolted together. There were—and still are—more of them in SoHo than anywhere else in the world.

Between 1950 and 1970, advances in manufacturing and transportation saw the bulk of SoHo's factories relocate to cheaper spaces out of town, where fewer workers were required. Consequently, the number of New York City residents employed in manufacturing jobs dropped from 29.5 percent to 20.5 percent and many of SoHo's cast-iron buildings emptied out. In the late 1950s, New York's so-called "Master Builder" Robert Moses, sensing an opportunity in all this, proposed construction of the elevated Lower Manhattan Expressway (LOMEX): a ten-lane superhighway connecting Long Island and New Jersey, which would have run right through (and thus obliterated) the Lower East Side, Little Italy, and SoHo, displacing 1,972 families and 804 businesses.

Local response was less than thrilled, and in 1962 the writer and activist Jane Jacobs, who had successfully fought Moses's attempt to build a road through Washington Square Park, spearheaded the Joint Committee to Stop the Lower Manhattan Expressway. Jacobs even got Bob Dylan to anonymously write an anthem for the group, "Listen, Robert Moses."

With the construction of LOMEX seemingly inevitable, SoHo landlords—whose vacant factory buildings seemed marked for demolition—had no interest in pouring money into properties they would soon lose. But the vigorous fight against LOMEX suggested that wholly abandoning them wasn't a great idea either.

Luckily, there was another option: let people live in them illegally. It was a win-win for the landlords: they were able to still make some money, but since illegal residents had no legal recourse, they also could neglect the buildings and refuse to offer basic amenities like heat, hot water, and even electricity.

Who would want to deal with a sketchy landlord, move into an unstable housing situation where they could be evicted at a moment's notice, and live in an enormous, freezing apartment where you had to boil water on the stove if you wanted to take a bath? Buddy, it's like you've never even met an artist!

The wide-open, empty factories were very conducive to the making and presenting of seemingly every kind of art. Visual artists had room to set up studios; musicians and dancers didn't have to worry about noise complaints from nonexistent neighbors. Artists of all stripes began trickling into the neighborhood, illegally occupying what had once been factory floors. Many installed blackout curtains and slept on easily hideable mattresses, so as not to attract the attention of authorities.

The artists were able to move in because the area's future was in flux. But it turned out SoHo was still just industrial enough, and home to just enough factory jobs, that some in positions of power did not want to see it gone. That, combined with Jacobs-led local activism, effectively killed off LOMEX by 1968; it was officially de-mapped in 1972.

In 1968, local artists, previously dwelling in secret but now seeing the possibility for something more permanent, formed the SoHo Artists Association—their name contracted "South of Houston" (referring to nearby Houston Street), thus rechristening the neighborhood.

The group began earnestly lobbying for their right to live in buildings zoned for manufacturing, and thanks to their efforts, the city rezoned SoHo in 1971 to allow for artists—and *only* artists— to reside with their families in joint live/work spaces on the upper floors of old industrial buildings. The neighborhood technically remained zoned for industrial use only, but, the thinking went, artists often work with industrial tools in some capacity (sure, why not). Artists would have to apply for certification from the city to prove that they were indeed artists, but many didn't bother. The end result was a weird liminal state where the dwellings were not quite legal (and landlords were able to remain negligent), but the city still acknowledged that people lived there and was cool with it.

Two years later, SoHo was designated a historic district, its cheap cast-iron sweatshops now considered culturally valuable landmarks.

In addition to being great spaces for creating visual art, the lofts in and around SoHo were perfect for hosting music of all stripes: Large audiences could fill the open floors, musicians could rehearse in their homes, and there was no preexisting community to complain about the noise—or about being displaced by the artists who were moving in. For those operating on the musical fringe, access to these cheap spaces could mean the difference between pursuing their art full-time or not. And best of all, landlords *had* to rent to them—it was artists or nothing!—so they couldn't possibly be gentrified out of there anytime soon. Of course they couldn't, right? Right? *Right?*

The Downtown live/work spaces that hosted live music during this period are typically associated with two genres: "Minimalism" and "Loft Jazz." As we'll see, these terms are both so vague that they're meaningless; several musicians from both camps bristle at the terms, and the boundaries between them were very permeable. I've opted to view them as components of a larger entity: experimental music.

LA MONTE

La Monte Young was born to a Mormon family in a log cabin in Bern, Idaho, in 1935, but by the time he graduated from high school in Los Angeles, he was a jazz saxophone prodigy. As a music student at Los Angeles City College in the mid-fifties, he befriended the acclaimed multi-instrumentalist and bandleader Eric Dolphy, who he reportedly beat out to get a seat in the school's renowned jazz band. As a working sax player around the LA jazz scene, Young played alongside legends such as Ornette Coleman and Don Cherry. But by 1958, when he moved on to further studies at UC Berkeley, his ambitions had shifted away from jazz and into something altogether different: a mix of modern avant-garde, classical, and traditional Asian music.

Young relocated to New York in 1960 to study with electronic composer Richard Maxfield at the New School for Social Research, taking an apartment at 119 Bank Street. By the end of the year, he was booking shows at Yoko Ono's loft and positioning himself at the nexus of Downtown's burgeoning avant-garde.

In 1962, Young formed a group called the Theater of Eternal Music (aka the Dream Syndicate). The group initially consisted of Young and light artist Marian Zazeela (the two married the following year), as well as photographer and Andy Warhol associate Billy Name and percussionist/calligrapher Angus MacLise. The group played a loose, improvisatory music inspired by both Young's jazz background and interest in Indian classical music. By '63, Name and MacLise had largely been replaced by violist John Cale (soon to be a founding member of the Velvet Underground) and violinist Tony Conrad. Under their shared influence, the group's music shifted toward long, sustained drones with uncommon, atonal intervals, played through electronic amplification. It was entirely without precedent.[i]

That same year, Young and Zazeela moved into a loft at 275 Church Street in what's now known as Tribeca. The loft hosted occasional performances by the Theater of Eternal Music but was also dedicated to a concept Young and Zazeela were formulating called "The Dream House," which Young later defined as "a place where live music and light can go on continuously on into time, and the work can evolve and develop."[24]

Young and Zazeela first actualized the Dream House concept in their Church Street loft in September 1966, using sine wave generators to create endless electronic drones, alongside Zazeela's light sculptures and slides. It ran continuously with few interruptions until January 1970. Where Yoko Ono's Chambers Street loft was the city's first residential space to host formal concerts, Young and Zazeela's Dream House became the first to present itself first and foremost as a venue—just one in which the couple happened to reside.

FLUXCITY

In 1963, visual artist George Maciunas—a friend of both Ono and Young's—moved into a loft at 359 Canal Street, which he dubbed Fluxus Headquarters. Maciunas had already begun applying the word "Fluxus" to a wide variety of endeavors, as well as using it as a genre descriptor for experimental, conceptual, and process-oriented artists of any medium with whom he felt a kinship. A storefront in the building became "FluxHall," hosting nightly performances and containing a store that sold Fluxus art.

Most of Maciunas's and Fluxus's work is beyond the scope of

---

i   Tragically, the music that Young, Zazeela, Conrad, and Cale recorded in the early 1960s remains unheard. Tensions developed between Conrad and Cale, who insisted that the group's music was collaborative, and Young, who insisted upon his sole authorship of the work. Even with Conrad's passing in 2016, the recordings remain in Young's exclusive possession to this day, as yet unreleased.

this book, except for one major thing: In 1967, with financial assistance from the National Endowment for the Arts and the J.M.
Kaplan Foundation, Maciunas began buying up freshly shuttered
factories in SoHo, beginning with a seven-story building at 80
Wooster Street. In flagrant violation of zoning laws, he converted
them into live/work spaces for artists which he dubbed "Fluxhouse
Cooperatives." The spaces, which were available to residents for
about $1 per square foot, were, per the Fluxus Foundation, "Maci-
unas's first realization of 'Fluxcity,' a Kolkhoz or collective estate
which offers the space for art to flourish."[25] Though stray artists and
musicians had been illegally living in lofts Downtown, Maciunas
was the first person to see the potential for SoHo's mass conversion from empty industrial district to artists' utopia, and take active
steps to help its buildings become legitimate housing for artists.

Maciunas converted sixteen buildings over the course of ten
years; his work set in motion activities that would culminate in
the legalization of SoHo lofts for artist residences, which have led
to him being informally designated as "The Father of SoHo."[26]

But it wasn't legal yet in 1967. Maciunas fell into trouble. One
anecdote has him chasing a building inspector into the street with a
samurai sword; others have him installing a guillotine blade above
his apartment door to ward off visitors, or leaving his house only
after dark, in disguise. Even after the lofts were legalized, Maciunas kept getting into sticky situations, culminating in his being
assaulted, allegedly by members of the Mafia, in 1975.

*Palestine: George was an asshole, and that was a Mafia area. He
was impolite to a whole bunch of Mafia people, so they got pissed off
and broke his legs. That was the beginning of his demise. He never
really recovered emotionally, physically, psychologically, after that.*

Following the assault, Maciunas relocated to Massachusetts. But
his vision for SoHo and Tribeca was already well on its way. Today,
it's tough to imagine purchasing real estate as a radical creative act
(especially when said real estate is now likely occupied by a designer

shoe store). But Maciunas's work had a direct hand in SoHo's brief tenure as a neighborhood in which artists and musicians *were* the endemic population, much like the Italian immigrant community was in nearby Little Italy. Maciunas couldn't possibly have foreseen his beloved SoHo transforming into the luxury neighborhood it is now, but wealthy celebrities like Kelly Ripa and Claire Danes wouldn't call it home were it not for this one weirdo artist who got NEA grants to buy up old factories.

MINIMALISM

Composers Steve Reich and Philip Glass had first met as class-mates at Julliard in the early 1960s, but reconnected in early 1967, when Glass attended a concert of Reich's at the Park Place Gallery (542 West Broadway). Reich had been experimenting with repetitive, rhythmic compositions inspired by encounters with La Monte Young's old collaborator Terry Riley; Glass, in turn, was blown away by Reich's new work and began pursuing similar musical ideas. Glass debuted this new direction in a concert on May 19, 1968, at the Filmmakers' Cinematheque at 80 Wooster Street (aka George Maciunas's first Fluxhouse Cooperative).

There was little reason to think that this music had any commercial prospects, and though living costs were low, Glass and Reich still needed to eat. To supplement their meager income from music, Glass and Reich co-founded Chelsea Light Moving, a moving company that only operated on weekends, with a rented van at that. Glass also worked as a plumber, cab driver, and (more glamorously) an assistant to sculptor Richard Serra. Waxing nostalgic, Glass later noted that in this era "you could work three days a week loading a truck or driving a cab, and you'd have enough money to live off of, but that's not true anymore."[27]

At this point in their still-nascent careers, both Glass and Reich had more friends in high places in the art world than either had in the music industry, and much of the work both composed in the late '60s and early '70s was performed in spaces in and around SoHo that were primarily devoted to visual art: Reich regularly performed at the John Weber Gallery (420 West Broadway) along-side exhibitions by his friend Sol LeWitt; Glass performed at avant-garde theater director Robert Wilson's space, the Byrd Hoffman School of Byrds at 147 Spring Street, Jeffrey Lew's 112 Greene Street gallery,[ii] and sculptor Donald Judd's loft at 101 Spring Street.

Both Judd and LeWitt, as well as Glass's erstwhile employer Richard Serra, were considered part of the "minimalist" art move-ment that had emerged out of the city, largely from artists' lofts in SoHo, in the 1960s. Minimalist art is more or less what it sounds like: art stripped of anything that could be considered clutter, often reduced to simple shapes, colors, textures, and ab-stractions, with lots of negative space. Glass and Reich, as well as predecessors like La Monte Young and Terry Riley and peers like Charlemagne Palestine and Meredith Monk, reduced their music to simple shapes and textures, leaning heavily on repetitive, cycli-cal phrases, rhythmic pulses, and/or drones. Inevitably, they too became saddled with the "minimalism" tag.

While minimalist visual art took off in SoHo in part because the area's cheap rents and wide-open lofts were conducive to it, minimalist music found a home there in large part because there was nowhere else for it to go. While other genres had their own dedicated venue systems in the city—folk had coffeehouses, rock had rock clubs, jazz had jazz clubs—minimalism was a contem-porary outgrowth of classical music, and traditional classical ven-ues were not interested in booking it. Minimalist musicians had to build their own venue system, from scratch.

Both Reich and Glass took full advantage of Downtown's bounty of ex-industrial loft spaces. By the early '70s, Reich had settled into a loft at 423 Broadway, just above Canal Street, which became both his home and a practice space for his band, Steve Reich and Musicians. Glass's Philip Glass Ensemble had been re-

ii   Glass also recorded several albums at 112 Greene Street's basement-level recording studio, Big Apple Studios, including *Music for Twelve Parts, North Star,* and *Einstein on the Beach.*

PHOTO BY THE AUTHOR, 2023.

10 Bleecker Street.

hearsing at saxophonist Dickie Landry's loft at 10 Chatham Square in Chinatown, but in 1972, Glass took over a top-floor loft space at 10 Bleecker Street (just north of Houston Street), which would become a transformative location for him.

During his two years at 10 Bleecker, Glass and his ensemble worked on a composition entitled *Music for Twelve Parts.* A handful of formal concerts were performed in the space, but the Glass Ensemble also held unofficial open rehearsals there on Sunday afternoons.

At these open rehearsals, the group would play in a circle, all facing each other, with audio engineer Kurt Munkacsi running the music through a punishingly loud quadraphonic surround-sound system—the sort of thing an unsoundproofed loft venue could only have had in an otherwise-empty building with few neighbors. Audiences sat on bleachers that were installed along the loft's walls. There was no cover charge, though donations were accepted.

The unconventional seating and informal nature of the shows allowed the music to develop into something far less uptight and formal than most contemporary classical music, which was almost never informed by the real-time feedback of a crowd of casual listeners at rehearsal. Despite only being in the space for two years, the Philip Glass Ensemble played more shows in the Bleecker loft than anywhere else during that entire decade.

By 1974, Glass had begun sharing the loft space at 10 Bleecker with another composer, Charlemagne Palestine. When the lease on 10 Bleecker Street ended in December 1974,[iii] Glass and Palestine relocated to a new building at 22 Reade Street, which was dubbed the Idea Warehouse.[iv] Palestine recalled staging several concerts in the space he and Glass shared there, but only a few months into its existence, a fire destroyed the building. Newly displaced, Palestine found a loft of his own at 64 North Moore Street.

Palestine: My loft was bizarrely constructed out of Sheetrock; I painted it all red and gold so it looked like a kind of Chinese temple. The rent was $500 a month, which was a lot, because when I was at 10 Bleecker with Phil Glass or at the Idea Warehouse at 22 Reade, we were [splitting] like $400 or $500. My mother helped me a little bit sometimes [financially], until a certain period where I began to help her at the very end of her life. But I needed help, because there was never very good financing for sound art.

Thanks to an association with SoHo's Sonnabend Gallery (420 West Broadway), Palestine was able to secure a top-of-the-line Bosendorfer piano for the loft, where he began staging regular, informal concerts.

Palestine: I had that space for about three years, and I invited a lot of other people to perform there on my instrument. It wasn't for any money, I just offered the space and the instrument, and they'd charge $5 or something like that.

---

iii   Later in the decade, the ground-level gallery space became a short-lived punk venue called Studio 10, which hosted the likes of Bad Brains, the dBs, DOA, and Johnny Thunders.

iv   Other tenants included experimental theater companies Mabou Mines and the Wooster Group.

64 North Moore Street.

PHOTO BY THE AUTHOR, 2023.

Beyond the confines of his loft, Palestine remembers nearby businesses being especially welcoming to—and forgiving of—working artists.

> *Palestine: Magoo's Restaurant [21 6th Ave., roughly three blocks away from 64 North Moore Street-ed.] would give us tabs which I would pay every several months when I would come back from a tour in Europe. The owner would send his daughter over and tell her "See if Charlemagne is back, because I don't want him to go anywhere before he comes here. He has to pay up his tab before he spends anywhere else."*

The seeds Yoko Ono, La Monte Young, and George Maciunas had planted were sprouting. Ono and Young presenting concerts in their homes had been novel at the time; but with others following in their footsteps, minimalism was becoming a fully-fledged scene in SoHo and Tribeca—one that existed almost entirely outside the confines of traditional venues, and one that arguably could not have existed had it been dependent on them.

LOFT JAZZ

The idea of house shows spread through other avant-garde music communities, too—particularly the jazz world.

A traditional jazz scene had been flourishing in the West Village since the '50s, and the Half Note at 289 Hudson Street in SoHo welcomed the likes of John Coltrane, Charles Mingus, and Billie Holiday. But the genre's avant-garde struggled to find footing: An Alphabet City club called Slugs' Saloon (discussed in greater depth in Chapter Seven) was a hub for avant-garde and "free" jazz throughout the '60s, but it was both sonically and geographically peripheral to the larger jazz industry. There was no club circuit for avant-garde performers to regularly book shows.

Some musicians took steps to open venues where avant-garde performers could play. In the middle of the decade, saxophonist George Braith opened Musart Spiral Foods in the basement of 149 Spring Street in SoHo, an organic restaurant that also hosted nightly avant-garde jazz shows. Ali's Alley, a small nightclub which opened at 77 Greene Street in SoHo in 1973, was owned and operated by Rashied Ali, a drummer best known for playing alongside John Coltrane during the final years of Coltrane's life. Ali covered the club's rent ($200 a month, which also covered his residence on the second floor) by serving alcohol and a full menu of soul food, so that musicians didn't have to fill the room just for the club to break even; Ali also gave performers 100 percent of the door. "All this club proves is that musicians can get up off their behinds, stop complaining to the air, and do something about their conditions," Ali explained. "Nobody's getting rich, but it's a start."[28]

For many musicians, the solution to the issue was to open up their homes as venues.

★ ★ ★

There is some debate as to what space should be considered the first jazz-oriented loft venue. As previously mentioned, live jazz had been a fixture of Harlem rent parties since the 1920s, and throughout the '50s and '60s, several apartments had functioned as twenty-four-hour open-door jam sessions for musicians, although few of those were open to the public. In 1967, drummer Warren Smith (best known to rock listeners as the percussionist on Van Morrison's *Astral Weeks*) started hosting occasional performances in his loft at 151 West 21st Street, a space he dubbed Studio WIS. But the "loft jazz" era arguably began in earnest in April 1968, when Ornette Coleman moved into 131 Prince Street in SoHo.

At that point, Coleman was already a world-renowned musician who was widely credited as the father of free jazz (at the very least, his 1961 album *Free Jazz* gave the subgenre its name), and in 1967, he became the first jazz musician to receive a Guggenheim Fellowship. And yet, he was rarely performing—not because he couldn't get bookings, but because, as writer Val Wilmer put it, he was "single-handedly...waging a campaign against the entrepreneurs who, he felt, had withheld from him the financial reward commensurate with his talent."[29]

Coleman had been largely itinerant, staying in a series of small apartments and hotel rooms around town, never for too long. 131 Prince Street, a co-op building where he remained until 1974, became his first stable residence in the city. Coleman took the first and third floors of the building, each over ten thousand square feet.[v] The third floor became his residence, in which he installed a desk, pool table, and fully functional sauna (the space was otherwise unheated); the first floor was converted into a practice space and music venue.

Coleman was also an old friend and collaborator of both Yoko Ono and La Monte Young's and close with the Philip Glass En-

---

v   Pioneering electronic music composer Emmanuel Ghent lived on the fifth floor.

PHOTO BY THE AUTHOR. 2023.

131 Prince Street.

semble's Dickie Landry, and he had attended several performances by Fluxus performers and minimalist musicians at loft spaces in and around SoHo. For an artist who was denying himself performance opportunities out of a principled refusal to enrich middlemen, the prospect of seizing the means of production and opening a loft venue of his own must have been extremely appealing.

While the notion that an artist of Coleman's stature and renown would open up their home to public performances is nearly unthinkable now, that's exactly what happened. Initially, Coleman's cousin James Jordan helped with booking and advertising shows at the venue, which was belatedly named "Artists' House" in 1972. But Coleman also allowed other musicians to come in and present their own shows in the space, and regularly hosted art shows and classes. Coleman even let other itinerant musicians crash there for extended periods, including saxophonists Julius Hemphill and Anthony Braxton, and violinist Leroy Jenkins.

Coleman's 1970 album *Friends and Neighbors*, recorded live on Valentine's Day at 131 Prince Street, is exemplary of his approach to the space: Liner photos show Coleman's group playing in an informal circle, while the audience sits in folding chairs and looks on; there is no stage of any kind, and no PA. The audience includes small children and elderly people; young hippies watch alongside saxophonist Pharoah Sanders. Uncharacteristically for Coleman, the opening title track features the audience singing a repeating chorus in unison, with a simple lyric celebrating the album's titular concept. All of which would have been a far cry from Coleman's pre–Prince Street performances in nightclub environments like the Five Spot or the Village Gate.

Though noise complaints from new tenants in the building forced Coleman to close up the first floor in 1974, he hosted a few more shows in his third floor living quarters before ceasing in 1975. But by that point, several other jazz musicians had adopted Coleman's live-in venue model.

In 1969, trumpeter James DuBoise took over a loft building at 193 Eldridge Street in the Lower East Side, which he'd had inherited from free jazz pianist Burton Greene. Conveniently, both Greene and DuBoise were able to live in the building rent-free, so long as they maintained it.

DuBoise and drummer Harold Smith worked together to renovate the six-floor space, fixing the roof, plumbing, and brick walls. DuBoise and Smith also installed a small stage on the sixth floor, and once the place was spruced up, they hosted jam sessions and concerts there. One show, advertised as "We—the 12 Groups in Concert," gave the space its name: Studio We.

Studio We's grand coming out party was a festival in July 1970 called "Three Days of Peace Between the Ears." The festival took full advantage of the space, with multiple performances on different floors—a feat that would have been impossible at a traditional venue. A few of the festival's performers—most notably, Sam Rivers and Rashied Ali—would go on to open venues of their own soon after.

From there, Studio We only improved, transcending the confines of a "loft venue" to become a full-fledged community cen-

PHOTO BY THE AUTHOR, 2023.

193 Eldridge Street.

ter. Percussionist Juma Sultan (best known for playing in Jimi
Hendrix's band at Woodstock) began running the space alongside
DuBoise, and set up a recording studio on Studio We's second
floor that other musicians could rent for cheap. DuBoise's brother,
Charles Hooks, opened a restaurant, Soul Food House, on the first
floor. At the time, DuBoise noted that "the restaurant keeps the
building together. It provides rent. And it's advantageous. To have
a restaurant, you have to keep the building clean so it's more apt
not to get torn down."[30]

Among the many young musicians finding their way to Studio
We in the early '70s was a keyboardist named Martin Reverby,
who would go on to shorten his last name to Rev and co-found
the synth-punk duo Suicide. But at the time, Rev was leading a
free jazz ensemble called Reverend B, as well as picking up side-
man gigs here and there.

*Rev: I was asked to do shows [there] with Steve Tintweiss, a bass
player who was already an active player on the avant-garde scene. So*

that's where Studio We kind of gravitated towards me, and I gravitated towards it very naturally. You saw an incredible array of the avant-garde in New York there—critical, major players of that world were coming through. It was a wonderful complex.

From 1975 to '78, a loft venue called Environ welcomed visitors to the eleventh floor of 476 Broadway in SoHo. The loft itself belonged to musician brothers Darius, Chris, and Danny Brubeck (sons of famed pianist Dave Brubeck), but was largely run by two nonresidents, John Fischer and Jay Clayton. Clayton was among the rare vocalists in the free jazz scene, as well as a member of Steve Reich's ensemble; Fischer was a pianist in a jazz group called INTERface, but was also known in the art world for his bread sculptures—literally, sculptures made out of bread. Fischer brought a similarly experimental approach to Environ, going so far as to serve anchovy-flavored ice cream and coffee with soy sauce in order to subvert audiences' sensory expectations.

A bit west of Environ, on the SoHo-Tribeca border, was 501 Canal Street, home to musicians Cooper-Moore, Alan Braufman, David S. Ware, and Chris Amburger. Cooper-Moore (then going by his given name, Gene Ashton) found the space on a tip from a photographer friend and got a ten-year lease on the building. Rent was a combined $550 a month for the entire five-floor building, split five ways between the four musicians and Cooper-Moore's wife. A street-level storefront became a rehearsal and performance space, straightforwardly named 501 Canal.

Cooper-Moore: I was able to play whenever I wanted to. I scheduled eight hours a day in the storefront playing piano—I usually played from midnight to 4:00 a.m. From 4 until about 8, I slept, took the kids to school, and came back home. I probably went to sleep at noon, got up at 4 p.m., and started all over again.

The front door downstairs would be open and unlocked, and people walked in all the time. I remember one morning after having been there for about five months, this guy, he doesn't even knock, he just walks on in. We're all having coffee or tea, or smoking a joint. This guy walks in, and we're like, "Hey man, how are you doing? Come on in!" He sits down at the table, we're like, "Do you want a joint? Have a joint!" Somebody rolled him a joint, and he started smoking it. I said, "Who are you? What do you do?" He said, "I'm a cop in this precinct. We knew somebody had moved in, I just wanted to see who y'all were." We're like, "Come by any time, man!"

Although jazz-oriented lofts were sprouting up downtown, the "loft jazz" scene arguably didn't coalesce until the 4th of July weekend of 1972. Promoter George Wein had relocated the Newport Jazz Fest from its namesake Rhode Island town to New York City, with a lineup that leaned heavily on middle-of-the-road acts: Count Basie, Weather Report, Herbie Hancock, Dave Brubeck, even Pete Seeger for some reason. Much to the dismay of New York's avant-garde jazz musicians, few of them were on the bill.

But since fans were going to be in town for the festival anyway, a group of Downtown musicians—including James DuBoise, Juma Sultan, Sam Rivers, Noah Howard, Milford Graves, Rashied Ali, Eddie Heath, and Ali Abuwi—organized the New York Musicians' Jazz Festival, which ran concurrently with Newport as either additional or counterprogramming, depending on how you looked at it. The festival included five hundred local musicians playing 180 events in eighteen locations throughout all five boroughs.

The festival heralded the arrival of what would become identified as the loft jazz scene, with musicians uniting to take control of how their music was presented and promoted. In an attempt to make the music as accessible as possible to as many people as possible, many of the events were free, held in parks, community centers, and lofts—including Studio We and Ornette Coleman's Artists' House, as well as a brand new one called Studio Rivbea.[vi]

Saxophonist Sam Rivers and his wife Bea had moved into the

vi   The following year, George Wein took the hint and invited the organizers of the New York Musicians' Jazz Festival to participate in the Newport Jazz Fest, a sign of the underground's growing influence. They accepted—while staging their own festival again, throughout the city.

24 Bond Street.

two-story loft space (ground level and basement) at 24 Bond Street, two blocks north of Houston Street, in 1969. The landlady, Virginia Admiral, was a painter and poet who had once worked as a typist for writer Anaïs Nin, and whose son Robert De Niro was on the verge of becoming a successful actor. Like George Maciunas, Admiral had been proactively finding and organizing low-cost housing complexes for working artists.

The Riverses lived on the ground level, and Sam used the basement space for rehearsals and giving lessons. But in 1972, he and Bea began using the space for performances as well, dubbing it Studio Rivbea (*Rivers + Bea*). In its infancy, Studio Rivbea hosted performances as part of the New York Musicians' Jazz Festival, which helped announce it to the community as a new, available venue.

Ahmed Abdullah (trumpeter): I played the very first night that Studio Rivbea opened in a band called the Melodic Art-tet. Sam didn't play, but that's how he was able to smartly build his place: You can

Bassist William Parker, drummer Rashid Bakr, and trumpeter Arthur Williams performing at Studio Rivbea, July 4, 1976.

build the place around yourself, but that is not necessarily going to give you the longevity that you might want it to have.

The Riverses had a good thing going: Sam booked the shows, Bea took care of the finances. Cover charges were typically in the $2–$4 range, and many accounts mention a free bowl of Beatrice's homemade soup included with admission.[vii] Musicians played for a cut of the door, although Sam and Bea took a small cut to help pay for rent and upkeep.[viii]

The Studio Rivbea Summer Music Festival, which Sam and Bea organized as counterprogramming to the 1973 Newport Jazz Fest and the New York Musicians' Jazz Festival, became an annual event, with the 1976 event recorded and released as *Wildflowers: The New York Loft Jazz Sessions*, a five-volume set on Casablanca Records.

Because of its breadth and quality, *Wildflowers* stands as the most comprehensive and definitive document of the loft jazz era—although it has little competition on that front, as few other such compilations exist—and was an introduction to the jazz lofts scene for much of the outside world.

In 1973, singer Joe Lee Wilson opened another jazz loft called Ladies' Fort, a one-hundred-seat ground-level space located one block west of Studio Rivbea at 2 Bond Street. The venue was named in tribute to singer Billie Holiday, a childhood hero of Wilson's whose nickname was "Lady Day."

Though Studio Rivbea got a grant from the New York State Council on the Arts, Wilson was unable to get outside funding, explaining to writer Stanley Crouch that "we pay the musicians by giving them two thirds of the receipts we take in at the door. The other third goes for the rent. Which is two months behind."[31] Despite that, Ladies' Fort was viable (friendly) competition for Studio Rivbea, with Wilson booking mainstream acts like Count Basie alongside avant-garde/free musicians.

---

vii Ahmed Abdullah, in our interview, insisted that Rivbea "never did food."

viii Among the regular guests at Studio Rivbea was the Riverses' upstairs neighbor, photographer Robert Mapplethorpe. Mapplethorpe's wealthy older boyfriend Sam Wagstaff had purchased the fourth-floor loft on his behalf in 1972 for $15,000. Mapplethorpe lived and worked in the space for the bulk of his career; his close friend Patti Smith was a regular visitor, and the cover for Television's *Marquee Moon* was shot there. Despite his grounding in the burgeoning punk scene, Mapplethorpe found the music at Rivbea compelling, and even took some shots of Sam Rivers.

PHOTO BY THE AUTHOR, 2023.

2 Bond Street.

Like many other loft venues, the Ladies' Fort relied on food sales to help pay its rent—in this case, organic popcorn. Bassist Hakim Jami, who took over the venue from Wilson in the late '70s, later recalled, "Being that I opened around midnight, a lot of my clientele were vegetarians. That was one of the only spots they could get organic food until eight o'clock in the morning."[32]

One block east of Studio Rivbea and two blocks east of Ladies' Fort was the Tin Palace, a legitimate bar and jazz venue run by poet Paul Pines. Pines opened the venue at 325 Bowery in 1970, but he didn't quite have a handle on what was taking place in jazz's avant-garde, which his bookings reflected. That changed in 1975, when two recent Californian transplants—saxophonist David Murray and drummer/writer Stanley Crouch—moved into the loft above it. Murray and Crouch began booking shows in their space, which they dubbed Studio Infinity. The pair befriended Pines, and in short order Crouch began booking an avant-garde jazz series on Sundays at the Tin Palace, including artists like James Blood Ulmer, Roscoe Mitchell, and Henry Threadgill.

The term "loft jazz" is less of a genre descriptor than an affirmation of a loosely knit community of experimental jazz musicians who were playing the same circuit of DIY venues. As Ahmed Abdullah put it, "You can work this loft here, and then you can work that one, and you could actually garner a reputation for yourself."

Still, it's not quite accurate to suggest that there was total cohesion or unity among the lofts, or that all the same people were playing at every place.

William Hooker (drummer): Each place had their own little group of people that ran the place, and if you fit in, you fit in, and you played. If you didn't, you didn't. I understand it completely now, but at the time when I was really trying to get gigs, it was difficult.

In 1975, bassist William Parker moved from the Bronx to an apartment on 6th Street between 1st and 2nd Avenue in the East Village. He found geographic proximity to the scene only increased his already-significant participation. Though loft jazz musicians were coming from as far away as the Bronx and Brooklyn, a substantial number were living around the Lower East Side, and as had been the case for folk musicians in Greenwich Village, they were regularly crossing paths in the neighborhood.

Parker: Any time I'd go out to the store to buy anything, it was, here comes Don Cherry down the street, here comes Frank Lowe, here comes Jackie McLean, here comes Clifford Jarvis. You'd have these summit meetings, standing on the corner, just talking. It took me three hours every time I went out to go to the store, because that's how many musicians were living in the Lower East Side.

My rent was $75 at first, and then it went up to $90. If your rent was over $75, [others would] say, "You're paying $90 rent? Man, you're getting ripped off!" Rent was so cheap that if your rent was $75, you could say, "I'll borrow $75 from my uncle to pay rent this month." Now, if your rent is $2,500, you can't borrow $2,500 from

your uncle. Your uncle will say, "Whoa, no, no, I'm not your uncle.
You only thought I was your uncle."

One difference in the motivations behind the minimalist house show and jazz loft scenes bears notice: in the largely white and leisure class minimalism scene, the loft venue was a deliberate choice, intended to draw a line between it and the less adventurous world uptown and beyond. La Monte Young, among others, purposefully issued few recordings to preserve the sanctity of his work, foregoing potential revenue streams in the process. Not to mention that wealthy benefactors—also white—were underwriting many of these artists and spaces with grants or commissions.

For Black artists, however, the lofts were a creative solution to a number of frustrations, most significantly entrenched systemic racism in the club scene. Most mainstream jazz clubs at that time had white owners, and though they did not have explicitly racist booking policies, bookings were given to musicians of a more commercial, crowd-pleasing stripe who were palatable to white, moneyed audiences. For Black musicians who wanted to push the boundaries of their art into something confrontational, these doors were closed, and by and large, the wealthy white donors who were underwriting minimalist composers weren't lining up to do the same for them. For these musicians, the lofts weren't just about making a statement or defining a new scene; some felt they were the only place they could consistently get gigs. Some found the lofts' lack of professionalism and meager payouts degrading; as pianist Muhal Richard Abrahams protested, "We didn't come to New York to play in lofts; we came to make a living."[33]

It's also worth noting that while the jazz lofts were predominantly Black-owned, the audiences were racially mixed, often skewing a little more white than Black. But the inverse was rarely true: white-run spaces devoted to minimalism attracted a largely white, leisure-class audience, with little attempt to reach out to other communities.

Put simply: in general, the stakes were much lower for the white musicians in the minimalist scene. Some Black members of the jazz scene addressed the disparity by operating explicitly Black-oriented spaces—most notably, John Dahl's Someplace Nice at 93 St. Marks Place.

Parker: John Dahl was a philosopher and a revolutionary thinker. In a way he mentored us, because he was always telling us to fill in the gaps about Black people owning grocery stores, how Black people don't have a laundromat, how we have to get our own businesses. At the other loft spots, if you didn't make any money, you didn't make any money, but when you left Someplace Nice, you'd always have money in your pocket. I don't know whether he had a little money or what, but he always gave us some money, even if nobody came.

SUICIDE

The Downtown loft scene was spawning other musical innovations, too. Martin Rev recalled being at Studio We in 1969 and seeing a poster for another show that had occurred at a venue called Museum of Living Artists, located at 729 Broadway. "I thought, that's an interesting name," Rev recalled.

Soon enough, Rev found himself with a gig at that very venue. It turned out to be a co-op art gallery run by a group of accomplished but underexposed visual artists, including one Baruch Alan Bermowitz, who would soon rename himself Alan Vega.

Though many jazz musicians had a great or even transformative time playing lofts, for Rev, "the scene in New York for jazz and avant-garde was not encouraging. If you wanted to be an active musician and play at least maybe once every couple of weeks, it would be tough after a while."

Increasingly disenchanted, he began collaborating on new music with Vega and friend Paul Liebegott, making their debut as a trio at Museum on June 19, 1970, under the name Suicide. Though based in improvisation, Suicide's music was decidedly not jazz. Instead, many of the group's early performances, both at Museum and the SoHo art space OK Harris (383 West Broadway), were advertised as "punk music"—the first instance of that word being self-applied as a genre descriptor.

By '71, Liebegott had left, turning Suicide into a duo with Vega on vocals and Rev on keyboards and drums, but their approach was new and alienating enough that gigs outside of Museum remained few and far between. In 1973, Museum relocated to 133-135 Greene Street in SoHo, just around the corner from Ornette Coleman's Artists' Space and two blocks up from Ali's Alley. Suicide continued rehearsing and performing their "punk music" in the new gallery's basement, where Vega also lived.

They weren't a comfortable fit in SoHo either. But as we'll see in other chapters, Suicide eventually found their niche in Downtown's nascent punk scene—which they'd named—and influenced the course of much of the music (rock and otherwise) that emerged in their wake. Still, it makes sense that the most confrontational and least commercial of the first wave of punk bands had roots in the loft jazz scene—though their sound didn't derive from it, their embrace of chaos and their self-expressive, outsider DIY philosophy certainly did.

CRASH AND BURN

Suicide are a unique example of the overlap between the music and art worlds around Downtown in the '60s and '70s, but that overlap was mostly within the minimalist camp—as previously noted, Philip Glass, Steve Reich, Dickie Landry, and Charlemagne Palestine all had close associations with and/or performances in galleries.

But by the late '70s, the SoHo art world had become infused with massive amounts of money—unlike music, visual art can be sold to the wealthy as a luxury good and/or investment opportunity. Suddenly, some minimalist artists who'd been living in the same unheated lofts as everyone else were wealthy art world superstars.

It was only a matter of time until, as Charlemagne Palestine put it, "The collectors began to see these [loft] spaces and said, 'Wow, why are we living in our bourgeois apartments, when there are all these fabulous spaces down here?'" For Palestine, "It became too humiliating to be a performer in the world of [galleries like] Mary Boone and Holly Solomon and Metro Pictures, because all these young artists were starting to make a lot of money, and there was no money at all for us [performers]."

As more money began flooding into SoHo and Tribeca, noise complaints followed suit and loft venues shuttered. But it would be misleading to lay the blame solely on gentrification, because there's another, more internal culprit: burnout.

If running a DIY space out of your home is a form of activism—and I believe it is—it's understandable that so many of the musicians running lofts began experiencing activist burnout. You give and give and give of yourself with little financial reward, and since the significance of that self-sacrifice is usually appreciated only long after the fact, it can feel like you're running yourself ragged for nothing. Couple that with the fact that these were active musicians with careers of their own to attend to, and you have a recipe for mass exhaustion.

Cooper-Moore: What you find out is that what you think of as a collective ends up being one person running it all. So I ended up doing most of the work. The roof was leaking, I had to go up and fix the roof. The side of the building was leaking, I had to go out and clean up the cement.

501 Canal was an early victim, with Cooper-Moore leaving the building, the city, and his music career (though he returned to the latter two in the mid-eighties) after a space heater he'd absentmindedly left running started a fire in the building.

Ornette Coleman moved out of 131 Prince Street in 1976, having already shuttered the first-floor venue space in '74 due to noise complaints. Coleman was again without a permanent home until 1982, when he bought a five-story schoolhouse building at 203 Rivington Street at public auction. Coleman attempted to transform the building into a "multiple expression center," with performances, galleries, and classrooms, but things didn't go as planned:

the surrounding Lower East Side neighborhood was rougher than SoHo had been, and Coleman was attacked and robbed twice in his home. He sold the building in 1986.

In Summer 1977, as Sam and Bea Rivers were staging the Studio Rivbea Summer Festival, Stanley Crouch booked a rival festival one block away at the Ladies' Fort, including many of the same musicians. Crouch was convinced that there was enough of an audience to fill both spots, but Sam Rivers was furious. He delivered an ultimatum: artists playing at Crouch's festival were unwelcome at his. Many sided with Rivers, in no small part because Rivbea was offering guarantees and Ladies' Fort wasn't. Turnout for both festivals proved to be meager, exacerbating tensions which culminated in Rivers punching Crouch in the face in the middle of Bond Street.

Rivers kept running Studio Rivbea for another year and a half, but between that frustration and his own career taking up more of his time and energy, he decided to close it in early 1979. Crouch continued booking shows at Ladies' Fort and the Tin Palace, but perhaps stung by the community rift that he had inadvertently engineered, by the end of the decade, he had turned his back on the loft scene entirely and began using his critical platform to champion much more traditional, middle-of-the-road jazz.

The dominoes continued to fall in swift succession. Environ closed in 1978; Ali's Alley shuttered the following year.

In the early '80s, New York State passed a new series of "Loft Laws" which granted full legality and rent stabilization for anybody (artists or otherwise) illegally residing in live/work spaces, with landlords required to bring them up to code. But by that point, prices for residential lofts in SoHo were climbing. As of early 2022, the neighborhood is technically still zoned as industrial, with residential exceptions exclusively for city-certified artists, but anyone who's spent ten seconds in the neighborhood knows what a farce that is. The city has never bothered to enforce the zoning, and the neighborhood is now among the city's richest and whitest.[ix] The billionaires in multimillion-dollar lofts could technically all be evicted en masse for not having artist certification, but that seems unlikely.

However, a proposed 2021 rezoning of the neighborhood—which, by the time you're reading this, will almost certainly be in effect—will dramatically increase the amount of new buildings that can be erected in SoHo and its surrounding areas, with restrictions in place that incentivize developers to construct (hypothetically) affordable housing instead of office or retail spaces. Unfortunately, a portion of the proposed rezoning called Mandatory Inclusionary Housing—which requires 30 percent of new residential units to be set aside for people making at least 80 percent less than the neighborhood's median income—was removed, with the explanation that other parts of the rezoning will already incentivize affordability.

Critics of the rezoning claim it will destroy the neighborhood's historic character (as if that hasn't already happened), and that long-term rent-controlled loft tenants will be displaced in order to make way for new construction, without creating enough new affordable housing to justify it. We'll see.

Though many other scenes discussed in this book are remembered as monuments to the spirit of DIY and artistic rebellion, I'd argue that that's truer for the minimalism and loft jazz scenes than most. These scenes proved that you can build something from nothing, especially if nobody intends to make a whole lot of money (although some like Philip Glass eventually did). Nothing about these empty once-industrial, now-residential spaces suggested that they would work as music venues, which they would probably never have become had these scenes not necessitated their transformation. It's a model that many successive scenes—from disco to indie rock—would adopt.

---

ix   A 2019 report by NYU's Furman Center showed that 68.4 percent of SoHo residents identified as white (https://furmancenter.org/neighborhoods/view/greenwich-village-soho, accessed June 3, 2022).

THE AFTERLIFE OF THE LOFT SCENE

Many of the spaces discussed in this chapter were residential and have remained so. Still, there have been some noteworthy transformations.

In 2021, a loft in George Maciunas's first Fluxhouse Cooperative at 80 Wooster Street sold for $3,200,000. The ground level, once home to the Filmmakers' Cinematheque, is now a brick-and-mortar outlet for the Real Real, an online purveyor of used luxury clothes.

After Charlemagne Palestine left 64 North Moore in the late '70s, the building was converted to a flashy but short-lived disco called Tribeca; it reverted to residential use. Palestine's old loft was on the market in 2022. Asking price: $2,700,000.

Ornette Coleman's ground-level performance space at 131 Prince has been subdivided into retail outlets—currently Faherty (a clothing store and "lifestyle brand") and TAFT (men's shoes).

The ground-level space at 77 Greene Street that once housed Ali's Alley is now devoted to AMI Alexandre Mattiussi, a French fashion house.

Studio We's corner storefront, which was once dedicated to Soul Food House, is now an unremarkable bodega.

Studio Rivbea, at 24 Bond Street, is now home to the Gene Frankel Theater, a small theater devoted to contemporary, politically progressive plays by living playwrights, especially playwrights of color and those from the LGBTQ+ community. The entire building was landmarked in 2008 as part of the NoHo Historic District Extension.

One block away, the old Ladies' Fort space at 2 Bond Street is now C'H'C'M', a "multi-brand men's clothing store specializing in contemporary American and Japanese designers." The old Tin Palace at 325 Bowery is now Bar Primi, a trendy Italian bar and restaurant.

501 Canal has long since been demolished; its site is now home to part of the Arlo SoHo Hotel.

The original Museum of Living Artists at 729 Broadway has also been bulldozed and replaced with Fresh & Co., a salad chain. The second location, at 133-135 Greene Street, is a retail space that is currently empty. Most recently, it housed Dior Homme.

But not all has been lost: against all odds, La Monte Young and Marian Zazeela have remained in their loft at 275 Church Street. In 1993, they reopened the Dream House as a permanent sound and light installation on the floor above their home, and it has remained open to the public ever since. Its future is perennially uncertain—Young and Zazeela are now elderly, and in recent years they've resorted to crowdfunding after the Dream House's primary backer pulled funding in 2015—so I encourage you to visit while you still can.

Suggested Listening

Tony Conrad—*Four Violins* (rec. 1964)

Ornette Coleman—*Friends and Neighbors—Ornette Live at Prince Street* (1970)

Philip Glass—*Music with Changing Parts* (1971)

Alan Braufman—*Valley of Search* (1974)

La Monte Young and Marian Zazeela—*Dreamhouse 78' 17"* (1974)

Various—*Jazz of the Seventies/Una Muy Bonita* (1977)

Various—*New Music for Electronic and Recorded Media* (1977)

Various—*Wildflowers: The New York Loft Jazz Sessions Vols. 1-5* (1977)

Abdullah—*Live at Ali's Alley* (rec. 1978)

Charlemagne Palestine—*Strumming Music* (rec. 197?)

3

THE BEGINNING OF A NEW AGE: MAX'S KANSAS CITY, GLAM ROCK, AND THE BIRTH OF PUNK

Jayne County: I'm like a freak magnet, I always gravitate toward the most outrageous, nutty, crazy, fun place there is in the city. That happened at Max's: I walked in and thought, "Oh wow, I belong here." What made Max's so great was that it wasn't just one kind of person, it was all kinds of people, but they were all there because they were in some way or another outcasts from society.

I didn't hang out anywhere else because there wasn't really any good reason to hang out anywhere else! I didn't even bother to find out if there were other places to hang out—I wouldn't have hung out there anyway.

When the story of Max's Kansas City is told, it's usually told as a tale of Beautiful People. Warhol superstars and art stars, actors, models, glam rock pioneers, Iggy Pop, and John and Yoko—Max's was the legendary, anything-goes party scene where they mixed it up late into the night. While all of this is accurate, it glosses over the true engine that made Max's run: food.

Not that the food served at Max's was good—by all reports, it was underwhelming at best. But as one of the only restaurants in the immediate vicinity of Union Square when it opened in 1965, Max's was able to make the bulk of its income serving lunch and happy hour cocktails to office workers in the afternoon. This allowed it to take financial risks in the evening, comping meals for a vast number of literally starving artists, booking unproven niche performers, and serving as a safe and inclusive place for members of the LGBTQ+ community, years before the Stonewall Riots. Without those office workers ordering the lunch special, none of it would have been possible.

While people often want stories of New York nightlife to be all about magic and kismet, Max's is a very down-to-earth story, with a very practical takeaway: if you want to serve an avant-garde community and support them as they take risks, it helps to have an alternate income stream.

Successful, influential venues typically open up in one of two locations. The most obvious location is in the middle of a growing artistic community, whose denizens use the club as a neighborhood meeting place—a sort of extended front stoop where people can catch up with each other while coming or going, and always feel like they're in the center of the action (e.g. the Greenwich Village folk clubs). The other is in the middle of fucking nowhere, where no one cares how much noise you make, who comes to your club, or what goes on in there.

When Mickey Ruskin first opened Max's at 213 Park Avenue in December 1965, it was very much the latter camp. The restaurant was on the northwestern corner of Union Square, a decidedly uncool and mildly terrifying area that Lou Reed memorably depicted as a drug addict's haven in the Velvet Underground song "Run Run Run."

But Ruskin was no naïf—the former lawyer had already owned

213 Park Avenue South.

or co-owned a series of artist-friendly cafes in and around Greenwich Village and the East Village, including the Tenth Street Coffeehouse, Cafe Deux Magots, the Annex, and the Ninth Circle. When he exited the Annex and the Ninth Circle, a noncompetition agreement with co-owner Bob Krivit prevented Ruskin from opening any new spots in the Village.[i]

Itching to open a new place outside that forbidden zone, Ruskin found a restaurant off Union Square called The Southern. The owner, an old man who was eager to retire, sold it to Mickey for a low fee. Its new moniker was suggested by a writer friend of

---

i   Krivit's son, Danny, went on to become a successful deejay and remixer during the disco era, and remains so to this day.

Ruskin's named Joel Oppenheimer, who proposed that "When I was a kid, all the steakhouses had Kansas City on the menu because the best steak was Kansas City–cut, so I thought it should be 'something Kansas City'...[And] wouldn't you eat at a place called Max's?"[34]

Max's' relative isolation ended up working in Ruskin's favor. As he later recalled, while there wasn't much preexisting nightlife nearby, "almost every major fashion photographer in New York had a studio within five blocks of the place,"[35] and there were several artist's studios in the area as well. It was only a matter of time before Max's became a regular destination for visual artists of all stripes.

Nick Marden (son of painter Brice Marden; bassist, the Stimulators): A friend of mine's father was in [art] school with my dad at Boston University, and one day he asked me, "How come your dad made it and mine didn't?" For some reason, it popped into my head, I asked him, "Was your dad hanging out at Max's?" and he said no. That had a lot to do with it: who you bumped into that day, whether you had the proper conversation, and whether you had made any connection at an artistic watering hole.

During the day, the area was also home to a stuffier assemblage of office workers and insurance agents, many of whom would dependably flock to Max's for the lunch special and happy hour drinks before heading back to their suburban homes at night.

Max's location was ideal for other reasons, too: though Union Square was not in the middle of any hip neighborhood, it was roughly located where four of them converged—Greenwich Village, the Lower East Side (a.k.a. the East Village), Gramercy, and Chelsea—each home to their own brand of artists and scenesters, all of whom could mix at Max's without too much effort.

Judy Collins: Max's Kansas City was sort of the bridge between Greenwich Village and everyplace else. It was more hip and drug-y than some of the places in the Village, but I loved it.

The bar was also more or less equidistant between the Hotel Chelsea and the Hotel Albert, the two major Downtown hotels where midlevel touring musicians would stay, and which a number of local artists and musicians called home. Of the two, the Chelsea (222 West 23rd Street) is far and away the better known, commemorated in song by Leonard Cohen, Bob Dylan, and Jefferson Airplane, all of whom spent significant chunks of time there alongside Janis Joplin, Chet Baker, Tom Waits, Velvet Underground members John Cale and Nico, and a prefame Patti Smith. Mickey Ruskin himself lived at The Chelsea on and off during his tenure at Max's.

The Hotel Albert (23 East 10th Street) gets less recognition these days than the Chelsea, but was roughly equal in stature during the late '60s. Bob Dylan (with the Band), the Lovin' Spoonful, Moby Grape, Lothar and the Hand People, and Tim Hardin all rehearsed in the basement, while musicians like Joni Mitchell, Tim Buckley, James Taylor, the Mothers of Invention, Jonathan Richman, Carly Simon, and Silver Apples' Simeon Coxe all called it home at some point. So did Warhol superstar Candy Darling, whose time there is commemorated in The Rolling Stones' song "Citadel."

As The Albert's star began to fade in the early '70s, musicians began staying with some regularity at the Gramercy Park Hotel, which was located even closer to Max's at 2 Lexington Ave. Notably, David Bowie—a dedicated Max's regular whenever he was in town—spent a considerable amount of time staying there in 1973, to such an extent that the hotel was nicknamed "The Glamercy."

Last but not least, Max's was located a mere four blocks from the Academy of Music, a major concert venue at 126 East 14th Street (it would be renamed the Palladium in 1976). During Max's' existence, the Academy/Palladium hosted major performances by the Band, the Grateful Dead, Lou Reed,[ii] Blue Oyster Cult, Iggy Pop, Frank Zappa, and Bruce Springsteen. Given the dearth of nearby

---

ii   Reed recorded two live albums there: *Rock 'n' Roll Animal* and *Lou Reed Live.*

bars catering to a younger audience, Max's was a perfect preshow and postshow destination for performers and fans alike.

All of these factors set Max's up for success, which came quickly. Within a year, it was an "it" venue, drawing a large clientele of artists and celebrities, both established and aspiring.

THE FOOD

Even if nobody had ever played a single note of music within its walls, Max's Kansas City would still hold a hallowed position in New York's music history for one simple, underacknowledged but stupidly obvious reason: every single day, Mickey Ruskin offered a free cocktail hour buffet for the price of a drink.

Yvonne Sewall (Max's waitress; married to Mickey Ruskin): There'd be chicken wings and chili and whatever else might have been leftover from [dinner] the night before. The Guardian Life Insurance Company and Chemical Bank was on the corner [next door], so cocktail hour was the one time where there would be a real mix of the "straight people" and the counterculture scene.

For the artists who hung around Max's, who were often pursuing transgressive and boundary-pushing work that couldn't be counted on to pay the bills, the free buffet at Max's was a godsend. For many, it was their only meal of the day. "That's how we survived," said Ruby and the Rednecks frontwoman Ruby Lynn Reyner. "Of course, it was horrible food; we always had the runs."[iii]

Despite his protestations that all of this was strictly business, Ruskin was generous with his regulars, especially in regard to food and drink. Visual artists weren't just drawn to Max's because it was convenient to their studios—Ruskin thought artists were impossibly cool, and let them know it, regularly allowing them to pay

---

iii   There were also free bowls full of dried chickpeas making the rounds at Max's, although Magic Tramps drummer Sesu Coleman remembered them mostly being used "for chickpea fights," rather than nourishment.

their bills with art. The result was that the restaurant's walls were covered with a museum-worthy art collection, and many Downtown artists got to eat there for free.

Reyner: Mickey would buy a drink for you on your birthday, and probably buy you dinner, too. He really wasn't that good of a businessman. I'd say, "Mickey, it's my birthday!," and he'd say, "Again??" It was always my birthday.

THE FRONT ROOM AND THE BACK ROOM

Ruskin's generosity toward artists makes a lot more sense when you consider that, as Sewall put it, "Owning the place gave Mickey a reason to be there. It gave him entry into that world he always wanted to be a part of. He never would have gone to Max's if he didn't own it."

Sewall: Mickey had this philosophy that "This is my living room, and every night I throw a party." He had this special talent for choosing very interesting, very unique people, and the blend was really quite special.

Though Ruskin endlessly nurtured the nighttime scene at Max's, it largely self-segregated into two camps, separated by interests, occupations, preferred intoxicants, and sexual orientations—each with their own distinct territory.

The front room was mostly occupied by artists who were heterosexual, at times obnoxiously so. The waitresses at Max's were outfitted in a proto-Hooters uniform of skimpy black miniskirts and low-cut tank tops; activist Abbie Hoffman tellingly described them as "the closest you could come to liking [Playboy] bunnies and get away with it, given the rise of women's liberation."[36]

The back room had a different vibe, not only because everyone was on speed instead of booze, but because that scene was dominated by gay and queer men, trans women, nonbinary people, and

others with little interest in sexually harassing the waitresses—all
lorded over by the one of history's least-likely social butterflies:
the shy, inscrutable Andy Warhol.

In 1965, the same year Max's opened, Warhol publicly "retired" from painting to focus his energy on pumping out a series of (mostly unwatchable) movies starring a clique of socialites
and glam outsiders he'd dubbed "superstars." It's sort of funny
that Warhol chose to start spending his "retirement" from painting at a known painter's bar, but by annexing the back room, the
ever-savvy Warhol could symbolically convey his own separate-
ness from the art world.

In December of that year, Warhol's filmmaking partner Paul
Morrissey introduced him to the Velvet Underground, then slog-
ging it out at Greenwich Village's Cafe Bizarre; Warhol began
managing them soon after. By '67, Velvet Underground members
Lou Reed, John Cale, and Sterling Morrison lived within a few
blocks of each other on East 10th Street and would all happily make
the short trek to Max's to eat on their benefactor's tab. Reed later
recalled that Ruskin "was personally responsible for my survival
for three years because he fed me every day."[37]

The back room's back left corner prominently featured a red
light sculpture by Dan Flavin, made in 1966 and titled "monument 4 for those who have been killed in ambush (to P.K. who
reminded me about death)." The political overtones of Flavin's
sculpture were largely lost on the crowd, many of whom identified it as the "Bucket of Blood" and noted the way it matched the
restaurant's red napkins, tablecloths, and chickpea bowls. Some
informally designated the round table beneath the statue as the
"Paranoia Booth," because it was the reddest part of the room,
but as Max's regular Tony Zanetta points out, the red light "made
everybody look fabulous."

Zanetta described the back room crowd as "a bit more of a freak
show," with Warhol hangers-on augmented by an endless stream
of celebrities and rock stars. With such a combustible mix, sex and
debauchery were de rigueur.

Reyner: Jane Fonda came around with [her husband, the film-maker] Roger Vadim looking for young women to screw, and I was approached. Vadim had a long, skinny dick, or so they said; Jane would be involved in arranging the whole thing, and then she'd watch. I was also almost fixed up with Warren Beatty there, but I thought, let me be the one New York chick who hasn't screwed Warren Beatty.

At the beginning of 1968, Andy Warhol relocated his studio, the Factory, from 231 East 47th Street to the Decker Building at 33 Union Square West—just a short stroll across the park from Max's, underscoring the Warhol clique's already-nightly presence.

Of course, beyond those two delineated scenes, there were other customers at Max's. On the more glamorous end of the spectrum were top-tier celebrities, who were seated in a private alcove: Yvonne Sewall recalled Cary Grant, Judy Garland, and John Lennon and Yoko Ono stopping by.

On the opposite end of that spectrum were the proletariat—a decidedly uncool, but necessary, component, who were seated out of the way of the Max scenesters. Although the second floor at Max's had initially been used as the waitresses' locker room, Ruskin soon opened it up as "Siberia," a place where he could seat tourists, bridge-and-tunnel types, and other boring normies who interfered with the hip vibe on the main floor. There, tucked away from the action, tourists helped underwrite the lives and art of the very hipsters they had come to peek at.

After the squares left for the night, the upstairs would often turn into a discotheque, and it also hosted the occasional musical performance or private party. But by the end of the decade it had largely fallen into disuse—so much so that Mickey lent it, for a time, to future mayor Ed Koch, who used it as headquarters for his 1969 congressional campaign.

JAYNE COUNTY

If there is a guiding spirit to this chapter, and to American glam rock in general, it's Jayne County. She's often passed over in the rush to anoint the better-known New York Dolls as America's sole glam pioneers, but County, her band, and her management often acted as the shock troops of glam and early punk, clearing the way for other acts to perform at venues where she appeared. Without Jayne, there'd be no American glam—or punk—as we know it. And to hear Jayne tell it, without Max's, there'd be no Jayne as we know her.

County first visited New York City in 1967, around the time she turned twenty. Assigned male at birth, she had grown up in Dallas, Georgia, a place as conservative and heteronormative as the deep South had to offer. Aware of her own gender noncon-formity from an early age, she fled Dallas when she was eighteen for the marginally more liberal confines of Atlanta, but still felt like a fish out of water.

County: New York was supposed to be a stop-off center for me—we were going to go to San Francisco to wear flowers in our hair. But on our way, we got sidetracked. We stopped in New York for a little bit on our way to San Francisco, and when we got there, we loved it so much, we couldn't get away. In New York City that summer, it was all about Andy Warhol and Lou Reed and the Factory and Max's Kansas City, and I thought, well, this is just as great as San Francisco.

A year after that first visit to New York, she and her friend, photographer Leee Black Childers, moved to the city for good. County fell in with the back room crowd, and she and Childers shared an apartment with Warhol superstars Jackie Curtis and Holly Woodlawn on East 13th Street between 1st Avenue and Avenue A.

Though certainly a step up from Georgia, New York was still far from an easy place to be queer. Homosexuality was illegal, as was cross-dressing. What gay bars existed in New York were largely owned and operated by organized crime, who used their muscle to (more or less) shield the LGBTQ+ community from police harassment, in exchange for using the bars to make and launder money—and to blackmail wealthy closeted patrons.

The birth of the gay rights movement is commonly traced to the Stonewall Riots, in which the Stonewall Inn, a mob-owned West Village gay bar, was raided by aggressive cops. The patrons revolted, and a crowd gathered to support them. The resultant riots lasted for six days; Jayne County and Holly Woodlawn were among the participants.

Max's wasn't a perfect queer paradise, but it was a place where LGBTQ+ people on the scene could relax, meet up, and hang out with friends of all sexualities, without worrying about police raids or Mafia shakedowns. Though County was still presenting as male at the time, Max's offered an especially welcoming and permissive environment in which to subvert and transcend gender norms.

UPSTAIRS REOPENS

From the time Max's opened, the upstairs "Siberia" space had sporadically hosted live music. Mickey Ruskin remembered the first live act being a local band called Jake and the Family Jewels, although the John-and-Yoko-affiliated group Elephants' Memory and the pioneering electronic band Silver Apples have both claimed the title for themselves. In 1970, the space hosted a run of legendary Velvet Underground shows during which front man Lou Reed quit the band.[iv] After that, things went quiet.

Ironically, it would take an old nemesis of Reed's to convince Mickey Ruskin to begin booking bands again. Eric Emerson, a Warhol associate whose image had been projected onto the band in the back cover photo for *The Velvet Underground and Nico*, attempted to sue after the album's release in a misguided attempt to get some dough. That little stunt caused the band's label, Verve Records, to pull copies from stores in order to airbrush Emerson out of the photo. By the time the album was widely available again,

---

iv   Reed's final show with the band was recorded by Warhol superstar Brigid
      Berlin and released in 1972 as *Live at Max's Kansas City*.

any momentum the Velvet Underground had built had largely subsided. Emerson didn't see a penny, and Reed blamed the incident
for derailing the band's chances for success.

After his failed attempt to sue the Velvets, Emerson relocated to
California and started singing in a band called Messiah. In 1971, a
bad earthquake left the band eager to relocate, and Emerson knew
exactly where to go.

*Sesu Coleman (drummer, Messiah/the Magic Tramps): Eric said,
"I know a place that we could probably play in New York. We can
work with Andy and he'll get us a gig, he'll talk to Mickey."*

*We were surprised when we got to New York to find out that
there were no rock 'n' roll clubs around. We got there at night, and
the next day Eric and I walked over to the Factory to meet Andy.
Andy said, "Eric, it's so wonderful to see you! What are you doing
here?" Eric said, "I've got a rock and roll band, we came here from
LA and we're gonna make this crazy New York rock 'n' roll." And
then [Warhol collaborator] Paul Morrissey came over and—I'll never
forget this—said, "Oh boys, rock 'n' roll will never fly in New York.
You've got to do cabaret."*

*We looked at him like, what? Everything was Off-Broadway, La
Mama, Jackie Curtis, and Candy Darling, the whole thing. "Would
You Like to Swing on a Star?" songs like that. So we said, "Ok,
we'll learn it."*

Morrissey wasn't totally off-base: New York's vibrant rock
scene of the mid and late sixties had largely subsided, and by 1971,
many of the venues where an unsigned band could get a gig had
closed. The few remaining West Village clubs were shells of their
former selves, and mostly hosted singer-songwriters. Though
larger venues like the Fillmore East and the Electric Circus still
drew significant crowds, there were precious few spots where
a band that was just getting started could play and begin to develop a fan base.

Coleman: After going to the Factory and meeting Andy, we walked across Union Square to Max's and went upstairs to see Mickey. Mickey always really liked Eric a lot. Eric said, "I got a rock 'n' roll band, maybe you'd let us play up here?" Mickey said, "No, I don't want music up here anymore. After The Velvet Underground thing... I can't deal with all the craziness that goes on with it." He had had the second floor closed up for a year, maybe more.

We worked on him somewhat, but he wasn't really going for it. The only way we got Mickey to give us the key to the padlock on that door [to the upstairs] was by telling him that we wanted to do a one-night showcase, just for Andy and the Factory crowd. It wasn't for the street crowd or anything like that. He gave us a key, and we went up and did one night. When we first got the door open, it was kind of like a ghost of the past: You knew that there was a lot that had gone down in that place over the years. It felt like we were opening up a dungeon.

It took a little time after that first show to play there again. We would work on Mickey, we went to visit him fairly often. He would just be friendly; we got along with him very, very well. So we kept saying, "What if, what if, what if," and he'd say "No, I've got a thing going on here." It took a while to get another show, but we convinced him.

The Messiah shows must have been somewhat lucrative for Ruskin, as he began to see the potential in reopening the space as a full-fledged music venue. Messiah—who soon rechristened themselves the Magic Tramps—became Max's' de facto house band for a spell. Ruskin wasn't particularly interested in music, though, and he needed someone else to book the acts. He found that in Sam Hood, former booker of the Gaslight.

Hood was in bad shape at the time. His wife, Alix Dobkin,

had come out as a lesbian and left him, taking their one-year-old daughter Adrian with her.[v] Postdivorce, Hood struggled.

> *Sewall: Sam Hood got into drinking a lot, that's all I'm gonna say. He was hanging out at Dr. Generosity's, which was a very popular bar up on the Upper East Side. It had an apartment upstairs, and I think Sam was living there. The owner of Dr. Generosity's said to Mickey, "You really ought to talk to Sam Hood and think about putting music up there. Sam really needs work, and he really knows the business." So Mickey went to meet him, and they really hit it off.*
> *Sam totally cleaned up his act, and he really did know the business very well. He was very good at what he did, and it became the most popular place for unsigned bands in all of New York, because there weren't that many places back then.*

Still, live music wasn't the primary attraction at Max's: Hood tended to book shows in fits and starts; Max's remained more of a clubhouse than a dedicated music venue.

> *County: Music happened, but it was always secondary to [visual] art; Mickey catered to artists. Bands would do two sets, and the audience would be sitting down in chairs at tables and eating and drinking while the bands were on. It was almost like dinner theater.*

Even so, Hood's booking skills were every bit as sharp as they'd been at the Gaslight.

Bruce Springsteen had several runs of shows at Max's, where he shared bills with both Hall and Oates and Bob Marley and the Wailers (the latter making their US debut). Other extraordinary pairings include Loudon Wainwright III with Steely Dan, Charlie Rich with Tom Waits, Jimmy Buffet with David Allan Coe,

---

v   Dobkin would go on to record several groundbreaking albums of explicitly lesbian music, most notably 1973's *Lavender Jane Loves Women*. She passed away on May 19, 2021.

and Waylon Jennings with Billy Joel. Big Star, Charles Mingus, Bonnie Raitt, Gram Parsons and Emmylou Harris (a one-time Max's waitress), Alice Cooper, Iggy and the Stooges, Willie Nelson, Sparks, and Tim Buckley all played Max's as well. The Philip Glass Ensemble performed at Max's in 1973, making Glass the first neo-classical composer to perform their work in a rock club. Hood also retained an affection for old friends that had played at the Gaslight during its heyday, booking the likes of Dave Van Ronk, Odetta, and Phil Ochs.[vi]

THE GLAM SCENE COALESCES

Despite the remarkable breadth of Sam Hood's bookings during the early '70s, Max's remains mostly associated with the city's burgeoning glam rock scene. Glam rock was largely a British export, courtesy of T. Rex and David Bowie—influenced to some degree by the Velvet Underground, but more overtly by the Rolling Stones (who had appeared in drag on the cover of their 1966 single, "Have You Seen Your Mother, Baby, Standing in the Shadows?"), the Kinks, and the Small Faces. But a uniquely homegrown take on the genre emerged downtown, coming together out of the back room at Max's, as well as a smaller after-hours bar in Greenwich Village called Nobody's.

Located at 163 Bleecker Street, Nobody's was a rundown and not especially popular bar owned by the Chin family. Ex-folkie Charlie Chin, a distant relative of the family, had played guitar and banjo in a band called Cat Mother and the All-Night Newsboys, who had gained industry attention after Jimi Hendrix produced their first album, 1969's *The Street Giveth...and the Street Taketh Away*. Chin left the band soon after and wound up becoming a bartender and deejay at Nobody's, where he started bringing in other friends of his from the music industry. The bar became a noted late-night

---

vi   Recall from Chapter One that Hood had promised Ochs he'd "see [him] on the way down." He was right.

destination for musicians, especially British ones like Led Zeppelin, the Faces, the Kinks, and the Who.[vii]

Of course, much like Max's, any place that attracts rock stars is also going to attract fans who want to be around them. Among those fans frequenting the place were two pairs of childhood friends from New York's outer boroughs—Rick Rivets and Arthur Kane from the Bronx, and Sylvain "Sylvain Sylvain" Mizrahi and Billy Murcia from Queens—as well as another Queens native, Johnny "Thunders" Genzale, and Staten Islander David Johansen. Sylvain, Murcia, and Thunders had been in a short-lived band together, but not much happened with it until Thunders met Kane and Rivets at Nobody's in late 1970. The three formed a band, Actress, and Thunders brought Murcia in as the group's drummer. In short order, Sylvain replaced Rivets, Johansen was brought in as a front man, and the group was rechristened the New York Dolls—named after the New York Doll Hospital, a toy repair shop at 787 Lexington Ave., across the street from a clothing store where Sylvain worked.

With a clear debt to the Rolling Stones,[viii] and aided by Sylvain and Murcia's fashion industry day jobs, the Dolls adopted a drag/camp aesthetic, despite being comprised entirely of heterosexual, cisgender men. Not quite fitting in anywhere, they struggled to find a venue that could serve as a home base: some early shows took place in gay bathhouses like the Continental Baths (in the basement of the Ansonia) and Man's Country in Brooklyn, but their most successful early gigs were rent parties they threw in the Chinatown loft that Thunders, Sylvain, and Murcia shared at 119 Chrystie Street, for which they charged $2 admission.

---

vii   British folk singer Bert Jansch celebrated Nobody's in the song "Nobody's Bar," off his 1971 album *Rosemary Lane*. The album's liner notes identify the bar as "the one good thing (or was it bad?) about the Village in New York."

viii Johnny Thunders, who idolized Keith Richards, is clearly visible in the Madison Square Garden audience in the Stones' infamous documentary *Gimme Shelter*.

County: All the bands were checking each other out to see who was wearing what. The Dolls were taking the lead for a while. When the Dolls started out, they were wearing secondhand clothes from thrift shops and stuff like that: They had those short, tight pants, women's shoes, and little children's shirts that were too small for them—that look became an "in" thing for a while. Once they started getting a little better known, they changed their look, but I preferred the early look because it was more of a downtown New York look.

County formed her first band, Queen Elizabeth, in 1972. Their live debut was a daytime show at NYU, an experience she remembers as "a nightmare":

County: All these students at NYU had come from out of town to New York, and there they are in the middle of the day, during their lunch break, being confronted with Queen Elizabeth. It freaked them out. There was this creature onstage fucking herself with a two-pronged dildo and a plastic vagina,[ix] and sitting on a toilet full of dog food.[x]

We got the plug pulled on us in the middle of the show by the Gay Liberation Front, because the show was so outrageous that they thought we were insulting women and gay people. They were screaming, "We will not allow NYU to be turned into a 42nd street smut shop!"

It was inevitable that Queen Elizabeth would perform at Max's, where the audience was already acquainted with County from her years of hanging around the place. She also worked as a deejay when the upstairs space became a discotheque, where she leaned heavily on *Nuggets*, a recently released compilation of '60s garage rock that was compiled by critic (and future Patti Smith Group guitarist) Lenny Kaye.

---

ix   A routine County would perform during the song "It Takes a Man Like Me to Fuck a Woman Like Me."

x   A routine County would perform during the song "Shit."

With the New York Dolls, Queen Elizabeth, and the Magic Tramps all gigging regularly by mid-1972, a glam scene coalesced— driven in no small part by other denizens of the Max's back room, including Leee Black Childers.

Zanetta: Leee Childers was kind of the glue that held a lot of this stuff together. Leee would take all these pictures of bands that nobody was interested in or wanted to see, and then he'd give them to Lisa Robinson for her magazine, Rock Scene. They would write these articles about them: "At Home with Blondie," or "A Night with David Johansen and [Johansen's wife] Cyrinda Foxe," or whatever. The scene kind of grew out of that magazine, really. It became self-perpetuating.

There was a [distinct] sensibility: a lot of irony, a lot of not taking things so seriously, a lot of defiance. You don't have to be a great singer, a great musician, a great actor. You don't have to be a [cisgender] woman to be a woman. You could be your fantasy. You could, period.

That accessibility and openness to reinvention were key, especially for younger participants in the scene. Mandy, Miki, and Paul Zone (real last name: Cilione) grew up as three gay brothers in working-class Brooklyn. They found salvation visiting Max's before forming a glam band of their own, the Fast.

Paul Zone: We would read about T. Rex or Alice Cooper in the Village Voice, *and how after their show, they went to a club called Max's Kansas City. A giant light bulb went off in our heads, like, not only can we go to the concerts, but maybe if we go places like that, that's where these people are.*

Mickey would stand at the front, where people were coming in, and he got to see us all the time. Every time we'd get there, he'd say, "Oh, here's the kids from Brooklyn," and he would talk to me. I guess he just thought I was a cute kid.

That's when I started meeting people like Debbie Harry,[xi] Eric Emerson, Holly Woodlawn, Leee Childers, and [Jayne] County. Depending on your outgoingness, who you're there with, and how you look, you could just become part of the scene. We would be going to these places five nights a week; our parents didn't care as long as I got up and went to school the next day.

Justin Strauss, who grew up in Woodmere on Long Island, also started venturing to Max's when he was fifteen. There, he met and befriended the Zone brothers, before joining a like-minded band in his hometown called Milk 'n' Cookies, who became a fixture at Max's. "Getting into the back room was the biggest thing in the world," Strauss recalled. "Iggy, Bowie, Todd Rundgren, all these insane Warhol people—everyone that I was reading about [in magazines] was there."

Manny Parrish, who would go on to fame as the electronic musician Man Parrish, saw the club as a way to escape a troubled home life in Bensonhurst, Brooklyn:

Parrish: At 12, 13 years old, I was going to Max's Kansas City just to stay away from home. You didn't have a bouncer outside checking to see who's coming in, it was just like going into a bodega or a supermarket: You just walked in, and as long as you didn't start a fight, nobody bothered you. Unless you were eight or ten years old, and probably even then I could have said, "I'm babysitting my nephew," and they probably would have been all right with that.

Most of the New York glam bands made little to no impact outside the scene, but interesting seeds were being planted. The Stilettos, led by Eric Emerson's partner Elda Gentile, featured future Blondie members Debbie Harry and Chris Stein, and future Television bassist Fred Smith. There was Sniper, whose singer Jeff Starship would become better known as Joey Ramone. Kiss were

---

xi   Before joining Blondie, Harry worked as a waitress at Max's.

keen students of both the New York Dolls and Jayne County, and made their Manhattan debut opening for Queen Elizabeth in a loft party at 54 Bleecker Street on May 4, 1973. Even a duo of recent Philadelphia transplants named Daryl Hall and John Oates, who had yet to arrive at the neo-soul style that would make them famous, were plastering on the rouge and making the scene at New York Dolls gigs.

THE MERCER ARTS CENTER

When the Grand Central Hotel opened at 673 Broadway in 1870, it was both the largest and the most expensive hotel in North America, boasting 630 rooms, three ballrooms, and two restaurants. But by 1970, its luster had decidedly faded: renamed the Hotel University to advertise its proximity to NYU, it had become a decrepit and dangerous flophouse. Still, the hotel's ballrooms hosted the occasional performance, including an early Velvet Underground show (when they were still known as the Falling Spikes) and a 1969 New Year's Eve gig by the MC5.

In 1970, nightclub owner Art D'Lugoff partnered with air-conditioning magnate and theater fan Sy Kaback to take over the Hotel University's ballrooms and restaurants and transform them into a theater complex, dubbed the Mercer Arts Center (its entrance, at 240 Mercer Street, was located in the back of the hotel).

The theater complex boasted two levels: the large Hansberry and Brecht theaters were located on the ground floor, while the second floor had three smaller theaters—the O'Casey, the Oscar Wilde Room, and the Shaw Arena—as well as the Blue Room Cabaret, a smaller space called the Kitchen, a bar called Obie Alley, three rehearsal rooms, and a boutique called Zoo that sold glam British fashions. The whole thing, which Tony Zanetta described as "the Lincoln Center of downtown," cost nearly $600,000 to build.

Much as they'd been at Max's Kansas City, the Magic Tramps were central to its conversion into a rock venue:

Coleman: We needed to make some rent money, and music wasn't quite doing it. Somehow we heard through the grapevine that there

*was a place that was going to be opening up, an Off-Broadway the-
ater, and they needed stages and a lot of work done, so we ended up
going down there. It was just a skeleton of a hotel from the 1800s,
and it was like walking into a dark excavated jungle. There were all
these chandeliers and mirrors and broken glass, and we had to get
shovels and wheelbarrows to shovel that shit out of there. It was really nasty, really gnarly, very dark, but you could tell at one time
that this place [had been] so luxurious.*

Though the Magic Tramps had simply shown up to earn some
cash, they soon realized that the space had potential as a music
venue.

*Coleman: We realized that there was a little place at the top of the
stairs that was tucked away in the corner, a place called the Kitchen.
It was sort of an artsy-fartsy place—you could videotape, you could
dance, you could stand up against the mirror, you could do anything
you wanted. We met the guy who was in charge of the space, and
we said, "Wow, this is such a cool place, can we play here?" and
he said, "Sure." So we played there as often as we could. That was
the only place we could actually use our own equipment and try out
new, exciting things. It was casual, it was fun, there was no pressure.*

Though the Mercer quickly became known around town as a
place to see cutting-edge music, much like Max's, it wasn't expecting to turn a profit on avant-garde tastes; instead, the music
was largely underwritten by theatergoers.

The band that would become most closely associated with the
Mercer Arts Center was the New York Dolls, whose first-ever paying gig was opening for the Magic Tramps there on May 5, 1972.
It must have gone pretty well, because a little over a month later,
the band began a Tuesday night residency at the Mercer which ran
from mid-June to October.

Suicide, who'd emerged from a more musically avant-garde
background, also became a regular feature at the Mercer. It was
the first venue to give them a regular gig outside of the Museum of

Flier for two Magic Tramps shows at the Mercer Arts Center's Oscar Wilde Room, November 1972. The photo shows the band in Washington Square Park. Left to right: Lary Chaplan (violin), Kevin Reese (guitar), Eric Emerson (vocals), Wayne Harley-Harley (bass), and Sesu Coleman (drums).

Living Artists, their home and practice space, located three blocks away at 133 Greene Street.

Martin Rev: I had already done a jazz show there with James Du-Boise; Sam Rivers was the other group playing, his trio or quartet. Later, Suicide went in there and tried to get some shows.

It wasn't easy at first, because the manager thought we were totally out-of-our-minds crazy. We had painted "Suicide" on the backs of our jackets, I had drumsticks in the loops of my belt with studs, we had some kind of hats. I put my foot in the doorway door arch as the manager was closing it, so he couldn't close it, and he started to get crazy. Then Sy Kaback, the owner, came out, and he wanted to know what the skirmish was about. [The manager] said, "Oh, these maniacs are here again."

Sy brought us into his office, and he asked us what we wanted. We said, "We'd just like to have a gig." Maybe 20 minutes later, he has a secretary draw up contracts for us to play four nights in the next month, one night a week in the Sean O'Casey Theater. We went from absolute rejection and denigration, to a contract being put in front of us. Sy was an independent entrepreneur, so he wasn't threatened at all by the little details of a music scene.

It's important to note that rock, though dominant, was far from the only genre of music being performed at the Mercer. There were frequent jazz shows in the cabaret theaters, as Rev alluded to—most notably, Charles Mingus. And the Kitchen, the Mercer's smallest performance space where the Magic Tramps had performed, was also helping nurture the avant-garde crowd that had already started to converge in SoHo, alongside video and performance art.

The Kitchen was run by a married pair of video artists, Steina and Woody Vasulka, alongside nineteen-year-old composer Rhys Chatham. The son of bohemian writer parents, Chatham had grown up around Greenwich Village and Gramercy Park, where he'd developed an interest in the musical avant-garde.

Chatham: I realized that there was a need for a place where people could play [experimental] music, because there were a lot of composers in SoHo presenting music in what were essentially people's living rooms. The Kitchen could be a step up from that, because we had a good sound system, a versatile space, a beautiful Steinway piano, and we advertised the concerts.

We charged $1 at the door, and gave 100% of the door to the musicians. Initially, the rent on the space came out of Woody and Staina's pocket, and then we got a grant from the New York State Council of the Arts. None of us got paid for working there, we were just doing it out of love because we wanted to make something happen. When I started out there, no one knew who I was when I reached out, and after one year, everybody knew exactly who Rhys Chatham was.

I really wanted to have La Monte Young play at the Kitchen, so I gave him a call. He was really, really nice, but I explained that it was for the door, and he didn't really see how he could do it. But I lucked out, because his wife, Marian Zazeela, said, "La Monte, we don't have any grocery money this week. Maybe we could sell our records there." So that's exactly what they did. They had The Black Record[xii] *out, that first album, so they sold that. The show was packed. La Monte had a record player, he put the needle down and played the record. And then he turned the record over. I was a little embarrassed, but he wasn't. They sold a lot of records afterwards.*

With all this activity going on, the Mercer Arts Center ought to loom larger in rock mythology, but tragically, its tenure was cut short on August 3, 1973:

Coleman: We were rehearsing there, and we were playing loud and really getting into the groove. It was the afternoon, like 5:00 or 5:20, something like that. And I kept hearing these noises, people yelling and things like that. We thought people were saying "Turn it down," so we turned it up to be even louder.

And then all of a sudden, the room got kind of foggy and dusty. We got up and looked out the window and saw a couple hundred people out there on the street, yelling "The building's collapsing!" We were like, "Shit, this is really happening." We just grabbed as much equipment as we could carry and scurried down the steps and

---

xii   The album's official title is *31 VII 69 10:26 - 10:49 PM / 23 VIII 64 2:50:45 - 3:11 AM The Volga Delta.*

out the door. We lost quite a bit of equipment, because we weren't allowed to go back in.

Four people—Herbert Whitehead, Kay Parker, and Arthur and Peggy Sherwin—died in the hotel's collapse. Had it fallen in the evening, as shows were occurring and hotel guests were slumbering, that number would have likely been much higher.

Reyner: The Mercer was fine, it didn't collapse at all, but it shared a retaining wall with the hotel that collapsed. It wasn't safe, so they had to destroy it. It was still new, everything in it was brand spanking new. It was beautiful, it was perfect, but it had to be torn down.

MAX'S CLOSES (FOR THE FIRST TIME)

By the time the Hotel University collapsed, according to Paul Zone, "there wasn't that much going on at the Mercer. People had moved on."

What a difference a year makes: By mid-1973, the New York Dolls had gotten signed to Mercury Records and experienced some success in the UK, but otherwise the glam scene was largely disintegrating. In his 1974 song "NY Stars," the scene's godfather Lou Reed dismissed what remained of the scene as "the faggot mimic machine" with "no surface, no depth."

"I'm just waiting for them to hurry up and die," he sings, "it's getting too crowded in here."

Things weren't much better at Max's. After the Mercer's collapse, Mickey Ruskin attempted to pick up the slack by bringing in a higher percentage of local, unsigned bands (including Suicide and Patti Smith). But by '73, the Warhol crowd had stopped coming, and with them went the attendant glamor. The visual arts scene had moved on as well.

Rev: We played at the first Max's two times, just before it closed, but we were never at home there. We were too hungry, too seedy. That

*was not our scene—the Warhol scene, as great as it was, attracted a
certain kind of clientele that was more fashion-oriented. Most of the
time they wouldn't even let us in, because we didn't look right. So
playing there, [I felt like] a guest, but not a welcome, embraced guest.
It was more like, "Well, we're gonna close soon, we have the space
open, we'll give it to you."*

Ruskin had also become a victim of his own generosity, with
many of his regulars' open tabs as yet unpaid. He declared bankruptcy and sold the restaurant in 1974. He continued to open and
operate restaurants and clubs in the city for years after, but none
recaptured the success of Max's.

Mickey Ruskin passed away from a drug overdose in 1983. Sam
Hood, whose extraordinary contributions to the city's music history have been mostly overlooked, moved to Woodstock in the
mid-seventies, where he became a longtime salesman for Pitney
Bowes. He died of cancer in 2007.

CLUB 82

As Max's was shuttering, glam rock was beginning its metamor-
phosis into what would be dubbed "punk"—in a new venue that,
ironically, perfectly suited the campy, queer glam aesthetics that
punk would shed.

Club 82, located in a former basement-level speakeasy at 82 East
4th Street, started its life hosting drag shows in the 1940s. As with
most gay and gay-friendly bars at the time, it was mob owned, in
this case by Vito Genovese, an associate of Lucky Luciano's. It was
largely run by Vito's estranged wife, Anna, who was broadly speculated to be a member of the queer community herself.

Rumor had the club existing primarily as a front for daytime heroin dealing. But the drag shows at Club 82 were high-production
revues, with glitzy costumes and music (a young Barbara Streisand
supposedly performed there as well, though presumably not in drag).
The club attracted celebrities looking to let their hair down outside of the public eye, including Judy Garland, Montgomery Clift,

PHOTO BY THE AUTHOR, 2023.

82 East 4th Street.

Elizabeth Taylor, and Errol Flynn, who, legend has it, drunkenly attempted to play the club's piano with his erect phallus.

By the early 1970s, Club 82's glory days were decidedly over. Campy drag shows had fallen out of favor in the LGTBQ+ community, which was newly politicized after the Stonewall Riots. The Genoveses sold the club; the new owners operated it as a gay disco, but began featuring local bands—initially on Wednesday nights, and then more regularly.

The club itself was the epitome of camp: The circular stage was flanked with light bulbs around the bottom, surrounded by mirrors and fake palm trees. A gold tinsel curtain at the back separated the stage from the dressing rooms behind it, allowing performers to make a dramatic entrance. Signed photos of movie stars on the walls, remnants of the club's past, emphasized its faded glamor.

As word spread, Club 82 became a popular destination for the same kind of rock stars who would once have ventured to Max's and Nobody's: David Bowie, Lou Reed, Mick Jagger, Pete Townshend, and John Lennon and Yoko Ono. And for noncelebrity musicians, the club's free Sunday night roast beef buffet was notably appealing (I wasn't kidding—free food really was part of what held this scene together).

While the New York Dolls famously appeared in drag (or something approximating it) on the cover of their self-titled debut album, their appearance at Club 82 on April 17, 1974, was the only time the group performed in full drag—excluding Johnny Thunders, that is, whose masculinity was apparently too fragile to handle wearing a cocktail dress for an hour.

In addition to hosting some of the remnants of the fading glam scene, Club 82 was a place to see some curious new bands like Television, Patti Smith, and Talking Heads. It was also home to a significant and transformative show by Jayne County and her new band, the Back Street Boys.[xiii] That show was attended by an old acquaintance of County's named Peter Crowley, who is about to become a central player in our story.

Crowley: After the show, I went backstage to say congratulations, how are you, all that stuff. [Jayne] was talking with Leee Childers, saying that [she] didn't know what to do about getting paid, because [she] booked the show [her]self and [she] hadn't discussed money. I piped up and said, "You don't know how much you're supposed to get?" [She] said no. I said, "Well, I'll go collect it for you, but it's going to be whatever the club says it is, because you didn't make a deal beforehand and you've already done the shows. It's too late to negotiate."

---

xiii Yes, you read that right: she performed under the name Wayne County and the Back Street Boys, decades before the boy band from the '90s. Why she never sued them is beyond me.

I went back to the office, and the club's owner, Peter Petrillo, gave me the envelope with the money; I went back and gave it to [Jayne]. It was $500, which was quite reasonable for one show at that time. And so I said to [Jayne], "Why don't you have a manager?" [Jayne] said, "Well, I used to—David Bowie's manager.[xiv] *But they just dropped me." And I said, "I'm gonna tell you right up front, I'm not a real professional manager, but if you don't have anybody else, I'll be glad to give it a try." So I took on the job of managing [Jayne] County.*

MOTHERS

As County's new manager, Crowley approached CBGB—a Bowery club nurturing the nascent punk scene, whose story is told at length in Chapter Five—about a gig, with little success.

Crowley: Almost every venue in New York City that hosted original bands without record contracts had closed, except for CBGB. And then Peter Petrillo died a few weeks after my encounter with him there, and the 82 Club closed up. I asked Hilly [Kristal, CBGB's owner] for a date for Wayne County and the Back Street Boys, and Hilly said, "Come see me in three weeks." I thought that was odd. I came back in three weeks, and he said the same thing. When he did it the third time, I went to [Jayne] and I said, "Is there a reason that I'm getting this runaround?" and [Jayne] said to me, "Well, Hilly asked me if I wanted to play, and I said I'd get back to him and I never did." I figured Hilly was feeling disrespected and was sort of biting off his nose to spite his face, because at that point, [Jayne] was second only to the New York Dolls in popularity.

I asked my friend Mike Umbers if he knew a bar where I could

---

xiv Bowie's manager, Tony Defries, briefly set up a New York branch of his management company MainMan, with Tony Zanetta overseeing operations. MainMan signed several New York artists, including Jayne County, avant-jazz synth player Annette Peacock, and singer Ava Cherry. By the end of '74, it was all over, and Jayne had little to show for it.

put on shows, and he said, "Yeah, I know a bar. They owe me money, too." So we jumped in his car and went up to 23rd Street. We walked into Mothers [267 West 23rd Street], which was a failed gay bar with no gay people in it: There was a bartender, the owner, some friends of the owner's, and a waiter, but no customers. [Umbers] said to the owner of Mothers, "This is Peter Crowley, and he's going to put on shows here."

You may have noticed a theme in this chapter that's often over-looked: a lot of New York's early punk scene took place at explic-itly gay bars and spaces. Once most of the city's small rock venues had shuttered, gay bars—especially old-fashioned drag bars, hurting for customers as entertainment tastes among the queer community changed—were among the few places willing to book unsigned rock bands.

Crowley: They had a tiny little stage where a drag queen could get up and lip sync to Supremes records—that was the only entertain-ment they had, and there was a tiny little PA system to play records on—but the owner said he would build a stage. I booked [Jayne] there for a week—it was a small place, I figured [Jayne] could fill it for a week. About four days before the first show, there was still no stage, so I went to the lumberyard and bought the lumber, hauled the plywood and whatever over there, and I built the stage.

I said to myself, now I have a venue and I can't just have [Jayne] County all the time; I might as well start booking available bands. Of course, 90% of them were CBGB bands. Essentially what hap-pened was that Hilly created his own competition. He wouldn't have had any if he had just given me a date.

Zone: Mothers was tiny, tiny, tiny. I think it lasted around eight months, which seemed like an eternity. It was the whole end of '74 into the beginning of '75. And everyone played there—we played every Thursday night for a month, and the Heartbreakers, Blondie,

Mink DeVille, Television, Ramones—it was a who's who of what was to become punk.

Crowley, who spent his days gainfully employed as a distributor for ESP Records, generously gave bands 100 percent of the door—in another one of the chapter's running themes, he was able to champion experimental art because he didn't expect it to turn a profit.

Crowley: It was such a small place that I felt it would have been really tacky for me to take any money away from these poor, starving kids. Even giving them 100% of the door, they weren't getting very much money there. There'd be maybe 50 people who paid to see Blondie and Mink DeVille, and the door charge was $3, so each band would get $75. If there's five people in the band, they were making 15 bucks apiece. I'm not going to take any money out of that.

Interestingly, Mothers was also across the street from Galaxy 21, a multilevel gay disco at 256 West 23rd Street where resident deejay Walter Gibbons held sway.

Zone: Everybody would finish up at Mothers, and then we'd go across the street to Galaxy 21, which was a crazy wild disco with lots of different rooms and flowing cocaine. It wasn't odd for us to go to gay discos—those [emerging genres] were all happening at the same time. There would be the gay scene in those clubs, but there would also be some glam and punk people who wanted to go somewhere where they felt that they wouldn't be discriminated against. You could go to gay discos at 2:00, 3:00, 4:00 in the morning, and you fit right in. I think that was a factor that brought a lot of those genres together.

MAX'S REOPENS

In 1975, as Peter Crowley was building a scene around Mothers, new life was about to be breathed into what had once been Mickey Ruskin's Max's Kansas City.

Crowley: Tommy Dean [Mills] was in Paris with his wife, Laura. They got the Herald Tribune one morning and saw an article saying that Max's Kansas City had gone bankrupt. So Tommy and Laura said to each other, "How could an iconic place like that go broke? That's impossible!" They called up their lawyer in New York and had him find out what it would cost to buy the place. They figured there'd be liens from the meat man, the liquor supplier, etc. But there was only one lien on Max's Kansas City, from Con Edison for $3,500. So Tommy bought Max's Kansas City for $3,500— one of the most unbelievable bargains of all time.

Tommy and Laura's background in the music business was limited to operating a lounge out by the airport, so they redecorated Max's until the place looked like an airport lounge, and they installed a live disco band upstairs.

They put ads in the paper that said, "Max is back," as if there ever was a Max, and everybody came running to see what was up with the new Max's Kansas City. So for about 10 days or so the place was packed, and then after that the place was empty, except for the disco nights on Friday and Saturday. The disco did well, because he had a very good live band playing all the latest disco hits, and it was only $3.50 to get in. It was packed, but not with Max's-type people: it was pretty much every Puerto Rican young person from the Lower East Side who couldn't afford the midtown discos that cost $20 to get into.

Tommy started going around asking people, "What did I do wrong? Why did everybody stop coming to Max's?" He asked me, and I said, "Get a legal pad, because you're gonna need a lot of space to write it all down." He made a few of the changes I told him to make, like he got rid of the fake Tiffany lamps over the tables, and he let me book Sunday, Monday, and Tuesday to start out. So for two weeks, I just did Sunday, Monday, and Tuesday, but I brought in the Ramones and Talking Heads and whoever, so it was packed. And of course I brought in [Jayne], right away.

There might have been a couple of weeks where I did both Max's and Mothers, but I quickly burned my bridges and just walked away and let Mothers atrophy. It got taken over by some of the kids who *hung out there, one of which was [actor] Rockets Redglare. He and his friends took it over, and the first brilliant idea they had was to change the name to Zepp's. They were open for a few weeks and then it just folded.*

Things didn't fully gel at the new Max's Kansas City until the spring of 1976, when Peter Crowley organized the Max's Kansas City Easter Rock Festival, with ten shows spread out across two weeks (he still wasn't allowed to book Fridays and Saturdays)—including Blondie, the Ramones, the Heartbreakers, the Mumps, and the Shirts. On the strength of the festival's success, Crowley was given free rein to book all seven days a week.

Where the original Max's was enamored with the Beautiful People, the new Max's allowed the outsiders to be insiders.

Miriam Linna (drummer, the Cramps, Nervus Rex, the Zantees, the A-Bones; owner, Norton Records): Max's made everybody feel like they belonged there. CBGB's was a great place to play and a great place to see bands, but you really didn't get that feeling that you got at Max's. I think a lot of that has to do with Peter Crowley, because he was a pretty incredible person. He was dealing with a lot of people like myself, being a younger person on the scene, and he didn't talk down to you. He really treated you like a human being, like we were people that mattered.

Zone: Peter was so much more influential when it came to bringing different bands onto the scene than Hilly was, without a doubt. Peter Crowley was the only smart one who would book Suicide. The Cramps didn't even pass their audition night at CBGB, and Peter took them on. Peter really had a good ear, and a good eye. He was so much more innovative than Hilly or CBGB.

The Heartbreakers—led by former New York Dolls Johnny Thunders and Jerry Nolan—were a cornerstone of Crowley's booking at Max's, with the group even recording a live album at the club in 1978.

James Marshall (writer, deejay): Bands like the Heartbreakers could do Friday and Saturday at Max's once a month or every two months, and that would keep four people and their drug habits alive. You could make three or four grand in a night.

Much like the first Max's, a new crop of young kids started showing up, thrilled by the possibility of getting close to their heroes.

Jack Rabid (editor, The Big Takeover; *drummer, Even Worse, Springhouse): [My high school friends and I] went to Max's Kansas City and ended up seeing the Heartbreakers about 17, 18 times. They would do five shows on weekends and we'd see all the shows, even though they started at 10:00 and 1:00, and the opening band would play both of them, so the Heartbreakers' second set wouldn't be until around 2:15. We would get there super early; they'd open around 8:30 or 9:00, but we'd get there at 6:00 and just park our butts up against that bank [next door], like we were waiting for Springsteen tickets.*

Under Crowley's stewardship, the new Max's Kansas City was explicitly a music venue, rather than the art world hangout with occasional gigs that Mickey Ruskin's Max's had been. The back room, once the club's pièce de résistance, was now a nonstarter.

Still, some vestiges of the old Max's remained. They kept the chickpeas, for one. The cocktail hour buffet was reinstated. Jayne County resumed her rightful role as the resident deejay. But arguably the most important factor that both eras of Max's shared was a dependence on nonbohemian lunch and happy hour customers to underwrite everything else that happened there.

Crowley: Max's had a very successful lunch and a tremendously successful happy hour, all coming in from people who worked in the office buildings nearby, so there would be $3-$4,000 in the cash register before I even did a sound check. Therefore, I had no pressure—I didn't have to deal with a club owner going, "I don't like that band, *they didn't bring any people, nobody bought beer," because the place made a ton of money before I even put a band on stage. I didn't have to worry about whether a band was already popular; I could put on a band that I knew was gonna get popular, and then build them up.*

The scene around Max's during the Tommy/Peter era is summed up perfectly in Jayne County's song "Max's Kansas City 1976," which she recorded with The Back Street Boys.

County: I thought Max's deserved to have a song written about it as a kind of historical document, naming bands and things. And then people could play the record and say, "Oh my God, listen to this song about this place that used to exist back in the '70s in New York City." I'm very proud of that song.

Crowley: I still had that problem, how do I get [Jayne] County on vinyl? I said to Tommy, "Would you like to put out an album that

Jayne County, 1978.

© GODDARD ARCHIVE/ALAMY

can advertise the club?" [Jayne] had the song already, "Max's Kansas City." Tommy liked that idea as a way to make some money, but mostly to advertise Max's Kansas City. So I put together the compilation [Max's Kansas City 1976, released on the club's in-house Ram Recordings label that same year]. We sold about 3,000 copies—that was the number of people who were interested at that point in time. We weren't well known anywhere outside of New York.

The compilation's cover is an extraordinary photo of all the bands on the record, gathered outside the club: Wayne County and The Back Street Boys, the Fast, Pere Ubu, Cherry Vanilla, the John Collins Band, Harry Toledo, and Suicide. Suicide's album-closing contribution, "Rocket USA," was their first commercially available recording, although the song had previously appeared on a commercially unavailable single which held a place of pride in the Max's Kansas City jukebox.

Rev: I was at Max's one night just talking to friends or whatever at the bar, and I heard Television's single ["Little Johnny Jewel"] come on the jukebox. I asked Tommy, "How did that get on?" and he said, "They made their own 45 and they put it on." I said, "Hey, what if we put out a Suicide single, can we get on a jukebox?" He said, "Yeah, just ask Peter." So we recorded "Keep Your Dreams" and "Rocket USA" on our little tape recorder, and then a few days later, I took the tape to 48th Street, to a studio where you could still cut acetates. You'd either record there or bring a tape, pay the fee, and then they'd press it for you and you could walk out with it. I had the guy cut two 45s, and then the next day I took it to Max's and gave one to Peter. It was on the jukebox by that night.

MAX'S CLOSES (FOR THE SECOND TIME)

Throughout his tenure as the booker at Max's, Peter Crowley remained first and foremost Jayne County's manager, and when opportunity knocked—in the form of punk's ascendance in the UK—he answered the call.

Crowley: I went to Tommy Dean and I got a bunch of money to go over to England in January of '77. And again, I burned a bridge: I walked away from my responsibilities at Max's in order to get [Jayne] County to England. Tommy, bless him, didn't get upset, because he understood that my allegiance was to [Jayne] before I'd ever come to Max's. My allegiance to [Jayne] had nothing to do with money, I never thought we would get rich. I thought that [Jayne] was the kind of artist that needed to be heard.[xv]

With Peter gone, Tommy Dean hired Terry Ork—Television's manager and the owner of Ork Records, who had been instrumental in booking early shows at CBGB—to be the club's new booker. Ork, in turn, brought in musician Deerfrance to share the responsibilities. By mid-1978, Ork had left and Crowley was back in New York. He resumed his booking role at Max's, briefly sharing the position with Deerfrance. But even after becoming the club's sole booker again, his dynamic with Tommy Dean had changed.

Crowley: I didn't have the same leverage that I had had in the beginning, because Tommy had discovered that he could get along without me. I felt like walking out, but every other time I'd walked out somewhere, there was another opportunity in front of me. By 1978, there were no other opportunities. I was old—I know my age wouldn't have made any difference, but the club owners want a younger person doing that type of work, because they think a younger person is more in touch with the youth or whatever. And there were already as many as 10 other major rock clubs at that point—Danceteria, Hurrah, Mudd Club.

Max's wasn't even the only rock club around Union Square anymore: Tramps had opened two blocks east from Union Square at 125 E. 15th Street in 1975. Three years later, Irving Plaza—

---

xv   In London, Jayne County formed a new band, the Electric Chairs, and appeared in two seminal punk movies: Derek Jarman's *Jubilee* and Don Letts's *The Punk Rock Movie*.

located just around the corner at 17 Irving Place—started hosting rock concerts (it continues to do so to this day). In 1980, The
Ritz—which regularly hosted the kind of midlevel touring bands
that would once have gravitated toward Mickey Ruskin's Max's—
opened up in the Webster Hall building at 125 East 11th Street.

On the other hand, Union Square was also no longer the ac-
cidentally perfect location it had once been. The scene had geographically expanded: of the clubs Crowley mentioned, none were
nearby, with Danceteria on 37th Street (it would relocate to 21st
Street after Max's closure), Hurrah on the Upper East Side, and the
Mudd Club in Tribeca. Union Square itself was also in the initial
stages of its revitalization, which started with the introduction of
the Union Square Greenmarket in 1976, followed by major renovations, rezoning, and high-rise construction over the course of
the 1980s.

With the back room scene long gone and the live music focus
shifted to local bands, Max's had ceased to be a destination for
glamorous rock star types—or the people hoping to catch a glimpse
of them (which is to say, the people who paid for food and drinks).

Nor was it particularly convenient for touring bands the way it
had once been. True, the Gramercy Park Hotel continued hosting
bands like the Clash, U2, and Siouxsie and the Banshees, and scene
stalwarts like Blondie's Debbie Harry and Chris Stein and Suicide's
Alan Vega had stints living there. But the Hotel Albert turned residential in 1977, and the Chelsea Hotel, already ramshackle during
its late '60s to early '70s peak, had only become rougher. In October 1978, New York punk scenester Nancy Spungen was found
dead in Room 100, allegedly murdered by her boyfriend, Sex Pistols bassist (and Max's regular) Sid Vicious,[xvi] bringing unwanted
attention to the hotel and its residents.

---

xvi After Vicious left the Sex Pistols, his only solo appearances prior to his death
took place at Max's in September 1978, with a backing band that included the
Clash's Mick Jones and the New York Dolls' rhythm section of Arthur Kane
and Jerry Nolan. According to Peter Crowley, Spungen booked these shows
by going behind his back to Tommy Dean. Lo-fi live recordings were later
released as *Sid Sings*, but they're basically unlistenable.

For all these reasons, Peter Crowley's reunion with Max's was a relatively short one. By the time it closed in 1981, Max's had become, in his evocative wording, "a real toilet." Worst of all, Max's' lunch and happy hour—the club's financial backbone—had ceased to be lucrative.

Still, as Jack Rabid points out, "Max's didn't close because they weren't having punters—if anything, in '81 they were far more crowded then they'd been in '79 and '80, when they had fallen out of favor. They started to realize that they couldn't compete [with other clubs] for the English bands and the California bands and stuff, so they would make their bones on the local scene"— largely young hardcore bands.

Crowley: The next to last week [of Max's existence], I had Walter Lure and Cheap Perfume booked, two relatively big names on the scene. That was going to be a really successful weekend, even though the club was going to hell. And then they both called me up on Friday to tell me that they can't play on Saturday; I don't know what their motivation was. For Friday, I had booked five hardcore bands, which would not have been a problem back when the restaurant was bringing in all that money, but the audience for hardcore didn't spend any money.

Probably 150 kids came on Friday. I remember Peter, the bartender, set up a hundred glasses of water on the bar, and then he went and sat on the beer cooler and gave me dirty looks all night long— he wasn't selling anything. Since I had a cancellation for Saturday, I asked the hardcore bands to come back and play again the next night, and one said yes.

Then Tommy called and said, "The club's closing tonight, everybody has to get their personal belongings and get out." Naive me thought he meant everybody when he said "everybody," but apparently it was just me. I packed up all my stuff, and I went home and called up everybody that was booked for the following few weeks to tell them all their shows were canceled.

For many years, I thought that the night I got fired was the last night. But people tell me that the following weekend actually happened, with Bad Brains and the Beastie Boys.[xvii] *The ad for that show was handwritten because there was no longer any money in the budget for typesetting. That's how low we'd sunk.*

But more than any of these factors, Max's final closure seems to have been the result of Tommy Dean's financial...well, let's say, clumsiness.

Crowley: *Tommy was also what you'd call a degenerate gambler, and when Max's closed, Tommy owed around a million dollars to the folks in Atlantic City. You don't want to owe them money and not pay it, for a number of reasons. Maybe you still want to be able to walk.*

He needed money desperately, and of course Max's wasn't making any money: for the last couple of years the restaurant was pretty useless, and upstairs just died a slow, lingering, horrible, cancer-like death. The money that I made him, and then Deerfrance continued to make him in the late '70s, made it possible for him to buy the building, which he had done. It was probably the only smart thing he ever did, and it was his only asset.

Tommy went to the woman who owned the office building next door and asked her if she wanted to buy Max's. She had a very good reason for wanting to, because she was sick and tired of cleaning up the blood and broken glass and vomit outside every morning. Tommy sold her the club and the building for a million dollars in cash, which paid his debt and saved his life. She immediately stripped all the signage off the front, and she made sure that there would never be another nightclub or restaurant there.

Jimi LaLumia (music journalist; singer, Psychotic Frogs): *Once Max's closed, there was no division anymore: You went to CBGB. But because Max's closed and CBGB was still open, the MTV gen-*

---

xvii The Beastie Boys had formed three months prior to the show and opened at
    Bad Brains' invitation; their three-song set was by all accounts unspectacular.

eration did not grow up knowing about Max's. When MTV made reference to the downtown scene, it was "CBGB, CBGB, CBGB." CBGB won the MTV crowd by default, because that's all they got to know. Max's was kind of a forgotten entity, even though Max's, in my opinion, was the birthplace of punk.

Though it's a little bit of a stretch to say that Max's has been forgotten, LaLumia is right that it's been eclipsed by CBGB. I would also say that its legacy has been misrepresented: Associations with Andy Warhol, the Velvet Underground, and glam rock have endured, and the Mickey Ruskin era has been commemorated in innumerable books and movies, but these often minimize or exclude the incredible stylistic breadth of Sam Hood's bookings. Even worse, the second era of Max's is often treated as an addendum to the glorious Mickey Ruskin era, with Peter Crowley's visionary stewardship of the punk scene known only to the most devoted fans.

THE AFTERLIFE OF THE GLAM ROCK SCENE

Since its closure, a succession of unspectacular delis have occupied the former Max's Kansas City space. Amusingly, the current tenant is named Fraiche Maxx—surely a coincidence, and not a veiled tribute. As for the luxury condos located above the old Max's space, at the time of this book's writing in 2022, they are being leased by Douglas Elliman agent Risé Cale, ex-wife to the Velvet Underground's John Cale.

In 1998, Tommy Dean Mills launched a new Max's Kansas City at 240 West 52nd Street. Though Peter Crowley was brought in to book bands, the new venture was primarily an overpriced seafood restaurant with little resemblance to classic-era Max's. Unsurprisingly, it closed almost immediately.

As Mills was attempting to launch his new Max's, he was successfully sued by Yvonne Sewall for ownership of the Max's trademark. Sewall used the trademark to launch the Max's Kansas City Foundation, a nonprofit that grants emergency relief for artists in need and sponsors economically disenfranchised kids to attend summer arts programs.

Around 2010, Sewall sold the trademark to investor Elliott Azrak, who allowed her to retain the name for the nonprofit. Speaking to the *Wall Street Journal*, Azrak laid out lofty plans for the trademark, including a series of boutique hotels which would "cultivate a playground for the creative class" and preserve "the DNA of the original place."[38] But as of 2022, no such hotels exist, and Azrak has done little else with the trademark.

In February 2019, Yvonne Sewall partnered with Bombay Sapphire Gin to build a simulacra of Max's on the Paramount Studios back lot, open to the public for three days as part of that year's inaugural Frieze Art Fair. In a room roughly the size of the infamous back room, Sewall displayed and sold pieces of Max's-affiliated memorabilia, photographs, and art, with all proceeds benefiting the Max's nonprofit. Instead of the classic Max's red and white color scheme, the walls were painted a deep blue (Bombay *Sapphire*—get it?), but otherwise it was a well-informed and roughly accurate tribute.

The space that previously housed Nobody's at 163 Bleecker Street was most recently Uncle Ted's Chinese Cuisine. The restaurant was ravaged by a five-alarm fire in 2021; its future is unclear.

What remained of the Mercer Arts Center was demolished after the building's collapse and replaced with NYU Law School's Hayden Hall dormitory. However, if you're on Broadway between Great Jones and Bond, you can see the outline of the Grand Central Hotel's roof and chimney, as well as a few remaining chunks of the hotel's wall, on the side of the next building, 665 Broadway.

Mothers (267 West 23rd Street) became Bonchon, a Korean fried chicken restaurant.

I've saved the best for last: Club 82 (in the basement of 82 East 4th Street) closed in the late '70s, and it's unclear what became of the space during the '80s. In 1990, Rolling Stones guitarist Ron Wood took over the space and operated it as a club called Woody's, which hosted the occasional indie rock band, but that club closed within a year. Following that, the space went full circle in a remarkable way, becoming an unadvertised gay porn theater called Bijou Film Forum. Hilariously, it attempted to maintain a facade of being a run-of-the-mill movie theater, with posters for *Scream 3, Eyes Wide Shut, The Bachelor,* and (cringiest of all) *The Rugrats Movie* adorning the entrance.

The Bijou Film Forum closed for good in 2018. I walked by a year or two ago while they were dismantling it, but all I could see inside was a poster for *Scream 3.* As of this book's writing, the space is being transformed by workers into something as yet unadvertised. Whatever that turns out to be will almost certainly not be worthy of its past.

Suggested Listening

The Velvet Underground—*Live at Max's Kansas City* (rec. 1970)

New York Dolls—*New York Dolls* (1973)

Bruce Springsteen—*Max's Kansas City 1973* (rec. 1973)

Wayne County—*At The Trucks!* (rec. 1974)

Milk 'n' Cookies—*Milk 'n' Cookies* (1975)

Various—*Max's Kansas City 1976* (1976)

Johnny Thunders & The Heartbreakers—*Live at Max's Kansas City* (1979)

The Magic Tramps—*Kickin' Up Moonlight Dust* (compilation)

The Fast—*Boys Will Be Boys* (compilation)

Suicide—*½ Alive* (compilation)

4

MAKE IT LAST FOREVER:
THE LOFT AND PARADISE GARAGE

Colleen "Cosmo" Murphy (deejay; founder, Classic Album Sundays): *I think the Loft attracts people that don't necessarily feel like they fit into traditional society in many ways, whatever it's because of gender, age, race, sexual orientation, or just mindset—I think of this old Claymation Christmas thing,* The Land of the Misfit Toys. *A lot of people that go to the Loft come from different economic backgrounds, whether they work for the city, some work as prison guards, some are blue collar, some are white collar, some are bohemian types. If you're supposed to be there, you'll find your way there.*

Freddy Bastone (deejay; remixer; producer): *It's always the Loft and Paradise Garage, like there were no other clubs. It's ridiculous.*

When the Broadway Central Hotel collapsed in 1973, it wasn't just the glam rockers and proto-punks at the Mercer Arts Center who found themselves displaced. A young record collector named David

Mancuso, who lived just down the block on the second floor of 645-647 Broadway, had been regularly throwing crowded parties in his apartment (known to regulars as the Loft) for three years, with little interference from the city. After the collapse, his parties were, suddenly, a natural target for police attention—especially after Mayor John Lindsay ordered housing and building supervisors to inspect the structures of all pre-1901 buildings. Inevitably, Mancuso was evicted.

For New York City music scenes, losing a primary venue is a blow almost impossible to recover from. In the time it takes to find a new space, trends change, and the original patrons scatter and move on. But for the Loft, almost the exact opposite was proven true. The loss of Mancuso's Broadway apartment was a catalyst not only for the Loft's subsequent expansion, but the development of the innumerable dance music cultures that sprang up in its wake—most significantly, disco and house. The closure of the first Loft made it clear that rather than being about a specific neighborhood or an exact cultural moment, the subculture it launched would be based on community—which gave it a longevity and flexibility unheard of in music history.

Unlike other scenes, or even other dance clubs that it inspired, there was never a moment when the Loft produced so many major stars that it hit a tipping point, became flooded with trend-hopping outsiders, and fizzled out. The Loft was never about providing a launching pad to wider success; it was fiercely DIY, falling somewhere between a club, a house party, and a community center. It was not really a scene that anybody could transcend without abandoning its principles—as became the case for Mancuso's best-known protégé, Paradise Garage deejay Larry Levan. The Loft was something that you were either a part of or not.

The fact that this fiercely supportive community was only possible through a strictly enforced invite-only structure is just one of the many contradictions that permeate the story. Mancuso and Levan have become venerated by subsequent generations, largely thanks to the work of author Tim Lawrence, whose 2003 disco history *Love Saves the Day* is an invaluable resource and remains the definitive book on the subject—but these complex, brilliant, tempestuous figures failed as often as they succeeded. Lawrence's work lovingly catalogs their ascents, but largely cuts the story off before their descents. But there's as much to learn from the ways these communities struggle as the ways they thrive.

THE LOFT

David Mancuso was born in Utica, NY, on October 20, 1944, the product of an affair his mother, Catilana Mancuso, had while her husband served in World War II. Two days after his birth, he was taken to an orphanage, where he spent the first five years of his life.

At the orphanage, Mancuso encountered a nun named Sister Alicia, who would have a profound effect on his life. As Mancuso later recalled, Sister Alicia "would find any excuse to have a party." She would play records for the kids to dance to, decorate the room with balloons and streamers, and serve fruit punch and birthday cake—all of which became hallmarks of the Loft experience. "I have a feeling that part of my influence for the Loft—why it was communical [sic], why I did it the way I did—has to do with that time back then," he explained.[39]

Douglas Sherman (deejay): I don't know that David started these parties with a full recognition of that aspect of his upbringing, versus it just being something that was just kind of wired in by the time he began doing the parties. Years later, one of the boys from that children's home tracked David down [and showed him] all these pictures that I don't think David had seen of them in the children's home with Sister Alicia. I don't think his childhood friend even understood the depth of what [those photos] meant. David had to step back and say, you know, there's some things maybe I didn't fully take into account.

Mancuso moved back in with his mother after his fifth birthday, but he ran away regularly, and even spent a year living in a reform school. When he was fifteen, Mancuso moved out on his own, dropping out of high school the following year. In 1962, having saved up a little money from a dishwashing job, he moved to New York City, where he worked menial jobs and spent his free time going to parties and clubs around the city, as well as indulging a newfound passion for high-end audio: after purchasing a pair of Klipschorn speakers from a hobbyist named Richard Long, there was no turning back.

In 1965, Mancuso moved into the loft at 645–647 Broadway at Bleecker Street, paying $175 a month for the roughly 25' x 100' high-ceilinged space. He couldn't have asked for a better location—not only was Broadway the border between trendy Greenwich Village and the edgy East Village, it was also just a couple blocks north of SoHo, which was still in the early stages of its transformation from an industrial zone to a functioning artists' colony. As with many of the loft spaces discussed in Chapter Two (including Studio Rivbea, which would open two blocks away from Mancuso in 1972), it was a formerly industrial building not zoned for residence, which meant that it was both cheap and less cramped than a tenement apartment.

Though Mancuso was likely unaware of the fact, it was an especially auspicious building, with a history that foreshadowed the Loft parties: 647 Broadway had once been home to Pfaff's Beer Cellar, a dimly lit, basement-level German-style beer hall. From the mid-1850s to the late 1860s, Pfaff's was *the* major hub for the city's bohemian underground (writer Alan Gurganus compared it to "the Andy Warhol factory, the Studio 54, the Algonquin Round Table all rolled into one"[40]). The crowds that regularly gathered around Pfaff's long communal tables were known for their progressive politics, avant-garde creativity, and sexual openness. Notably, poet Walt Whitman was a member of the Fred Gray Association, a group of openly gay men who regularly convened at Pfaff's. Whitman reportedly first explored cross-dressing at Pfaff's, and it's where he met Fred Vaughn, who is believed to be one of Whitman's long-term partners and the inspiration for several poems.[i]

---

i   Whitman wrote an unfinished poem, "Two Vaults," about Pfaff's.

645–647 Broadway.

Around the time he moved to the Broadway loft, Mancuso became personally acquainted with LSD guru Timothy Leary. Already fond of the drug, Mancuso began regularly attending Leary's
LSD-based meditation center League for Spiritual Discovery (get
it?) at 551 Hudson Street, as well as Leary's private house parties,
where acid consumption was accompanied with music and food.
Inspired, Mancuso began throwing his own Leary-inspired LSD
parties in his loft, where a small group of friends would drop acid,
lie around, and listen to music on his high-end stereo. But in 1966,
Mancuso removed one of the loft's few walls in order to expand
the space for dancing. The music he played at his parties began to
reflect a shift from languid psychedelia toward something more ecstatic and physical—soul, rock, Afro-Cuban music, and early funk.

Mancuso's vision coalesced at a private party he threw on Valentine's Day, 1970. Invitations featured Salvador Dali's painting *The
Persistence of Memory* and the phrase "Love Saves the Day" (once
again: get it?). Around one hundred people attended, after which

Mancuso began throwing all-night parties with increasing regularity; within six months, they were a weekly affair.

Dance clubs existed in the city at the time—traditional discotheques in the pre-disco sense of the word, where deejays would put on records and people would dance. The majority were devoted to heterosexual audiences, but even the ones that weren't positioned themselves as catering to very specific groups—white patrons, Black patrons, Latinx patrons, wealthy patrons, working-class patrons. And they all sold liquor, which meant they had to close after last call.

The Loft, from the very beginning, was an inversion of these elements. There was no alcohol, which meant that they could go all night, much as the West Village folk coffeehouses did. The lack of liquor license was also key in its egalitarian philosophy—when the Loft first opened, it was technically illegal in New York City for two men to dance together in a place where alcohol was served. (This shamefully remained the case until December 1971, when Mayor John Lindsay's administration overturned the rule, thanks in large part to a swell of post-Stonewall activism.) Loft patrons, who came from all walks of life and all ethnic backgrounds, were free to dance with whomever they wanted, all night long.

Also unlike traditional nightclubs, the Loft was not open to the public—these were private parties, and one needed to be on Mancuso's mailing list or be the guest of someone who was to get inside. Mancuso even stationed trusted confidants at the door to screen unfamiliar faces who arrived as guests of guests, making sure everyone was fully vetted.

Murphy: It was about self-policing: OK, you're coming into my home, you have to be responsible for yourself and your guests. You were vetted, and if you had a guest with you that misbehaved, that would be noted the next time you wanted to come.

Once you got through the door, in the words of *Village Voice* writer Vince Aletti, "It was like being at someone's—everyone's—

birthday."[41] There were balloons and streamers everywhere, colored lights, a large mirror ball, and a year-round Christmas tree. Some dancers would shake tambourines and maracas in time with the music. Mancuso would spend Wednesday, Thursday, and Friday preparing the space, the food, and his mental state for the Saturday parties, with the intention of creating the most welcoming, positive environment possible.

Mancuso had few ambitions as a disc jockey—for most of his life, he exclusively played records in his own home. In fact, he abhorred the term "deejay" and preferred to view himself as a "musical host."

"Socially, I'm an introvert, I'm very shy," he told the *Village Voice* in 1975. "But I had to do it—no one else was going to."[42]

Mancuso sought a spiritual self-erasure when playing records that would prove to be drastically at odds with the innovations of some of his protégés. Still, the "musical host" handle is a bit of an understatement: Mancuso played not just with sound, but with the senses, regularly playing with the lighting and temperature of the room to emphasize a record's specific qualities or dictate the flow of the evening. As the Loft's groundbreaking auteur and star, Mancuso was the Orson Welles of dance music.

Mancuso viewed the entire night's party as a journey and structured the music accordingly; taking inspiration from Timothy Leary's book *The Psychedelic Experience*, Mancuso adopted Leary's model of the psychedelic trip as a movement through three states, or "bardos." The first bardo, which typically kicked off around midnight, would be devoted to quiet, meditative music (Van Morrison's *Astral Weeks* and Alice Coltrane's *Journey in Satchitananda* were favorites), which would gradually build into something rhythmic. The second bardo was all about cathartic, ecstatic dancing, propelled by high-energy music. Finally, the third bardo was a gradual comedown and reentry into reality, with the party typically wrapping up around 6:00 a.m. Breakfast would be served, and Mancuso frequently signed off with Nina Simone's cover of the Beatles' "Here Comes the Sun."

It was important to Mancuso that once the admission fee was

paid (it was soon raised from 50 cents to $2, and then $3, and eventually $4), no other money would be exchanged within the club. A substantial spread of organic foods, fresh juices, and sweets were included with admission. In the event that an invitee couldn't afford the cover charge, Mancuso granted infinite IOUs. "I want a situation where there [are] no economic barriers," he later explained, "meaning somebody who didn't eat that day or only has a few dollars in his pocket can eat like a king, drinks are included, you see your friends[.]"[43]

Mancuso also banned attendees from dealing drugs inside the Loft. Psychedelics were available free of charge, although Douglas Sherman insists that legends of the fruit punch being laced with LSD are false—the last thing Mancuso wanted was for someone to have a psychedelic experience by accident.

Sherman: LSD was a very free-flowing thing at the Loft. When I say free-flowing, it wasn't in a reckless way, but if it was something you wanted to pursue, it could be had. Between LSD and mescaline, you could have this experience that intensified the moment and led to what for some could be a transformative experience, with the music and the dance and everything.

The community that developed around the Loft was undefinable by design, in a decidedly hippie-ish, utopian way. There was a significant gay male population, but plenty of straight men and women were at the parties as well. Although Mancuso and several of his guests were white, a large portion of the dancers were Black and Latinx.

Murphy: For some Black people, it was the first time they were able to talk to a white person and become friends with a white person who wasn't a co-worker. This is hugely significant. A place where you can dance with a man, make out with a woman, whatever, and it's acceptable. There was one woman I know, she was a single mom who'd just come from Mexico and didn't speak any English—David allowed her to bring her kids.

That is perhaps what most set the Loft apart from the other dance clubs when it opened—the overwhelming utopian philosophy with which it operated. That said, West End Records executive and Paradise Garage co-founder Mel Cheren ascribed an earthier motive to Mancuso's invite list, as "David Mancuso had a strong sexual attraction to black men." Still, Cheren acknowledged that whatever Mancuso's reasoning, the Loft ultimately served as "a crucial link between a moneyed, mostly white group of gay men eager to party with tribal abandon, and a mostly black gay world suffused with music and style."[44]

THE BEST OF FRIENDS, THE SANCTUARY, AND THE FIREHOUSE

Although contemporary scholarship tends to position Mancuso's Valentine's Day Loft party as the birth of disco, the truth is it was one of several seeds being planted around the city.

Beginning in 1968, a group of college friends from Queens began promoting dance parties for a heterosexual, largely Black crowd, calling themselves the Best of Friends (TBOF). Their parties were thrown at venues all over the city, and much like the Loft, they were primarily promoted via a well-curated mailing list; a strict dress code was designed to keep out undesired guests. Unlike the Loft, alcohol was sold and drugs were strictly prohibited.

Like Mancuso, TBOF's resident deejays, Danny Berry and Charles "CP" Perry played a mix of soul, funk, and Latin music—Eddie Kendricks's "Girl You Need a Change of Mind" and Manu Dibango's "Soul Makossa," both frequently played at the Loft, were TBOF mainstays. They also independently developed turntable tricks that other deejays of the era were simultaneously creating, all without knowledge of each other. These tricks, which included primitive beat matching[ii] between records, and overlaying parts of different records atop each other, provided the groundwork for

---

ii   Making the tempos of two different songs align so that the transition between the two is as seamless as possible.

many of the vinyl-based musical developments that would follow—including disco, house, hip-hop, techno, and their myriad offshoots.

In 1971, the TBOF organizers recognized an opportunity in sleepy Midtown Manhattan: white flight had led many white office workers to move to the suburbs, but many Black professionals still lived within the city and had few nightlife options after work. They began promoting weekly Thursday parties at the Ginza (40 East 58th Street), a nightclub with a heavily white and Asian customer base which they folded into their own following. By '73, they were opening nightclubs of their own (including their flagship, Leviticus) which were among the first significant Black-owned dance clubs in the city.

At the same time, deejay Francis Grasso was developing his own reputation at the Sanctuary, arguably New York's first overtly gay dance club, which opened in 1969 in a former German Baptist church at 407 West 43rd Street. The church's communion table was converted into Grasso's deejay booth, and owner Arnie Lord (that name's a bit on the nose, isn't it?) had the club adorned with a pornographic mural of a devil surrounded by fornicating angels, as well as a large wooden statue of Satan, to really underscore the church's deconsecration.[iii] Grasso—who, unlike the club's clientele, was straight—played a mix of funk, soul, rock, and Afro-Cuban music (James Brown, Led Zeppelin, Santana, and Babatunde Olatunji were favorites). Simultaneous to the TBOF parties, Grasso independently arrived at the same early mixing techniques.

But even more than Grasso's technical innovations, the Sanctuary was significant in that, unlike the underground gay clubs that preceded it, it wasn't owned by the Mafia.

The mob weren't too keen on this development. This led to some kerfuffles, including Grasso being kidnapped at gunpoint from his deejay booth and beaten up. To be fair, the mob were never confirmed as responsible for Grasso's assault, but many sus-

---

iii   The club's interior, complete with Grasso in the deejay booth, is prominently featured in the 1971 Jane Fonda/Donald Sutherland movie *Klute*.

pected they were—especially after the deejay declined to file a police report. Still, it's impossible to overstate how liberating it was
for the gay community to finally have non-Mafia-owned spaces
in which they could let loose without fear of blackmail or assault.

In 1971, the Gay Activists Alliance—an organization that had
coalesced after Stonewall, splitting from the more politically radical Gay Liberation Front to form a group that could work with the
political establishment—opened their headquarters in a converted
firehouse at 99 Wooster Street in SoHo. They held weekend parties, making it the rare dance space that was exclusively and explicitly gay owned and operated. Like Grasso, deejay Barry Lederer
primarily played a mix of soul and rock, including The Rolling
Stones, Bill Withers, and the Detroit Emeralds. Unlike the Sanctuary, the Firehouse was a private party, not a club, which meant
that like the Loft, it was exempt from the licensing that hampered
bars. Tragically, the Firehouse closed in 1974 after it was devas-
tated by a fire that had been set by vandals to cover up the theft of
expensive electrical equipment.

There is a superficially obvious detail common between all of
these clubs and parties that's worth unpacking: Mancuso, Grasso,
Lederer, and the TBOF deejays were all playing commercially released records that were not proprietary to them. Some of it was
made in New York, but much of it wasn't. And though Mancuso,
Grasso, and Lederer were all white, much of the music they played
was primarily made by and promoted to Black people. The multiracial, Downtown, LGBTQ+ community gets much of the credit
for early disco, but their innovations were, strictly speaking, not
musical—they were social, environmental, technical, and proce-
dural. The records had a life of their own far beyond a few underground parties in New York City.

THE LOFT COMMUNITY FORMS

As other deejays were perfecting their beat-matching techniques
and layering records on top of each other, David Mancuso was
heading in the opposite direction. Though he'd initially dabbled

in mixing techniques, he recalled, "[O]ne day I just said to my-self, 'What am I doing? It's like having a painting on the wall. I shouldn't change the colors; I should leave [sic] as it was intended, let it stand on its own.'"[45]

Mancuso viewed himself as a conduit rather than a performer and chose to play the records exactly as they were recorded, from beginning to end, without tweaks or interruptions. Already a high-end audio enthusiast, he delved further and further into the pos-sibilities of sound in order to present as faithful a reproduction of the music as possible—and to consciously diminish his own role in the presentation.

To that end, Mancuso partnered with sound system designer Alex Rosner. A Polish-born Jew, Rosner had been imprisoned at Auschwitz as a child and survived thanks to his ability to entertain Nazi guards by playing accordion alongside his violinist father.[iv] By the time he met Mancuso, Rosner had begun making a name for himself building nightclub sound systems, including the one at Max's Kansas City.[v]

When Rosner finally attended a Loft party, he was impressed by the thoughtful way Mancuso arranged the party.

Rosner: It was an intimate party room: dimly lit, very romantic, and very, very peaceful. It was not a club atmosphere. And he played a wide variety of music, not the kind of music that you hear in clubs anywhere. And it wasn't just for dancing, it was for listening as well.

By 1972, Mancuso's Loft parties were big enough that they began attracting attention from the authorities. After a police raid, Man-cuso was arrested on the charge of running an unlicensed cabaret. His legal defense was sound, though—the parties were private, and

---

iv   Rosner's accordion is now on display at the United States Holocaust Memorial Museum in Washington, DC.

v   Rosner recalled Max's as "a small club with a few people dancing, nothing special."

no alcohol was being sold. The judge ruled in his favor, but the NYPD continued to target the Loft—so much so that Mancuso installed a sophisticated warning system, so if someone working the door saw cops coming, they could flip a switch that triggered a light in Mancuso's booth, allowing him to turn the music off and let the cops walk into a quiet, seated affair.

Police be damned, the Loft community was growing, and significant people were entering Mancuso's orbit—including Brooklyn native Larry Levan. Born Lawrence Philpot on July 20, 1954,[vi] Levan had begun deejaying when he was five years old, at a birthday party. "He was so small they had to put the record player on a low chair so he could reach," his mother, Minnie, later remembered.[46] As a gay Black teenager, he struggled to find community until he encountered Harlem's drag ball scene, which had been thriving in the neighborhood since the late 1800s. While making costumes for the balls, he met another gay Black teenager, Bronx-born Francis Nicholls Jr., better known as Frankie Knuckles. The two became inseparable.

When Levan was seventeen, he met Mancuso at a club called the Planetarium on 2nd Avenue between 10th and 11th Streets (Mancuso's friend Richard Long—later a key collaborator of Levan's—worked the door), and the two began dating. The relationship didn't last long, but they remained friends, and Levan became a regular at the Loft parties. He was particularly enamored with Mancuso's sound system—as he later explained, "I was never interested in being a DJ...[but] I was always interested in stereo equipment."[47]

In the summer of 1973, Levan ran into Knuckles at the Planetarium. The two hadn't seen each other in months, and after closing the club down together, Levan brought Knuckles to the Loft. Knuckles later recalled the dancers were "moving in such a tight rhythm that all the bodies felt like one... I never witnessed, let

---

vi   Philpot was his father's name; Larry's parents never married and Larry was raised by his mother, Minnie, whose maiden name he reverted to.

alone, been apart [sic] of this kind of madness...and to this day, my life hasn't been the same."[48]

THE GALLERY

Levan and Knuckles weren't the only teenagers sniffing around the Loft. Nicky Siano and his girlfriend Robin Lord were already hanging out at the GAA Firehouse when an ex-girlfriend of Siano's older brother Joe brought them to Mancuso's party. Around the same time, Lord and Siano—both sixteen—moved to Manhattan from their native Brooklyn, sharing a one-bedroom apartment on Bleecker between Broadway and Mercer (just around the corner from the Loft) for $280 a month.

During his second visit to the Loft, Siano later recalled, "I was dancing and all the lights had gone out, apart from a lamp... All of a sudden, the horns came in on the song and the lamp just dimmed and went out. Everyone went crazy." It was a transformative moment for Siano, who "realized David was controlling everything in the room—the sound, the light, the air conditioning. I said... [']I have to do this.[']"[49]

Lord helped Siano get a job deejaying at a flailing club called the Round Table, but the pair dreamed of opening a spot of their own, something like the Loft but oriented toward heterosexual dancers (ironically, Siano had recently come out as gay, although the pair remained intermittently involved).

While walking around Chelsea, Siano and Lord came across a "for rent" sign outside 132 West 22nd Street. The 5,300-square-foot, second-floor loft could be had for a mere $360 a month, and it was an ideal space in which to realize their dream. With Siano's brother Joe pitching in $10,000 that he had won in an insurance settlement, the pair took over the space and dubbed it the This & That Gallery, soon shortened to the Gallery. Given their Loft origins, Alex Rosner was brought in to design the high-end sound system, which accounted for $6,500 of their budget.

The Gallery opened in February 1973; the following month, Siano turned eighteen. Their attempt to operate a straight version of the Loft struggled to gain traction, but then, that June, Mancuso closed the Loft for the summer in order to vacation in Europe. At the last party before Mancuso's trip, Siano and Lord handed out cards that said, "What are you doing this summer? Come to the Gallery," and as Siano recalled, "The next week there were 500 people at the Gallery."[50]

The Gallery shifted from a struggling straight club to a thriving gay one. Where Mancuso sought to remove any interference with the music, Siano bent the music to his will. A natural performer, he took the innovations that Francis Grasso and TBOF's deejays had developed and built upon them, extensively manipulating records. He'd cut back and forth between two different records, use multiple copies of the same record to loop portions of it, and pioneered the kind of dramatic filter sweeps that are now colloquially known as "bass drops." He even installed a third turntable in his booth to use for sound effects records during song transitions. In his own way, Siano's deejay sets were as technically proficient and improvisational as any jazz.

Though Mancuso was also gay, his musical hosting conveyed something a little more asexual and cerebral. Siano's deejay sets, on the other hand, were unquestionably *gay* and profoundly horny, the way only an eighteen-year-old boy can be. As deejay Kenny Carpenter, a Gallery regular, noted in his memory of Siano's sets, "When you hear music played from a gay perspective, it's just very different [from] when you hear somebody straight playing music. There's a feeling: it's the knowledge of being a man and the strength you need to be a woman at the same time, all wrapped up into a deejay set."

In expressing those sentiments, Siano was drawn to much of what would come to sonically define disco—lyrics about love and sex, with vocals from soulful singers (mostly Black female singers) laid atop a tight rhythm section and ornamented with lush strings and punchy horns. Much of it came from Philadelphia's Sigma Sound Studios, including Siano's signature song, MFSB's "Love Is the Message."

Around the time the Loft closed for the summer, both Frankie

Knuckles and Larry Levan began working at the Gallery. The pair would blow up balloons, decorate the space, run the lights, and (ahem) distribute hits of LSD.[vii] Levan and Siano grew especially close and briefly lived together as a couple, although Siano later recalled Levan as being essentially asexual.[51] The couple frequently spent off-hours at the shuttered Gallery, where one day Levan asked Siano for a crash course in the basics of deejaying. Levan was a natural, and Siano soon noticed that his new boyfriend was meticulously and flawlessly copying his patented turntable tricks.

When Mancuso left for his Europe trip in June '73, he could not have anticipated the hell to which he'd return. Despite his well-intentioned efforts—which included soundproofing, installing sprinklers and security lights, and giving other residents in the building free entry to his parties—he was not unreasonably loathed by his neighbors. After the Broadway Central Hotel's collapse, they were concerned that crowded parties in Mancuso's second-floor loft (from which he'd recently removed a non-load-bearing wall) might result in a similar catastrophe.

As the building was legally nonresidential, unwanted attention from law enforcement was less than ideal. Still, six of Mancuso's neighbors were concerned enough to alert city agencies, which resulted in the police, fire, buildings, and health departments all paying Mancuso a visit during one of the Loft parties. On May 31, 1974, Mancuso was officially evicted by the Department of Buildings on account of his overcrowded parties and DIY wall removal. A couple of months later, the fire department evicted the Gallery from their equally illegal space on 22nd Street, citing the lack of sufficient fire exits.

By that point, Larry Levan had broken up with Nicky Siano and taken the lighting skills he'd developed at the Gallery to the Continental Baths, an infamous gay bathhouse in the basement of the

---

vii   Unlike the Loft, the Gallery's fruit punch *did* contain a significant amount of the drug. Some of the pieces of fruit were also laced.

Ansonia Hotel that doubled as an unconventional music venue.[viii]
When the resident deejay, Joey Bonfiglio, quit on Memorial Day
weekend, Levan was handed the job. In short order, he brought
Frankie Knuckles onboard as his co-deejay.

In the spring of 1974, on Mancuso's recommendation, Levan
was invited by Richard Long to deejay at the new club that Long
was setting up in his apartment at 452 Broadway. Long intended
the club, which he dubbed SoHo Place, to be a showroom for the
audio equipment he was building. With both the Loft and the
Gallery now out of commission, SoHo Place was also designed to
be a replacement.

Levan, then nineteen, turned SoHo Place from a struggling club
to being "so crowded you couldn't walk," as he later recalled.[52]
With a deejay booth and crowd that were now all his, Levan honed
his own unique style. Disinterested in technical perfection, he
would stop songs in the middle and cross-fade between records
with clashing tempos.

*Antonio Ocasio (deejay; producer): Anybody could tell you that
Larry's mixes weren't great. Sometimes he was on, but a lot of times
the mix was off and it didn't even matter because the music was so
good. That's one of the things I learned about deejaying [from David
Mancuso and Larry Levan], was that nothing is more important than
the music. The sound of course is number one, you need great sound.
You can mess up a mix—everybody messes up a mix, even the best
deejays. If the music is great, you could be forgiven.*

DISCO BLOWS UP

By this point, the seeds that had been planted at the Loft, the Sanctuary, the Firehouse, TBOF parties, and the Gallery were bloom-

---

viii The bathhouse hosted a broad range of performers that included the New
York Dolls, Bette Midler (with Barry Manilow on piano), Andy Kaufman,
Yma Sumac, Leslie Gore, and the Manhattan Transfer.

ing into a full-on musical movement. Other deejay-oriented dance clubs, with varying degrees of legality, had been opening around the city throughout the early '70s: Tamburlaine at 148 East 48th Street, the Tenth Floor at 151 West 25th Street, Galaxy 21 at 256 West 23rd Street, the Barefoot Boy at 309 East 39th Street, Le Jardin at 110 West 43rd Street, Better Days at 316 West 49th Street, 12 West at 491 West Street.

Some were licensed bars, some were members-only parties in the Loft mode. The music these clubs played was largely aligned with what Nicky Siano had been playing at the Gallery—rhythmic, soulful songs with simple, uplifting lyrics, largely performed by Black singers. And now it had a name: disco.

Disco is often remembered (especially by rock fans of a certain age) as frivolous and cheesy, eternally tied to the image of John Travolta's white suit and finger-pointing dance moves in 1977's *Saturday Night Fever*. It's also remembered as apolitical, which could not be further from the truth. In its racial and sexual politics, it was arguably the most socially groundbreaking genre of music to have emerged at that point. And as King Crimson guitarist Robert Fripp, of all people, noted, "Instead of saying 'Screw the system, it doesn't work,' [disco] says, 'The system doesn't work, we will ignore it,' and the political platform is the dance floor…disco to me is a political movement which votes with its feet."[53] The parties gave people from marginalized groups spaces where they could safely be themselves and enjoy the pleasure of dancing, without mob interference or the threatening presence of bigots.

So regardless of the cheesy commercial sheen that would come to burden it, make no mistake—early disco was a grassroots, underground, politically charged movement developed by and for marginalized people.

MOVE TO SOHO

In November 1974, Nicky Siano reopened the Gallery at 172 Mercer Street, in a building that spanned an entire block along Houston

PHOTO BY THE AUTHOR, 2023.

172 Mercer Street.

Street between Mercer and Broadway and held multiple addresses. As that description suggests, the new location was massive, and sixteen hundred revelers came out for its opening night.

Less than a month later, promoter Michael Fesco, who had previously run gay dance clubs on Fire Island, moved into the second floor of the same building (with an entrance at 599 Broadway) and transformed it into a totally unrelated disco, the Flamingo. Like its predecessors, the Flamingo was invitation only and didn't serve alcohol, but unlike the Loft or the Gallery, the crowd that gathered there was almost exclusively white gay men of means. With their differing clienteles, the proprietors of the Flamingo and the Gallery weren't terribly bothered by each other's existence—there was very little audience crossover. Nevertheless, the two created a disco mini-district on one SoHo block.

In 1975, they'd be joined by David Mancuso, who moved into a two-story (street-level and basement) space at 99 Prince Street

99 Prince Street.

at Mercer[ix]—just down the block from the Gallery, and only four blocks southwest of the original Broadway Loft. Mancuso came to the Prince Street space on the recommendation of Loft regular Penelope Grill, who lived in the building; the landlord leased the space to Mancuso on the condition he bring it up to code.

Mancuso did not find himself particularly welcome in SoHo. Where the Gallery and the Flamingo were located along the always-bustling Houston Street, 99 Prince Street was within SoHo's new residential quadrant. Many of the neighborhood's loft-dwelling and ostensibly liberal artists—who had raised few qualms when Philip Glass played loud concerts in Donald Judd's Spring Street home, or when an already-prestigious Ornette Coleman performed to largely white audiences at Artists' House on Prince Street (one block west of the new Loft), or even when Suicide per-

---

ix　Prior to Mancuso's arrival, the basement space had been a studio belonging to artist Lloyd Cross, a pioneer in holographic art.

formed their aggressive synth-punk in the relocated Museum of Living Artists on Greene Street (just around the corner from the new Loft)—were now concerned about the incoming presence of a weekly dance party that just so happened to have considerable Black, Latinx, and LGBTQ+ constituencies.

Community uproar against the Loft's move to Prince Street was organized by Michael Goldstein, editor of the ostensibly hip Downtown publication *SoHo Weekly News.* And wouldn't you know it, it turned out that Goldstein had himself been eyeing the Prince Street space for *SWN*'s new offices prior to Mancuso's arrival. Goldstein's first shots were fired in a *SWN* article entitled "What's Going On at 99 Prince Street?" in which he described the Loft as "an after-hours, drug-oriented club"—which, to be fair, *was* technically accurate. Soon after, Charles Leslie of the SoHo Artists Association declared the Loft's appearance "the beginning of an invasion."[54] A picket line even appeared outside the new Loft, with one protestor's sign reading "No New 8th Street," a reference to a loud, club-lined West Village street.

Granted, the GAA Firehouse had already been throwing large dance parties in SoHo, but *Village Voice* writer Vince Aletti speculated that "it would not have been politically correct in liberal SoHo to attack a gay organization," while the superficially apolitical Loft was fair game.[55] "I don't see many young artists," Mancuso told Aletti when assessing his new neighborhood, "just lofts for the rich who are concerned about dog leashes and the crime rate."[56] What had been a welcoming neighborhood for cutting-edge artists and musicians at the start of the decade had already become something stodgier.

Undaunted, Mancuso (with his landlord's approval) set to work fixing up the space. He received a significant financial boost from none other than Yves Saint Laurent, who paid him $850 to rent out the new Loft for a fashion show. As far as I can tell, Mancuso's neighbors didn't seem to take much issue with the attendees of that particular event.

Aware of the precarious nature of the Loft's legality, Mancuso applied for a cabaret license this time around, despite having no desire for one. After what he described as "the longest hearing in the history of consumer affairs,"[57] his application was denied on the grounds that he was not running a cabaret because he did not sell alcohol. All had gone to plan, and Mancuso was ecstatic—he now had legal grounds to run his parties free of police interference.

With two floors of space spanning most of its block on Prince Street, the new Loft was larger than its predecessor. During Loft parties, the ground level served as the primary dance floor, while the basement level was a hangout space with food and beverages. Mancuso ran the parties at 99 Prince Street in much the same manner as he had at the original Loft, but in a winking tribute to his new address, he adjusted the entry fee.

Sherman: I think when I started going, it was $5.99, but it quickly went up to $6.99. But it always was whatever-.99. David kept a little bowl of pennies at the cashier's booth; you'd take your penny change, and then nothing else was for sale.

The newly legal Loft officially reopened on October 20, 1975, with a party that drew roughly a thousand revelers. Crowds briefly ebbed after that—the scale of the new Loft meant that the party lacked the same degree of intimacy, and the sound system was no longer as potent as it had been in the smaller Broadway space. Aware of the need for an upgrade, Mancuso invested a whopping $250,000 in his sound system, going so far as to outfit his turntables with $3,000 Koetsu cartridges. Both Alex Rosner and Richard Long were called upon to assist; the resultant sound system put Mancuso's contemporaries to shame and won back many of the regulars.

And there was a new crop of people coming in, many of whom would go on to become musical hosts and deejays themselves. Nineteen-year-old Douglas Sherman first visited the Loft as a friend's guest shortly after the relocation to Prince Street.

Sherman: I had already been to a number of commercial clubs, but when I went to the Loft for the first time, I saw something that was unlike anything else I had ever experienced. There were moments that were just explosions of, I could only describe it as "love," because it was everybody coming together on a dance floor around a particular moment in a record. It was a little overwhelming. I'd never heard such a clean, clear sounding system anywhere, and when I left, I didn't have tinnitus. I left before the last record, because it was already after 10:00 in the morning, but the damage was done. I just wanted to go back after that.

Another teenager, Bronx native Antonio Ocasio, had an especially eye-opening introduction to the Loft around 1977.

Ocasio: I was blown away by the music, like Cymande and Santana. There was this couple, a white guy and a Black girl, they were dancing and I was just watching them and listening to the music. They were dancing for a long time to a lot of music, and they were drenched in sweat. The next thing you know, they were having sex on the dance floor. I was like, "This is it! This is it!" Because the Loft was never a sex club, it was just that it felt so free. Nobody made a big deal out of it, I don't even know if other people noticed it.

As a kid growing up on the Upper West Side, Victor Rosado was obsessed with clubbing from a young age. When he was thirteen, he met Kenny Carpenter, then working the lights at Downtown dance clubs like Galaxy 21 and Inferno. The two became fast friends, and eventually, Carpenter brought Rosado along to Prince Street.

Rosado: Kenny took me as his guest in 1980 or '81; I was about eighteen. I'd heard about [the Loft] for many, many years, but I also knew that it was a private membership thing, so I hadn't gone because I didn't want to be embarrassed if they said, "You can't come in."

When I walked into that room, it sounded so beautiful. He was playing the Main Ingredient's "Happiness is Just Around the Bend."

I said, "Wow, I have this record, but it doesn't sound anything like this." It brought tears to my eyes.

I met David, and David took a liking to me. He invited me back and gave me a comp card, and I went every Saturday after that. He was just such a nice person, so together, different, eclectic, out of phase with the universe, and there were so many things I learned from him. He changed my life.

Both Rosado and Douglas Sherman were so taken by their experiences at the Loft that they began regularly assisting Mancuso at the parties.

Rosado: I started bringing records, certain things that David may have forgotten or lost that I had in my collection, like Don Ray's "Standing in the Rain." I did lights for him for a little bit, I did coat check, I did balloons, I did mailing, I did every job there was to do there. [My family] donated furniture to the Loft, and my mom came and cooked at the Loft. There were times where he would call me and ask me to cover for him, so I had to jump in a town car and bring two cases with about three hundred records. And then he wouldn't have anybody to do the kitchen, so I would do the kitchen, put on a record that's fifteen minutes long, go back and refresh the kitchen, put out punch, cookies, food, whatever it was, and then go back and play more records.

Not all of the Loft's visitors found it to be a transcendent experience. Richard Vasquez, who would soon begin his own deejaying career, felt unwelcome during his visits to the Prince Street Loft. To Vasquez, "the people there that were having the party were very cliquey, and the other people [felt like] observers." A few other deejays, including Danceteria's Freddy Bastone and the Mudd Club's Justin Strauss, found Mancuso's aversion to mixing to be underwhelming. Writer Fran Lebowitz found the DIY informality of the Loft to be a bit much, noting that "people would fold their coats and put them on the floor so they could kind of keep an eye on them. Then other people would sit on them, have sex on them... Even thinking about it now, I become anxious."[58]

In addition to the Loft parties, David Mancuso, with the help of deejays Steve D'Acquisto and Paul Casella, used the Prince Street Loft to pioneer the concept of a record pool—essentially, an organization in which deejays from clubs across the city are given equal access to promotional records from participating labels, rather than turning against each other in a battle for exclusivity. The New York Record Pool officially formed on June 2, 1975, with Mancuso, Larry Levan, and Frankie Knuckles among the 65 deejays that were its charter members (that number ballooned to 183 by the end of the month). For a $2 monthly membership fee that covered administrative costs, deejays from across the city had access to every hot (and not-so-hot) new record the moment it was released.

Mancuso was elected to be the Record Pool's president, and the Loft doubled as a distribution site where deejays could come collect their new records every week. The record pool concept, rooted in the same all-for-one mentality as the Loft parties, proved to be a winning one. Mancuso continued to run the New York Record Pool until 1977, when the financial and emotional burdens of running the organization out of his home began to take their toll. To help manage the organization, Mancuso brought in Judy Weinstein, a Loft regular since the Broadway days.

Though she eased Mancuso's burden, and for a time even lived with him at 99 Prince Street, Mancuso came to believe that Weinstein (who was pointedly *not* a deejay herself) was angling to oust him. Whether this is true remains unclear, but regardless of Weinstein's intentions, Mancuso's paranoia eventually actualized itself—Weinstein left, and the New York Record Pool fell apart in her absence. In early 1978, Weinstein opened her own record pool, For The Record; to Mancuso's chagrin, many former New York Record Pool members were more than happy to join.

THE GARAGE

SoHo Place, Richard Long's factory showroom/dance party, was forced to close in 1975 after his long-suffering neighbors took legal action to put an end to the noise. Luckily for Larry Levan, a man named Michael Brody offered him a job deejaying at a new venue in Tribeca, Reade Street (143 Reade Street), which was consciously modeled after the Loft and came equipped with an Alex Rosner–designed sound system. Levan accepted and brought his small but growing crowd of devotees with him.

Reade Street was not long for this world, closing in early 1976 after Brody had a dispute with the landlord. But as Brody saw potential in Levan, he wisely asked the young deejay to hold off on taking other gigs, and set off looking for a new spot.

He found what he was looking for at 84 King Street. The large, two-story structure had once been Fred's King Street Garage; more recently, it had housed a short-lived disco called the Chameleon. At the time Brody came to see it, the first floor was still set up as a parking garage, while the ten-thousand-square-foot top level was being used for truck maintenance. Conveniently, the building was geographically isolated—the once-industrial area was as yet undeveloped, so there were no neighbors to annoy. Plus, its Hudson Square location bordered both SoHo and the West Village, each home to large gay enclaves and popular clubs.

It was dubbed the Paradise Garage.[x] The club's new logo said it all: A muscular, curly-haired, ethnically ambiguous man flexing his left arm. He clutches a tambourine, suggestive of parties like the Loft where dancers would occasionally wield percussion instruments and play in time to the music. Below his arm are a whistle (again, frequently used by revelers at the Loft) and a popper.[xi]

As with Reade Street, the Paradise Garage was modeled after the

---

[x]   It wasn't music history's first significant establishment bearing that name. In 1971, the Paradise Garage at 420 King's Road in London was an early iteration of what became Malcolm McLaren and Vivienne Westwood's seminal punk clothing store Sex. In 1975, McLaren assembled the Sex Pistols as a means of promoting the shop.

[xi] A small tube of nitrate which, when inhaled, creates a temporary high, increases blood flow, and relaxes sphincter muscles, all of which made it popular within the city's gay club scene as both a stimulant and an aid for anal penetration.

Loft, to such an extent that both Brody and Levan initially lived in the space.[xii] It also operated on the same membership model. Brody wisely continued to operate the first floor as a parking garage, which helped him pay the substantial rent as he was setting the club up. But short on funds after paying five months' rent up front and adding to his sound system, he decided to open the club in stages. Beginning in January 1977, the Paradise Garage had a soft opening with a series of construction-themed parties (orange cones, sawdust, hardhats, etc.) held in the nine-hundred-square-foot Gray Room, a small space enclosed within the larger second floor.[xiii]

Alex Rosner was brought in to expand upon his Reade Street design, but after a financial dispute, Brody forced Rosner out and brought in Richard Long. Long delivered a doozy of a sound system: where the Loft's sound was crystal clear but not overwhelming, the Paradise Garage sound system was so loud[xiv] and so bass heavy that dancers could quite literally feel it in their bones. Long, who had lost his showroom when SoHo Place closed, also got to use the club during the day to show his handmade sound equipment off to potential customers. Larry Levan took to regularly upgrading and adjusting the club's sound.

Richard Vasquez (deejay; co-founder, The Choice): Larry managed to put in all kinds of controls in the sound system, so that if he was not deejaying, the sound system was pretty mediocre. He was brilliant, and knew all the tricks for survival.

---

xii   Brody later found an apartment for Levan on Gold Street and routinely paid the deejay's rent just to get some time away from the guy.

xiii Brody would later redesign the Gray Room and rechristen it the Crystal Room. Surprisingly, some of the best documentation of this portion of the club can be seen in Woody Allen's 1987 film *Radio Days*, where it serves as radio stars Roger Daley and Irene Draper's Manhattan townhouse.

xiv   135 decibels, supposedly. According to the CDC, prolonged exposure to anything above 120 decibels can lead to permanent hearing damage and considerable ear pain.

When the finished club officially opened on February 17, 1978, it was an unmitigated disaster. Michael Brody had designed the club for a financially well-heeled white gay crowd, and that crowd turned out in significant numbers. Unfortunately, a delay in the delivery of necessary sound equipment forced said crowd to wait outside for an hour—and in a snowstorm, no less. When they were finally allowed inside, the space was just as cold as it was outdoors. Many swore they would never return.

But although the A-listers didn't come back (at first, anyway), a less moneyed but more sympathetic crowd came in to fill the void—one which was largely Black and Latinx. Brody recognized the importance of a club that could serve such a clientele: Mel Cheren, Brody's former lover who helped finance the club, later wrote that up to that point, "most of the spaces that welcomed minority gay men were basement dungeons, cheap walkups, firetraps." The Paradise Garage, Cheren explained, was "the first big-time, mainstream gay club to enthusiastically court Black and Latino gay men[.]"[59]

The Garage was unquestionably a gay club (it was frequently referred to by those in the know as the "Gay-rage"), but as more and more heterosexuals were drawn to it, Brody decided that Friday nights could be open to both straight and gay men, while Saturdays would only be open to gay members. Those members could bring as many as four guests with them, but only one of those guests could be a woman (even then, some regulars often griped about there being too many women). And no guests under twenty-two were allowed, at least hypothetically.

Joey Llanos (head of security, Paradise Garage): The straight [people] weren't as forgiving or easygoing as the gay party. The music was even different Saturday night—it was a more serene atmosphere. Fridays were sometimes busier, but it was tense, because you had the straight guys and the girls. Sometimes guys would get overly aggressive with the women, and we would have to squelch that.

Paradise Garage had adopted David Mancuso's invite-only format, but with a twist: you only got an invite if you were a member, and to be a member you had to pay a membership fee—on top of which, there would be the evening's door fee.[xv] Interested parties had to apply for memberships in person during specific—but unadvertised—time frames, which meant you had to have been passed along the details by a member. And even then, you'd have to prove your merit: through the years, it was reported that several straight men attempted to pass as gay in an attempt to curry Brody's favor and get Saturday night passes, though they rarely succeeded.[xvi]

The Garage took after the Loft in other ways as well. Significantly, it didn't serve liquor, which meant that they could legally remain open all night and well into the next day. Going without a liquor license made sense for Mancuso, who was hosting comparatively intimate parties in his home, but for a massive nightclub like the Garage, it was a bold move—that's quite a bit of potential income to forgo for a nightlife business with considerable overhead. But the lack of alcohol and resultant all-night hours created a more passionate, devoted community of regulars explicitly there to dance.

True to Mancuso's influence, once you paid the cover, you were treated to a lavish spread of fruit, juice, punch,[xvii] coffee, and snacks. As music journalist Frank Owen wrote, "Most people— black, white, gay, or straight—who came were far from wealthy; some could barely afford the $10 or $15 admission. But Levan and owner Michael Brody gave them a lot for their money[.]"[60]

---

xv Members paid $8 and were entitled to four free nights a year. Guests paid $15. For both, there was an additional fee whenever the club hosted live performances.

xvi That said, Levan reportedly had a penchant for coming around when Brody was conducting interviews, opening the door up to all the hopefuls and deejaying for them, much to Brody's chagrin.

xvii As had been the case with the Gallery, the punch was initially spiked with LSD. But within a few years of the club's opening, the community had grown too large and the spiked punch created too much of a liability, so the practice was discontinued. Clubgoers looking for drugs usually had no trouble finding them elsewhere.

Despite its many similarities with the Loft, the notion of Paradise Garage as a party and not a full-fledged nightclub is sort of ridiculous. Sure, they adopted the aspects of the Loft that made it impervious to licensing requirements, plus a dollop of David Mancuso's customer service, but there was little of what had made the Loft so warm and intimate. For Antonio Ocasio, there was no comparison between the two: "I'm not saying that other people couldn't feel that feeling of family at the Garage, but for me it was just too big."

This is not to diminish it in any way; rather, we can better appreciate its unique contributions and significance in a nightclub context rather than by viewing it as simply the Loft writ large. And as nightclubs go, it was a phenomenal one.

It's hard not to notice that the dance scene's focus on community and attempt to conjure a good time instead of commenting on the city's decline was somewhat singular among the music scenes of the era. In contemporaneous New York City scenes, like punk and no wave, the city's neglect was often embraced by musicians and fans, its deterioration seen as a source of inspiration or creative freedom (we'll go into that in depth in the next few chapters).

While many of the people who made up punk and other rock-oriented scenes were New York transplants and were largely white, the dance music scene was a home for many native New Yorkers of color, often from parts of the city where urban blight wasn't intriguing or artistic; it was simply a fact of life. Hip-hop, which involved musicians and performers from the same neighborhoods, began as a lighthearted disco offshoot, but starting in 1982 with Grandmaster Flash and the Furious Five's "The Message," rappers focused on confronting and addressing the city's decay, and the way poor New Yorkers and people of color were expected to bear the brunt of it.

For patrons at the Loft and the Garage—especially people who weren't opting in to New York for artistic reasons, but simply lived there because it was where they were from—these spaces offered relief from the more punishing aspects of city life, allowing patrons to exist briefly in a utopian world, where all different groups mixed together, all needs were cared for, and your true self was accepted. When the AIDS epidemic hit the city, this became doubly true—nights out in these spaces offered joy in the midst of horror.

Michael Brody was the owner, but Paradise Garage was unquestionably *Larry*'s club. Brody wisely built the club around the needs, preferences, and whims of his star deejay, allowing Levan to control every aspect of the environment: the sound, the lights, the video screens, even the temperature. Victor Rosado recalled that Levan's enormous deejay booth even included a custom-built "carousel of records" which Levan would spin to find the one he was looking for.

With the entire club at his disposal, Levan came into his own as a deejay. Few would argue that he was the most technically skilled mixer (in fact, nearly everybody I interviewed for this chapter stressed the opposite), but like Nicky Siano before him, Larry would make *his* records and *his* crowd bend to *his* will. Various ingenious tricks were deployed: He would play with EQs until the whole room was engulfed in nothing but bass frequencies, and then tease them with hints of treble. He would upgrade his turntables' cartridges over the course of the evening, so that the sound quality subtly but appreciably improved, building up to a sonic peak. He would play two copies of a record simultaneously but milliseconds out of sync to create a swirling echo effect. He would build the crowd's energy to a fever pitch, and then throw on an a cappella track or a slow ballad (a sort of musical blue-balling, if you will). He brought in keyboard player Michael DeBenedictus to improvise live along with the records. And when he was really feeling it—which was often—he'd come down from the booth and dance in the crowd to his own selections.

Other top-tier deejays in the city—including Freddy Bastone, Johnny Dynell, Justin Strauss, Sharon White, François Kevorkian, and Danny Krivit—were especially impressed, with many heading to the all-night Garage after their own shifts ended at 4:00 a.m. Unique among them was Richard Vasquez, a former graphic designer who'd only started deejaying in his early forties.

Vasquez: I was looking for a very rich, abundant social life. I had missed all kinds of fun in high school, and I didn't have the money to go to college, so I missed that fun as well. I just worked really, really hard, and by the time I got to my forties, I owned a nice building, I was pretty much set, and I could goof off.

Vasquez had gotten his feet wet at the after-hours club Berlin, where he'd offered graphic design services to the club for free in exchange for a plum deejaying gig. By the time he started going to the Garage, he was deejaying regularly at the Cat Club (6 East 13th Street), which was primarily a post-punk and metal venue. "I wasn't crazy about a lot of the disco Larry was playing," Vasquez explained. "I would just be waiting to hear the [post-punk] records that I was playing in clubs that had shitty sound systems, to hear what they sounded like at Paradise Garage."

In time, Vasquez came to appreciate the disco records he was hearing at the Garage—and Levan, who made a point of identifying his regulars' individual tastes, took notice. "My favorite record was 'Dr. Love' by First Choice," he recalled, "and Larry told me at one point, 'Whenever I see you on the dance floor for the first time, I try to program 'Dr. Love,' because I know you love that record.'"

The fact that Larry Levan was playing punk and new wave records was significant—while disco became trendier to play at white rock-oriented clubs like the Mudd Club and Danceteria, punk and new wave never became commonplace at Black and/or gay discos. Mancuso would delve into rock from time to time, but Levan's tastes were harder-edged: Pat Benatar's "Love Is a Battlefield," Van Halen's "Jump," Stevie Nicks's "Stand Back," the Clash's "The Magnificent Dance," and the Who's "Eminence Front." He was reportedly also a huge Aerosmith fan and expressed a desire to remix the band (which went tragically unconsummated).

On the other hand, Levan had no qualms about playing commercial disco records that the underground largely derided.

Ocasio: This is the difference a sound system makes: Me and my cousin were listening to Larry play, and then "You Should Be Danc-

ing" by the Bee Gees came on. We started laughing at him, like, look at this stupid shit he's playing. And then, not even a minute into the song, we were dancing, and we were screaming and yelling. It blew me away. That was the first and last time I ever made fun of him.

Levan was also massively influential in the music industry, with the power to single-handedly make or break a hit. He developed a close relationship with the popular radio deejay Frankie Crocker at WBLS; Crocker paid attention to Levan's selections at the Garage, and records that Levan premiered were often heard on Crocker's show the next day. Levan also cultivated a relationship with Vinylmania, a record store located just a few blocks north of the Garage at 30 Carmine Street. Vinylmania supplied Levan with whatever new releases and imports he wasn't already getting for free, and once he played them at the Garage, they'd fly off Vinylmania's shelves.

Judy Weinstein, who as head of For The Record had become a power broker in her own right, was also regularly booking live performers into the club. Paradise Garage didn't publicly advertise the shows, which usually took place around 4:00 a.m., so few outside the club's inner circle knew they were occurring. But those in attendance were treated to an extraordinary range of acts, including Diana Ross, Cyndi Lauper, ESG, Patti LaBelle, Klaus Nomi, Wham!, Grace Jones, Divine, Duran Duran, the Pointer Sisters, Whitney Houston, Madonna, New Order,[xviii] Tim Curry,[xix] and Nu Shooz.[xx]

---

xviii Both Madonna's music video for "Everybody" (1982) and portions of New Order's video for "Confusion" (1983) were filmed at the Paradise Garage.

xix Curry released a song about the club, called "Paradise Garage," in 1979.

xx There was also a bizarre one-off punk/no wave show on June 18, 1978. Advertised as "Hell in Paradise," the show was headlined by Richard Hell and the Voidoids, with the Senders, Teenage Jesus and the Jerks, Contortions, and the Stimulators opening. According to documentarian Pat Ivers, it didn't go well: "If there were 100 people there, I'd be surprised. The electricity went out at least once. It was a real clusterfuck."

Though disco had receded from the mainstream after its late-seventies overexposure, there was no shortage of incredible new dance records coming out. Perhaps out of a desire to distance this new music from disco's bad name, much of what Levan played became known locally as "Garage music." But at the same time, Levan's old comrade Frankie Knuckles had begun playing similar sounds at a Chicago club called the Warehouse, where it became known as "Warehouse music," which was soon shortened to the name that would encompass all of it: house music.

THE THIRD LOFT

By the end of the 1970s, SoHo was unrecognizable from what it had been a decade earlier. Though plenty of artists' lofts remained, rents were rising. Galleries and artists' shops were joined by upscale boutiques and fine dining establishments. The rise in bourgeois businesses was accompanied by a rise in thefts at said bourgeois businesses, which was in turn accompanied by explicit racism directed at the Black community. In 1984, *New York Magazine* reporter Patricia Morrisroe claimed that "the vast majority of [SoHo's] robberies have been committed by blacks, and many shopkeepers are now refusing to allow them into their stores. For a neighborhood made up mostly of the young and the liberal, this is a particularly painful dilemma."[61]

In that *New York* article, several store owners, managers, and security guards openly admit to an increased suspicion toward Black shoppers, often refusing them entry. The bias and hysteria also extended to members of the LGBTQ+ community, with neighborhood merchants supposedly concerned about how "[f]or years, SoHo has been besieged by transvestites, many of whom [are] ripping off stores."[62]

A growth in neighborhood suspicions toward Black and gender-nonconforming people was bad news for the Loft. Even though David Mancuso had persevered against early attempts to prevent him from opening at 99 Prince Street, he saw the writing on the wall. In 1979, his landlord gave him a chance to purchase the building, but Mancuso found the neighborhood's direction dis-couraging enough to reject the offer. When the landlord sold it to another buyer for a couple million, Mancuso began searching for a new home.

He found it in the area commonly known as "Alphabet City," due to its lettered (rather than numbered) avenues. The roughest area in Lower Manhattan, it was at the time infamous for drug dealing, gang activity, and a sizable homeless population, but (as we'll see in Chapter Seven) also had a significant artistic and mu-sical community.

The building Mancuso found at 240 East 3rd Street between Avenue B and Avenue C was, much like the Broadway Loft, aus-piciously located. Built in 1913 as the six-hundred-seat American Movies Theater, the building had since been renamed the New Pilgrim Theater. The building to its immediate left had housed the seminal jazz club Slugs' Saloon in the '60s and early '70s; the Nuyo-rican Poets Cafe, a beacon for artistic expression of all stripes for the neighborhood's Puerto Rican community, was to the right.[xxi]

Mancuso acquired the theater in 1982 with a $25,000 down pay-ment, viewing it as a step toward self-sufficiency. He removed the seats, leveled the theater's sloped floor, and converted the projec-tionist's booth into residential quarters, all the while continuing to throw parties at 99 Prince Street. Once the new space was ready, Mancuso held his final party at 99 Prince Street on June 2, 1984.[xxii]

As had been the case with Yves Saint Laurent's showcase at

---

xxi The New Pilgrim itself had been home to a ten-day music festival in 1981 billed as "New Music for Millions," featuring Sonic Youth, R.E.M., DNA, Wall of Voodoo, Love of Life Orchestra, 3 Teens Kill 4, and the Bloods, among others. Despite its phenomenal lineup, the festival was plagued with issues typical of the neighborhood at the time: according to Love of Life Orchestra's bandleader, Peter Gordon, "I didn't find out until after our show that the night before, [the Bloods] had been playing, and four guys came in with guns and robbed the whole club."

xxii In 2016, artist Martin Beck made a film and accompanying book called *Last Night*, cataloging every song Mancuso played at the final Prince Street party, in sequence.

99 Prince Street, the new Loft at 240 East 3rd Street got an early financial and promotional boost from a commercial entity, as Mancuso was hired to premiere Pink Floyd's new album *The Final Cut* on his immaculate sound system. There were special events for the Loft community as well; beyond the usual Saturday night parties, Konk bassist Jonny Sender recalled playing a daytime barbeque there soon after the reopening.

The dancers that followed Mancuso to the new Loft location were as passionate as they'd ever been. For Kenny Carpenter, the East 3rd Loft was his favorite yet, with a sound system that improved upon the already remarkable one at Prince Street. And it was around this time that the expressive, athletic, improvisatory dancing that some at the Loft had pioneered became known as "Lofting."

But much of the Loft community found crime-ridden Alphabet City to be a harder sell than SoHo had been.

Sherman: He had a good turnout for the first party, but then he lost maybe two-thirds of his following. People didn't want to park in that neighborhood, and it was a good hike from the nearest train. It was such a shit-upon neighborhood because of the demographics and the way the city allocated resources.

Murphy: You could not walk down a block without being propositioned three times—body bag, body bag, body bag. I was young, but for people that had gone to Prince Street, they were getting older, their jobs were getting more serious or they're having children. The last place they want to go is this heroin-infested neighborhood.

Beyond Alphabet City's dangerous reputation, there are two other factors that likely contributed to Mancuso's shrinking audience. One is purely geographic: 99 Prince Street is roughly a ten-minute walk from 84 King Street, home of the Paradise Garage. But King Street and Alphabet City are on opposite sides of the island; it takes twenty-five to thirty minutes to make the journey.

Whatever overlap existed between the Garage and the Loft would have been strained by the distance, and with its inherent familiarity, density, commerciality, and neighborhood safety, the Garage had the clear upper hand.

The other factor, of course, is much bigger and infinitely more devastating: the emergence of HIV and AIDS.

GAY MEN'S HEALTH CRISIS

In 1977, Dr. Donna Mildvan and Dr. Dan William at Beth Israel Medical Center began noting similarities in the symptoms of several gay male patients; two years later, Mildvan began identifying a form of severe diarrhea that she noticed in these patients as "Gay Bowel Syndrome." By 1981, rumors of a "gay plague" began circulating in New York City; Dr. Lawrence Mass[xxiii] published a report in the local gay newspaper *New York Native* warning the community that this still-mysterious disease was being spread through unprotected sexual activity between men.

The following year, Dr. Mass was involved in co-founding the Gay Men's Health Crisis (GMHC), a nonprofit that provided legal services, crisis counseling, and other supportive services to men with the disease, while educating those outside the community about its painful realities. The organization began operating out of Colonial House, a townhouse at 318 West 22nd Street belonging to West End Records co-founder and early Paradise Garage funder Mel Cheren.

At the time of GMHC's formation, the new disease was identified as Gay-Related Immune Deficiency, or GRID, but by the end of 1982 it would be known as acquired immunodeficiency syndrome, or AIDS.

Man Parrish: We were all freaked out, and there were all kinds of rumors. I didn't want to go to a bar and touch a doorknob or sit on a

---

xxiii Dr. Mass is the brother of Mudd Club owner Steve Mass, who we'll discuss in Chapter Six.

toilet seat, because maybe you can get it from a toilet seat or a door-knob. There was no CDC giving us advice, because it was a bunch of fags, so who cares?

New York's overflowing hospitals were of little help, too. Dying men were turned away, and because the modes of transference weren't firmly established (and, doubtlessly, because of institutional homophobia), those lucky enough to get interred were treated like lepers.

AIDS decimated New York's gay community. Over the following decades, several leading lights in the Downtown art and music scenes would be lost to the disease: artist Keith Haring, singer Klaus Nomi, musician Arthur Russell, artist David Wojnarowicz, photographer Robert Mapplethorpe, performer John Sex, B-52s guitarist Ricky Wilson, Teenage Jesus and the Jerks bassist Gordon Stevenson, Mumps front man Lance Loud, actress and writer Cookie Mueller, singer Sharon Redd, Danceteria doorman Haoui Montaug, Stimulators singer Patrick Mack, Miki and Mandy Zone from the Fast, dancer Wili Ninja, Studio 54 owner Steve Rubell... the list goes on and on. All the while, powers that be like NYC mayor Ed Koch (himself a closeted gay man) and President Ronald Reagan refused to acknowledge it.

At least five Paradise Garage staffers died of AIDS. A disproportionate number of the people interviewed for this chapter are heterosexual, in large part because so many of the gay men who were involved with the scene died. Nearly an entire generation of LGBTQ+ elders was decimated.

The impact on the city was immediate. As writer Sarah Schulman observed, "Real estate conversion was already dramatically underway when the epidemic peaked and large numbers of my neighbors started dying, turning over their apartments *literally* to market rate at an unnatural speed."[63] For Kenny Carpenter, "After the AIDS epidemic, that's when gentrification started setting in. A lot of people that would have been there to help fight the battle were gone."

At least one disco originator found a new purpose after AIDS's emergence. Nicky Siano, who had retired from deejaying in the early '80s, became a certified social worker, working closely with HIV/AIDS patients. In 1993, as Nick Siano, he published a book, *No Time to Wait: A Complete Guide to Treating, Managing, and Living with HIV Infection*, exploring both traditional and alternative medical treatments, as well as the emotional and psychological impacts of the virus. "That, for me, was the most important work I did in my life," Siano later said.[64]

FAREWELL TO THE GARAGE

Though he'd eventually play a significant role there, Victor Rosado's first visit to the Paradise Garage had been less than encouraging.

> *Rosado: I started to dance with a friend of mine that I went to the club with, and we were dancing the hustle. Over comes this big, dark-skinned guy—Joey Llanos, the head of security. He told us, "Larry told me to tell you that you can't dance that dance here. You have to stop." Can you imagine? A club for dancing, but you could only dance what they allowed you to dance. I was a little embarrassed and turned off by it, but not mad enough to not come back.*

At the same time, Rosado was continuing to assist David Mancuso at the Loft in a wide variety of capacities, which included serving as one of Mancuso's trusted backup musical hosts.

> *Rosado: On Friday nights at the Loft, we would do "homework" to test the new records—he'd get them in the mail, or I'd go shopping. He'd either tell me yes or no, and then we'd move on to the next record. One Friday, around May of '86, David went upstairs to his apartment; he could hear the music from his window, so I just kept going.*
> *All of a sudden, the door from upstairs opened up, and in comes*

Larry. I said, "Larry, I didn't know you were upstairs," and he said, "Yeah, I'm hanging out with David, we were talking and listening to you go through the music." As he was leaving, he said, "Why don't you come to the club tomorrow? Come as my guest, I'll leave your name, and you can bring whoever you want." And then he turned around and said, "And bring some records!" I said, "Larry, why would I bring records? You don't even know if I play." He said, "Just because you didn't know I was here doesn't mean I haven't heard you play. I've heard you play many times."

After that visit, Rosado and Levan developed a close bond.

Rosado: *I started hanging out at the Garage every week, though I also kept my relationship at the Loft. [One time,] Larry said, "Why do you like playing music?" I said, "Larry, I just love it. It makes me feel complete, like I have a purpose." He said, "Why do you play with David?" I said, "Even though he doesn't have money to pay me, I play for free because it makes me happy." He said, "You should care about the money—when you play like you do, you should be making money." And then he asked me, "What's one of your biggest wishes?" I said, "I dream about someday playing at a club like this, on this scale, to make people dance and feel a certain way with my music." He said, "Wow, that's powerful."*

A couple of months later, it was Larry's birthday celebration—his is July 20th, mine is the 23rd. I had four or five crates of my records there. The festivities start, it's crowded, Larry's playing. And then he tells me, "I've got to go to the office to take care of some stuff. I'll be back." I said, "But Larry, the record's going to finish." He turns around and looks at me and says, "Happy birthday. Play." He leaves, and my hands are shaking. I'm left with a gigantic sound system, a room full of 3,000 people, and the record's playing.

I pull out Jimmy "Bo" Horn's "Spank." The crowd goes crazy. I queued up the next record, which was Xavier Gold's "You Used to Hold Me," but I got nervous and confused, and when I picked up the needle to cue the record, I picked the needle up off of "Spank."

COURTESY OF VICTOR ROSADO.

Larry Levan deejaying at the Space Lab Yellow nightclub in Tokyo, Japan, ca. 1988.

The room screamed, and I'm shaking and nervous. I put the nee-dle back down on ["Spank"], it went right into the break, and they screamed even louder. Then I went into Xavier Gold, and they fucking went bananas. They started screaming "Larry! Larry!" and then they looked over [and realized it was] me. I carried the night for about two hours.

The rest was history. We worked together until he passed away.

As Levan was forging a bond with Rosado, his relationship with his boss, Michael Brody, was disintegrating. Communication be-tween the two men had long been tense, as each implicitly under-stood that their own success was heavily dependent on the other's. But as the two bickered over matters small and large, they became increasingly vicious. One fight—either over an expensive piece of audio equipment that Brody refused to buy, or Brody conspiring to get rid of Levan—resulted in Levan dropping to all fours and biting Brody's leg so hard that he drew blood.

Both men are now dead, so it's impossible to get the full story as to why their relationship broke down the way it did. But by all accounts, Levan's success and popularity had exacerbated some of his more entitled qualities; he'd also been consuming prodigious amounts of heroin and cocaine.

Levan's erratic behavior wasn't the only ominous sign. The Hudson Square area had been drawing higher-income residents and businesses, who viewed the Paradise Garage as a public nuisance. In 1985, Tishman Speyer Properties announced the construction of a new eighteen-story building at 375 Hudson Street—less than a block from the club—with the top nine floors going to the Saatchi & Saatchi advertising agency. As the firm's senior vice president Richard M. Mumma told the *New York Times*, "Hudson Street is much farther south than anyone else [in advertising] has ever gone... But for creative people the galleries, shops and restaurants there are a more exciting concept than being across from the General Motors Building."[65]

According to Joey Llanos, there had been "a lot of pressure from the community board to shut us down, but it was difficult because we didn't have liquor, so there wasn't a lot that the city could do." But with Brody's ten-year lease on 84 King Street coming to a close in 1987, he was informed by the building's owners that it would not be renewed. Instead, the building would go to New York Telephone, for use as a private garage in which to repair and store their vehicles.

It was around this time that Brody contracted HIV. As the illness took hold, he became a spectral presence at the Garage. When he got the news about the club's unrenewed lease, he saw little reason to rally what minimal energy he had left to keep his club alive.

Levan took the news especially poorly; at the staff meeting where Brody announced the club's closure and his own imminent death, Levan stormed out of the room, went into his deejay booth, and turned the sound system's volume up high enough to blow the whole thing out. In an especially cruel twist, things between the two had deteriorated to such a degree that Brody refused to bequeath any element of the club to Levan—not even the deejay's custom-designed sound system.

Richard Vasquez made a valiant but unsuccessful attempt to salvage the club.

Vasquez: I was trying to get Keith Haring and Mark Josephson, who ran Rockpool [a record pool], to become my partners and keep the Garage going as our business. Keith and Mark were interested in doing it, but at that point Michael Brody was unapproachable and nobody would let anybody visit him, so we could never get to him to make the proposition.

Mel Cheren, among others, believed that Brody "wanted his Paradise Garage to die with him" in order to cement his legacy. Had the club continued without him, Cheren speculated, "the passing of Michael Brody would be just another tragic blip[.]"[66]

The closure of the Paradise Garage was announced with an invitation to the club's final weekend, which would run from September 25 through 28, 1987. The closing weekend was by all accounts an emotional experience, equally joyful and tragic. Several Garage favorites, including ESG and Liz Torres, performed live. Keith Haring flew in from Japan especially to attend; Levan's mother, Minnie, brought a mountain of homemade soul food and held court by the buffet tables. Unfortunately, it was also punctuated by a violent stabbing outside the club on its penultimate night.[xxiv]

Two months later, Michael Brody died from AIDS. After Brody's passing, a few former employees attempted to open a spin-off called Paradise Ballroom in a converted theater on 43rd Street, boasting the famous Paradise Garage sound system. But as most would have predicted, it failed to recapture what had made the Garage so special.

After the Garage closed, an unidentified friend of Cheren's stumbled across the club's famed neon sign waiting to be picked up with the trash. The friend passed it along to Cheren, who gave it a place

---

xxiv Several recordings of Levan's final sets at the Garage have since been commercially released with varying degrees of legality, and there is some grainy but compelling footage on YouTube.

of pride on the sun deck of Colonial House. After Cheren passed away in 2007, the sign went along with the rest of his archives to NYU's Fales Library, currently stored in an offsite warehouse.[xxv]

After Paradise Garage closed, things went from bad to worse for Larry Levan. At the Garage, he'd reigned supreme; few other deejays before or since have been acquiesced to by both the club's staff and its dancers to the degree he'd experienced. Removed from the bosom of his club, an insecure and drug-addled Levan made the rounds of other clubs in the city that would have him, including Studio 54, Irving Plaza, the Palladium, Mars, Tracks, and the World.

Freddy Bastone: Larry played the best I ever heard him play at the Palladium. He wasn't playing anything that he played at the Garage, but he was making everybody go crazy. If somebody is a great deejay, they can play in different atmospheres. He was out of his element, but he made it his own.

By this point, Levan was largely deejaying with borrowed records. His enormous library at the Garage had been packed up and put into a Chelsea storage facility where the monthly rent was a reasonable $100, but out of stubbornness, obliviousness, or both, Levan continually neglected to pay. After a final warning, Levan's record collection was auctioned off. Garage devotee Danny Tenaglia, a reputable deejay in his own right, reportedly bought some of the rarer ones and gave them back to Levan, but most were gone. Even after that loss, Levan continued selling what few records remained for drug money.

Though many in New York now viewed him as a has-been, Levan's reputation had spread to Europe and Asia, and he found himself invited to deejay at legendary clubs like London's Ministry

---

[xxv] Though hypothetically available for any interested party to view, multiple requests from this author were ignored.

of Sound. But Levan was struggling financially, and he would go for stretches without a residence of his own, relying on the kindness of the few remaining people with whom he hadn't already burned bridges.

In July 1992, as he was getting ready to leave for a tour of Japan, Larry Levan ominously told his mother that he only had six months to live. He overestimated: on November 8, 1992, shortly after his return from Japan, he passed away from endocarditis, an inflammation of the heart's lining, exacerbated by years of heavy drug abuse.

THE LOFT IN EXILE

In the late '80s, David Mancuso had decided that, nearly two decades since the first Loft parties, it was time for a break. His associates from this era tend to speak vaguely about their mentor's troubles, but it's clear that the diminishment of the Loft community, his subsequent financial struggles, and the loss of many friends and associates to AIDS had all taken a toll on him, and he was self-medicating in some capacity. Mancuso turned his East 3rd Loft over to Richard Vasquez and Joey Llanos—who transformed it into their own successful club, the Choice—and retreated to a house he owned upstate.

Mancuso came back from his self-imposed exile in the early '90s with a renewed verve, but it didn't last long, as he discovered that his lawyer had swindled him out of ownership of 240 East 3rd Street. All the money, time, and passion he'd poured into the building had been for naught. Though the lawyer—who'd run similar scams on other clients—went to jail for his crimes, the building had already been legally sold by that point, leaving Mancuso without recourse.

From there, Mancuso bounced around between rented apartments in Alphabet City.

Murphy: The 1990s were not a good time for the Loft. We were constantly having to move him, we were doing fundraisers, and the spaces were getting progressively smaller.

The Downtown Mancuso was being forced to navigate was very different from the one he'd established himself in. This was partially because so many apartments had turned over as a result of the AIDS epidemic, alongside Mayors Dinkins and Giuliani cracking down on nightlife. The city also undertook specific actions to gentrify Alphabet City in the '90s, which we'll get into in Chapters Seven and Nine. The end result was an East Village that wasn't especially welcoming to, say, an underground party in a residential building full of POC and LGBTQ+ dancers grooving to a top-of-the-line sound system.

There were other issues as well. Mancuso's already-significant financial struggles were exacerbated by the loss of his property. Where many of his devotees had gone on to have successful careers as traditional deejays and remixers, Mancuso's uncompromising vision and lack of business sense left him destitute.

Murphy: David was brilliant in some ways. When it came to money? No. He could make it and he could lose it.

Robert Clivillés (C+C Music Factory), Victor Rosado, and David Mancuso at South Street Seaport, ca. 1997–98.

COURTESY OF VICTOR ROSADO.

There was also the matter of the music he was playing. By the '90s, Mancuso had established a clear canon of Loft records. Though he remained open to new sounds, both Mancuso and much of his audience had aged; inevitably, their tastes were colored by a degree of nostalgia.

Ocasio: It was still the Loft, David was still there, but there was a change. The main reason I would go to Loft was to get turned on to music, and there came a time for me where David stopped being the teacher. I don't know how else to say it. He wasn't turning me on to amazing music as often. He would always drop some dope shit, but it just wasn't the same.

After being forced out of a short-lived space on Avenue B, Mancuso moved into a small apartment and ceased throwing parties in his home. "Everything went into storage, and he was living day-to-day, hand-to-mouth," Douglas Sherman recalled.

Murphy: I thought David should do a compilation for somebody; that would be a good revenue stream. So I mentioned it to him, and he said, "Colleen, I'll only do it with you." I was quite taken aback, because I didn't have a record label, and I was just getting ready to move to the UK. But I had relationships with different labels in the UK, and I thought it would be better on a UK label—they'll put more money into it, it'll be produced better, it'll be marketed better, it will sell better. If he had put it out on a New York label, I don't think that he would have gotten that kind of level of artistic integrity and that audience.

Nuphonic Records released the resultant compilations, 1999's *The Loft* and 2000's *The Loft Volume 2*. The track lists are a crash course in Loft classics: Manu Dibango, Loose Joints, the Orb, Eddie Kendricks, Crown Heights Affair. Not all Loft devotees were thrilled—as Victor Rosado put it, "David would never play CDs, yet he made CDs to sell? How are you going to sell something that you yourself are totally against playing?" But even so, the compilations had the intended effect—they put some money in Mancuso's pocket and helped spread his reputation beyond a niche community in New York, leading to lucrative offers for Loft-style parties in Japan and the UK. "All of a sudden, people started signing up for the mailing list and it had the capacity to become successful," said Murphy. "He was able to make a living."

Sherman: Somebody mentioned this rental space on 2nd Ave.[xxvi] *David fell in love with it immediately, and the rent that was being asked for it was perfect for him. The chairman of the board that operated the space hit it off with David, and they became fast friends. They knew we were a steady source of income for them and we weren't going to destroy their place, and because of that they gave us a lot of leeway to do things.*

It's where the Loft has the longest residency of any address; I think it's been eighteen years. When we got into that space, we were doing parties three times a year, and it eventually grew to four. So we went from parties every Saturday for 52 weeks a year, to doing zero, to doing three, and eventually four times a year. As a result, we had to increase the contribution that we asked for. What had been an affordable contribution for many became excessive for some: David went up upwards of $55, because that's what it costs to pull off.

Some of the more seasoned folks would balk at spending that much money for the party, because they felt like they had always supported David for so many years, and now it's $55—that's like a Broadway show! But it's not like he walked away with a handsome profit. David made just enough money to carry him between parties—his rent, food, maybe a few comfort things, and he was getting Social Security as well. He never got rich off this thing. He lived in a rent-stabilized, fifth floor walk-up apartment with no elevator. He had

---

his music, and a TV in his room because he liked to watch the news. He didn't need a whole lot.

As Mancuso's parties were finally taking root again, his own health was failing. There were aches and pains, his vision was getting blurrier. He gradually began outsourcing the job of musical host to acolytes like Sherman and Murphy.

Sherman: He would do setup, he would open the party, and then he would say "Douglas, take over," and he'd leave. For the last seven years of the party, David essentially just stopped playing, and he didn't even come for the last year and a half; he just stayed home. But he would be on the phone driving us all crazy.

David Mancuso passed away in his apartment on November 14, 2016. No cause of death was ever made public, but multiple members of the Loft community have pointed to the devastation he felt after Donald Trump's election—the antithesis of everything Mancuso and the Loft stood for.

While the accessible DIY spirit of folk and punk made the boundaries between performer and audience more permeable, disco and house music did away with those boundaries altogether, upending the established hierarchies of nightlife and the music industry. Deejays could be performers without adhering to any traditional aspects of musical performance, or even drawing attention to themselves; they served instead as facilitators or guides, and lived or died on the strength of their curatorial ear. Dancers could be the central focus of the entertainment, despite their lack of a traditional stage, name recognition, or remuneration. Those responsible for the actual music being played were mostly absent and unaware of the way their work was being consumed; those that did come to the clubs could experience the success or failure of their work from a spectator's vantage point, often going unrecognized by an audience who'd only absorbed their work aurally. The nuances of the PA systems played as significant a role as the records they amplified—and in the case of the Loft and Garage, arguably more significant. No single element dominates over the others; the true star of the night is the alchemy of it all.

It is a noble goal and, when it succeeds, it provides an unparalleled experience of communal transcendence. And yet, the central paradox of every democracy is that someone becomes elevated above everybody else. In the end, David Mancuso's repeated insistence on his self-erasure as the musical host has mutated into a near deification, no doubt exacerbated by his Christ-like visage.

And much like Jesus, some of his closest disciples have scattered, each claiming to be his true spiritual heir, or that their interpretation of what is and isn't "the Loft" is definitive. Love is still the message, but it coexists with a perceptible amount of bad blood.

Still, the extraordinary community that Mancuso built has continued to exist without him. On Valentine's Day, 2020, the Loft celebrated its fiftieth anniversary.

Sherman: That was really the milestone we wanted to achieve. David must have been looking down on us with angel eyes, because we were able to have that 50th Anniversary Valentine's Day weekend when the [Covid-19] pandemic was already raging. Right after that party, everything shut down. But we had over 900 people in attendance, when we normally have a little over 400, and it went beautifully. Nothing but smiles for miles.

Because of the restrictions of the rented space, Loft parties are no longer an all-night affair; they start at the polite hour of 5:00 p.m. and run until midnight. But most traditions have remained in place: It's still invite only, there's a large spread of free food, balloons are everywhere, and the music is presented in Mancuso's three-bardo structure. The records are mostly drawn from Mancuso's canon, and each time, his prized sound system is brought out of storage.

I first had the privilege of attending the Loft in 2019; though

PHOTOGRAPH BY THE AUTHOR.

Balloons at the Loft, 2019.

I'd already researched Mancuso's story, nothing could have prepared me for the real thing. There was a degree of warmth between strangers that's all but impossible to find in present day New York City, and the mix of people was remarkable: there were seasoned Loft dancers whose laugh lines belied their agility and stamina, sweaty twentysomethings in tank tops flipping out to records twice as old as they were, Ann Taylor–clad moms conspiratorially dropping ecstasy together. Even in his absence, David Mancuso's vision remains startlingly intact.

The Paradise Garage community has persevered as well, to a lesser degree. In 2021, I attended the annual Paradise Garage reunion at the Bushwick, Brooklyn, club Elsewhere. Levan's old compadres David DePino and Joey Llanos deejayed; as with the contemporary Loft, the set list was somewhat predictable but in no way diminished by its obviousness. Unlike the contemporary Loft, these reunions are ticketed and open to the public, there is alcohol available, and the Elsewhere sound system is excellent but hardly as bone rattling as the storied Garage PA. The dancers were roughly a fifty-fifty split between Black and Latinx people over fifty who had been there, and white people under fifty who hadn't; they shared the space harmoniously, but the two groups rarely seemed to mingle. Still, drenched in sweat and dancing to Stevie Wonder's "As" at 3:45 a.m., my critical thinking had long since fallen to the wayside and I felt pure, transcendent joy.

THE AFTERLIFE OF THE LOFT AND PARADISE GARAGE

David Mancuso's original Loft 645-647 is still residential. The second Loft at 99 Prince Street is now part of the Mercer Hotel, which advertises itself as "the first hotel to offer an authentic taste of loft living."[67] The ground and basement levels that once housed the Loft have been subdivided into a high-end restaurant called Mercer Kitchen and a cluster of luxury retail spaces; the Loft ethos of class mixing is decidedly absent.

After Mancuso's lawyer sold the building, the third Loft at 240 East 3rd Street became a rehearsal and production studio for Blue Man Group. They remained there until 2017, when the building sold for $12 million and was demolished.

After the Paradise Garage closed, the building at 84 King Street became a series of warehouses; most recently, it housed Verizon service trucks. In early 2018, the building was bulldozed to make way for a luxury condo building called 77 Charlton. An ongoing campaign to rename the block Larry Levan Way has been so far unsuccessful.

The original location of Nicky Siano's Gallery at 132 West 22nd Street is now part of the Irish Repertory Theater, an off-Broadway theater specializing in Irish and Irish-American plays. The Gallery's second location at 172 Mercer Street is now an American Eagle store.

The Sanctuary (407 West 43rd Street) closed in 1973. The building briefly became a methadone clinic but was soon transformed into an off-Broadway theater—which it remains to this day.

The Gay Activists Alliance Firehouse at 99 Wooster Street is currently empty; most recently, it was a Victorinox Swiss Army store.

In 1985, Mel Cheren turned Colonial House (his townhouse at 318 West 22nd Street which also served as headquarters for the Gay Men's Health Crisis) into a bed and breakfast called Colonial House Inn, which is still run by and primarily serves gay men.

Suggested Listening

MFSB—*Love Is the Message* (1973)

Larry Levan—*Live at the Paradise Garage* (rec. 1979)

NYC Peech Boys—*Life Is Something Special* (1983)

Various—*David Mancuso Presents: The Loft Vols. 1 & 2* (compilation)

Various—*Journey into Paradise (The Larry Levan Story)* (compilation)

Various—*Larry Levan: Genius of Time* (compilation)

Various—*Love Is the Message: A Night at the Gallery 1977* (compilation)

5

TODAY YOUR LOVE, TOMORROW
THE WORLD: CBGB & OMFUG

Genya Ravan (singer; record producer): People have to learn how to play, and they need bars where they can do that and [hear themselves on] good sound systems. So it was a great place for people to go and be able to make mistakes.

Brooke Delarco (live/recording engineer, The Feelies, Patti Smith, the Heartbreakers): CB's was a local hangout; we all lived basically within two or three blocks of it. You'd walk down Bleecker Street on any given night and you would run into any number of people on their way there-[Television guitarist] Richard Lloyd, [Patti Smith drummer] Jay Dee Dougherty, we all lived off Bleecker Street. It really was like that song that Richard Hell wrote, "Down at the Rock and Roll Club." CBGB had those big, swinging saloon doors; you'd open the door and this rush would hit you in the face. I don't want to say "Star Time," but yeah, it was Star Time.

So much ink has been spilled over the CBGB story, from every imaginable angle, that it would be reasonable to assume that the corpse has been picked clean by now. What more could there possibly be to say?

A lot, actually. Though there are many narratives that give an accounting of the club's glory days, most accounts skim over the club's embarrassing twilight years, or mischaracterize the morally complex circumstances that led the club to finally close in 2006. And there's the matter of its afterlife: How has a place revered as one of the most authentic rock clubs in American history found itself mostly remembered in the public imagination through cheesy T-shirts and a theme restaurant at the Newark International Airport?

And the biggest question of all: What made this shithole bar such a culture-defining, world-changing place that you're willing to read *yet another* history of it? Though you'll mostly hear that it had to do with owner Hilly Kristal's vision or a magical meeting of the right people and the right time, there's another factor that often gets overlooked: Remember that in talking about Max's Kansas City, I said that most successful clubs are either located smack-dab in the middle of a community or in the middle of nowhere? CBGB was both—clumsily inserted onto one of the most foreboding, crime-ridden streets in Manhattan, but also mere blocks from the homes of some of the most important musical talents in the city's music history. Existing in these two spaces is what gave CBGB the freedom to take risks, foster community, and allow artists to grow—though it also brought up complex issues of gentrification that would prove to be part of the club's undoing.

HILLY'S

CBGB & OMFUG, located at 315 Bowery, opened in 1971 as Hilly's on the Bowery. Its owner, thirty-nine-year-old Hillel "Hilly" Kristal, was a frustrated musician who had come very close to signing with Atlantic Records in the late '50s, after which he worked as a manager and booker at the Village Vanguard through the early 1960s. He opened his first bar, a cabaret club that was also called Hilly's, at 62 West 9th Street for a few years in the mid to late '60s (a third Hilly's briefly existed at 104 West 13th Street after the Bowery location had already opened).

The Bowery had once been a theater district for lower-class patrons, but for the bulk of the 1900s, it was practically synonymous with homelessness and substance abuse. An instructive example: around the turn of the century, a popular bar just a few doors south of where CBGB would open gained the name McGuirk's Suicide Hall because many area sex workers literally drank themselves to death there. By the early '70s, the area had become home to the occasional bohemian looking for ultracheap rent, but it remained relatively unchanged.

315 Bowery itself housed the Palace Hotel, a flophouse which, almost too perfectly, shared both a name and mise-en-scène with the one in John Steinbeck's *Cannery Row*. Since its opening in 1949, it had become the Bowery's largest flophouse, offering 105 windowless cubicles and 224 dormitory beds, which could be had for as little as $2.85 a night. Upwards of 600 men crammed in each night, sharing one bathroom per floor.

When Kristal moved in, 315's street-level storefront housed the hotel's namesake bar. With a bare minimum of redecorating, it was transformed into Hilly's on the Bowery, serving two primary client bases: the Bowery's homeless population, who didn't have much money to spend on booze, and the neighborhood chapter of the Hell's Angels—long headquartered around the corner at 77 East 3rd Street—who essentially ran a protection racket that allowed them to drink for free.

Granted, Kristal had been drawn to the Bowery because he had noticed a trend of artists moving into the area and buying lofts—not to mention that the Tin Palace was already located a few doors up on the corner of Bowery and East 2nd, drawing jazz fans and tourists to the area well before CBGB. In that sense, it wasn't totally virgin territory, but it was far from a bustling nightlife district.

Hilly's bar fell into dire financial straits pretty quickly, but given his background in music, live bands seemed like a good fix. Kristal's personal tastes ran toward traditional American roots music, so he began inviting country, bluegrass, and blues artists to come play. It worked well enough, and in 1973, he changed the bar's name to reflect its new direction (Country, BlueGrass, and Blues = CBGB, and Other Music For Uplifting Gourmandizers = OMFUG, dig?[i]).

Not only was Kristal trying to make a country bar work on the Bowery, he was pushing it as a *morning* venue, with the club serving a hearty breakfast as the country musicians played. Unsurprisingly, it never caught on.

The club also presented a good amount of jazz (which would fall under "OMFUG"). This was a logical move, given the location: besides the Tin Palace, Hilly's was also two blocks southeast from Studio Rivbea and three southeast from Ladies' Fort. Bassist William Parker, who regularly played at Hilly's with drummer Rashied Ali, recalled Tuesday nights being the major draw for jazz heads.

TELEVISION VS. THE MAGIC TRAMPS

How exactly CBGB began its transition into the world's most famous punk club, however, is a bit of a *Rashomon*-like story, with competing narratives. The most famous version of the story, the one you've probably heard, goes like this: On the day Kristal was putting up his bar's new awning, members of a recently formed band called Television happened to be walking around the Bowery (the question of which specific members were there depends on which of them is telling the story). An aggressively uncommercial band whose members had hung out at the Mercer Arts Center, Television were having trouble finding places to play since that venue's collapse.

After asking Kristal about his bar's unusual name, one of the band members fibbed and claimed that Television was in fact a

---

i　　Though "Uplifting" is canon, some recollections from those around in the club's early days have it as "Undernourished."

country and/or blues outfit.[ii] Without bothering to investigate, Kristal invited them to come play on March 31, 1974—a Sunday, his quietest night. They weren't a country and/or blues band after all, and they didn't draw well, but manager Terry Ork bought enough drinks on his own for Kristal to see some value in inviting them back. From there, they began playing on a weekly basis.

The gambit worked. Ork and guitarist Richard Lloyd began booking Sunday night shows that saw Television headline over a variety of other unknown local bands, with all the door money (initially $1/person, soon raised to $2) divided amongst the performers. On Easter, less than a month after that first Television gig, Patti Smith and her bandmate Lenny Kaye came to check out Television while on their way to visit William S. Burroughs, who lived a couple blocks south of CBGB at 222 Bowery. Smith and Kaye were so struck by the club's potential that in short order, they began playing there, too. Things just sort of snowballed from there.

It's a great story—one that's both roughly accurate *and* misleading, bordering on disingenuous. Television certainly played a large role in building CBGB into the legendary venue it became, but it was hardly virgin territory for boundary-pushing rock bands when they first darkened its doorway.

In fact, the very first live act to play in the space—punk or otherwise—were the ever-intrepid Magic Tramps, who had already been responsible for both reopening Max's Kansas City to live music, and bringing glam rock to the Mercer Arts Center.

And, once again, their fortunes hinged on their willingness to work with lumber.

Sesu Coleman: Eric and I were walking over to the Mercer from the east side in the late afternoon, and there was Hilly out there, cleaning the canopy. Eric knew him, so he said, "Hilly, how's it going?" I hadn't met him before, so there was an introduction, all that kind of

---

ii   Guitarists Richard Lloyd and Tom Verlaine, bassist Richard Hell, and manager Terry Ork have all been credited in one account or another.

stuff, and then we went inside. It was a really stinky, smelly, funky biker bar, with dogs shitting everywhere.

Eric said, "You should let us play here, Hilly," and Hilly laughed and said, "Yeah right! This is a biker bar, Eric, not whatever you're doing there." And Eric said, "That's okay. We can do anything, we can learn anything." Hilly said, jokingly, "If you build a stage, you could play here." Joke joke, ha ha. But we said, "OK, we'll do that."

So we went out and found these little plywood boards in the garbage, maybe left over from some construction or something, and a whole bunch of other crap that people had thrown in the street. We took it over to Hilly's, laid down a bunch of boards and carpets, and we created this funky, makeshift—I guess you'd call it a stage. If you looked at it now, you'd say, "That ain't no stage," but it was more than was there previously.[iii]

We said, "There!," and Hilly goes, "You're too much. I'll tell you what, I'll let you play one night, but it's not going to be rock 'n' roll. I don't want any rock 'n' roll stuff in here, only blues, jazz, bluegrass, all that stuff." We said, "We don't care, as long as we can [play]."

Next thing you know, we were playing the grand opening with Jeremy Steig, who was a jazz flute player, and a couple of other really big names from the jazz world. We were the only rock band, we opened the show up for the jazz night, and then went back to Mercer. We were always looking for a new gig to make a few bucks here and there and just get the name out, and this was just one of the places. We thought it was kind of a fluke.[iv]

Coleman's claim is backed up by a flier advertising Hilly's' grand opening as a music venue on October 19, 1972, which lists the

---

iii   Television's Richard Lloyd also claimed to have built the stage, although his then-bandmate Richard Hell disputes this assertion. Hilly also claimed to have built the stage himself at one point. The history is unfortunately somewhat blurry; it's possible that they all could have built short-lived stages. The one Coleman and Emerson constructed doesn't sound like it would have lasted too long.

iv   Emerson died in 1975, just as things at CBGB were starting to take off.

Flier for the grand opening of Hilly's on the Bowery, October 1972.

Magic Tramps as the opening act for Jeremy Steig, Ralph Towner, and Miroslav Vitous—rendering his version of the story definitive.

Other glam and proto-punk bands also played the club before the first Television gig. Jayne County appeared early on with her band Queen Elizabeth. Musician and journalist Jimi LaLumia recalls seeing the proto-glam drag troupe the Cockettes at Hilly's. Leather Secrets, a quasi-S&M-themed glam band, played there at least once. The Fast's Paul Zone and Suicide's Martin Rev both recalled their respective bands playing multiple shows together at Hilly's. But Rev described the bar at that point as unspectacular, "just an empty space with some people drinking beer." So while other bands did technically get there first, CBGB didn't find its identity as a venue until Television's initial run there.

THE BAR

The strongest argument for CBGB (rather than Max's or Club 82) being the first "punk club" was that, unlike its predecessors, it was wholly removed from glam rock's decadent, campy, queer vibe—it catered to what *New Musical Express* writer Charles Shaar Murray described in 1975 as "chopped-down, hard-edged, no-bullshit rock and roll, totally eschewing the preening Mickey Mouse decadence that poleaxed the previous new wave of NY bands."[68] In contrast to Max's druggy vibe, booze was often the preferred intoxicant, and unlike Max's mixed crowd, the initial CBGB audience was predominantly straight, cisgender men, accompanied by a smattering of female band members and girlfriends.

As Shaar Murray also noted, CBGB was in many ways an abysmal bar, or rather "a toilet... It looks as if the proprietors kick holes in the walls and piss in the corners before they let the customers in."[69] In fact, "toilet" is a word that comes up over and over when discussing the club's vibe. It famously boasted the most disgusting bathroom in New York City (and possibly the world). It often seemed as though nobody bothered to clean the bathrooms at any point during the club's thirty-three-year run.[v]

Miriam Linna: You were lucky if there was some TP in there, and the mirrors were all smudged from people writing all over them and stuff like that. I don't think the taps were really running.

---

v   According to a 2020 social media meme, "if you ever used the bathroom at CBGB, you're immune to the coronavirus."

For Kristal's dog, a large saluki named Jonathan, the entire club was a toilet. He would defecate when and where he pleased, up to and including on the stage while a band was playing. The club's decor was largely befitting of a place awash in honest-to-god feces: the bare walls were gradually covered in graffiti, stickers, and flyers, until it arguably became the club's visual signature.

But to some extent, that grime was part of what made CBGB so appealing to musicians. As Ten Wheel Drive singer and record producer Genya Ravan recalled, "When I first walked in there, I felt comfortable immediately. It smelled like a bar, it looked like a bar, and it *was* a bar." While more glamorous spaces like Max's could feel intimidating, the lack of pretension in CBGB's design could help make unknown bands feel comfortable. And much of the grime was intentional—remember, as Sesu Coleman mentioned, Hilly's was a biker bar *by design*. Kristal even spray-painted the neon beer signs hung above the bar to make them look older and more worn out than they were (until, eventually, they actually were).

But whether or not musicians personally found CBGB's seediness appealing, as Talking Heads front man David Byrne pointed out in his 2012 book *How Music Works*, Hilly also instituted "a few simple rules...that made it possible for a whole scene to emerge."[70]

First, artists were required to play original material—though plenty of bands worked covers into their sets over the years, full-on cover bands were a no-go. Though Kristal frequently claimed it was about supporting the proverbial "little guy," this policy was not a wholly altruistic gesture: the rule existed at least in part because Karen Kristal—who was not only Hilly's ex-wife but also the designer and painter of the club's iconic awning, its sometime bartender, door person, cleaner, cook, and general-interest rule enforcer, and (due to Hilly's spotty financial track record) the club's actual legal owner and holder of its liquor license—didn't want to pay dues to ASCAP, an organization which collects royalties for published music.

But for new bands, this was a godsend. When CBGB opened, entry-level acts had few options: Most small bars were only interested in crowd-pleasing cover bands. Max's Kansas City was still mostly booking more-established acts, and its first incarnation shuttered soon after CBGB opened. Club 82 only presented bands once or twice a week; music was never its primary focus. The Mercer Arts Center was gone. For a newly formed rock band—unwelcome at folk clubs and jazz lofts alike—where else was there to go?

The second policy was that, initially at least, CBGB paid bands fairly. The deal was usually that bands kept 100 percent of the money made at the door; Hilly made his money on drinks. The significance of this can't be overstated—most small venues take a cut of the door or have a basic "room fee" that needs to be met before performers get paid. But at CBGB, if only ten people paid the $2 cover, a band could still walk away with $20 (adjusting for inflation, that's a solid $122—a damn good payout for an under-attended gig). Unfortunately, this ceased to be true once the club started to take off, but we'll get to that in a bit.

Unlike most of the other clubs that came before (or after) it, CBGB was a one-room club. There was no antechamber, no bar in a different room from the stage, no quiet corner where you could go have a conversation. There was never a VIP area, and for the first several years, there wasn't even a backstage; when one was finally installed in the club's former kitchen space, it was meager and insufficient. This meant that bands really had no choice but to watch each other and mingle when they weren't on stage, which helped forge relationships. Even as the club and bands grew in popularity, Kristal made few overt concessions to any sort of music industry caste system or diva behavior.

Emily Armstrong (documentarian): The band would be hanging around the bar, and then they'd pick up their guitar and step on the stage. There wasn't a lot of division; the musicians were the fans.

Finally, bands that had played CBGB a couple times were allowed to come in for free, and beloved regulars were often given free beer as well. In and of itself, this isn't especially notable, as many clubs discussed in this book extended this courtesy. But unlike the Greenwich Village folk clubs, which were subsidized by their tourist audiences, or Max's Kansas City, which was subsidized by its daytime diners, there was no large group of paying customers to offset the losses from free admission and booze. The early audience at CBGB was largely just bands watching each other night after night, free of charge, at a place that was spitting distance from their homes.

Justin Strauss (singer, Milk 'n' Cookies; deejay): It was a really small scene. It was basically just the bands. Everyone would go see everyone else's shows [free]. I don't know how anyone made any money.

THE FIRST WAVE OF BANDS

Given all of that, one does have to note that the first two acts to make CBGB their home base—Television and Patti Smith—did not live in the immediate neighborhood. Patti Smith lived at 107 Mac-Dougal Street at the time, on the same block that had once housed the Folklore Center, the Gaslight, and the Commons. However, after Patti Smith Group's initial performances at CBGB, guitarist Lenny Kaye moved across the street from the club, becoming a regular fixture at CBGB for the better part of two decades.

Television's base of operations was manager Terry Ork's Chinatown loft on East Broadway, somewhere near Market Street, where the band rehearsed and guitarist Richard Lloyd lived. Ork would go on to play a major role at CBGB over the course of the next several years after that first Television gig, as he (with assistance from Lloyd) became the club's primary booker; it was only after things began to pick up at CBGB that Kristal decided he could do the job himself.

Even after Television and Patti Smith descended upon the space, the transition to punk mecca didn't happen overnight. Nor was the club instantly lucrative: until 1975, Kristal had to subsidize it by running a moving business (also called "Hilly's") during the day, and he lived on a cot in the back of the club for approximately two years before moving to an apartment around the corner on East 2nd Street. That said, by the end of 1974, CBGB was almost exclusively presenting rock music. Kristal told journalist Roman Kozak, "It was not what I liked in music. But what I liked was that these people...were very sincere and they really believed in themselves."[71]

On August 16 of that year, five months after Television's CBGB debut, the Ramones played their first gig at the club. Though the band members had all grown up and formed their band in Forest Hills, Queens, Joey (born Jeffrey Hyman) and Dee Dee Ramone (born Douglas Colvin) were living on and off with their friend Arturo Vega in his second-floor loft at 6 East 2nd Street, just steps away from the club. Before finding their way to CB's (at Jayne County's recommendation) they had held rehearsals and even some early public performances in Vega's loft. Looking across the street out of Vega's window, they would have had a clear view of Extra Place, the alley behind CBGB where bands could load in and out (and where they would later shoot the cover for their third album, 1977's *Rocket to Russia*).[vi]

So it was practically inevitable that the Ramones would become a regular presence at CB's, as both performers and spectators. By all accounts, their first CBGB performance left something to be desired, with the band bickering onstage throughout their fifteen-minute set, seemingly unable to agree on which songs were being played when. But Kristal must have seen potential beneath the rampant unprofessionalism, because over the three months that followed, the Ramones played at CBGB twenty-four more times. According to writer Legs McNeil, Vega's loft became "kind of the green room for CBGB."

The fact that the Ramones were given plenty of follow-up shows despite a disappointing initial set gets at another key element of CBGB's success. Though many people want punk to be the prod-

---

vi   The cover for their self-titled debut album was also shot nearby in Albert's Garden, a quaint community garden on the same block as Arturo Vega's loft.

PHOTO BY THE AUTHOR, 2023.

6 East 2nd Street.

uct of savant-like skills and "right place, right time" magic—and CBGB to be a holy ground that transforms you into whatever it is you want to become—the truth was that it was just a crappy room with a good PA where you could become what you wanted to become by working hard. The club nurtured these bands by giving them a place where they could improve by playing multiple sets a night, multiple nights a week. That it was a community hangout meant that people would show up no matter who was playing, so bands that were still working the kinks out were able to gain invaluable live experience. No one wants punk to be hard work, but the story of CBGB proves that it inarguably is.

Chris Stein and Debbie Harry had first performed at CBGB as members of a band called the Stilettos, opening for Television on May 4, 1974.[vii] On August 16—the same night the Ramones made their debut at the club—Stein and Harry played CBGB with their

vii The Stilettos also included bassist Fred Smith, who would go on to replace Richard Hell as Television's bassist.

new band, Angel and the Snake. By October, they'd rechristened themselves Blondie.

McNeil: Blondie sucked in the beginning. The great thing about Blondie was you got to see them get better and better, because they would open for the Ramones every two weeks. They became fantastic, right in front of your eyes.

In 1975, Stein, Harry, and bassist Gary Valentine moved into 266 Bowery, a four-story building two blocks south of CBGB. They lived with a rotating cast of friends, paying a combined $350 a month for the entire building (minus the ground-level liquor store). The band also used Harry and Stein's apartment as their rehearsal space; Hilly Krystal's moving service helped get a piano up the stairs for them.

Like Arturo Vega's loft, 266 Bowery became another unofficial VIP area for the club. In a demonstrative moment of scene unity, the cover photo for Richard Hell and the Voidoids' *Blank Generation* album was taken in Stein and Harry's apartment by photographer Roberta Bayley, who also worked the door at CBGB.

A block east of Blondie's loft, Talking Heads' David Byrne, Chris Frantz, and Tina Weymouth were also paying dirt cheap rent—$289 per month, according to Frantz's book; $150, according to Byrne's—to live on the ninth floor of 195 Chrystie Street. On the recommendation of Weymouth's brother Yann, the group bypassed conventional housing options and instead found their twelve-hundred-square-foot dwelling in the *New York Times* industrial real estate section.

Their kitchen consisted of a hot plate and a toaster oven, and there was no hot water (though they could warm some up on the hot plate) or heat after 5:00 p.m., and no shower or bath of any sort. Luckily, they could bathe at their college friends Jamie and Susan Dalglish's apartment in a residential building at 52 Bond Street, where Byrne had first stayed when he came to New York—located, conveniently, a block away from CBGB.

266 Bowery.

There were plenty of other bands around from the beginning, as Mudd Club doorman Richard Boch pointed out: "It was very hit and miss. You could see Blondie or Television or Patti Smith in the early days, but you could go there on another night and there would be some band from New Jersey playing and there'd be five people in the club."

Many of those bands probably worked just as hard, under just

195 Chrystie Street.

PHOTO BY THE AUTHOR, 2023.

as miserable conditions, and in the end, didn't get anywhere. But it's those five—Television, Patti Smith, the Ramones, Blondie, and Talking Heads—who gave CB's its reputation, and it's nothing short of remarkable that they all lived nearby, especially the latter three, who all lived within blocks of the club. More than any sonic similarities, that was really the thread that ran through CB-GB's initial crop of successful bands: they lived in the same cheap, shitty neighborhood and hung out at the same cheap, shitty bar.

It only got called "punk" later,[viii] but grouping all these bands

---

viii   Technically, Suicide had been calling their music "punk" since 1970, but it wasn't used as a catchall genre name until much later in the decade.

together aesthetically doesn't totally check out. Television, with their fey lyricism and jazzy guitar solos, do not even remotely sound like the loud, fast, stupid-but-smart-but-stupid Ramones. Patti Smith sounds nothing like Talking Heads, and neither of them sound much like Suicide. Nor were these bands a unified front by any means, as Byrne wrote, "There wasn't much camaraderie among the bands at CBGB…everyone wanted to stake out their own creative territory, and aligning oneself with others might have run the risk of dilution."[72]

Jimi LaLumia: New York punk wasn't so much about how the songs were played or what the subject matter was, it was the fact that the conventional record labels snubbed their nose at everybody that was not taking the conventional approach. More than the sound or the speed of the records, punk was an attitude, and it was how we approached the industry: Do it yourself.

The dilapidated, undesirable East Village—especially the foreboding Bowery—granted all of these bands the necessary space to do just that.

The Ramones performing at CBGB, February 1977.

Linna: There's no words to describe how desolate and undesirable the Lower East Side was to people at that time. The first time I came, I walked down the street and it was so dirty. I mean, there was just garbage and rats everywhere, and there were tons of bums. I busted out crying and thought, Oh, my God, what have I done? But you get used to it very quickly.

McNeil: [It was] like a movie set from one of the Batman *movies, just dark and gritty. I just loved it, I think most of us did. Downtown was deserted; there weren't any people out except bums standing by trash cans that were lit on fire to stay warm. They would try to beg for money from people who didn't have any (at least, I didn't have any). Above CBGB was the Palace Hotel, where they used to throw bums out of the windows for stealing each other's shoes.*

The Bowery's nightmarish environs offer an extreme example of transformation taking place all over the city. In 1975, the city went bankrupt, the culmination of a slow burn of both white flight and the exodus of manufacturing jobs. With those losses went much of the tax revenue, and because the city's debts were somewhere in the ballpark of $11 million, it was unable to borrow more to compensate.

President Gerald Ford's initial refusal to grant New York financial assistance gave birth to the immortal *New York Post* headline "Ford to City: Drop Dead." The resultant PR nightmare got him to change his mind and sign the New York City Seasonal Financing Act that same year, giving the city $2.3 million over the course of three years with the stipulation that it would reduce the number of municipal jobs, cancel a proposed wage increase for those workers who didn't get laid off, and raise prices on public services.

By 1977, New York had paid off its short-term debts, although it would take until 1985 for its finances to fully recover. But in the interim, the city experienced a uniquely permissive lawlessness. A not-unearned reputation for crime and dirt kept tourists at bay, rents remained low, and those willing to endure the trials and tribulations were rewarded with a chance to do pretty much whatever they wanted until the city's recovery began to take hold. Bands could focus on their music, to the exclusion of almost everything else.

Of course, this neighborhood wasn't empty when these young artists showed up—even in its most nascent stages, the CBGB scene was starting to displace the poor and homeless people who called the Bowery home.

Arto Lindsay (singer/guitarist, DNA; solo artist): The Lower East Side was really cheap, and kids poured in and shared space with people who couldn't afford to live anywhere else or weren't allowed to live anywhere else. So it wasn't innocent, even back then. You could say that the punk and post-punk movements on the Lower East Side were a kind of gentrification.

This is clearer nowhere than in the fact that CBGB was able to hold shows late into the night, every night, beneath a residential hotel where people were trying to sleep. Many of the people interviewed for this chapter recalled having had little or no awareness of the Palace Hotel and its patrons, beyond occasional panhandling or violence between the hotel's residents in front of the club. It's difficult to imagine that CBGB could have had loud rock shows every night if the people who lived above it weren't members of society's least powerful class.

And even if CB's patrons didn't notice the way their presence was changing the neighborhood, another group, with values that ran counter to those CBGB seemed to champion, definitely did. As Karen Kristal noted in the late '80s, "From time to time I talked to the police and they have told me that CBGB has done more than anyone or anything else to clean up the area and bring safety."[73]

By 1975, there was enough interest in the club that Hilly began using Mondays—a traditionally slow night—as audition night; those that passed would be booked for "real" shows on better nights. That system remained a cornerstone of CBGB's booking for the remainder of its existence. Excruciating as that might sound, according to Brooke Delarco, "Monday audition night, that was a big night. You'd just go down early, hang out, have some drinks with your friends and see who was playing."

Joshua Fried (musician; sound tech, CBGB): There would be seven bands on the show, and it was grueling. Sometimes there would just be me and the cocktail waitress in the main body of the club. The big secret was that when you played audition night, the person who reviewed you was the person at the door. [They] sat there with a notebook and listened, but wouldn't watch, except maybe a few seconds, because [they were] facing the door taking people's money. And I was told, "Don't tell the bands, we don't want them to know who to kiss up to."

Peter Crowley, who started booking Max's Kansas City that same year, admits to regularly haunting CB's audition nights in order to snipe new bands for his own calendar.

Crowley: When the Cramps did their audition there, there were maybe 30 or 40 people there. Hilly came over and poked me, he pointed at them and he goes, "You think they're serious?" I looked at him and I said, "I don't know if they're serious, but I think they're fabulous." He just looked at me like I'd completely lost my mind. They were absolutely terrible, and so awfully out of tune that it was painful to listen to, but the basic idea of the band was so fucking brilliant that I was blown away.

Inspired by the Newport Jazz Festival's presence in the city, Kristal staged the CBGB Rock Festival in July 1975. Originally planned for eleven days, the festival's success saw it extended in real time to just shy of three weeks. Over thirty unsigned bands played—with six sets every night—including Blondie, Television, the Ramones, Talking Heads, Mink DeVille, the Heartbreakers, and the Shirts (Patti Smith, already signed to Sire Records, was naturally excluded).

In-house accounting for a show at CBGB on March 21, 1979, featuring the Feelies and Chris Stamey and the dB's.

Things really started to take off for the punk scene in 1976, when the Ramones and Blondie both released self-titled debut albums. Television, Talking Heads, Richard Hell and the Voidoids,[ix]

___

ix   Hell had quit Television in 1975, and after a short stint playing with the Heartbreakers, formed his own group in 1976.

the Dead Boys, and Suicide all followed suit one year later. With one band after another being catapulted from CB's to commercial success and international renown, 1976 was the first year when CBGB started paying for itself. Kristal was able to end his daytime moving business, but the income only really kept the lights on—he was still broke. Kristal's generosity was a big part of why these bands were able to find audiences in the first place, but he wasn't getting a cut.

THE SECOND WAVE OF BANDS

As CBGB's reputation took hold and the first wave of bands started to outgrow it, a second wave arrived. The two most notable among those bands had shared roots in Ohio: the Cramps and the Dead Boys.

The Cramps' core members, singer Lux Interior (born Erick Purkheiser) and guitarist Poison Ivy Rorschach (born Kristy Wallace), had come to New York from Akron in 1975. Strangely, the couple put down roots on the Upper East Side rather than anywhere Downtown, moving into an apartment at 322 East 73rd Street that became the band's headquarters. A record store job introduced Interior to guitarist Bryan Gregory (born Gregory Beckerleg). Miriam Linna, a Cleveland resident on vacation in the city, was recruited to be the band's drummer (despite having never played the instrument) and duly moved into an apartment at 406 East 9th Street.

The Cramps made their live debut at a CBGB audition night on November 1, 1976, alongside the Dead Boys, who Linna knew from their shared hometown. The Dead Boys had gotten their gig at CB's in part through the generosity of Joey Ramone, who met singer Stiv Bators (born Steven Bator) after a Ramones show in Youngstown, Ohio. Relocating to New York on the strength of that show, the Dead Boys all moved into Linna's cramped 9th Street apartment.[x]

---

x   After parting ways with Linna in 1977, the Cramps moved into a practice
      space they shared with the Fleshtones and Alex Chilton in the basement of
      344 Bowery—very conveniently, one block north of CBGB.

The Dead Boys represent a turning point for both CBGB as a club and punk as a genre. Musically, they're arguably the point at which "New York punk" becomes codified as a sound and image, rather than a group of sonically unrelated bands playing at the same club. In fact, alongside the Cramps, they are among the first CBGB-oriented bands to have been influenced at their outset by another CBGB band: the Ramones. That influence was then filtered through the Dead Boys' Midwestern cultural touchstones and came out a little less artsy and a little more aggressive.

With the Dead Boys' ascent came a new audience. Bartender Maureen Nelly told Roman Kozak that prior to the band's arrival, the audience at CBGB had been "people in their late twenties, people who lived in the city." As the Dead Boys became a fixture at the club, Nelly claimed that the audience became discernably younger, and "the older regulars started to maybe not come in as often."[74]

Jayne County: There were kids coming in from Jersey and other places outside of Manhattan, dressing up and pretending to be punks. I actually caught some once when I was just walking by: These people had parked their car nearby and were changing into their punk clothes that they had brought with them and then going to CBGB's. They had their CBGB's costume in order to be a part of CBGB's.

Of course, for some of those kids, wearing that CBGB costume was an act of profound self-discovery.

Nick Marden (bassist, the Stimulators): We had friends who'd come into the city from wherever, and they couldn't wear that leather jacket at home. They'd get it out of the trunk of their car when they got to the city.

Suddenly, CBGB was no longer a neighborhood place—it was a destination for people all over the country. For writer and deejay James Marshall, who moved to New York from his native Florida in 1977, "It almost seemed like there was a beacon on top of the Empire State Building that was calling every damaged, fucked-up kid in the world to come here. You'd see them arriving by the day."

In 1977, Kristal took out a bank loan to upgrade CBGB's PA system. The result was a state-of-the-art, thirty-eight-piece, 4,500-watt, $100,000 system designed by CB's soundman Norman Dunn, who had previously designed custom PA systems for the likes of Grand Central Station. It was one of the best decisions Kristal ever made. Though every other aspect of CBGB remained ramshackle, no other club of its size sounded as good.

> *Rhys Chatham: That's why people would play at CB's—the place sucked, you were lucky if you got paid $5, but the sound system was the best in New York, and you'd sound great. A lot of sound people in rock clubs can be really awful, but even if you were the lowest on the totem pole, you got a good soundcheck at CBGB.*

In order to make back the money invested into the PA, bands were charged a fee to use it (the exact dollar amount of those fees seems to have fluctuated). For a few extra dollars, they could also walk away with a professional-quality tape of their performance. But as Mumps drummer Paul Rutner pointed out, the PA fee "always struck me as kind of bullshit, as if you could play an un-amplified show there for free. That PA must have been paid for a thousand times over."

(ATTEMPTED) EXPANSION

In 1977, as many of CBGB's flagship bands outgrew the club, Hilly (with financial assistance from Sire Records' Seymour Stein) ac-quired the nearly 1,735-seat Anderson Theater at 66 2nd Ave. as a potential next-rung venue. In the late '60s, the former Yiddish theater had hosted concerts by the likes of the Grateful Dead and Gladys Knight and the Pips, but by the mid-seventies, it had been dormant for years and was in serious disrepair.

Kristal reopened the Anderson as the CBGB 2nd Avenue Theater on December 27 with a concert by Talking Heads, the Shirts, and Tuff Darts. A number of his old favorites proceeded to take the stage over the next few days—Richard Hell and the Voidoids, the Dictators, Patti Smith Group, the Cramps, and the Dead Boys—but thanks to a combination of unforeseen structural problems, angry neighbors, and Kristal's unwillingness to book bands he didn't already know, the CBGB 2nd Avenue Theater shuttered within a week.[xi] The total loss amounted to somewhere in the ballpark of $150,000-$160,000.

By the early '80s, the fire that had been lit at CBGB had spread throughout the city, and established bands that would once have been confined to CB's and Max's were presented with larger, better-funded options in clubs like Hurrah, the Ritz, Danceteria, Mudd Club, Rock Lounge, and Peppermint Lounge, which could offer bands upfront guarantees instead of CBGB's cut of the door. With these bands lured away, Kristal was once again forced to throw the proverbial spaghetti at the wall.

Marshall: CB's got kind of bad kind of fast, because once the first string of bands were on the road regularly, Hilly came up with this formula: If he had five bands who brought ten friends who bought two drinks, he would make money. So he started having five bands a night, and the quality of the bands got worse.

The area around the club was changing, too. In the early and mid-eighties, with CBGB as part of its magnetic core, the East Village began to draw a more moneyed class of residents who viewed the once-foreboding neighborhood as exciting and youthful. The telltale signs of gentrification—sushi bars, clothing boutiques, new construction—arrived like clockwork. A 1983 *New York Times* article entitled "New Prosperity Brings Discord to the East Village" reported that "[The gentrification's] beneficiaries are largely the artists and young people who see the area as an inexpensive place

---

xi   It briefly reopened for two shows by the Jam in March '78.

to live, and the entrepreneurs who feel it is a good place to invest," while longtime residents and small local businesses got the short end of the stick.[75]

BLACK ROCK COALITION

In her essay "Beastie Revolution," the writer Lucy Sante noted that "it wasn't until 1978 or so that it even occurred to the regulars at CBGB that almost everybody who played there was white."[76] There were a handful of exceptions, including the all-Black punk bands Pure Hell and Bad Brains, Voidoids guitarist Ivan Julian, and Neon Leon. But Sante's point still stands: the scene was overwhelmingly white. This wasn't unique to CBGB, to be fair—in the years since Jimi Hendrix's ascent in the 1960s, the music industry had become disinterested in Black artists who played hard rock—an issue that was exacerbated by the rise of commercial funk and disco in the 1970s.

> *Greg Tate (music journalist; guitarist, Burnt Sugar Arkestra):*
> *Black bands doing rock were not being signed by major labels, [because they] were totally flummoxed and bewildered by the whole prospect. They would frequently tell Black bands doing rock, "We wouldn't know how to market you." Then Living Colour blew up—like, these are the people you can't figure out how to market?!*

Living Colour were formed in New York in 1984 by guitarist Vernon Reid. He had already made a name for himself Downtown as both an experimental jazz musician and a member of the band Defunkt, and from the outset, Living Colour were playing CBGB regularly.

In 1985, Reid, Tate, and music producer Konda Mason formed the Black Rock Coalition and began holding regular meetings at the Just Above Midtown (J.A.M.) Gallery at 503 Broadway in SoHo. After an initial showcase at the Kitchen in 1986, the Black Rock Coalition organized the Stalking Heads Festival at CBGB on February 11 and 12, 1987, showcasing New York–based Black rock bands including Living Colour, Eye & I, J.J. Jumpers, and Cookie Watkins.

> *Tate: Hilly really, really liked Vernon. So when we came to him [in 1987] and said that we wanted to do a two-night music festival, they were completely open. Naming the festival "Stalking Heads," there was kind of a reverse colonialism thing going on. It was a nice little pun that said a lot.*
>
> *The remarkable thing about those shows was that that was probably the first time that many Black people had ever been inside CBGB, because we pretty much packed it. And then after that, our bands would regularly play CB's.*
>
> *People try to act like [music downtown] stopped at a certain point [in the late '80s], because it stopped for the young white rebels of the time. But that's when BRC and hip-hop were just getting started.*

EXPANSION

In 1987, Kristal acquired a neighboring storefront at 313 Bowery (previously a shoe repair supply outlet) and converted it into the CBGB Record Canteen, a combination record store and cafe. It was roughly the same size and shape as the club, but the vibe was more tranquil. The record store—whose managers included two members of the band Action Swingers: Ned Hayden and Julia Cafritz[xii]—was by most accounts decent in pricing and selection. The cafe sold no booze, only coffee, soda, and snacks—because of that, in a throwback to the Greenwich Village coffeehouses of the '60s, it was able to stay open well past last call. The cafe was especially popular during the Sunday all-ages hardcore punk matinees that CBGB began hosting in 1981, both because young kids would come over to buy sodas—which were slightly cheaper at the Record Canteen than at CBGB proper—and because it offered chaperoning parents a relatively quiet and comfortable place to wait.

---

xii Cafritz was also a member of the noise rock band Pussy Galore.

The Record Canteen only lasted a couple of years before it was turned into CBGB's 313 Gallery, an art gallery and performance space for (comparatively) gentler music. Among other things, it hosted an unplugged Guns 'n' Roses promotional appearance, Cat Power's first NYC show, regular appearances by folk/blues singer Toshi Reagon, and a weekly goth night called Alchemy.

In 1989, Kristal expanded his empire further by annexing the storefront at 317 Bowery and opening the CBGB Pizza Boutique, which served pizza (duh) and beer, had pinball machines and a pool table, and sold the full complement of CBGB shirts and memorabilia.

Between the club proper (which also started hosting occasional shows in the basement, glamorously dubbed the "CBGB Downstairs Lounge"), the pizza boutique, and the gallery, Kristal had refashioned a nice little chunk of the once-nightmarish Bowery.

Which is not to say that the club was thriving, exactly. At some point in either the late '80s or early '90s (accounts vary), the building's owners presented Kristal with an opportunity to buy the property for around $4 million. He seriously considered it, but passed due to a lack of funds. It was arguably the biggest mistake he ever made.

After the club celebrated its twentieth anniversary in 1993, Kristal became uninvolved with regular operations, and his longtime assistant Louise Parnassa-Staley became the club's primary booker. Though CB's bookings had been a grab bag from the outset, they became increasingly questionable in Hilly's absence. For example, that same year, the Bloodhound Gang—a Pennsylvania-based frat-boy pop-punk band—began a monthly residency at CBGB, at a time when no other venue would book them (can you believe nobody else recognized the potential in the geniuses behind the 1999 album *Hooray For Boobies?*). Despite being the lucky recipient of this patronage, front man Jimmy Pop felt compelled to say that he'd "seen cavemen with better clubs."[77]

Pat Noecker (bassist, Liars, N0 Things, These Are Powers): I remember playing CB's in '98, at the Gallery. It was almost embar-

rassing to say I played there. Liars never played CB's. Paul Smith
[from Mute Records] wanted us to play there, and talked about how
there was a line around the block when Sonic Youth were playing
there in the '80s. We're just like, "Paul, it's dead, man. It's done."

In 1993, the same year CBGB celebrated its twentieth anniversary, the Palace Hotel finally closed. A television exposé and outcry from neighbors and community boards had resulted in a police raid and the city no longer offering vouchers for homeless people to stay there. The hotel had become overrun with hard drugs, especially crack cocaine. One tenant, Coles Jackson, told *New York Times* reporter Bruce Lambert that the Palace Hotel had gotten "really crowded and a little dangerous...if a guy didn't pay up, they would cut his leg to get the money."[78]

Into the void stepped the Bowery Residents Committee, a social services organization that had been working with the local homeless population since the early '70s, who took on a forty-five-year lease of the former hotel space. During their renovations, BRC filled up five industrial-sized dumpsters with the remnants of the hotel's recent past—hypodermic needles, crack vials, empty beer bottles, and bedbug-infested mattresses. BRC executive director Eric J. Roth stressed that BRC was "trying to raise conditions to much more supported, humane housing" without raising the Palace Hotel's nightly fee.[79]

Josh Lozano started interning at CBGB in 1997 as a seventeen-year-old high school student. After graduating, Kristal invited him to stay on. Like many a CB's employee, he took on several roles, including booking. As he recalls it, at that point, booking the club had become something of a lose-lose proposition. They were one of the only clubs in town that booked unsigned bands at the time, and certainly the best known, so they were deluged with bands trying to get stage time.

At this point, the club was mostly trading on its name and counting on seats to be filled by curious tourists, rather than trying to cultivate a particular sound or scene.

Lozano: It got to a point where you couldn't really prioritize putting a good show together. We just slapped together these bills. We'd put some out-of-town ska band on first, and then we'd have a local band playing second, but they're some other genre. It was just, "Okay, this band really wants to play, and they've called enough times." We had [bad] bands that played somewhat regularly just because they were persistent, or they would manage to swing by right when somebody else canceled and we'd ask, "Can you play in three days?"

Sometimes we'd have promoters who would come by and say, "Hey, June 29, can we have this entire night?" Ok, you're a stranger, we don't even know you, but we're gonna put this night in your hands because it's just a relief for us that we won't have to deal with it.

CLOSURE

Unexpectedly, the thing that began to threaten CBGB's survival in the early '00s was not the neighborhood's increasing gentrification or the club's declining reputation for quality. It was the BRC, which was aiming to provide better accommodations for the Bowery's homeless population than the Palace Hotel had offered.

Lozano: The neighborhood was definitely getting kind of nicer and fancier, but you really couldn't tell, because right above the club was the BRC. We had junkies nodding out, crackheads fighting each other, knifing each other, people barfing and bleeding and doing all kinds of shit right in front of the club at all hours of the day and night. So even while the neighborhood was changing a lot, our block still just seemed like the Bowery. Once in a while, they'd have someone pass out or die in the shower up there, and the shower would overflow and start pouring down onto our stage; they never really cared. I don't fault them for it, I think they had their hands full.

In 2000, BRC hired a new director, Muzzy Rosenblatt, who, in trying to get BRC's affairs in order, informed Kristal that he in fact owed BRC upward of $300,000: apparently, there had been several rent increases since BRC took the building over, although nobody had bothered to make Kristal aware of that fact. Tensions escalated from there. A 2003 safety inspection revealed several violations on both CBGB and BRC's part. Kristal claimed that "Anything that had to do with safety, I fixed within a week,"[80] while noting that BRC were slower to act. In 2005, for example, Kristal told the *Village Voice* that 315 Bowery had not had a working furnace for three years, and he'd had to resort to electric heaters to warm the space.[81]

In 2005, with the club's lease expiring, Rosenblatt offered Kristal a new lease that more than doubled the current rent, from $19,000 to $41,000. The pair began sniping at each other in public. In a *New York Magazine* interview, Kristal noted that Rosenblatt's salary was $150,000 a year—"That's more than I pay anyone on my staff, including myself."[82] In a *Spin Magazine* interview from the same year, Kristal also claimed that BRC paid the building's owner less rent than they had in turn collected from CBGB, meaning in effect that the club subsidized the shelter.[83] Rosenblatt told *New York Magazine* that "I'd love for them to stay. My wife and I—we had our first date there. We had our first *kiss* there."[84] But, speaking to the *Village Voice*, Rosenblatt was clear that he was "not going to subsidize a for-profit nightclub. The money I should be using to help homeless people I'm having to pay to lawyers just to get Hilly to meet his obligations."[85]

Unexpectedly, then-mayor Michael Bloomberg got involved. In August of 2005, the New York City Mayor's Office offered to help renegotiate the lease, and, if that didn't pan out, help CBGB find a new space.[86] But in the end, Bloomberg's intervention didn't help—especially after the club had been a victim of the mayor's own nightlife crackdowns over the previous few years.[87]

Lozano: Bloomberg came and posed for a picture wearing a "Save CBGB" T-shirt, but he didn't even buy it. He didn't actually do anything at all. That was something that people respected him for; like, "Oh, you've got the mayor helping you out." No, the mayor has shut down every other club in this area and is probably thrilled that we're closing.

He did to us what he did to [a lot of other clubs]: He would send this mayoral task force that would come down and raid us on a Friday night, make the band stop playing. They'd measure the doorways, and suddenly this doorway isn't 32 inches wide, it was only 31 inches. So there's a $1,000 fine for this, and you have to fix it. To make the doorway one inch wider, it would cost us thousands of dollars, and then they'd come back a few weeks after all that work was done and find something else wrong with it.

Various celebrities spearheaded efforts to save the club—notably, E Street Band guitarist "Little Steven" Van Zandt organized a "Save CBGB" rally in Washington Square Park, with performances by Blondie, Public Enemy, Bouncing Souls, and Bush front man Gavin Rossdale. Though some efforts were genuine, others were merely an attempt to get in on a cause célèbre.

Lozano: One band that I will say, fuck that band, was the Offspring. They were coming through on Warped Tour and they decided that they wanted to do a "Save CBGB" benefit, but they demanded $3,000 to do it. I don't even know why we said yes. We got roped into it by whoever they were being booked by; we could have just burned that bridge at that point. And then the kicker was that they wouldn't let us promote it, because Warped Tour wouldn't let them. So the Offspring played to maybe 60 people, and then we paid them $3,000.

But even with his myriad financial difficulties, Kristal had one certifiable cash cow—the logo. And he milked it for all it was worth, as was his right. In 2005, Hilly told *Spin Magazine* that the merchandising brought in $2 million a year, but was quick to clarify that "the money we make from [CBGB T-shirts] is going into the business. It's not going in my pocket... If not for fashion, it would be a break-even business."[88]

For most of the CBGB's lifespan, the shirts were only available for purchase in person at the club. But at some point around the turn of the century, with the advent of the internet and the need for additional funds, they became available everywhere. And suddenly, they were omnipresent: Mischa Barton wore one on *The O.C.* in 2003; the following year, Mark Ruffalo wore one in the rom-com *13 Going on 30*. The shirts could now adorn posers worldwide who had never once set foot in the club—including, at one point, this book's author.[xiii]

BRC took Hilly to court in 2005 over $90,000 of outstanding back rent. Hilly claimed that this was the result of BRC's having failed to inform him of incremental rent increases, which Rosenblatt conceded to. Judge Joan M. Kenney ruled in CBGB's favor.

Having lost in court, Rosenblatt simply declined to renew CBGB's lease. By the end of that year, Hilly and BRC reached an agreement allowing CBGB to stay open at 313-315 Bowery until October 31, 2006. Upon the lease's expiration, Rosenblatt released a statement pleading with the club to "vacate the premises both voluntarily and expeditiously and avoid costly eviction proceedings that will further hinder our thirty-five-year mission to help the homeless."[89]

Convenient as it would be to say that CBGB's closure in 2006 was a product of gentrification, to do so would be reductive at best and a fallacy at worst. CBGB's landlord was—and I really can't stress this enough—*a homeless shelter.* I'm writing this and you're reading this because music has given profound joy and meaning to our lives, but let's try to not lose sight of the bigger picture here. BRC's methods might have been needlessly cruel. But if there's anything the city needs more than a past-its-prime nightclub that's largely coasting on a decades-old reputation, it's a homeless shelter.

It is perhaps more notable that CBGB's was able to hang on to

---

xiii I was sixteen. What the fuck do you want from me? I went there eventually. My shitty band even played there. Jesus Christ, calm down.

that space as long as it did, as the area around it was transformed by the remorseless forces of New York City real estate. In the decade-plus since CB's closure, while the Bowery's expensive boutiques are forced out and replaced by even more expensive boutiques, the BRC building has not been sold or demolished. It is the only business on its block that does not explicitly cater to the rich.

The final run of shows at CBGB saw several familiar faces return: Bad Brains, the Stimulators, the Dictators, Fishbone, Bouncing Souls, and even an acoustic duo set by Blondie's Debbie Harry and Chris Stein. The final act to play at CBGB, on October 15, was Patti Smith, who performed two back-to-back sets. Paying tribute to others from the club's initial scene, Smith and her band peppered their set with covers of the Dead Boys, the Ramones, Blondie,[xiv] and Television, whose guitarist Richard Lloyd joined Smith for his band's "Marquee Moon." As one might imagine, the club was packed well beyond its legal 350-person capacity.

Richard Boch: I still have my all access pass from that closing night. But I probably hadn't been there for a decade prior to that.

Ruby Lynn Reyner: I went there on the last day, and they didn't even let us in. They had all the press and the uptown people there, but they didn't let in the people who made it what it was.

Around the time of the club's closing, Kristal seriously entertained an offer to relocate the club—including all of its original fixtures—to Las Vegas's schlocky Fremont Street.

Lozano: He was just sort of desperate to have anything, he just didn't want his baby to die. When we got the word that the club was closing, I watched him get sicker and sicker, and he was too sick to pursue

---

xiv Technically, the song Smith covered, "The Tide Is High," was first recorded by the Paragons, but Blondie's cover is the best-known version.

the Vegas thing. Not even six months after the club closed, he died.
The club closing broke his heart, and it killed him.

Hilly Kristal passed away on August 28, 2007, from lung cancer complications, less than a year after CBGB closed. He was seventy-five years old.

The endurance of the CBGB shirt raises an interesting, seemingly contradictory point: looking back at some of Kristal's failed ventures (e.g. the 2nd Avenue Theater), one could argue that his inability to exploit and expand the CBGB brand during its heyday probably contributed to the club's long-running reputation for integrity and artistic purity.

Still, it would be misguided to say that he was simply a poor businessman: after all, CB's was one of the longest-running venues of its size in the city, and among the very few to exist under the same ownership for several decades. Clearly, he was doing *something* right.

That success can be attributed to a number of factors. For one, much of CB's significance can be paradoxically attributed to its lack of curatorship. Anybody could get on that stage and perform at an audition night, regardless of genre or skill. And then, if Kristal or a trusted employee recognized a compelling artist in their most nascent form, they would happily get out of the way and allow that artist to assume their own shape and build their audience from the ground up.

CB's prolonged success may have also had something to do with the accidental perfection of its location. Though all the areas around it were just called "the Lower East Side" when the club first opened, 313-315 Bowery is conveniently located at the approximate nexus point of several newly defined and obnoxiously rechristened neighborhoods that more or less gentrified in succession—the East Village, Nolita, SoHo, NoHo, Alphabet City, and the (current) Lower East Side. This meant that CB's remained within a short walk of at least one cheap, artist-friendly neighborhood for decades. It was only after the Lower East Side became fully gentrified in the early '00s that CB's survival was challenged. The fact that it was on Bowery—a street with a reputation as the worst in Manhattan—probably helped slow things down as well, as some new Downtown transplants might have remained leery.

More than anything, though, CBGB's longevity is a testament to Hilly Kristal's innate menschiness and generosity. Taking stock of his legacy, Kristal wrote on the CBGB website, "I certainly didn't love every band that played CBGB's but I did love to encourage them to do their own thing."[90]

Of the numerous employees, performers, and regulars that I interviewed for this book, both on and off the record, none would say a bad word about the guy, uniformly portraying him as a loving, benevolent father figure. That said, it is worth noting that a significant number of the people I spoke to were willing, and in some cases quite eager, to go off the record disparaging Karen Kristal, who was portrayed as a puritan, a scold, a hard-ass, and just straight-up mean. Though I can't speak authoritatively to her character, a reasonable interpretation would be that Hilly and Karen's good cop/bad cop dynamic, intentional or not, probably helped keep the lights on for so long. Karen's willingness to play the villain and tell patrons to put away their drugs or refrain from doing anything else that might attract police attention or endanger the club's liquor license (which was in her name) meant that Hilly's interactions with his staff and clientele could largely remain compassionate and supportive, and his role as the bighearted champion of the underground mostly went unchallenged.

THE AFTERLIFE OF CBGB & OMFUG

In 2005, when the club's closure was looming, Hilly Kristal finally became CBGB's legal owner: Karen Kristal signed 100 percent of her shares of the club and the liquor license over to him. She received no compensation, and it is unclear who instigated the transfer. When she was later shown the contract that she and Hilly (but no witnesses or legal counsel) had signed, the eighty-two-year-old Karen (who in recent years had been struggling with cognitive and memory issues) reportedly said, "Did I sign this? That's my signature?"[91]

At the time of the signing, Karen and son, Dana Kristal, were under the impression that, with the business eternally struggling, Hilly possessed no significant assets. When Hilly passed, he left $100,000 to Dana in a trust, and left everything else he owned to his daughter, Lisa, who he made co-executor of his will. Karen, who claimed Hilly had promised her a share, got nothing.

But after Hilly's passing, new revelations began to leak out: He was worth $3.7 million. He had purchased a house in Asbury Park, NJ, for $600,000.[xv] It was all because of those damned T-shirts—Hilly owned 100 percent of CBGB Fashions, a merchandising company he had secretly established. That logo that Karen designed had earned her ex-husband a small fortune (one which he claimed to have largely reinvested in the club, but still).

Karen and Dana took Lisa to court; at one point during the proceedings, Lisa reportedly threatened to place Karen in a legal guardianship. In 2009, the family settled out of court, but not for much: after debts and taxes were paid, the estate was reduced to less than $1 million, with Lisa retaining the bulk of the inheritance.[xvi] The *Village Voice* noted at the time that "anyone who had to get paid by Hilly knows that fighting over money is actually an integral part of the legacy."[92]

At some point just before the closure, Hilly Kristal also sold ownership of all the club's assets and trademarks to CBGB Holdings LLC—aka marketing professionals James Blueweiss and Robert Williams—for which he was paid $1.1 million along with a promissory note for more. It was a sale that would not have been possible had he not gotten full ownership of the club in 2005. It

---

xv   For what it's worth, Hilly had freely admitted to buying the Asbury Park house to *New York Magazine* in 2005, explaining that it was, "the first place I've ever owned. Actually, the bank owns it. I'll own it outright when I'm 103." (Gessen, "Between Punk Rock and a Hard Place.")

xvi   Karen passed away in 2014, at the age of eighty-eight.

was CBGB Holdings who profited off the logo in Kristal's wake, but they declared bankruptcy in 2010, blaming the family's lawsuit for devaluing the trademark. The estate of Hilly Kristal—which for all intents and purposes meant Lisa—was granted the legal right to foreclose and repossess everything.

After CBGB's closure, Elliott Azrak—who, you may recall, also owns the Max's Kansas City trademark—bought the lease for 313-315 Bowery under his Rebel Rebel Capital group. According to their website, Rebel Rebel is "a private investment firm that targets investments in real estate, emerging companies, cannabis, cyber security, facial recognition, [and] content acquisition as well as iconic brands." Their address is publicly listed as 313 Bowery.

Into the club's old space came John Varvatos, clothier of choice for every middle-aged investment banker who wears ill-fitting pleather pants to their skybox seats at the Aerosmith concert. Varvatos, to his credit, has bent over backward to preserve much of CBGB's aura in the store, but part of me wishes they had just gutted the joint and turned it into a Starbucks. Varvatos's appropriation of CB's husk perverts the club's legacy in a shameless and embarrassing attempt to assuage the guilt of the moneyed class that helped put it out of business. To wit, millionaire golfer Alice Cooper (who was really more of a Max's guy back in the day) endorsed the venture in its initial press release, suggesting that "now all the old CBGB punks will become the best dressed CBGB punks in the world."[93]

Seaton "Raven" Hancock (saxophonist, Murphy's Law, the Stimulators): John Varvatos, my ass. All those fucking rock and roll sellouts who wear his shit, I'm pissed at them all. Iggy [Pop] too, man! I've met Iggy, he's a nice guy. But I want to kick his ass now [for wearing Varvatos's clothing].

For a time, Azrak also opened a lounge and venue in the basement of the old club called, confusingly, "Extra Place by Max's Kansas City." The space, which hosted private events and secret performances, and proudly proclaimed in its press release that it

PHOTO BY THE AUTHOR, 2023.

The John Varvatos store at 315 Bowery.

was "never open to the public," contained a CBGB "shrine," aka the wall and sink of the original bathroom.[94] Beyond a handful of shows and parties, it amounted to very little.

The cultural necrophilia doesn't end there. When restaurateur Daniel Boulud opened a burger restaurant on the Bowery in 2009, he had the balls to name it DBGB (*"Daniel Boulud Good Burger,"* naturally). An intellectual property lawsuit forced Boulud to remove the restaurant's logo, which mimicked CB's unmistakable font, but the restaurant kept the smug, appropriative name until its closure in 2017.

In 2011, local pizza chain Two Boots, with assistance from Patti Smith Group's Lenny Kaye, unveiled the "CBGB (OMFUG)" pizza slice—*C*hicken, *B*roccoli, *G*arlic, and *B*asil pesto (they lazily didn't bother trying to add OMFUG ingredients, which is a real missed opportunity to include onions, mozzarella, figs, urgelia, and guanciale—you're welcome).

When Target opened its flagship East Village branch on 14th Street in 2018, the exterior included a fake CB's awning, reading

"TRGT" in the iconic font ("OMFUG" was replaced by, simply, "BANDS"). *Vanishing New York*'s Jeremiah Moss referred to it as "the most deplorable commodification of local neighborhood culture I've ever witnessed."[95] The outcry was substantial enough that the chain removed the offending awning and issued a noncommittal apology. And yet, the residential building that houses said Target continues to go by the moniker[96] EVGB ("*East Village's Greatest Building*").[xvii]

None of this is to suggest that the logo's current owners have done right by it. In 2011, Lisa Kristal Burgman sold all the club's assets at auction—including all associated intellectual property, as well as remnants of the physical club, disassembled and kept in storage—to a group of anonymous investors. The following year, said investors launched the CBGB Festival, a three-hundred-band, multivenue music and film festival, culminating in a Times Square performance by Jane's Addiction (who, as far as I'm aware, never played CBGB proper).

After its closure, CBGB also became the unexpected muse of a certain cheesy corner of Hollywood. In the 2010 film *Sex and the City 2*, the club is name-checked as the former workplace of publicist/sex addict Samantha Jones (Kim Catrall); in a 2013 episode of the Showtime series *Californication*, star David Duchovny is shown, in a painfully awkward and wig-filled flashback, meeting his first wife at the club. 2013 also saw the release of the movie *CBGB*, directed by Randall Miller, co-produced by Lisa Kristal Burgman, and starring Alan Rickman as Hilly. This film is required viewing for all the wrong reasons. But stunt casting and historical inaccuracies aside (although both are multitudinous), the movie's greatest failure lies in showing how hard Kristal worked

---

xvii Another luxury residence on 13th Street introduced itself to the neighborhood in 2019 with this unintentionally hilarious, chronologically challenged advertising campaign: "First we had the Ramones, then the Velvet Underground, and now there's Eve East Village: Designer Studio, One and Two Bedroom Rental Residences."

without ever giving a hint as to his motivation. Rickman's Hilly just seems miserable the entire time.

McNeil: It's a piece of shit. The guy who played Hilly got him down, but Hilly wasn't CBGB! Hilly was a big part of CBGB, but he wasn't why everybody went there. I went there because of the Ramones and the Dead Boys and Talking Heads and Patti, and the people who played them were just so boring.

I've saved the worst for last. In 2015, a CBGB burger restaurant and bar opened in Newark Airport's Terminal C, complete with a replica of the awning and a grand piano covered in bumper stickers and fake graffiti. An accompanying shop sold CBGB-branded ChapStick and heavily marked-up LPs by the likes of Taylor Swift, alongside the traditional punk fare of neck pillows and *Us Weekly* magazines. The one time I had the misfortune of flying out of Newark, I saw reality TV star Spencer Pratt at the restaurant, taking phone calls on his Bluetooth and eating a burger alone. Unsurprisingly, it has since closed.

In spite/because of it all, those shirts still sell like hotcakes. The club's branded apparel currently runs between $25 and $60 at the official CBGB online store, while John Varvatos hawks an appliqued version for $98. Best of all, the Los Angeles–based designer Lauren Moshi offers a sweat suit with the logo festooned across both shirt and pants, accompanied by stylized safety pins, a menacing skull with sunglasses on, and incongruous rainbow-colored racing stripes, for a cool $308.

It's easy to want to be offended by all of this. But it's hard to say that these businesses are defiling the CBGB legacy, simply because it was too late for that. By the time they arrived on the scene, the club's legacy was already confused and mangled by years of decline in quality as a venue, by outsiders' attempts to impose their own meaning onto it, by legend building that undermined the values the club championed, and by uncertainty about what its legacy was. None of this is meant as an insult to CBGB or Hilly

Kristal—it's hard for a club to exist for even three or four years in New York City, so if you stay open for over thirty, a lot is going to happen, and probably most of it won't be that great. It's more to say that whatever happened there has been inflated to such absurd proportions in the popular consciousness, and become so divorced from what made it so powerful, it no longer means anything at all.

Suggested Listening

Television—"Little Johnny Jewel" single (1975)

Blondie—"X Offender" single (1976)

Various—*Live at CBGB: the Home of Underground Rock* (1976)

The Ramones—*Ramones* (1976)

The Dead Boys—*Young, Loud, and Snotty* (1977)

The Shirts—*The Shirts* (1978)

The Cramps—*Gravest Hits* (1979)

Bad Brains—*Live at CBGB* (rec. 1982)

Living Colour—*Live from CBGB* (rec. 1989)

Agnostic Front—*Live at CBGB* (1989)

6

CONTORT YOURSELF:
NO WAVE, MUTANT DISCO,
AND THE ARRIVAL OF HIP-HOP

*Johnny Dynell (deejay; singer): Living downtown really meant
something then; you were really in a whole world. By five o'clock at
night, when everyone went home [from work], it was desolate down
there. But it was safe, it didn't feel dangerous or anything.*

When New York City went bankrupt in 1975, it was a culmination of several forces, including decades of white flight and the end
of the city's manufacturing industry—which, as you may recall
from Chapter Two, is what allowed the loft scenes in SoHo and
Tribeca to flourish. Mayor Abraham Beame, who had only been
elected a year prior, had been dealt a hand that was all but un-
playable, especially after President Gerald Ford refused to bail out
the city. Backed into a corner, Beame publicly mused about cost-
cutting measures that could keep the city running, one of which

was laying off significant numbers of municipal workers, including police, corrections officers, and firefighters.

The public perception of New York City at the time is well represented by classic New Yorksploitation films like 1974's *Death Wish* and 1976's *Taxi Driver*: desolate, derelict, dangerous, seedy, filthy, nightmarish, laid to waste by crime and class warfare. And honestly, that wasn't far off. But parts of Midtown and Uptown Manhattan remained as bourgeois as ever (see Woody Allen's late seventies films *Annie Hall* and *Manhattan*, in which the city's massive infrastructure problems are little more than a peripheral inconvenience). And tourism remained a reliable source of income for the city, with upward of 10.5 million tourists continuing to stream into New York each year.

The municipal workers whose jobs were on the line were aware of that fact and used it to their advantage. In June 1975, a group called Council for Public Safety—comprising twenty-eight unions of police, corrections officers, firefighters, and the like—began distributing a pamphlet to visitors at the airport entitled *Welcome to Fear City*. And if that title wasn't foreboding enough, the cover also bore a gnarly illustration of the Grim Reaper. The pamphlet opened with a few splashy crime statistics, ripped into Beame's proposed job cuts, and then got to the point: "Until things change, stay away from New York if you possibly can."[97]

The pamphlet went on to offer visitors advice, some of which were reasonable ("Conceal property in automobiles," "Be aware of fire hazards"), but most of which were exaggerated fearmongering: "Stay off the streets after 6 p.m.," "Do not walk," "Do not leave Manhattan."

It was true that violent crime and theft numbers had ballooned in the city between 1965 and 1975: the number of murders and assaults more than doubled, rapes and burglaries more than tripled, and there were ten times as many robberies. But encouraging tourists to engrave (not write, mind you, *engrave*) their name and phone number on all belongings and "never ride the subway for any reason whatsoever" was straight-up ridiculous.[98] Mayor Beame certainly thought so, calling it "a new low in irresponsibility."[99]

If the goal of *Welcome to Fear City* was to save municipal jobs and/or fight the city's escalating crime rates, it failed: fifteen thousand city employees (including thousands of cops) were laid off on June 30, 1975. Over the next five years, the NYPD shrank by 34 percent and violent crime increased by 40 percent (although correlation doesn't equal causation).

But if *Welcome to Fear City*'s goal was simply to scare the shit out of potential tourists and make Mayor Beame's already untenable situation even worse, boy did it succeed! The national press piled on as well, reporting an endless stream of NYC crime statistics with a near-pornographic salaciousness. The PR crisis was substantial enough that the city dispatched representatives to London, Paris, Brussels, and Frankfurt with a fifteen-minute slideshow illustrating how safe and fun New York still was.

Elliott Sharp (multi-instrumentalist; composer): The art tourists from Europe and Japan were our main audience, because most Americans were deathly afraid of New York City. Every day in the paper there was, "Five Tourists Stabbed in the Subway" or whatever. It was daily fodder for the press.

But as the rest of the country continued to steer clear of the city, a new punk offshoot was blooming downtown, which wore the city's ruin like a badge of honor. Unlike Patti Smith, Talking Heads, and other punk bands who'd had mainstream commercial ambitions from the outset, many of these new bands were proud to make music which seemed to have zero chance of reaching listeners above 14th Street, let alone outside the city. Rather than introduce the outside world to NYC culture, as their predecessors had, these new bands mostly seemed interested in telling New York about itself.

In defiance of early punk's back-to-our-roots garage rock base, these new bands—which included Teenage Jesus and the Jerks, Contortions, DNA, Mars, Rhys Chatham, and Theoretical Girls, among others—were more visceral, noisy, cathartic, and downright menacing. Musically, these musicians were largely untrained, and lyrically, they often took a dispassionate, at times even smirking stance toward destruction and urban blight. These bands delighted in presenting a phantasmagoric New York straight out of *Welcome to Fear City*, handily earning the antagonistic genre name they were soon saddled with: "no wave."

But when you look closely, some funny little wrinkles appear: a decent component of this new development was taking place in and around the newly named Tribeca, a part of Downtown that, while aesthetically rough, was generally pretty placid and safe. Many of the participants were recent transplants to the city with fancy art school educations, and the scene was supported in part by the posh art world that was spilling over from neighboring SoHo. Music that was framed (at least by music press, if not by the bands themselves) as brutal dispatches from the edge of civilization was often a dispatch from a small group of pretty civilized musicians and artists who were, by and large, having a blast.

THE KITCHEN (AGAIN)

This story starts in SoHo, with our old friend, the Kitchen— formerly part of the Mercer Arts Center. When the Grand Central Hotel collapsed in 1973, taking the Mercer down with it, the Kitchen was already in the process of relocating to a 7,500-square-foot gallery and performance space on the second floor of 59 Wooster Street and 484 Broome Street (two addresses for the same building). Originally founded by video artists Woody and Steina Vasulka and composer Rhys Chatham, the Kitchen was now run by a gallerist named Robert Stearns, with composer Jim Burton booking the musical acts. Though the Kitchen's musical programming largely stuck to the minimalist template that Chatham had established, Burton's successors—composers Arthur Russell and Garrett List—started expanding the parameters of what precisely "minimalism" could be. In 1975, Russell booked the Boston proto-punk band the Modern Lovers; the following year, List (at Russell's suggestion) booked an early show by a then-unknown Talking Heads.[i] Punk was slowly entering the mix in avant-garde SoHo.

Chatham: Peter Gordon [composer and founder of the band Love of Life Orchestra] was the first person that I knew to merge rock with classical techniques. One evening, Peter and I were walking back home from rehearsal on Bleecker Street, because we both lived in the East Village at that time. He said, "Have you ever in your entire life been to a rock concert?" and I said "No." I knew what rock was, but I had never been to a rock concert. He laughed and said, "There's a good group playing tonight at this club called CBGB's, why don't you come down and we'll listen to them tonight." This was May 1976, and the group was the Ramones.

What I saw changed my life. It just seemed so romantic and bizarre, these rail thin guys on stage with their moves all down. The music was a little more complex than what I was doing—they were working with three chords, I was working with one—but I felt a lot in common with what they were doing.

I became music director [at the Kitchen] again in 1977, or at the end of '76, something like that. During my [second] tenure in the Kitchen, I mixed things up with—I don't like to call it "experimental rock," but that's what it was. Patti Smith, Talking Heads, Blondie, that was all very exciting, but for the generation that came immediately after—because generations happen much more quickly in rock than in the other forms of music—things had gotten really experimental.

NO WAVE

In the mid and late '70s, most of the neighborhoods encompassed by Community District 1—including Tribeca, the Financial District, and Battery Park City—were in a state of flux. Like SoHo, Tribeca was full of disused former factory buildings that artists had started converting into lofts (recall Yoko Ono, La Monte Young, and Charlemagne Palestine's lofts there from Chapter Two). But

---

i   This show is on YouTube in its entirety, and is incredible.

unlike SoHo, those loft buildings were not part of a protected historic district, meaning that the city and developers could demolish them at will.

The area was zoned for redevelopment in the 1960s, and by the '70s, there was already a concerted effort to revitalize Tribeca with new construction, including the massive Independence Plaza housing complex (completed in 1975) and the Borough of Manhattan Community College (completed in 1980). Older commercial and office buildings like the iconic Woolworth Building, which had been rotting for decades, were also being renovated.

The Civic Center area—encompassing City Hall, NYPD headquarters at One Police Plaza, federal agency offices, courthouses, and jails—is also steps away from Tribeca, and of course the Financial District was bustling with various financial activities, all of which added to the area's foot traffic.

That is, until 5:00 p.m. when the workers went home. After that, one could walk several blocks at night and not see another living soul.

In 1977, a pair of adjacent, derelict buildings at 81 and 83 Warren Street (in the Financial District, just a hair over the line from Tribeca) were home to some of the first stirrings of what would become the no wave scene. 81 Warren Street, where future Contortions members Don Christensen and Jody Harris lived, was the first to be occupied; it also served as a rehearsal space for the Cramps, Teenage Jesus and the Jerks, Richard Hell and the Voidoids, and critic Lester Bangs's band Birdland.

83 Warren—an abandoned building where Teenage Jesus and the Jerks' frontwoman Lydia Lunch and drummer Bradley Field, Cramps drummer Miriam Linna, writer/deejay James Marshall, and the members of the band Mars all lived—was christened "The Hole" and/or "The Home for Teenage Dirt."

Linna: We were totally squatting there. There was no running water at all, so we had to figure out where to take showers and stuff like that. It had electricity, but barely—it was just enough to plug the amps in.

The residents at 81 and 83 Warren Street had all been hanging out around CBGB and Max's Kansas City: Linna was regularly playing at both with the Cramps, and Mars were starting to play around (initially under the name China). Lunch (née Koch) had found her way to CBGB as a sixteen-year-old runaway from Rochester, befriending Suicide and the Dead Boys[ii] before forming her own band, Teenage Jesus and the Jerks, with Field as her drummer.

Prior to her stint on Warren Street, Lunch had lived in a cramped storefront in the East Village with another Teenage Jesus bandmate, saxophonist James Chance. Unlike many of the musicians populating the no wave scene, Chance (née Siegfried) was a conservatory-trained saxophonist from Milwaukee; upon his arrival in New York in 1975, he made tentative simultaneous inroads into both the punk and loft jazz scenes, even playing with pianist John Fischer at his loft venue, Environ.

Chance found his way into the nascent no wave world through a girlfriend, Nancy Arlen, who was also the drummer in Mars. In addition to Arlen and vocalist Sumner Crane, Mars included a couple, guitarist Connie Burg and bassist Mark Cunningham. The two had formed the band after moving up from Florida alongside Cunningham's college roommate Arto Lindsay (soon-to-be front man for DNA) and Lindsay's girlfriend Robin Davis.

As you may have surmised, the roots of the various bands that made up the no wave scene—principally, Teenage Jesus and the Jerks, Contortions, Mars, DNA, Theoretical Girls, and Rhys Chatham, though there were several others—are too tangled to unpack here. But suffice it to say there was a good deal of bandmate swapping when these bands were in their infancy.

Chatham: Arto had never played guitar before, and he purposely put together people who had never played their instruments and were the most unlikely people possible.

---

ii   She is immortalized in the Dead Boys' song "I Need Lunch."

Thanks to Lunch's suggestion, Lindsay met performance artist Robin Crutchfield, who had recently been gifted his roommate's old electric piano. The two formed DNA in 1977 with friends Gordon Stevenson and Mirielle Cervenka (sister of X frontwoman Exene Cervenka).

Crutchfield: [Gordon and Mirielle] had a loft we could rehearse at for free. Arto knew Terry Ork of Ork Records, and was told that Terry was booking new band nights at Max's Kansas City at the end of September, he'd heard Arto had a band and [invited him] to participate in that. Arto asked when the gig was, and we were told that it was twenty-eight days later. Despite just starting, with no training, and no material, we said yes. But, our other two members panicked and jumped ship, leaving Arto and I to find another member and another rehearsal space.

The residents of 81 Warren Street were evicted after only a few months, not because of any financial issues or encroaching gentrification, but because the building's owners didn't like that Lunch was displaying graphic, disturbing paintings in the windows. Lunch, Bradley Field, and Sumner Crane left Tribeca for a second-floor loft above a Chinese movie theater on Delancey Street in the Lower East Side (according to Arto Lindsay, "It was a kung fu movie theater, and you could hear the movies through the walls"). Teenage Jesus and the Jerks, Contortions, Mars, DNA, and the Mumps all used the loft as a practice space, and it was there that Lindsay and Crutchfield found their new drummer in time for their Max's gig.

Crutchfield: The only person hanging around rehearsals that wasn't in a band at the time was the girlfriend of Teenage Jesus and the Jerks' Japanese bassist. Ikue [Mori] couldn't speak much English and didn't own any drums, but we managed to borrow equipment from Nancy Arlen of Mars for her to use, and communicate through gestures and diagrams and sound. Somehow we managed to put together a 20-minute set for Max's by the deadline, settling on the band's name [DNA] not very much before that.

James Chance, having been kicked out of Teenage Jesus and the Jerks, had started his own band, Contortions, with guitarists Pat Place and Jamie Nares, keyboardist Adele Bertei, drummer Chiko Hige, and the mononymous Reck on bass.[iii] In stark contrast to Chance's conservatory training, none of the other band members had much experience with their instruments.

Place: I hadn't been playing guitar—I really didn't play an instrument until James asked me to join the band, [but I figured] I can play like Connie Burg or Arto or Lydia, so I got a guitar at a pawn shop. The first rehearsal was on Delancey Street, where Lydia Lunch and Sumner from Mars were living, and then we played [our first show] at Max's Kansas City. That gig was insane. I came off stage and there were two strings on my guitar, my hands were completely bloody and there was blood splattered all over the guitar because I didn't even really know how to strum properly. We were playing so frenetically and I was so into it that I didn't even notice I was ripping my hand up.

A second faction of no wave bands came from more traditional musical and performance backgrounds. One such band was Theoretical Girls, whose members included the classically trained composers and guitarists Glenn Branca and Jeffrey Lohn. Like Rhys Chatham, Branca and Lohn had been disinterested in rock music until they discovered early punk bands like Suicide and the Dead Boys, which led them to pursue an artier, noisier, minimalist take on punk. Conveniently, Lohn lived in the first-floor storefront at 17 Thompson Street in SoHo, which doubled as an early venue

---

iii   Hige, Nares, and Reck all left soon after the band formed, replaced by bassist George Scott III and Lydia Lunch's old neighbors, drummer Don Christensen and guitarist Jody Harris.

for numerous Theoretical Girls gigs, as well as performances by Laurie Anderson and Rhys Chatham.

Having had his "come to Jesus" moment with the Ramones, Chatham became intrigued by the prospect of merging the minimalism he'd learned from the likes of La Monte Young and Charlemagne Palestine with the volume and aggression of punk. To that end, Chatham got a crash course in the rock vernacular by playing electric guitar in his friends' bands, Gynecologists and Arsenal, before debuting his new sound with the 1977 composition "Guitar Trio."

> *Chatham: The first time we played "Guitar Trio" at Max's, I remember being hugely nervous, because I didn't fit into this Johnny Thunders model of having tattoos and a hypodermic needle sticking out of my arm and stuff like that. I was afraid I was gonna get lynched.*

Where bands like the Heartbreakers, Richard Hell and the Voidoids, Suicide, and the Dead Boys adopted effortlessly cool, street-tough personas, many of the no wave musicians—despite an often-impeccable film-noir-meets-nouvelle-vague-on-a-budget aesthetic—seemed unable to fully shed their innate nerdiness, befitting their backgrounds as either art students or conservatory-trained musicians. Even James Chance, an admitted junkie with a penchant for violently attacking audience members midset, was a scrawny Midwestern jazz nut with a ridiculous pompadour who looked like he was seventeen years old, tops. Only Lydia Lunch, an honest-to-god teen runaway, came across as genuinely threatening in her persona; the rest seemed to be working quite hard to achieve their coolness.

It might seem like working hard to cultivate an aura of danger and mystery is at odds with no wave's freeform, unstudied vibe. But they're both part of the scene's DIY ethos: you didn't need to be born with the innate badassery of Patti Smith or Alan Vega in order to be in a band, just like you didn't have to have any musical training or ability. No wave was proof that anybody—truly, anybody—could come to New York, live on the fringe, start a band, make art, and be part of a scene. You just had to do it.

In short time, the no wave bands were regularly playing at CBGB and Max's and accumulating enthusiastic followings. None of them were making much in the way of money from these gigs, although expenses were low, and as Place notes, they were making "enough to get a slice of pizza once a day."

But unlike the bulk of their punk predecessors, the early no wave bands—whose ranks also included the Communists, Jack Ruby, Terminal, and Ut—were also finding gigs at highbrow venues like the Kitchen and at gallery spaces around SoHo and Tribeca, at least in part because many of the band members came from art school backgrounds. For Johnny Dynell, who played bass in Terminal, "I knew nothing about music, I didn't play any instruments. I was in art school and I was thinking of it as performance art."

Arto Lindsay: For a gig at CBGB's, you put up the posters yourself and you played for the door. A gig at the Kitchen or at [the Tribeca gallery] Artists' Space was a different ballgame: Their money came from grants, they would give you a guarantee, and the New York Times *would write about it. Everyone in the audience would be very passive, because they were already endorsing it just by being there. It's not such a physical relationship with the audience.*

Beyond gigs, guitarist Elliott Sharp (who moved to the city in 1979, in part because he was a Contortions superfan) recalled that the galleries also sustained the scene in another way: by offering free wine and cheese at art openings, which musicians were all too happy to partake in.

NO NEW YORK

There is some debate as to where the term "no wave" originates. An obvious rejection of new wave—aka the more commercial end of the punk scene, like Blondie and Talking Heads—it might have been something first said in an interview by Lydia Lunch, or Mofungo drummer Chris Nelson. It might be a reference to French New Wave filmmaker Claude Chabrol's remark, "There are no waves, only the ocean."[100] But the most likely origin story is that it came from a zine called NO-*Instant Artifact of the New Order*, which Teenage Jesus and the Jerks bassist Jim Sclavunos[iv] put out with some of his friends from NYU: *NO*'s second issue had a photo of a surfer on the cover with the headline "New Wave, No Wave."

Given these bands' overwhelming lack of commercial potential, it's very possible that none of this would be remembered were it not for Brian Eno. The former Roxy Music keyboardist had been spending time in New York while producing records for Talking Heads, and decided to relocate to the city from the UK in 1978. By May of that year, he was subletting an apartment on West 8th Street from an amateur filmmaker named Steve Mass.

Through Mass, Eno met Anya Philips, a Taiwan-born fashion designer, professional dominatrix, and CBGB regular. Philips was managing and dating James Chance, and along with *New York Times* music critic John Rockwell, she encouraged Eno to come check out Chance's band on May 5 at Artists' Space, a gallery located at 105 Hudson Street in Tribeca.

That particular show happened to be day four of a five-day no wave festival. Contortions were sharing the bill with DNA; the previous three nights had included Terminal, the Communists, Gynecologists, Theoretical Girls, Daily Life, and Tone Death.

Eno was blown away by what he saw and came back the following night to catch Teenage Jesus and the Jerks and Mars. Convinced that something extraordinary was afoot, he convinced his label, Island Records, to bankroll a compilation of the four bands he'd seen. "I think he really wanted to capture the spirit of the bands' live performances," said Robin Crutchfield. "He had the

---

iv Sclavunos would briefly become the drummer in Sonic Youth, and is now a member of Nick Cave and the Bad Seeds.

sense that time was of the essence and that the energy and enthu-siasm and outrage of the bands would likely burn out quickly if not captured by someone."

The resultant compilation, *No New York*, was released by Is-land's Antilles subsidiary in November 1978.[v] Its legacy is decidedly mixed: On the one hand, it's an extraordinary artifact of a short-lived and otherwise underdocumented scene that has proved mas-sively influential. It gave a rock star's seal of approval and a major label's worldwide distribution to music that would have otherwise had no commercial potential.

But the success of the record also proved to be the scene's end. Eno helped push four bands as the worldwide faces of no wave, which meant that bands who played the first three days of the fes-tival weren't included on the album or in the national press that surrounded its release, and have mostly faded from the public con-sciousness as a result. The larger scene was reduced, in the historical imagination, to the four bands who were taken to be the stand-outs of the scene. But many of the bands that were excluded were just as central; several were understandably pissed about being ex-cluded. Though the no wave scene's impact would be felt in the city (and elsewhere) for decades to come, Eno had inadvertently delivered it a death blow.

THE MUDD CLUB

Joey Kelly (doorman, The Mudd Club): Steve was one of those kinds of guys where you never know if he's full of shit or he's really that crazy.

---

v   The recording sessions took place at Big Apple Studios, located in the basement of a gallery at 112 Greene Street in SoHo, where much of Philip Glass's work had been recorded. The studio was later rechristened Greene Street Studios, and several classic albums were recorded there during the '80s and '90s, including Public Enemy's *It Takes a Nation of Millions to Hold Us Back*, Sonic Youth's *Daydream Nation*, and A Tribe Called Quest's *The Low End Theory*.

While Eno was assembling *No New York*, Steve Mass—his Bleecker Street roommate/landlord—was hard at work on a venture of his own in Tribeca.

Mass had made a good amount of money working for his family's private ambulance business, but he had also studied philosophy, creative writing, art history, and anthropology, and had briefly operated an independent publishing company. By the time he was living with Eno, he'd become a self-styled filmmaker, and was palling around with underground directors like Jack Smith and Amos Poe.

Through Poe, he met Anya Philips, who in turn introduced him to filmmaker and conceptual artist Diego Cortez (born Jim Curtis). Philips and Cortez had already been toying around with the idea of opening a club that would combine the punk world from CB's and Max's with deejays, film screenings, and visual and performance art. They convinced Mass to join in as the club's financial backer. Depending on which account you're getting, Mass either sold a home he owned in Massachusetts or borrowed money from his family's business to do so.

Mass and Philips found an old textile warehouse at 77 White Street that had been converted into a residential building. The owner, painter Ross Bleckner, lived on the sixth floor, and he took some convincing—Cortez, who had been a tenant of Bleckner's, assured him that the club would be oriented around conceptual and performance art, and definitely wouldn't feature loud rock bands, no sirree.

The building's otherwise-unadorned exterior had the letters *MCL* inscribed on it, so Philips and Cortez proposed the hilarious name "Molotov Cocktail Lounge." Mass disagreed, insisting upon "Mudd Club Lounge," named for Dr. Samuel Mudd, the physician who treated John Wilkes Booth in the aftermath of Abraham Lincoln's assassination. This disagreement, and others, led to a falling out between Philips and Mass, who continued building the club without her.[vi]

---

vi   Philips passed away from cancer in 1981.

77 White Street.

Among the construction crew building the club were members of a Brooklyn-based band called Aviation, whose ranks included singer Joey Kelly. He recalled that during the construction, "Steve got to know and trust us, and he assigned us all jobs" once the Mudd Club opened. For Kelly, that meant getting "stuck [working] the door."

The Mudd Club's location was central in its success. Tribeca was desolate, much as Union Square and the Bowery had been, but 77 White Street was only two blocks removed from the trendier SoHo; plenty of young artists and musicians were already living in the general area. Though many patrons avoided the subways, nearly every Manhattan-based subway line stops at Canal Street, just two blocks north of White Street.

The Mudd Club was also one block west of the New York City Civil Court, and spitting distance from the city's Civic Center, a complex which included the New York County Supreme Court and the newly-erected Metropolitan Correctional Center—not a particularly rock 'n' roll location, but perhaps one that helped some patrons feel more comfortable traveling to a deserted area late at night.

Kelly: White Street was at that vortex, where it was near many lofts, and you had the courts down the block, so it was pretty much clean there. People were never threatened or bothered, and during the day on White Street, there'd be nothing there. It turned out to be one of the best locations they ever could have found.

After a few low-key parties, the Mudd Club officially opened on Halloween 1978 with a headlining performance by the B-52s. "No one had ever heard of them before," Kelly recalled. "They totally blew us away."

For all the ways the Mudd Club deviated from the punk club template, arguably the most significant was its adoption of the selective door policy, previously a hallmark of swanky Uptown discos like Studio 54. Sure, they framed it as performative irony, but the underlying concept was the same: make sure only the most deserving people were admitted.

Dynell: The whole idea behind the Mudd Club was a joke, kind of a punk satire of Studio 54. They put velvet ropes outside the door,[vii] they hung a mirror ball, they had a deejay, but it was sort of like performance art, really tongue-in-cheek. And the crazy thing is, it took off. Putting these velvet ropes up and not letting anybody in was just

---

vii   In keeping with the club's industrial aesthetic, they used a bike chain rather than an actual velvet rope.

making fun of Studio 54, and next thing you know, there's lines of people trying to get in for real.

Kelly: *My job was to come out every 10 or 15 minutes and go, "You, you, you, you, you, you, you," and then go back in and disappear because the people that weren't getting in would be pissed off at me. We knew from the beginning of the evening who was going to get in and who wasn't, so this poor guy that's standing in front of me for two and a half hours, you'd think that I would have the audacity to tell him, "Look, just go home, it's not happening." But we didn't do that. Poor guy, I felt so bad for him, but there were 50 or 60 of him every night.*

It's kind of bizarre to think that all these punks who had come up through CBGB's egalitarianism saw a club with a doorman and just accepted it as the new cool spot. But the fact that it happened speaks to the seductive power of exclusivity. An underground club with a doorman can seem silly—until said doorman decides to let you in. *Then*, it's awesome.

Not to mention, it sounds like one hell of a party.

Jonny Sender (bassist, Konk; deejay): *At the Mudd Club, you'd have the scene people, you'd have downtown people that were not necessarily in the scene, you'd have a few odd businessmen, a couple drag queens, and one or two Hasidic regulars who'd be out on the floor with their [tzitzit] sticking out of their pants, sweating and freaking out to the music. It was basically a white scene, but it was a very bizarre, mixed scene.*

Of course, they couldn't *only* let the coolest or most famous people in—after all, most of the too-cool-for-school regulars weren't paying the $3 cover *and* Steve Mass was regularly supplying them with free drinks (and other intoxicants). All of that made for a great party, but the club did have to at least try to earn some kind of profit.[viii]

Michael Holman (filmmaker; artist; booker, Negril; musician, Gray): The cool kids got in for free, and all the squares had to pay. They kind of supported us.

Though the Mudd Club occupied the first two floors of 77 White Street, the rest of the building remained residential. Bleckner lived on the sixth floor; the fourth floor was home to Rosie Shuster, a writer for *Saturday Night Live* and estranged wife to the show's creator, Lorne Michaels. Shuster's live-in boyfriend at the time was one of the show's stars, actor Dan Aykroyd; both became Mudd Club regulars. (According to Richard Boch, who alternated with Joey Kelly as the club's doorman, "Dan was fine if he was hanging at the bar, but if he had to come in and out through the crowd outside, he had very little patience.")

MUSIC AT THE MUDD CLUB

Holman: I had already been going to Studio 54 every weekend. Studio 54 was this big, slick, expensively produced, interior redecorated, hedonistic, cybernetic experience that was glitzy and huge and exciting and expensive, with lots of celebrities. They played what I consider the worst kind of disco music—not R & B Black disco, just radio disco. I still liked to go to Studio 54 because I just wanted to go where the action was, to see and be seen.

---

viii Among the Mudd Club's regulars were several actual children. Although the drinking age was eighteen in New York State at the time, IDs were never checked, and a mix of neighborhood kids and outer-borough teens getting away from rough home lives were welcomed and embraced. This brigade of underage regulars included three future movie stars: Debi Mazar (who even worked at the club as a sixteen-year-old), Dylan McDermott, and Eszter Balint.

Singer Klaus Nomi and Mania D drummer Karin Luner at the Mudd Club, 1978.

> *When I first went to the Mudd Club, it was just a complete an-*
> *tithesis to Studio 54. It was a small hole in the wall; no money was*
> *spent on its decoration. It was tiny, stuffy, and dark. The deejays*
> *played great rock and roll and soul, and music from ten or twenty*
> *years before. They played James Brown, and they played Funkadelic.*
> *It was heaven, because the music was so great. Between 1979 and*
> *1981, which were the best years there, I must have gone to the Mudd*
> *Club 300 days out of each year.*

Though live music played a sizable role at the Mudd Club, it was
decentralized—a stark change of pace from what CBGB and Max's
Kansas City had been doing of late. As *Washington Post* reporter

Gary Kenton noted in 1979, "Even when there is a group performing at the club, few seem to come expressly for that purpose."[101]

> *Boch: You could just sort of pass [through without being] conscious
> of the fact that a band is going to be playing. Whatever happened
> during the course of a night at the club was just part of being at the
> Mudd Club. So you weren't consciously going to see music.*

Bands usually didn't go on until around 2:00 a.m. (the club
didn't even open until midnight), and many acts took the Mudd
Club stage unannounced, which meant you never knew what
to expect. Early bookings leaned heavily on some of the more
obvious punk and no wave bands—both local (Suicide, Talking
Heads, Rhys Chatham, the Feelies) and international (U2, Bow
Wow Wow, Psychedelic Furs)—but there were also '60s provoca-
teurs (Frank Zappa, Joni Mitchell, Captain Beefheart, Marianne
Faithfull), salsa (Tito Puente, Eddie Palmieri), beloved oldies (the
Crystals, Mary Wells, Sam and Dave, Screamin' Jay Hawkins,
Percy Sledge), country (Ernest Tubb), reggae (Burning Spear, Steel
Pulse, Lee "Scratch" Perry), and funk (George Clinton, the Brides
of Funkenstein). This commitment to musical diversity and not
announcing acts in advance meant there was the opportunity for
thrilling surprises—as well as serious disappointments.

> *Kelly: One night, Glenn [McDermott, who booked bands at the
> club] decides he wants to book Judas Priest. What a fucking disas-
> ter. Nobody knew who was playing that night, so you have all these
> cool, chic, groovy people hanging out, expecting something like the
> Cramps. Lo and behold, here comes Judas Priest on stage. Everybody
> stopped, froze, looked at each other, turned around, and walked out.*

The Mudd Club wasn't the first punk club to have a deejay; they
were just barely beaten to the punch by Hurrah, the self-proclaimed
"rock disco" at 36 West 62nd Street, which we'll discuss in Chapter Eight. Hurrah was explicitly a rock-oriented dance club which

also hosted live bands; their deejays focused exclusively on punk and new wave records.

So did the Mudd Club deejays, at first. David Azarch, Danny Heaps, Howie Pyro, and Sean Cassette played a mix of punk, new wave, no wave, and glam rock; Azarch would play some soul, and Pyro dipped into his vast collection of children's novelty records. But the Mudd Club's unique musical voice emerged when Anita Sarko, a college radio deejay (and secret trust fund kid) from Detroit, began working the decks.

When Sarko deejayed, the very notion of genre lost all meaning. Alongside the requisite punk, new wave, and no wave, a typical Sarko set might include funk, rockabilly, novelty records, dub reggae, American Songbook crooners, industrial, Afrobeat, disco, cheeseball exotica, early hip-hop, opera, spoken word, and ambient field recordings. With Sarko kicking the door wide open, the Mudd Club's identity became that of a musical omnivore.

Once Sarko kicked the door open, other deejays with omnivorous tastes started working at the Mudd Club. Johnny Dynell (née Savas) had moved to New York in 1975 to go to the School of Visual Arts, and fell in with the nascent no wave scene. He and Robin Crutchfield had played together in an unnamed early version of what became DNA, after which he joined the no wave band Terminal. But at the same time, Dynell had been getting into disco and regularly visiting the Loft and the Gallery.

Dynell: I never wanted to be a deejay, just like I never wanted to be in a band. But Steve Mass was like Caligula, saying "You do this, you work at the door, you're a bartender," and I got "deejay." I had never deejayed before, I didn't know anything about it, I didn't even have any records. I just went around and borrowed a bunch of records from people and started on a Saturday night.

In the early '70s, Justin Strauss had been the singer in the power-pop band Milk 'n' Cookies, playing CBGB and Max's Kansas City alongside the Ramones and Blondie. But after a failed attempt to relocate to Los Angeles, the band broke up, setting off a series of events that led him to the Mudd Club's deejay booth.

> *Strauss: I was talking to my ex-girlfriend, and she said, "There's this club that just opened called the Mudd Club, and it's so cool. You should deejay there." I said, "I don't deejay." I had a lot of records, but I'd never thought about being a deejay. She said, "Just come. I'll introduce you to David [Azarch]—he's the deejay there—and see what happens."*
>
> *I came back to New York, I went to the Mudd Club, and I met David Azarch. He asked me if I would like to try it one night. I was nervous as hell, my hands were shaking putting the records on. I guess I did OK, and Steve Mass asked me if I wanted to do a night there.*

Like Dynell, Strauss had been frequenting discos like Studio 54 while participating in the punk scene and thought nothing of switching back and forth between what were ostensibly "rock" and "dance" records.

This is the Mudd Club's greatest contribution to music history: it wasn't the first rock disco, but it was the first club to say that the lines that demarcated rock, disco, and every other genre were no longer needed. If the music was good, it was worth dancing to. And as we saw with David Mancuso's Loft—where rock, soul, funk, Latin, and jazz all blended into what would become disco—there's a certain amount of genre cross-pollination that works best when the audience doesn't even realize it's happening.

According to Steve Mass, music journalist Robert Christgau once referred to the Mudd Club as a "citadel of dilettantism."[102] It's a reasonable critique, given Mass's own occupation-hopping background, or the fact that he was randomly assigning friends and acquaintances to jobs for which they were wholly unqualified. But even beyond that, the Mudd Club offered its regulars a permissive environment to try something weird and new, even if they didn't totally know what they were doing. A few of these regulars—

including Tina L'Hotsky, B-52s singer Fred Schneider, and Michael Holman—even staged elaborate theme parties.

Holman: I did one called the Soul Party, which was a huge hit. We brought soul food down from Harlem, and we got Clarence Carter to perform. The upstairs was made to look like a pimp's bedroom, with black velvet posters. Steve Mass was from the south, so he really loved the southern edge that I brought to that party, and he kept it up for six weeks or something like that.

Holman also performed at the Mudd Club with his band Gray, whose ranks included an up-and-coming painter named Jean-Michel Basquiat and a would-be filmmaker named Vincent Gallo. Like DNA and Teenage Jesus and the Jerks before them, none of the band's members had any musical training, and they branded their music as "ignorant."

The scene's permissive vibe was also evident to Chandra Oppenheim, daughter of conceptual artist Dennis Oppenheim, who lived on Franklin Street, in a loft building abutting the Mudd Club (Diego Cortez had briefly worked as Oppenheim's assistant). By the time she was eight, Chandra was already staging performance art pieces at the Kitchen. As a ten-year-old, she hooked up with members of a band called the Dance, who were friends of her fathers', and formed a new band called Chandra (later renamed Chandra Dimension). Inevitably, they made their live debut at the Mudd Club, by which point Chandra had turned eleven. "I remember the deejay played Jackson Five's 'ABC' as our walk-on music, and I loved that they picked that," she recalled.

But where the club's attitude toward art and performance was all-inclusive, its attitude toward patrons was becoming more exclusive. Celebrities were already a big part of the club's regular clientele—and its appeal to the greater public—and a side entrance on Cortlandt Alley was turned into a covert VIP entrance. But even being among the plebes who'd made the cut to get in was too much for some. For them, the club's second floor—initially a dressing room for bands—was converted into an VIP area, though Richard Boch stressed that "It was never ever called a 'VIP room,' you just knew it as 'the second floor.'"

Of course, one person's glamor is another person's phoniness, and the conspicuous presence of a VIP area full of celebrities in a club that's already impossible to get into has a funny way of alienating people.

Denise Mercedes (guitarist, the Stimulators): Screw those people! What the fuck are you that you're so much better than everybody else? If you're a rocker, you didn't need to go there, there were so many other options where people treated you nice when you got there.

TIER 3

One such place was Tier 3, a short-lived club that you've likely heard little or nothing about unless you used to hang out there. But while Tier 3 is often treated as a minor blip in New York's nightlife history, I would argue that its significance, when it comes to actual impact on musicians, is equal or greater to the Mudd Club: Tier 3 was a genuine incubator for Downtown's post–no wave scene, acting as ground zero for the development of a sound that defined Downtown in the early '80s. Several bands played there in their infancy, musicians of all stripes hung out regularly, and many recall it as their favorite club—plus, it was the rare venue owned and primarily operated by women. Its virtual erasure from greater New York music history says something about who constructs our music history narratives (by and large, the people who got rich and/or famous) and how the vast contributions of women to the no wave and post–no wave scenes have largely been overlooked.

Tier 3 (often stylized as "TR3") began its life in the late '70s as a less than promising, vaguely Japanese-fusion restaurant/jazz venue/art gallery, located three blocks west of the Mudd Club at 225 West Broadway in Tribeca. That soon changed, thanks to a waitress named Hilary Jaeger. An East Village native who'd got-

PHOTO BY THE AUTHOR, 2023.

225 West Broadway.

ten swept up in the punk scene, Jaeger began waiting tables at Tier 3 in 1979.

Jaeger: During the day, I was serving fried porgy to workers from the tombs and the court system, and at night there was a jazz band. It wasn't long before they stopped serving lunch, staying open only on weekends. Around this time they started talking about closing— it was the spring of 1979. There had been a floating party called Stinky's that had lost their space and had a sound system and crew, and I knew some of them.

While Jaeger was waitressing at Tier 3, a group of her friends— including her sister Angela Jaeger, Bob Gurevics, Perry Brandston, siblings Michael McMahon and Amy Rigby, and the band Mofungo—had started running an informal, unlicensed club called Stinky's in the basement of 94 St. Marks Place. Mostly students from NYU and the New School, they were looking for a place where they could dance to punk records, and neither Hurrah or the Mudd Club quite fit the bill.

McMahon: [Stinky's] was only open for a couple of months, and the police shut it down pretty much every night, because it was in a completely residential building.

Jaeger: They had lost their space, and they had a sound system and crew, so Jim [Geiger, Tier 3's bartender] and I got the idea to approach [Tier 3's] owners and let us try and run a club. They agreed if we'd lend them $500 each to pay their bills, so we did.

Rigby: Maureen [Cooper] and Kathy [Giarratano, Tier 3's owners], we called them "the older women." They were maybe in their mid-thirties.

It was called Tier 3 because of the bizarre layout. The rooms weren't big and they were all on different [floors]. As a restaurant, maybe it really didn't make the best sense for someone to be like running food up or down the stairs.

According to Jaeger, in a bit of serendipitous continuity, the restaurant's bar had been a fixture at the Broadway Central Hotel, home to the long-gone Mercer Arts Center. There was no stage initially, and when one was finally installed, it could only be a foot high due to the low ceilings. Like the Mudd Club, the second floor was a hangout space, and also hosted art shows. The third floor was what McMahon referred to as "the disco floor."

"It was like a kind of big, dark disco lounge that had banquettes and disco lights," he recalled. "It was closed to the public generally, but I think it was kind of a sex room?"

Beyond the similar multilevel layout, Tier 3 took after the Mudd Club in that it was two blocks away from the NYPD 1st

Precinct headquarters, and one block away from a firehouse, Hook & Ladder 8.[ix]

Rigby: You read about how dangerous the city was, but there was the police station right around the corner, so it always felt very [safe]. There was really no reason for criminal activity to be going on in that part of the city, it was mostly offices that were closed at night. So it did feel kind of like a playground.

Hilary Jaeger became the nascent club's booker, which opened on May 17, 1979, with a performance by the Stimulators. The band was connected to Tier 3 through one of the club's bartenders, Rose Feliu: her sister Denise Mercedes was the band's guitarist, and her twelve-year-old son, Harley Flanagan, was the group's drummer. The following night featured a short-lived band called Stare Kits, aka Stinky's co-founders Amy Rigby, Michael McMahon, Angela Jaeger, and Bob Gurevics.[x] Angela Jaeger moved to England soon after, but the other three assumed jobs at Tier 3: Gurevics as a deejay, Rigby at coat check, and McMahon as a barback. ("It was not a demanding job," he recalled. "I don't even know if I got paid for it.")

Though the club lasted for less than two years, every musician I interviewed for this book who set foot in Tier 3 at some point professed their love for it, with many even claiming it to be their favorite club of all time.

Bob Bert (drummer, Sonic Youth, Pussy Galore): Tier 3 was my favorite place. They had great deejays, and great bands—it was

---

ix   The firehouse was later used as a central location in the 1984 movie *Ghostbusters*, starring Mudd Club regular Dan Aykroyd.

x   After Tier 3's closure, Rigby, McMahon, and Jaeger would go on to form the punk-country band Last Roundup, and all three have remained active musicians: Amy Rigby co-founded the Shams in the late '80s, and has gone on to have a successful solo career; Michael McMahon fronts the rockabilly band Susquehanna Industrial Tool & Die Co.; Angela Jaeger was a member of the British post-punk bands Drowning Craze, Pigbag, and Instinct, and collaborated with The Monochrome Set and Bush Tetras.

right in that post-punk era, so they would get Bush Tetras, 8-Eyed Spy, the Raybeats, all that downtown stuff. It wasn't the kind of place that even sold tickets in advance, but you never had to worry about getting in.

It wasn't only that they had great shows, it just had a great, down-home, post-punk vibe. I'm not a big drinker or a bar guy, so there aren't a ton of places I like to go to just to hang, but that was one of them. I would just go there on a Tuesday night and sit at the bar. One time, I was there on a rainy weeknight and the only two other people at the bar were David Bowie and Joe Jackson.

Like Peter Crowley at Max's Kansas City before her, Hilary Jaeger's taste was impeccable enough to help develop and drive a scene, and she took pains to treat musicians fairly. And much like Crowley, she was open to bands that were not getting gigs else-where or had yet to amass followings—an openness to the new that's crucial for any scene to develop.

Jaeger: Everybody was forming bands. I'd listen to the tapes, or people would come in and if I knew them and they had a band, I'd book them. Sometimes I booked people if they came in and just looked interesting, and I was always partial toward any band that had women in it.

Cynthia Sley (singer, Bush Tetras): Of all the people that ran clubs, Hilary was definitely the most like us. She was really supportive of bands, and she wasn't in it for the money. It was more that we had a place to be and hang out and support each other.

Bush Tetras formed in 1979, with guitarist Pat Place, who had recently left Contortions, joined by drummer Dee Pop and a pair of recent Ohio transplants, Sley and bassist Laura Kennedy. Bush Tetras made their live debut at Tier 3 on February 1, 1980, and went over so well with the crowd that they played their entire seven-song set all the way through twice. They began regularly

A flier listing upcoming shows at Tier 3, made by Hilary Jaeger. Note the map in the upper righthand corner, which also points out the locations of the "Mudclump" and Baby Doll Lounge.

gigging at Tier 3 almost immediately, all but becoming the club's house band.

Though the original no wave scene was already disintegrating, Bush Tetras were part of something new that was emerging in its wake, a post-punk subgenre that the Mudd Club and Tier 3 were actively incubating. These new bands—which also included Liquid Liquid, Konk, Pulsallama, ESG, the Bloods, James White and the Blacks, Dark Day, Dinosaur L, and Lizzy Mercier Descloux—

Bush Tetras performing at Tier 3 on March 20, 1980.

welded no wave's seedy noir ambiance and take-all-comers approach to instrumentation with a more traditional, accessible pop
music core. At the time, Bush Tetras bassist Laura Kennedy called
her band's sound "rhythm and paranoia," while writer Lucy Sante
later defined the subgenre as "anything at all + disco bottom."[103]
It would eventually become known as "mutant disco," which first
appeared as the title of a 1981 compilation on ZE Records.

In addition to these burgeoning local bands, Jaeger brought in several British acts with similarly omnivorous post-punk sounds, including the Slits, Madness, the Raincoats, Young Marble Giants, Bauhaus, and New Order—all playing some of their first shows in New York.

Like the Mudd Club, bands at Tier 3 alternated with deejays (including residents Bob Gurevics, Simeon Gallu, and Sara Salir alongside several guest deejays), and there were a variety of other events, including film screenings and poetry readings.

McMahon: In the beginning, because it was a restaurant, there wasn't a deejay booth, they just put a table with the turntables on it in the middle of the floor. But people were tripping over wires, and people could make requests. As any deejay knows, it's not the cool people who are making a request for something you want to play, it's always somebody walking into a punk rock club and asking, "Can you play some Foreigner?" So we built a deejay booth, and it had a plywood extension built around the top which made it like six feet high, so there was no way to even see the deejay, let alone pester them. I painted a mural on it of an imposing-looking Russian border guard in a big fur hat, with a German shepherd on a leash and a rifle slung over his shoulder—clearly: do not enter.

McMahon's deejay booth was one of three murals in the club; the other two were painted by up-and-coming artists Kiki Smith and Jean-Michel Basquiat.

McMahon: There was one night where Kathleen was running out of the ladies' room, which was right around the corner from her perch at the end of the bar, and she was just screaming "That's it! He's 86'd! He's on the floor barking like a dog with a tampon in his mouth!"

Jean-Michel was in the ladies' room with probably half a dozen 18-year-old girls who are just hanging out, putting on makeup in the mirror, whatever, and he's on all fours amusing them by barking like a dog with the string from a tampon hanging from his mouth.

It was probably not the first time Kathleen had seen him do some kind of shenanigans, but it was perfectly harmless fun—who hasn't barked like a dog with a tampon hanging from their mouth to amuse some pretty girls? But whether he was actually 86'd after that incident, I doubt.

Despite the thriving scene around the club, tensions did arise between the club's owners and the younger staff—especially Hilary Jaeger.

Jaeger: Very early on, the owners decided to cut the bands' take from 100% down to 75%. Then it was cutting out bands on Saturdays, so they could just pay a deejay and still charge to get in. That made it hard to keep booking the bands I wanted to. I guess the writing was on the wall.

As we've seen over and over, one of the key elements that allows a scene to develop is for venues to have other income streams, so that they can take risks with bands who don't bring in large amounts of cash. Tier 3 didn't really have that: It was a restaurant during the day, but not a successful one. As the owners became more dependent on the club's profits for their bottom line, the leash tightened. Jaeger saw the band payouts get smaller and smaller, and staff amenities get chipped away, even though business was going well.

The first sign that the Mudd Club and (to a lesser extent) Tier 3 had spawned a monster came in 1980, when Howard Stein and Peppo Vanini, who had previously co-owned a garish and touristy Midtown disco called Xenon, opened a knock-off club called Rock Lounge (that name—*yikes*) at 285 West Broadway, two blocks north of Tier 3. Their clientele was a confusing mix of would-be Downtown hipsters who couldn't get into the Mudd Club and mildly adventurous bridge-and-tunnel disco types.

Throughout the second half of 1980, tensions between Tier 3's owners and its staff were coming to a head—exacerbated by the sudden appearance of bigger, slicker, and better-funded clubs like Rock Lounge.

In December 1980, on top of everything else, Tier 3 received an eviction notice.

McMahon: My sister and I went home to Pittsburgh for Christmas in 1980, and while we were gone, the marshal shuttered it. We both deejayed there, so that was where we kept our records—when the marshal padlocked the place, those records just went in the dumpster.

It's a little unclear what exactly happened after Tier 3's closure, but it seems that for a brief window, it reopened as a country-western bar called Frontier 3 (oof) where the centerpiece was a mechanical bull. After that, it became a club called Stillwende, which mimicked Tier 3's post-punk vibe, booking acts like Sonic Youth and Beastie Boys. That, too, was short-lived.

HIP-HOP ARRIVES DOWNTOWN

By the end of the decade, another homegrown sound was entering the mix among Mudd Club and Tier 3 regulars. Hip-hop[xi] has its roots in the Black and Latinx communities in the Bronx and Harlem; for geographic reasons, the story of its birth is beyond

---

xi   The terms "hip-hop" and "rap" are often used interchangeably, but they are not the same thing. "Rap" is a specific musical form in which lyrics are rhythmically spoken over a (often sample-based) musical backdrop; "hip-hop" is a larger artistic culture that contains rap alongside deejaying, graffiti, break dancing, and fashion. I've done my best to use the different terms where appropriate, but the discrepancies are often in the eye of the beholder: for example, rap records that include visual or lyrical nods to graffiti, break dancing, or hip-hop fashion become hip-hop records by definition. Many hip-hop clubs foregrounded rap performance and excluded some of the other elements, but because clubs incubate a cultural community in which all of these things exist, I've chosen to identify them across the board as hip-hop rather than rap venues.

the scope of this book.[xii] But for the purposes of this chapter, it's important to know three things: First, most of the people responsible for inventing hip-hop in the '70s were teens and preteens (in fact, legend has it that deejay Grand Wizzard Theodore invented record scratching when he was all of *twelve*). Second, the elements of hip-hop (rapping, deejaying, break dancing, and graffiti) initially existed as separate art forms with only occasional overlap in personnel. And third, early rappers in the '70s were essentially acting as hype men for deejays, and many of the earliest rappers didn't conceive of themselves as musicians in the traditional sense. It wasn't until the Sugar Hill Gang's 1979 single "Rapper's Delight" that most of the genre's originators realized that rapping could be commercially released as music in its own right.

But it's possible that hip-hop as we know it might have taken a completely different route to its eventual mainstream success were it not for two Mudd Club regulars: Michael Holman and Fab 5 Freddy.

Holman had come of age as a multiracial American kid on army bases across Europe before settling in California. While an undergrad at the University of San Francisco, he joined the new wave band the Tubes (of "White Punks on Dope" and "She's a Beauty" fame), taking a year off to tour with the group. Upon graduating in 1978, he moved to New York, and through a connection from the Tubes, he wound up in a young banker's training program at Chemical Bank.

Holman: I think my salary was around $30,000, which was a fortune back then. I would be working at the bank during the day, and then going out every night to all the coolest clubs—Max's Kansas City, CBGB, Tier 3, and eventually the Mudd Club.

In the daytime, I was kind of struggling to be involved in this world

---

xii   I'd especially recommend Joseph C. Ewoodzie Jr.'s 2017 book *Break Beats in the Bronx: Rediscovering Hip-hop's Early Years*, which analyzes the birth of hip-hop using a geographic, economic, and historic perspective similar to the one I've employed.

of banking and Wall Street. One day, maybe eight or nine months into my job at Chemical Bank, this drop of water hit the sheet of paper that I was working on, and the ink started to spread. I'll never forget it. I looked up at the ceiling, and then another drop hit. So I touched my face, and I realized I was crying because I was so miserable. I was trying to do the right thing having a job, but I realized, I can't do this. This isn't me; I'm an artist. I got up, put my jacket on, went to my boss's office, and quit at that moment. I walked out and never looked back at that world.

Holman was already spending a good amount of time hanging out with British-born artist Stan Peskett, a Tubes associate who had a loft at 533 Canal Street—a handful of blocks away from Tier 3. In early 1979, Holman was flipping through a copy of the *Village Voice* and came across an article about a graffiti crew called the Fabulous 5. The group's spokesman was Fred Braithwaite, an artist who went by the name Fab 5 Freddy. "His number was right there in the article," Holman recalled, "so I called him up and invited him over to Stan Peskett's loft, and the three of us started hanging."

A Bed-Stuy, Brooklyn, native, Fab 5 Freddy was practically guaranteed to be cool from the second he left the womb: his godfather was the legendary jazz drummer Max Roach, and other jazz giants would regularly drop by the Braithwaite house, including Thelonious Monk and Bud Powell.

Holman, Peskett, and Fab 5 Freddy decided to throw a party for the Fabulous 5 crew at Peskett's loft—dubbed Canal Zone—on April 29, 1979, inviting "the whole downtown art scene," as Holman put it. "That was really the very first time that the downtown scene rubbed shoulders with the uptown [Harlem and the Bronx] scene, that party. That was where Fab 5 Freddy and myself met Jean-Michel Basquiat for the first time."

At the time, Basquiat was only known for his omnipresent graffiti, which bore the tag "SAMO." Basquiat hit it off with both Fab 5 Freddy and Holman right away; the latter formed the band Gray with Basquiat that same night.

At the same time, Freddy was already paying attention to what was coming out of the Bronx and Harlem, listening to live recordings of rappers and emcees and going to see performers like Grandmaster Flash and the Furious Five. Inspired by the connections he saw between graffiti and this new music, Freddy soon began bringing some of his Downtown friends up to the Bronx, including Blondie's Debbie Harry and Chris Stein. In a 2022 podcast interview, Harry recalled, "It was like folk music to me, although musically it wasn't like folk music…it was a vox pops kind of situation[.]" In the same interview, Stein said, "I was very excited because, on a socio-political level, it was…all these marginalized kids finding a voice."[104]

Stein and Harry began evangelizing for hip-hop. From November 21-23, 1980, the art critic Edit d'Ak threw a multiday festival at the Kitchen called "Dubbed in Glamour"; though the event mostly featured Downtown mainstays like Bush Tetras, Anita Sarko, and actress/writer Cookie Mueller, it also saw Harry introducing a performance by the rap group Funky 4+1—the very first time a Bronx hip-hop act performed downtown. A few months later on Valentine's Day, 1981, when Harry hosted *Saturday Night Live*, she insisted on bringing the Funky 4+1 with her as a musical guest. Their performance of their signature song, "That's the Joint," was hip-hop's television debut.

In January 1981, between the Kitchen gig and the *SNL*, Blondie also released their single "Rapture." The song is one of Blondie's best, right up until the moment Harry starts rapping, at which point it becomes almost painful to listen to. But it was (technically) the first rap record to go to #1, and the first rap video shown on MTV. It's sad that it took a new wave band named for a hair color that only white people have to break those specific barriers on hip-hop's behalf, but not surprising in the least—it's the American music industry in a nutshell.[xiii]

---

xiii The "Rapture" video included appearances from Fab 5 Freddy and fellow graffiti artist Lee Quinones, as well as Jean-Michel Basquiat in the role of a deejay (he wasn't one, but Grandmaster Flash failed to show up).

Kool Moe Dee (rapper, Treacherous Three): Even though Blondie came from the downtown thing, she was aware of us, and I remember that being a big deal. I remember feeling like we must be making some kind of headway because now white artists are mentioning us.

As Grandmaster Flash told writer Jeff Chang, Freddy "was like one of the town criers. He would come into the hood where whites wouldn't come and then go downtown to where whites would, and say...'You gotta book these guys.'"[105] In April of 1981, Freddy curated an art show at the Mudd Club called "Beyond Words: Graffiti-Based, -Rooted, and -Inspired Work." The show made a case not only for graffiti as fine art, but for hip-hop culture and punk culture being simpatico, with Freddy including works by Iggy Pop and Suicide front man Alan Vega alongside graffiti artists like Lee Quinones, Rammellzee, Lady Pink, and Dondi. The show's opening night, April 9, included a hip-hop showcase on the club's main floor, with performances by Cold Crush Brothers, Fantastic Freaks, and Afrika Bambaataa's Jazzy Five MCs (an early iteration of what would become the Soulsonic Force).

Holman was similarly "getting deeper and deeper into this hip-hop world," he recalled. In the fall of 1981, Peskett introduced him to Malcolm McLaren, former manager of the Sex Pistols and current manager of the new wave band Bow Wow Wow. "Stan said, 'Michael's been involved with this Uptown culture,'" Holman said. "So I invited [McLaren] up to the Bronx to a Bambaataa throwdown park jam." Blown away by what he saw, McLaren asked Holman to assemble a hip-hop showcase as the opening act for Bow Wow Wow at The Ritz (125 East 11th Street; now Webster Hall) on September 15, 1981.

The resultant show included music from Afrika Bambaataa and the Soulsonic Force and DJ Jazzy Jay, break dancing by the Rock Steady Crew, and footage Holman had filmed of break-dancers and graffiti artists. And there it was: For the first time ever, the four defining elements of hip-hop (rapping, deejaying, break dancing, and graffiti) were presented together as a single culture…at a Bow Wow Wow show.

In attendance that night was Ruza Blue, a British expat who had been part of the post-punk "new romantic" scene at London's famed Blitz Club. In New York, Blue was working at McLaren's SoHo boutique, World's End, but had also taken over hosting Thursday dub reggae nights at a two-hundred-capacity, basement-level East Village club called Negril (181 2nd Avenue). Struck by what she witnessed at The Ritz, "She asked me to bring my hip-hop revue to her club," Holman recalled. "That was historic, because that was the first time that all the hip-hop elements came together in one club."

By the end of the year, Blue's Thursday night series at Negril was wholly devoted to hip-hop, with Holman sharing the booking duties. Afrika Bambaataa and Jazzy Jay became the club's primary deejays, Rock Steady Crew would break-dance, and performers like Cold Crush Brothers, Treacherous Three, Funky 4+1, and Rammellzee would come through and rap.

181 2nd Avenue.

Negril's Thursday night series was a hit, although as Kool Moe Dee noted, hip-hop's audience in the Bronx and Harlem "wouldn't venture downtown just because the artist had a chance to go downtown. One or two guys that you knew maybe would get on a train and go downtown, but most of the Harlem cats and the Bronx cats stayed in Harlem and the Bronx." Instead, the series drew an audience of (mostly white) Downtown scenesters, including David Byrne, Andy Warhol, Joey Ramone, John Lydon, Keith Haring, and Madonna.

In January 1982, Holman profiled Afrika Bambaataa for the *East Village Eye*, in a section called "New York Chillin' Out" that also featured an interview with Fab 5 Freddy, a break dancing photo spread, art from graffiti artist Futura 2000, and street fashion tutorials (the latter also by Holman). In his written intro to the Bambaataa interview, Holman referred to the "hip-hop, b-beat scene," and then defined hip-hop as "the all-inclusive tag for rapping, breaking, graffiti-writing, crew fashion-wearing street subculture."[106] It was the first time the scene was explicitly branded and defined in print.

Claude "Paradise" Gray (producer, X-Clan; hip-hop archivist): The acceptance that hip-hop music and culture got from the punk community and the gay community that those clubs were primarily serving—a lot of diverse people were so accepting of hip-hop partially because they understood what it was like to be discriminated against. So they gave us access to spaces that we didn't have traditionally. People with access and money started taking notice.

I want to be very clear here: This is not a "white savior" narrative. The embrace of hip-hop—a culture by and for teenagers of color—by an audience of mostly white adults is a loaded subject, to say the least, and really a book unto itself.[xiv] But it's unequivocally true that a number of mostly-white post-punk outsiders—whose

---

xiv   Specifically, Dan Charnas's 2010 book *The Big Payback*.

minds and ears had already been expanded by the Mudd Club deejays and mutant disco bands—played a crucial role in helping get
hip-hop music and culture onto the larger world stage. Whether
that's a sign of vibrant cross-cultural exchange, a sign of how little
power young Black people wielded in the music industry at the
time, or both, is a much larger discussion.

Unfortunately, Ruza Blue and Michael Holman's run at Negril
didn't last long—the two had a falling out, and Negril was temporarily shuttered in February 1982 after the fire department raided
the club for being over capacity. But neither of their stories end
there—we'll pick them back up in Chapter Eight.

SONIC YOUTH

When Sonic Youth first formed in 1981, they were somewhat awkwardly part of the mutant disco camp, fusing no wave guitar noise
with a danceable rhythm section—although that dance element reflected the influence of their mutant disco peers and British post-
punk bands more than any sort of direct disco influence. To that
end, the band's drummer, Richard Edson, was also a trumpeter in
mutant disco kingpins Konk—a more successful band at the time.

Soon after forming, Sonic Youth's guitarist Thurston Moore
and keyboardist Ann DeMarinis organized Noise Fest, which ran
from June 16-24, 1981, at White Columns, a gallery at 325 Spring
Street in SoHo. The festival seems almost like a direct sequel to
the 1978 Artists' Space festival that spawned *No New York*: the
lineup featured several bands from (or descended from) the initial
crop of no wave bands—including Rhys Chatham, Glenn Branca,
Ut, Robin Crutchfield's Dark Day, Y Pants, and Mofungo. Underscoring no wave's art world roots, the gallery displayed an art
show with pieces from several musicians on the scene, including
Robin Crutchfield, DNA's Ikue Mori, Sonic Youth's Kim Gordon, Liquid Liquid's Richard McGuire, Suicide's Alan Vega, Ut's
Nina Canal, and Glenn Branca.

It was a transformative event for Sonic Youth: DeMarinis was
already planning to leave, and it was at Noise Fest that Sonic Youth

found her replacement, guitarist Lee Ranaldo. Ranaldo, who had been playing in Glenn Branca's band, had his first rehearsals with Sonic Youth in the White Columns space after the festival's conclusion, and became a core member of the band. Edson was on his way out, as well—he was more interested in Konk's punk/disco/Latin fusion and felt that the no wave bands at Noise Fest had been "too straight and too white and too middle class, so I didn't take it that seriously."[107] [xv]

With Ranaldo on board, and Tier 3 regular Bob Bert as their new drummer, Sonic Youth shed the mutant disco influences and delved deeper into no wave's artier, noisier side. As mutant disco began to separate back into post-punk and dance music factions in the mid-eighties, Sonic Youth would become no wave's most successful descendants by a mile.

Bert: No one gave two shits about them at the time, and no one could foresee the future of what they would become. If you would have told me in 1985 that I would still be talking about Sonic Youth in 2014, I would have thought, "What are you, fucking nuts?"

THE DECLINE

DJ Mojo (deejay; doorman, Hurrah, Berlin, Pyramid Club): If you want to talk about a club dying a slow and painful death, that was the Mudd Club.

In 1981, interesting things were still happening at the Mudd Club, not the least of which was the transformation of 77 White Street's third and fourth floors into the Mudd Club's very own art gallery, curated by up-and-coming artist Keith Haring. Still, the regulars were moving on, and it was tangibly transforming into the very

---

xv Edson would go on to find success as a character actor, appearing in *Ferris Bueller's Day Off, Good Morning Vietnam, Platoon, Do the Right Thing, Stranger Than Paradise,* and *Howard the Duck,* among other films.

thing it set out not to be: a trashy hub for starfuckers and bridge-and-tunnel types.

According to a few people I spoke to, Steve Mass was also becoming harder to work for. By this point, Mass had moved into a loft at Franklin and Broadway, spitting distance from the Mudd Club, and installed closed-circuit security cameras so that he could keep tabs on the club's activity from his apartment. Most of the club's star deejays (including Justin Strauss, Johnny Dynell, and Anita Sarko) had left for greener pastures, as had Joey Kelly and Richard Boch.

> *Boch: Steve wasn't coming to the Mudd Club as much. I think there was a lot of paranoia on so many levels; he didn't have people there who he trusted any more. By '82, I think Steve had moonlighting cops [working the door]. When the cops were just acting as security they were the best, but as far as doing the door, forget it.*

Looking to inject new blood into the operation and/or ride another club's coattails, Mass did a bulk hiring of people affiliated with Club 57, a bar and art space located in a church basement at 57 St. Marks Place (no relation to Club 82). Run by actress and singer Ann Magnuson, Club 57 was another home for a social circle which overlapped heavily with the Mudd Club and Tier 3 scenes (most notably, Keith Haring, Klaus Nomi, and the B-52s were Club 57 regulars). Although it was largely known for elaborate theme parties, art installations, campy movie screenings, dance parties, and performance art, the tiny basement space occasionally hosted bands—including Liquid Liquid, the Misfits, the Fleshtones, Plasmatics, and Sonic Youth.[xvi]

Among the Club 57-ites Mass hired was one of their resident deejays, Dany Johnson. Johnson had grown up in Cheshire, CT, "the same town Legs McNeil is from." Though Johnson was younger, the two remained friends, and she would come down to

---

xvi Club 57 also promoted larger shows at Irving Plaza.

visit McNeil and see shows at CBGB and Max's. "They weren't checking anyone's age at the time," Johnson recalled. "I looked like I was about 12."

After high school, Johnson relocated to the city and started hanging out at the Mudd Club, Tier 3, and Club 57—all of which had working female deejays. "Seeing Anita Sarko and [Club 57 deejay] Naomi Regelson and [Tier 3/Hurrah deejay] Sara Salir really gave you the idea in that scene that women can do it," Johnson noted, "because otherwise you wouldn't have even thought it was a possibility." She made her debut at Club 57 in 1980, and swiftly became that club's main deejay. For Jonny Sender, who also had his first deejaying experiences at Club 57, "Dany was the best deejay of all the deejays."

After Anita Sarko left the Mudd Club, Johnson was brought in as her replacement.

Johnson: I was paid $60 a night. I didn't really like working there that much. I didn't like that the deejay booth was in the bar and people would be hanging over it trying to get drinks. People were messy there. Some of your friends would show up and it would be fun, but bridge-and-tunnel [people] were in there too.

After a while you just get sick of hearing, "I want to hear [Devo's] 'Whip It,'" "Come on, play 'Whip it!'" I was such a bitch, I would say, "Oh, sure," and then I'd play [Dazz Band's] "Let It Whip" instead. Or I'd be a total bitch and say, "Oh, how does it go?" And then some drunk person would be singing it really terribly. "Oh, I didn't catch that. How does it go again?"

Mass's attempt to revitalize the Mudd Club with the Club 57 personnel didn't go as planned. By late '82, the Mudd Club had stopped charging admission; Mass knew things were coming to a close there, and he was planning to open a new club (it never materialized). The Mudd Club finally closed its doors in early 1983; having bought the building from Ross Bleckner in 1980, Mass sold it back to him and walked away.

AREA

Legendary clubs in New York (and elsewhere) can largely be divided into two camps: exclusive and inclusive. The Mudd Club,
with its tight door policies and VIP areas, epitomizes the former;
Tier 3, with its welcoming, all-for-one clubhouse feel, is a perfect
example of the latter. If it wasn't already obvious, this author's admitted preference is for the inclusive clubs, but scenes often re-
quire a give-and-take between the two to flourish: the exclusive
clubs give a scene the necessary space to define itself, and the inclusive clubs grant outsiders the opportunity to become insiders.
Of course, it really helps if the two are as geographically close as
the Mudd Club and Tier 3 were.

It's worth emphasizing that neither the Mudd Club nor Tier 3
closed as a direct result of gentrification. Rather, they were victims of their own success: they were so influential that they bred
larger, swankier, better-funded clubs with whom they simply could
not compete. It's market capitalism 101. As Mass put it, "Here,
this idiot took a loft...and built one of the most notorious, publicized nightclubs in the world... People said, 'If this jerk can do
it, why can't I?'"[108]

Another club was far more pivotal in Tribeca's gentrification:
Area, which opened in 1983 at 157 Hudson Street, just a few blocks
north from where Artists' Space had been. Founded by Mudd Club
regulars Shawn Hausman and Eric Goode, along with Darius Azari
and Goode's brother Christopher Goode, Area was Tribeca's first
megaclub. Taking over a 12,500-square-foot space that had once
been pony express stables, Area was the Mudd Club's punk/art/
elitism mix on steroids. The club contained several large glass display cases that displayed thematically linked art installations, which
were overhauled every six weeks.

Area also hired familiar faces from the Mudd Club days, including deejays Justin Strauss, Johnny Dynell, Anita Sarko, and Dany
Johnson, as well as Jean-Michel Basquiat (who also became a deejay there). Strauss remains in awe of his time at Area, referring to it
as one of his two favorite clubs of all time, alongside Paradise Ga-

rage. Johnson is more muted in her assessment, noting that "Area at least was fun. I've got nothing bad to say about Area."

Sender: Area pulled from everywhere. It just seemed like everybody you knew was working there. Despite all the great things people say about Area, I found that it looked like a suburban mall inside, with these big display cases that were like the display cases at a department store. Despite all the installations they would do, it never really changed the internal environment that much. It felt like money had entered the scene at that point in a way that it hadn't before. I think that something was really lost there.

Like the Mudd Club before it, Area drew a mix of celebrities and Downtown scenesters. But it was especially magnetic for Downtown's new class of suddenly wealthy art stars like Basquiat, Haring, and Julian Schnabel—and for the agents, dealers, investors, collectors, fashion industry bigwigs, and advertising execs that glommed on to them. Where music had been a decidedly second-tier element at the Mudd Club, it was even further demoted at Area—wealth, celebrity, and spectacle were the real attractions.

By the time Area opened, celebrities had started moving to Tribeca in droves. This was largely thanks to actor Robert De Niro, who became an evangelist for the neighborhood after "discovering" it while preparing for his role in 1980's *Raging Bull*. De Niro has been waving Tribeca's flag ever since, and he owns a piece of several high-end restaurants and hotels in the area. Now Tribeca has practically become New York City's Celebrity District—the kind of neighborhood where, for example, Taylor Swift might buy Dominique Strauss-Kahn's old house at 153 Franklin Street for $18 million (as she did in 2017).

Boch: I stayed in my loft until 2005. The neighborhood's changes are one of the things that made me not feel sad about leaving. It became a suburb for kids and young adults who grew up on Park Avenue and

*got married and had their kids, and their parents bought them a loft
on Warren Street or Murray Street or North Moore Street.*

Though few of the no wave and mutant disco bands found much
in the way of mainstream success, interest in these Downtown mi-
croscenes has only grown in the twenty-first century, with a steady
stream of books, documentaries, museum exhibits, high-profile
compilations, and gussied-up reissues commemorating their legacies. But some elements have been, if not wholly omitted, then at
the very least underacknowledged. Tier 3, for one, should be in the
pantheon of great New York venues, but it's been largely ignored
in favor of the more overtly glamorous Mudd Club.

I suspect that part of Tier 3's historic dismissal has to do with
the fact that, where the Mudd Club was owned and run by one
attention-loving man, Tier 3 was owned and run by down-
to-earth women. Hilary Jaeger, one of the most influential and
pivotal nonperformers on the scene, has rarely been acknowledged
as such in the decades since the club's closure. It is my hope that
this book can play some small part in elevating both Jaeger and
Tier 3 to the venerable positions they deserve.

But even beyond Tier 3, it's important to note that the no wave
and mutant disco scenes were uniquely female driven, more so
than any other communities or genres discussed here. Anya Philips was instrumental in the Mudd Club's conception, although she
was driven out before she could glean the benefits. Anita Sarko,
Dany Johnson, Naomi Regelson, and Sara Salir led the charge from
their respective deejay booths. All four bands on the *No New York*
compilation had female members, and unlike the male-dominated
punk scene that preceded it, there were several all-female no wave
and mutant disco bands, including Pulsallama, Ut, Y Pants, ESG,
and the Bloods (the latter of which is widely acknowledged as the
first rock band to have all members identify as lesbians). And although Bush Tetras had a male drummer, their musical and lyrical perspective was pointedly female-driven.

But of course, the music industry is obnoxiously male-driven.
Dany Johnson acknowledged that throughout her deejay career, "I

was always paid less than the guys—I knew, because they'd tell me what they would get." She was also a target for harassment from male employers. "The things people would just say right to me, you wouldn't believe," she said. "But when you see a full dance floor, it's worth it."

While there is a long lineage of male musicians and deejays growing into elder statesmen, that's a luxury few women are afforded. Of the many people discussed in the chapter who are still alive, the majority of the men remain professionally involved in the music industry in one way or another. Very few of the women can say the same.

> *Johnson: A woman in her thirties is old. You know, these [male deejays] can keep going 'til they're seventy, but you don't see any women. That's something that Anita was also struggling with, that was upsetting her. Of course, you don't kill yourself just because you don't get invited to parties anymore.*

Anita Sarko went on to deejay at Danceteria and the Palladium; by the '90s she was largely deejaying at fashion shows and working as a journalist for outlets like *Interview* and *Paper*. In 2010, she was diagnosed with both ovarian and uterine cancer; she beat them both, but there were lingering pains. She was also struggling professionally, with gratifying work growing increasingly scarce. According to *Village Voice* writer Michael Musto, Sarko found that "employers were looking for recent college grads, not old-timers with history and personality," which left her feeling "discarded and unappreciated."[109]

Anita Sarko died by suicide on October 15, 2015. She was sixty-eight years old.

AFTERLIFE OF THE NO WAVE/MUTANT DISCO SCENE

In 2005, Ross Bleckner sold the old Mudd Club building at 77 White Street for $6 million; it has since been converted into luxury condos. In 2016, the fourth floor—once Rosie Schuster and Dan Aykroyd's apartment, later the Mudd Club's art gallery—sold for $3,600,000. A makeshift plaque on the building, courtesy of the public arts organization Creative Time, reads "The Mudd Club— 1978-1981," which is incorrect. The Mudd Club closed in 1983.

In 1990, Steve Mass opened a restaurant called Cannes 46 on Church Street, not far from the Mudd Club's old home, but it only lasted a few months. Later that year, Mass moved to Germany, and in 2001, he opened a new Mudd Club in Berlin at Große Hamburger Straße 17. It closed in 2011.

Tier 3 (225 West Broadway) became a series of other nightclubs—Stillwende, the Night Gallery, Garbo's, and Birdland West—before turning to quieter options as the neighborhood changed. Hilary Jaeger noted that Tier 3 seemed to be comprised of two awkwardly conjoined buildings; they have since been redivided. Their respective storefronts currently house Rigor Hill Market, an upscale grocery store, and Terra, a wine bar and Italian restaurant.

Jaeger: I always thought, I wonder if they know there's a Jean-Michel Basquiat under that painted wall that's probably worth millions? Should I say anything?

The Kitchen is alive and kicking, although it relocated to 512 West 19th Street in 1986. The Kitchen's old Tribeca space is now home to the Owen James Gallery.

In 1994, the former Artists' Space at 105 Hudson Street became the first-ever location of the upscale sushi restaurant Nobu, which is now a multinational chain (Robert De Niro is part owner). Nobu relocated in 2017; the space has remained vacant ever since.

Negril (181 2nd Avenue) is now the basement level of Village East Cinemas.

Area (157 Hudson Street) closed in 1987 and became a series of other clubs—most significantly, the house music club Shelter.

The ground floor is now Officine Gullo, an Italian purveyor of bespoke kitchens; the rest of the building is residential.

Suggested Listening

Rhys Chatham—*Guitar Trio* (1977)

Various—*No New York* (1978)

Glenn Branca—*The Ascension* (1981)

Grandmaster Flash and the Furious Five—*The Message* (1982)

Sonic Youth—*Sonic Youth* (1982)

Liquid Liquid—*Optimo* (1983)

Treacherous Three—*The Treacherous Three* (1984)

Gray—*Shades Of* (rec. 198?)

Bush Tetras—*Rhythm and Paranoia* (compilation)

Konk—*The Sound of KONK* (compilation)

7

THE BIG APPLE ROTTEN TO
THE CORE: MUSIC AND CONFLICT
IN ALPHABET CITY

Lee Ving (singer/guitarist, Fear; bartender, Slugs' Saloon): It
was a war zone. That neighborhood was rotten, rampant with heroin addicts, and the violence that accompanies it was everywhere. It
was a pandemic.

Harley Flanagan (drummer, the Stimulators; bassist, Cro-Mags):
I have no interest in even being around that area anymore. I think
people really romanticize a lot of it. For me, it was really fucked up,
and I have really bad PTSD from life down there. I spent a lot of
years really fucking high on drugs trying to deal with that shit—a
lot of PCP, huffing glue, heroin, crystal meth, you fucking name it.
That neighborhood really fucked me up.

On the far eastern edge of the East Village is the area known colloquially as Alphabet City, so named because while the major-

ity of the city is laid out on a numeric grid system (i.e. 1st Street, 2nd Avenue), the four short avenues that comprise the area's main thoroughfares are instead named after letters—Avenues A, B, C, and D. At the neighborhood's heart lies the 10.5-acre Tompkins Square Park. Bordered by Avenue A to the west, Avenue B to the east, East 10th Street to the north, and East 7th Street to the south, the park has been a hub of activity for the immigrant neighborhood since it first opened in 1850. Some of that activity is the kind you'd find in any city park—kids playing, old people feeding the pigeons, community groups gathering for meetings, athletes playing basketball or handball—and some of it reflects the area's rich creative history, like the many concerts staged in the park's legendary band shell.

But it's tough to talk about the history of Tompkins Square Park without also talking about its long life as a place of unrest.

In 1857, seven years after the park first opened, German immigrants protesting food shortages and mass unemployment were met with force from the police. In 1863, the park was at the center of the New York Draft Riots, a five-day violent uprising of working-class whites ostensibly sparked by the nationally instituted draft for service in the American Civil War, but which quickly transformed into a racially charged assault on Black people, homes, and businesses. With an official death toll of 119 (though the actual number is likely ten times that), it remains the deadliest riot in US history. In 1874, thousands of unemployed locals, infuriated about the lack of employment opportunities, clashed with the NYPD. In 1877, five thousand locals who'd peacefully assembled to hear communist orators were attacked by police and the National Guard. Most relevant to our narrative is the 1988 Tompkins Square Park riot, when police charged a crowd protesting a park curfew and a violent melee broke out, leaving forty-four people injured.[110]

And those are just the big ones. But this isn't to place blame for this history on the residents of Alphabet City. From early on in the neighborhood's existence, the fact that immigrants called it home led it to be neglected by the city, which led to a lack of resources

that made living there difficult. Police often seemed more interested in fighting residents than protecting them.

But when hippies began moving to the neighborhood en masse
in the '60s, the neighborhood suddenly had a new stress to deal
with—one that would loom in the background of every story of
every band the neighborhood produced: the tension between those
who were born into poverty and those who had entered into it as
a lifestyle choice.

For much of the 1800s, Alphabet City was part of a larger German immigrant neighborhood in what's now the East Village,
often referred to as *Kleindeutschland*, or "Little Germany." But the
neighborhood experienced a sudden, drastic change on June 15,
1904, when the PS *General Slocum*, a ship carrying 1,342 *Kleindeutschland* residents to a church picnic, caught fire and sank in the
East River. Only 321 of them survived; until the attacks of September 11, 2001, it was the deadliest incident in the city's history.
With much of its population decimated, *Kleindeutschland* became an
ever-changing patchwork of low-income immigrant communities,
which at various points included Irish, Eastern European Jewish,
Polish, Greek, Russian, Ukrainian, and Puerto Rican residents.

But with its cheap rents and no single community claiming
dominance over the area, it became attractive to bohemians: folk
singer Lead Belly lived at 414 East 10th Street between C and D
for much of the '40s; saxophonist Charlie Parker lived at 151 Avenue B from 1950 to 1954; around the same time, Beat poets and
then-lovers Allen Ginsberg and William S. Burroughs lived together at 206 East 7th Street between B and C (Jack Kerouac was
a frequent houseguest). And as noted in Chapter One, folk singers
Noel Paul Stookey and Tom Paxton lived together at 629 E. 5th
Street, between B and C, in the early '60s.

In 1964, poet Ed Sanders leased a former kosher butcher shop at
383 E. 10th Street between B and C for $50 a month and opened
the Peace Eye Bookstore. In addition to selling poetry chapbooks
and subversive literature, the Peace Eye was home to regular rehearsals and occasional performances by Sanders's band, the Fugs.

His bandmate Naftuli "Tuli" Kupferberg conveniently lived next door at 381; Sanders himself moved to the neighborhood in 1966 with his wife and daughter, renting an apartment at 196 Ave. A. Sanders later recalled that at the time, "the streets were safe enough to go down to the park and let our kids dance in the water fountains."[111]

In 1966, a band shell was erected in Tompkins Square Park, with Jimi Hendrix and the Grateful Dead among the early performers to grace its stage. Those shows were indicative of a larger shift within the neighborhood: As journalist Pete Hamill later wrote, "Many middle-class kids started coming to the neighborhood, to play for a while at poverty and rebellion. The truly poor resented them, because if they got into any real trouble they could always call Daddy for a check."[112]

It was around this time that the phrase "East Village" was first applied to the portion of the Lower East Side above Houston Street—positioning the area as a hip alternative to Greenwich Village, whose bohemian stock was declining amidst the influx of tourists and Johnny-come-latelies. And of course, those tourists drew an increased NYPD presence that paid especially close attention to the sale and consumption of narcotics; the comparatively unpoliced "East Village" held no such risks for drug users. By 1967, the media and real estate industry had adopted the "East Village" designation, reconfiguring the public perception of the area from a working-class immigrant neighborhood to an edgy bohemian enclave.

Rents skyrocketed, and tensions between locals and new arrivals came to the fore. On Memorial Day, 1967, a noise complaint from a nearby resident led to a clash between two-hundred NYPD officers and a group of peaceful guitar-and-bongo-playing hippies in Tompkins Square Park, with forty-one people arrested. Those cases were unilaterally thrown out by criminal court judge Herman Weinkrantz, who claimed that "this court will not deny equal protection to the unwashed, unshod, unkempt, and uninhibited."[113]

During a band shell performance by the psychedelic band the Group Image a few days later, the *Village Voice* reported, "A group

of Puerto Rican youths, upset by the hippies' newly-won dominance of the park, rained rocks and beer cans on the musicians."
Soon after, the *Voice* noted, during another performance by an unidentified folk rock band, "Puerto Ricans came to the band shell
and demanded Latin music," resulting in another scuffle between
longtime residents and newly-arrived hippies.[114]

In an attempt to ease tensions, a group of hippies and Puerto
Rican activists staged a concert in the park with performances by
Cuban percussionist Mongo Santamaria and folk singer Len Chandler, emceed by activist Carlos "Chino" Garcia. The concert itself
was successful, with a mixed audience of hippies and Puerto Rican
people enjoying the music. But the Memorial Day clash and its
aftermath kicked off a cycle that would play out in the neighborhood over and over again in the decades to come.

SLUGS'

As hippies were streaming into the neighborhood, Alphabet City
was also nurturing a thriving avant-garde jazz scene. This was in
large part thanks to Slugs' Saloon, a cramped bar and jazz venue
at 242 East 3rd Street between B and C, which was opened in
1964 by owners Jerry Schultz and Robert Schoenholt. The name
was, apparently, a nod to the "three-brained beings" mentioned
in G.I. Gurdjieff's *Beelzebub's Tales to His Grandson*; as for the "Saloon" portion, it was swiftly removed when the owners were no-
tified that their establishment did not meet the Liquor Authority's
criteria for saloon-ship. It was renamed "Slugs' in the Far East."

Slugs' became a regular destination for local musicians, who
would come to watch each other, hang out, and network. Many
of them just happened to be some of the best and most renowned
players in the world: legend has it that saxophonist Hank Mob-
ley lived in the building when the bar opened and was responsible for convincing Schultz and Schoenholt to book live jazz in
the first place. Neighborhood regulars included Jackie McLean,
the first live act booked at Slugs', who lived nearby at Avenue D
and Houston Street. Bassist Henry Grimes, clarinetist Perry Rob-

242 East 3rd Street.

inson, and drummer Tom Price all lived together at 272 E. 3rd, one block away from the club, and pianist Cecil Taylor lived two blocks northeast, at 344 E. 4th Street.

But perhaps most significantly, from 1962 to 1967, the members of the Sun Ra Arkestra lived, rehearsed, and recorded together in a townhouse at 48 East 3rd Street. From 1966 until the club's closing in 1972, the Sun Ra Arkestra played at Slugs' every Monday night, with sets typically running for six uninterrupted hours, from 10:00 p.m. until the club closed at 4:00 a.m. The length and regularity of the gigs gave the group the space and flexibility to experiment with different approaches and angles. At times, the group would play in total darkness, other times they'd project films behind them. One night, the music would be all percussion, with the Arkestra members playing all kinds of hand drums and gongs; another night, they'd all be playing exotic stringed instruments. Band members often fanned out across the space during performances, with some even performing inside the club's bathroom.

Ving: When Sun Ra would come in, Slugs' would turn into a festival. He'd start on the stage, and then pretty soon he's off the stage and he's dancing and walking around Slugs' with all of his singers and all of his musicians, there might have been thirty of them. And he'd have dancers, four or five or six women, and they're all dancing around the perimeter of the room and singing "Space is the Place."

Still, rent at 48 East 3rd was consistently difficult to make; a *Newsweek* article from 1966 has the band being paid $117 for one night's work at Slugs', which was then split among eleven band members. In 1968, the Arkestra relocated to Philadelphia—again moving into a group townhouse at 5626 Morton Street, where surviving members of the Arkestra reside to this day—but they maintained their Monday night residency at Slugs', driving up each week, playing for six hours, and then heading back to Philadelphia at around 5:00 a.m.

Bartender Lee Capallero—who would later rename himself Lee Ving, front the notorious LA hardcore punk band Fear, and act in both *Flashdance* and *Clue*—began working at Slugs' in the early '70s. Ving was already a working rock musician, having fronted a blues band called Sweet Stavin Chain in his native Philadelphia, but he was also a devoted jazz fan who studied under famed guitarists Jim Hall and John Abercrombie.[i]

Ving: As I'm working there, I'm seeing all my heroes that I had never seen before, from McCoy Tyner and Charles Mingus on down. It was a magical thing for me, a musical education. Even though it was in a hellhole of a neighborhood, people from all over the [world] would come to the bar; they'd get out of their taxis from Copenhagen and come right in to Slugs'.

---

i   Ving later wrote Fear's classic 1982 song "New York's Alright If You Like Saxophones" in reaction to some of his experiences around Slugs', especially the pretentious anti-rock sentiments harbored by many jazz afficionados.

By that point, the city's economic fortunes were declining, and Alphabet City had become progressively more crime ridden. The gruesome and highly publicized murder of socialite-turned-hippie Linda Rae Fitzpatrick and her boyfriend James "Groovy" Hutchinson in the basement of 169 Avenue B in October 1967 had put a swift end to the Summer of Love in the city, and the neighborhood's tide of hippies soon began to recede.

Things at Slugs' took a turn for the worse on February 19, 1972, when trumpeter Lee Morgan was shot and killed at the club by his common-law wife, Helen Morgan. Schultz and Schoenholt sold the club to doorman Ernie Holman, who ran it for another few months before it shuttered.[ii]

LOISAIDA

Throughout the '50s and '60s, the Puerto Rican immigrant community in the Lower East Side had grown. From the outset, they were met with open racism from both the NYPD and the Eastern European immigrant communities they lived alongside. Carlos "Chino" Garcia was a member of that Puerto Rican community in Alphabet City. He moved to the city at the age of five in 1951, and by the time he was ten years old, he had joined the Assassins, a local Puerto Rican gang who were part of the city's large teen gang culture. But though he was initially drawn to gang life "to protect ourselves from other nationalities," Garcia soon realized that the problems his community faced were in fact coming from "a society [that] is attacking us through the Board of Education, housing situation, jobs."[115]

Garcia's parents sent him to live with relatives in Puerto Rico for a time, where he was exposed to new political ideologies; when he returned to New York, he was determined to fight systemic racism. In 1964, Garcia and fellow activist Angelo González co-

---

ii   It is significant that Holman was Black—making him briefly one of the very, very few Black jazz club owners in New York (and likely the world) at the time, despite the music's Black roots.

founded the Real Great Society, a youth collective organized to help people in their community obtain education, job training, and self-sufficiency. In 1965, Garcia—along with Humberto Crespo, Angelo Gonzáles, Roy Battiste, (Moses) Anthony Figueroa, and Sal Becker—formed a splinter group called CHARAS (named for their first initials), which aimed to address larger issues, including arts, environmentalism, and housing.

By the early '70s, with Eastern European families and hippies both leaving the neighborhood, the Puerto Rican community became predominant within the neighborhood. Unfortunately, this shift coincided with the city's mounting economic misfortunes. At the same time, the mass exodus of industries from Lower Manhattan—especially the garment industry—put a considerable number of Alphabet City residents out of work. It's depressing but not surprising that those in power opted to invest what little money they had in maintaining services in better-off (which is to say, predominantly white) neighborhoods. With the number of police in the city reduced, their presence in Alphabet City declined substantially, and crime escalated—especially drug dealing.[iii]

On top of it all, local landlords were finding it more lucrative to burn down their buildings (sometimes with tenants still inside) and collect insurance money, or to simply abandon them to rot, rather than pay taxes and maintenance. The city systematically repossessed these technically uninhabitable buildings, but due to the ongoing economic distress, they were unable to do much of anything with them. Slowly but surely, the husks of these forgotten buildings began to attract squatters who would break in, live rent-free, and rehabilitate them.

Despite it all, the 1970s were something of a golden age for Puerto Rican culture in the area. Local actor and poet Bittman

---

iii   A popular mnemonic device to guide outsiders through the area noted "A is alcohol, B is blow, C is crack, D is death." You may have also heard it as "A for aware, B for beware, C for caution, D for death," or "A, you're adventurous, B, you're bold, C, you're courageous, and D"—yup, you guessed it—"you're dead."

"Bimbo" Rivas even bestowed a new name upon the neighbor-hood in his 1974 poem "Loisaida"—a heavily accented Spang-lish pronunciation of "Lower East Side." As Chino Garcia noted, "[T]he Latinos on the Lower East Side had a hard time always say-ing Lower East Side. So by saying Loisaida in Spanglish, it created a word for them to use...and it's a sense of identity that you get from naming a neighborhood."[116]

In 1973, poet Miguel Algarín, who had been hosting poetry readings in his apartment for years, co-founded the Nuyorican Poets Cafe at 505 East 6th Street. The club, which went on to play a major role in the development of slam poetry, is still going strong to this day, though it relocated to a larger space at 236 East 3rd Street in 1981.

In 1976, Eddie Figueroa—an actor and member of the gang-turned-activist group the Young Lords—took over the storefront at 101 Avenue A. Originally a German beer hall, it had recently housed two short-lived jazz venues, the East Village In and the Jazz Boat. Figueroa transformed it into the New Rican Village, a venue that showcased local Puerto Rican musicians (including Manny Oquendo, Mario Rivera and the Salsa Refugees, and the Fort Apache Band) alongside art, theater, dance, and poetry from the Loisaida community. It remained in the space until 1979, when it closed due to financial problems.

At the end of the '70s, CHARAS was headquartered in the Christodora Building, located at 143 Avenue B. The Christodora had been built in 1928 as settlement housing for low-income and immigrant tenants, aiming to provide them with food, shelter, work, and education. Its imposing sixteen-story frame cost over $1 million to build, and it contained a music school, a gym, a swimming pool, offices, and workshops. But by 1948, the finan-cial difficulty of operating such a complex led the Christodora's management to sell it to the city for $1.6 million.

The city intended to use the building as a welfare agency and community center, but for whatever reason never got around to doing it. Instead, the building stood empty for years, during which it hosted numerous squatters, including both CHARAS and the

Black Panthers (it also reportedly served as a set for numerous low-budget porn movies around this time). But the city sold it for $63,000 in 1978; CHARAS, naturally, were evicted.

They didn't have to look far for a new home. In 1979, CHARAS began squatting in an abandoned public school, PS 64, at 605 East 9th Street—one building over from the Christodora. The school ceased operations in 1977, and in the two intervening years the building had fallen into disrepair and become a shooting gallery for junkies. Under CHARAS's direction, PS 64 became *El Bohio* ("the Hut"), a community center that served the neighborhood in a wide variety of ways, hosting everything from bicycle repair workshops to English lessons to twelve-step meetings to martial arts classes. Luís Guzman and John Leguizamo both studied acting there. Though it predominantly served the Puerto Rican population, *El Bohio* welcomed all comers: it was the longtime home of the Czechoslovak-American Marionette Theater, a teenage Spike Lee had his first film screening there, and it rented out rehearsal spaces to a wide range of musicians over the years, including loft jazz mainstay Jemeel Moondoc and the scuzzy rock band Pussy Galore.

When musicians (especially white musicians) talk about coming to Alphabet City in the late '70s and '80s, they often describe a dangerous, desolate, and derelict neighborhood that more or less doubled as an open-air drug supermarket—all of which is fundamentally true. But it's important to remember that theirs was an outsider's view. For many of them, Alphabet City's lawlessness was part of the attraction—loud music, late hours, and underage drinking were all A-OK, not because there wasn't anybody around to complain (as had been the case in SoHo and Tribeca), but because the locals were treated as second-class citizens by cops who simply didn't give a shit. But the music scenes that took root in Alphabet City during that period weren't springing up in a total cultural vacuum. There was a preexisting, flourishing Puerto Rican bohemian culture onto which these predominantly white artists were (at times unwittingly, at times apathetically) superimposing themselves.

THE STIMULATORS

In the '70s and '80s, 437 East 12th Street, between Avenue A and 1st Avenue, was known as the "Poet's Building." Its most famous resident was Allen Ginsberg, who lived there with his partner and fellow poet Peter Orlovsky. Other longtime tenants included author Lucy Sante, and musicians Richard Hell (of Television, the Heartbreakers, and the Voidoids), Susan Springfield (the Erasers), Rhys Chatham, and Arthur Russell. In the mid-seventies, the building was also home to a pair of sisters, Rose Feliu and Denise Mercedes, as well as Rose's young son, Harley Flanagan. Feliu and Mercedes, both consummate scenesters, had been associates of Ginsberg's since the mid-sixties.

Mercedes: It was kind of like the rock and roll dormitory. It was very inexpensive—I think people in that building were paying [around] $250, $350. It was still in a dangerous neighborhood at that point; there was some gang activity on the block which made it scary. [David Bowie guitarist] Mick Ronson once came over when me and Rose were having some party or something, and he said it was the scariest place he'd ever been. He really respected me for wanting to rock 'n' roll and living there in order to be able to do it. It still makes me laugh a little bit, because we didn't see it as that bad.

By the mid-seventies, Mercedes had already played in a glam rock band called Stutz and jammed with the likes of Link Wray and Iggy Pop. Around 1975, Ginsberg brought her into Bob Dylan's orbit. Dylan brought her and Ginsberg along on his fabled Rolling Thunder Revue tour that year, and she appears in Dylan's semifictional 1978 tour movie *Renaldo and Clara.*

Her credentials were etched in stone, but as for the punk scene that was exploding at CBGB and Max's Kansas City, Mercedes recalls, "I had seen many of the New York bands that were considered the punk bands, and I wasn't feeling terribly energized by it." It wasn't until she tagged along with a friend to see the British punk band the Damned at CBGB that everything clicked into place for her. "From the second they started, it was pure pandemonium," she recounted, "but pure energy, pure exhilaration, such authenticity."

Invigorated, Mercedes teamed up with bassist Anne Gustavsson and singer Patrick Mack to form the Stimulators. The band went through a series of drummers—including the Dead Boys' Johnny Blitz and New York Dolls/Heartbreakers' Jerry Nolan—before Mercedes realized that the best option was (literally) right under her nose. After Blitz failed to show for an out-of-town gig, Harley Flanagan, then all of eleven years old, became the band's new drummer. By that point, he was already well acquainted with the punk scene, as he'd been regularly tagging along with his mother and aunt to CBGB, Max's, and Tier 3.

Nick Marden, the son of painter Brice Marden and nephew of folk legend Joan Baez, lived a couple blocks away from the Poet's Building on 13th Street. Like Harley Flanagan, he had tagged along to Max's Kansas City with his father, where his mind was blown by an early punk band called the Testors. By the time he was seventeen, he was deep into punk and regularly hanging out at Max's on his own. Denise Mercedes introduced Marden to two teenage friends of hers from New Jersey, Jack Rabid (née Corradi) and Dave Stein, who were both devout punk fans. With Marden, they formed a band called Even Worse with the express purpose of opening for the Stimulators.

Rabid: Nick called Dave and said, "Hey, the Stimulators don't have someone opening for them. If we put together a band, we can play," and being eighteen and stupid, we were like, "Great!" The first Even Worse rehearsal was in the Stimulators' rehearsal room on April 30th, 1980, two days before our first gig opening for the Stimulators at Tier 3.

The music that the Stimulators, Even Worse, and peers like the Blessed and the Mad were making was indebted to punk predecessors like the Dead Boys and the Ramones, but with a new edge that emphasized the genre's speed and volume. This new style would eventually become known as hardcore punk, but Nick Marden articulated it perfectly with a homemade article of clothing.

Marden: "Loud Fast Rules" just popped into my head one day. Eventually, I got some white shoe polish and just [wrote] it on the back of my jacket. At first it said "Stimulators," "Bad Brains," and "The Mad" on the top, because they were the triumvirate for me at the moment in New York, and I started putting other bands on there. The Stimulators had that song ["Loud Fast Rules"] written already but they didn't have a title for it, and then I went to Max's to see them and wore that jacket, and they were like, "That's it!"

When Anne Gustavsson left the Stimulators, Marden was an obvious pick to replace her. Saxophonist Seaton "Raven" Hancock also found his way to the band.

Hancock: I went to see the Stimulators at Max's. I had my horn with me, I was sitting in the back, and they were so loud that I assumed no one could hear me [when I started playing along with them]; I was wrong. They brought the volume down to dub style, with just bass and drums, and said, "You with the saxophone, do that!" So that's how I met Denise, Nick, and Harley, and on that day I joined the Stimulators.

As a diehard Stimulators fan, Jack Rabid suggested to Dave Stein that the two of them start a zine devoted to the band, as well as fellow travelers Bad Brains and the Mad—none of whom were getting the press coverage Rabid felt they deserved. The resultant zine, *The Big Takeover*, soon transcended its Stimulators-oriented roots and became a full-fledged magazine covering all manner of punk and indie bands. Rabid continues to publish it to this day, and it's distributed worldwide.

Rabid: Issues two through six, the Stimulators paid for because they saw the value in it. We were casting them as a central player in the scene, which they were. In issue six, they started writing their own things without telling me—things I did not agree with, like insulting the Ramones and stuff. I was starting to have a falling out with them anyway, because their reaction to the new hardcore bands was to go slower and more metal. I didn't want to be a part of the Stimulators' camp anymore because I felt like they weren't in tune with the new scene. But they had been these great mentors, helpers, catalysts—I can't give them enough credit.

The Stimulators' role as scene catalysts had a lot to do with the fact that their young drummer was bringing other kids to come see them.

Marden: We had Harley playing drums, he was thirteen and fourteen, so we had a contingent of thirteen-to-fourteen-year-olds who'd come and see us if we could get them in. That would be very annoying to the older patrons, but as far as having a bunch of fourteen-year-olds ricocheting around the room, that just brought the energy level to a whole different place.

For young kids looking to make a lot of noise, burn off energy, and experiment with booze and drugs, the notoriously lawless Alphabet City was an imperfect but enticing fit.

171A

North Carolina natives Jerry Williams and Scott Jarvis moved to New York in 1979 from Raleigh with their punk band Th' Cigaretz. In September 1980, Williams began renovating a storefront at 171 Avenue A that had previously housed a glass shop; he planned for it to be a space for Th' Cigaretz to live and rehearse, so he installed the band's PA system, and built a small stage and sound booth. By November, Th' Cigaretz had broken up, but Williams decided to keep the space, opening 171A (as it became known) as a venue and regularly hosting shows on Friday and Saturday nights—not that they had any sort of licensing, mind you.

PHOTO BY PENNY RAND. COLLECTION OF HARLEY AND LAURA FLANAGAN.

John T. Davis, Harley Flanagan, Denise Mercedes, and Jerry Williams outside 171A, 1981.

The weekend shows didn't last long: after a rival club (it's unclear which one) tipped off the cops about 171A's lack of a liquor license, it was shuttered by the fire department just before a New Year's Eve show. But Williams continued to operate 171A as a community hub for the local punk scene. An accomplished engineer, Williams used the space as a recording studio, occasional venue, and practice space, where bands like the Stimulators, Konk, Richard Hell and the Voidoids, Bad Brains, Subhumans, Cro-Mags, and Angry Samoans rented it out for $6-$8 a pop. The Californian band Black Flag even used the place to audition DC-based singer Henry Rollins.

In 1980, Williams and Jarvis were joined by two other southern transplants: Boca Raton, Florida's Donna "Day-Z" Parsons[iv] and Cathy "Fish" Fitzsimons. Parsons had started publishing a

---

iv   Throughout her involvement in the hardcore scene, Parsons was presenting as male. She later came out as transgender and began using the names Donna and Day-Z.

zine called *Mouth of the Rat* (a very literal translation of "Boca Raton") back in Florida; after relocating to New York, Parsons and Fitzsimons took over the basement at 171A and transformed it into a record store they dubbed Rat Cage, in a nod to Parsons's zine.[v] Parsons often kept the store open until 4:00 a.m., so that kids who were coming to shows in the area could come hang out and buy records while they were at it. Rat Cage even spawned a record label in 1982, with Parsons and Fitzsimons releasing pivotal early records by Agnostic Front, Beastie Boys (who started out as a hardcore band before pivoting to hip-hop), the Young and the Useless (featuring future Beastie Boy Adam Horovitz), and Heart Attack.

171A is best remembered now as the place where the Beastie Boys recorded their debut EP, 1982's *Polly Wog Stew*. But at the time, the band that loomed largest there was Bad Brains. Bad Brains formed in 1978 in Washington, DC, as a jazz fusion group, but soon discovered punk and Rastafarianism and embraced both. As the rare punk band in DC at the time, and one of the very few all-Black punk bands anywhere in the world, they struggled to make headway in their hometown. New York's scene, however, had already welcomed them when they'd come up for early gigs at Tier 3 and CBGB. So in 1981, Bad Brains relocated to New York, and 171A became the band's crash pad, practice space, and frequent venue.

With Jerry Williams producing, Bad Brains recorded their self-titled debut album at 171A in 1981. When it was released on cassette by ROIR Records the following year, Donna Parsons drew the iconic cover art of the United States Capitol Building being struck by lightning.

Rabid: When they made that album, I attended all the recording sessions and sat on those couches watching them record. I hadn't really seen a real recording studio, so I didn't know that this is not how you do it. They had a stage at one end, so the band was set up on the

---

v   In addition to records and zines, Harley Flanagan recalled Parsons also selling skateboards and LSD.

stage. There was almost no separation at all between the drums and the guitarist—it wasn't Phil Spector doing "River Deep, Mountain High." It was really a live album. I heard them play the same set I'd heard them play a hundred times before, with no let-up in velocity.

Also hanging around 171A at the time were high school friends John Berry, Kate Schellenbach, Jeremy Shatan, and Michael Diamond, who had formed a post-punk band called Young Aborigines in 1981. As Berry, Schellenbach, and Diamond began to embrace hardcore, they, with Adam Yauch on bass, formed a second, hardcore-oriented band called Beastie Boys.

Shatan: The Beastie Boys were partially a parody of hardcore; they were kind of making fun of it. There is a comedy aspect to hardcore, but the majority of the bands didn't think so. The majority of the bands were very, very serious.

A7

Four blocks south of 171A, across the street from the southwestern corner of Tompkins Square Park, was a bar called A7 (112 Avenue A; it was named for its location at Avenue A and East 7th Street). Owner Dave Gibson opened the venue in 1980 in a former Polish social club. Brian Butterick, who booked bands at Pyramid Club across the street (which we'll get to in a moment), later recalled that A7 "was essentially this guy's living room with broken down sofas. It was filthy. You didn't ever make any money. Admission was $3 but no one paid."[117]

Though it's largely remembered as a hardcore venue, A7 hosted a diverse range of musicians throughout the week: Tuesdays were given over to "experimental funk," there was reggae on Wednesdays and Sundays, new wave on Thursdays, and hard core on Fridays and Saturdays—the two nights most suburban teenagers could go out, natch (the club was closed on Mondays).[118]

Elliott Sharp (multi-instrumentalist; composer): A7 was a place where people who didn't fit in anywhere else came. Dave pretty much gave me Tuesday nights to do whatever I wanted, so I tried to invite a lot of people from different scenes there. We were all friends: all the no wave people, the more adventurous free jazz people, a lot of the early electronic noise and industrial people. We all hung out with each other, because there weren't that many people doing weird shit in New York in those days.

A7's hours were more closely aligned with all-night dance parties like the Loft or Paradise Garage than any rock venues, though not because it shared those spots' utopian nightlife philosophies; A7 seemed to keep late hours—and a broad, diverse booking policy—simply due to its chaotic management. Shows began at 1:00 a.m. and frequently ran until (or past) sunrise. One could spend six hours or more watching as many as ten bands in a row, for a pittance—not because of any specific booking agenda, but because Gibson wasn't really interested in curating the lineup.

PHOTO BY THE AUTHOR, 2023.

112 Avenue A.

Rabid: The bands playing there [mostly] had just walked up to him that night and said, "Can we play?" At 5:00 in the morning they would still be presenting some band, because Dave wouldn't turn people away. He wouldn't say "No, I'm sorry, we're full up," it was, "Well let's see, you could play at 4:30, does that sound good?" I think that's how the Beastie Boys played their first gig there; they weren't booked or anything, or certainly weren't advertised. It would irritate the booked bands. I was there to see the Effigies and Dave kept putting other bands on before them that weren't booked. Eventually they said, "It's 2:30, we're done, we're leaving." They never played. Stuff like that used to drive me up the wall.

The burgeoning hardcore scene first made its way to A7 via Doug Holland (née Lozito), guitarist in the band Kraut (and later a member of Cro-Mags). After eighteen-year-old Holland began working as a bartender and manager at A7 in 1981, he gave jobs to other friends from the hardcore scene, including Murphy's Law's Jimmy "Gestapo" Drescher, Warzone's Raybeez (born Ray Barbieri), and Agnostic Front's Roger Miret.

Though the nascent community was first nurtured at 171A and Rat Cage Records, it arguably only became a full-fledged *scene* once A7 was in the mix. With the two venues only four blocks apart, and both allowing bands to come in and rehearse during the day, they formed a small but vibrant hardcore district along Avenue A. As if to make the subtext text, on May 16, 1981, the Canadian hardcore band DOA famously played a set at A7, then went over and played a set at 171A, and then returned to A7 to play their third set of the night.

From '81 until its closure in 1984, A7 hosted the likes of Bad Brains, Beastie Boys, Agnostic Front, Black Flag, Cause for Alarm, Scream (featuring a young Dave Grohl on drums), Heart Attack, SS Decontrol, the Undead, No Thanks!, and Murphy's Law. Kevin Crowley, singer in the Abused, regularly gave haircuts in the bathroom during shows. And since nothing says "local scene" quite like territorialism, graffiti on the club's exterior read, "Out of town bands remember where you are!"

> *Hancock: You could see the writing on the wall, literally. There was a backlash reaction to the new wave scene, and you saw such graffiti as, "Black Flag Kills Ants," in reference to Adam and the Ants.*

That sense of territorialism—both good and bad—led Kevin Crowley to come up with the famed New York hardcore symbol: A large X with four smaller letters written in its crevaces—N on top, Y on the bottom, H on the left, and C on the right. That symbol has been mimicked and parodied to no end, and innumerable successive waves of local hardcore bands and fans have adopted it as their own. But viewed in its original context, it's remarkable: an identifiable logo that stood for *an entire scene*, beyond any one band, record label, or venue. As far as I'm aware, such a thing had never previously existed.

THE HARDCORE KIDS

For the most part, the kids in the hardcore scene were actual, honest-to-god *kids*. Adults like Jerry Williams, Donna Parsons, Denise Mercedes, and Bad Brains were the exceptions—the bands and fans at A7 and 171A were predominantly high school–aged or younger. Heart Attack's front man, Jesse Malin, was twelve when the band formed and sixteen when they broke up. Harley Flanagan, already a seasoned pro from his years with the Stimulators, was fourteen when he co-founded Cro-Mags. Todd Youth (née Schofield) was twelve when he joined Agnostic Front and fifteen when he joined Murphy's Law. Freddy Cricien, whose older brother Roger Miret sang in Agnostic Front, started performing with that band when he was all of seven years old; he formed his own band, Madball, when he turned twelve.

As such, a significant quadrant of the scene still lived with their parents, largely in middle- and upper-class neighborhoods (as was the case for all three Beastie Boys). Many came in from Brooklyn and Queens, others took the train in from Long Island, Upstate New York, New Jersey, and Connecticut.

As the scene progressed, a number of those kids moved out of their parents' houses into Alphabet City squats, of which the C-Squat at 155 Avenue C is far and away the best known. The derelict five-story building became a major hub for young punks: Harley Flanagan and his Cro-Mags bandmate John Joseph McGeown shared an apartment there, where their seminal 1986 album *Age of Quarrel* was written; Raybeez was also a tenant, and others would come by to party.

Apartment X, in the basement of 188 Norfolk Street (just below Houston), was packed: Flanagan and McGeown also put time in living there, as did Cause for Alarm's Keith Burkhardt, Agnostic Front's Rob Kabula and Roger Miret, and Cavity Creeps' Steve Poss. Heart Attack lived and rehearsed in a storefront at 162 Avenue B.[vi] And of course, there was a steady stream of people crashing at 171A and A7. Some people would vacillate between squats, and kids from New Jersey and Connecticut would stay with their friends in the neighborhood when they came in for the weekends.

Most of these kids were likely too naive to grasp the socioeconomic situation into which they had inserted themselves. Unsurprisingly, the hardcore kids were far from a welcome presence in the neighborhood for many locals. They were especially disliked by many young Puerto Rican residents who had spent their entire lives in Alphabet City: To them, hardcore kids likely read as interlopers who were there by choice and not circumstance—which was largely true. Many in the hardcore scene had little interest in the cultural aspects of Loisaida that didn't impact them, and thus often viewed the locals as a threat to be avoided or fought—which,

---

vi   The storefront is now a bar called Dream Baby, owned by Heart Attack front man, Jesse Malin.

since punks found themselves attacked by neighborhood gangs, was also often true.[vii]

> *Flanagan: When the hardcore scene and the punks started hanging out on Avenue A they got fucked with a lot. That's when shit started getting a little wild, because the local Puerto Rican gang saw us as some sort of new imposing gang, so hardcore kids and punk rockers used to get jumped regularly, stabbed regularly. That's why the second-generation New York hardcore kids started being a little bit more tough, and the New York hardcore kids actually wound up being some of the tougher hardcore kids in the country: Because we actually had to deal with real life drama shit in a neighborhood that was not very welcoming.*
>
> *I was always the one that was super scary in the New York hardcore scene, because I grew up fighting, I grew up huffing glue, I grew up dealing with being in that hood. I used to get picked on like crazy there, until I came of age where I wouldn't take anybody's shit anymore. I went from living a life of being fearful and really, really hating growing up on the Lower East Side to kind of thriving and doing really well there, because I became really violent and aggressive. But then you had all these other clowns who started trying to emulate me, and then the scene just got really ugly and stupid.*

Flanagan's growing reputation for unchecked aggression preceded him—famously, he'd attack people by swinging around a cue ball inside a sock (among other weapons) over even the most meager of perceived slights.

By 1984, New York's hardcore scene had perceptibly changed, with a swelling number of kids drawn to it in large part *because* of its reputation for violence. It had also outgrown the neighborhood: A7 and Rat Cage Records both closed that year; the date of

---

vii   Ironically, the scene around A7 and 171A had a sizeable Latinx contingent. Still, by virtue of their punk affiliation, many of these kids likely read as white to Loisaida natives.

171A's closure is unclear (likely due to its unofficial and multipurpose nature) but it was around the same time. Hard core migrated to CBGB and larger Downtown venues like the Rock Hotel and the Ritz. There would be periodic hardcore shows in Alphabet City, but as the scene got bigger, their location mattered less and less—with so much of the audience commuting in from outside the city proper, a specific location was less important than it would be for an older crowd.

Rabid: Hardcore killed punk for me. All the punk bands I liked couldn't make a living anymore because they weren't hardcore, and the rest of the scene didn't want to go see them. It just killed all the bands with any subtlety. All the punk rock bands I knew had a gigantic array of influences, and then all the hardcore bands, all they liked was punk rock—and a very, very narrow subset of it. It was inevitable that they were going to paint themselves into a cul-de-sac, and they did very quickly. A thousand bands that all sounded alike— how is that punk rock? Hardcore really sapped a lot of the energy of the underground scene, and it became all these separate scenes. When you do that, you decrease the draws, because [the audiences] only go to see that type of music.

As the first wave of hardcore venues shuttered, another venue, just across the street from A7, was thriving. Instead of celebrating the aggressive end of punk, the Pyramid Club celebrated avant-garde art, queerness, camp, and a lighter musical palette. But the fact that several core musicians and employees from A7 found themselves working at the Pyramid Club is a testament to how the neighborhood's chaotic nature could bring together subcultures, too.

PYRAMID

After the New Rican Village closed in 1979, the storefront at 101 Avenue A was taken over by one Richie Hajguchik and transformed into a resoundingly unspectacular bar called Pyramid

PHOTO BY THE AUTHOR, 2023.

101 Avenue A.

Cocktail Lounge.[viii] But in 1981, boyfriends and recent South Carolina transplants Bobby Bradley and Alan Mace (along with a third business partner, Vincent Sapienza) persuaded Hajguchik to let them take over his bar on Thursday nights.

Bradley and Mace (who was already performing drag under the name Sister Dimension) had been unceremoniously fired from their busboy jobs at the nightclub Interferon. Instead of looking for new busboy gigs, they decided to start a club of their own. Their vision was to combine aspects of both the artsy Downtown post-punk

---

viii Reportedly, Hajguchik had a silent partner who was a cop—which is wildly illegal, but which also meant that the club was never targeted by the NYPD.

clubs like the Mudd Club and the seedy Meatpacking District gay bars like the Anvil. Only in Alphabet City, far from preexisting gay club districts, were they able to realize this vision.

They kicked things off on December 10, 1981, with a party they dubbed "On the Range"—the titular range being Alphabet City, where few dared to go. Admission was $3, Mace deejayed, and the night featured drag queens, go-go dancers, musicians, and performance artists. The place was packed, and the bar's owner was sufficiently impressed that he gave Bradley, Mace, and Sapienza Fridays and Saturdays, with Sundays added soon after, and eventually the whole week. They could keep and distribute all the money made from the door, while the owners would keep what was made at the bar.

Pyramid Club, as it came to be known, was uniquely positioned at the intersection of post-punk music, drag performance, and avant-garde art. Some practitioners of all three had already been living in the neighborhood since the '60s, but Pyramid was the first time any of them had a neighborhood joint to call their own. As Brian Butterick later wrote, "The Pyramid was a rejection of the 'gay ghetto' disco club scene of the late seventies and a place where gays and straights, men and women, freaks and the few remaining Ukranian [sic] customers all mingled[.]"[119]

Joshua Fried (sound tech, Pyramid Club; musician and composer): The Pyramid was so hot and so popular that they would book what they thought was cool, and the crowd would come anyway. Not only did it have performance art stuff, but they also had theater, like John Jesurun's early [plays],[ix] which would happen at 7:00 at night, and they had the Red Hot Chili Peppers and the Beastie Boys and They Might Be Giants, and then they would have the drag queens, and the deejay dancing was also very serious there.

---

ix   Jesurun's serialized 1982 play, *Chang in a Void Moon*, was staged at Pyramid, and featured the acting talents of an unknown Steve Buscemi alongside Pyramid regulars like Ethyl Eichelberger and John Kelly. Buscemi also appeared in an experimental production of Shakespeare's *Titus Andronicus* staged at Pyramid in 1983, alongside Ann Magnuson and John Sex.

Drag was an especially key component of Pyramid Club's identity in the early days. Bradley, Mace, and Sapienza had been given the freedom to staff the place with their friends, and an early advertisement proudly read, "Pyramid is solely owned and operated by drag queens"—not *quite* true, as they didn't own the place, but certainly true in spirit. Drag performers like Ru Paul, Lady Bunny, Mistress Formika, Ethyl Eichelberger, Tanya Ransom, Tabboo!, and Lypsinka all took early steps there; booker Brian Butterick created his own memorable persona, Hattie Hathaway, while working at the club. In 1984, a group of regulars including Lady Bunny, Wendy Wild, and members of the garage rock band the Fleshtones concocted the idea of staging a festival in Tompkins Square Park; the resultant show, a drag extravaganza called Wigstock, was staged there annually until 1991, when it was relocated to Union Square.

As you may recall from Chapter Three, punk, drag, and performance art had previously mixed at Max's Kansas City. But by the time Max's closed, it had long ceased to serve that population, and until Pyramid, no other spot filled that role. Max's devotee Jayne County found Pyramid to be a worthy successor.

County: I felt strange when I first moved back to New York [in the '80s]. I had been living in London for a while and I just wanted to go back to London, because for the first time, New York felt like alien territory to me. But I got a gig playing at Pyramid Club, and I felt really at home there. The show was packed, and everyone was just on my side from the minute I opened my mouth. They knew every song. I was absolutely amazed. I guess I really didn't feel at home in New York City until I found the right hang out—you find that niche of people who are like you and you make it your home for a while. So I made Pyramid Club my home for a while.

By 1984, Bobby Bradley had become difficult to deal with, thanks in part to a growing heroin addiction. As Fried recalled, Bradley "got kind of nutty and off the wall and self-satisfied and difficult and maybe capricious and insular and hard to deal with."

Pyramid Club advertisement, 1985.

That year, the rest of Pyramid's staff forced him out (he received a $15,000 severance package); Alan Mace and Brian Butterick assumed his responsibilities.

At the same time, the club was growing in popularity, appearing in the likes of *People Magazine*. Larger crowds at Pyramid meant larger crowds on Avenue A, where few nonlocals would have dared to tread just a couple years earlier. Butterick, who himself played in the experimental band 3 Teens Kill 4,[x] had a distinctly post–punk sensibility. Under his watch, live music became a dominant element at Pyramid, and the wide range of acts he booked included They Might Be Giants, Sonic Youth, Beastie Boys, Bush Tetras, Elliott Sharp, Butthole Surfers, Liquid Liquid, Nico,[xi] Red Hot Chili Peppers (in their NYC debut), and Gwar.

---

x Famed artist David Wojnarowicz was also a member.

xi Funnily enough, the former Velvet Underground singer had lived in the apartment above the club during her tenure with that band in the mid-sixties.

But for Pyramid's doorman DJ Mojo (born Jim Smith), the club's transition to a full-fledged music venue was its undoing.

DJ Mojo: When the Pyramid started, it had the most diverse customer profile—you had the gay crowd, the punk crowd, the new music crowd, the old guys in the neighborhood would come by in the afternoon and drink. When it lost that broad palette of identities in the late '80s/early '90s, it lost what I felt made it great. When Pyramid started doing rock 'n' roll shows and CMJ shows, that was pretty much game over.

When Pyramid first opened, its relationship to the hardcore scene at A7 across the street was relatively friendly. Elliott Sharp remembers the two clubs as having "pretty separate constituencies," although DJ Mojo claimed that the two were "like one community. It wasn't like you were crossing the Louisiana Purchase to cross the street, it was pretty much the same kind of vibe."

I suspect there would have been a degree of distance, if only because there was a quadrant of homophobia within the hardcore scene. But by the late '80s, any tensions that may have existed between Pyramid and the hardcore scene had largely dissipated, and a few of A7's former employees and regulars began working at Pyramid. Jimmy Gestapo and Raybeez both worked the door, as they had at A7; Raybeez and Youth of Today's Ray Cappo booked Saturday afternoon hardcore matinees; fifteen-year-old Todd Youth became a barback.

With the Pyramid Club along the western side of Avenue A (making it closer to the rest of the East Village), the bleak reality of Alphabet City seems to have intruded upon it a tad less than it did across the street at A7. Though one might assume that drag queens would have trouble in a neighborhood that was often unwelcoming to outsiders, there are a lot more stories of neighborhood gangs getting into fights with hardcore kids than Pyramid's staff or customers.

In the late '80s, however, another music scene would take root

in the neighborhood—one that often seemed to take the harsh-
ness of Alphabet City life as its muse.

PIGFUCK

Michael Gira moved to New York City from California in 1979. By
1981, he was in a floundering post-punk band called Circus Mort
and living in a deconsecrated Puerto Rican Pentecostal church in
a storefront at 93 Avenue B, paying $100 a month. He shared his
new living space with a rotating series of bandmates, friends, and
girlfriends (the latter category reportedly including one Madonna
Ciccone). "You couldn't live there legally," Gira later remembered,
"There was a toilet but no shower, no kitchen—nothing, just a
concrete box, 800 square feet total and no windows."[120]
     The following year, Gira formed the band Swans; they rehearsed
regularly in his storefront, which was dubbed the Bunker.[xii] The
space had limited and somewhat ineffectual soundproofing; complaints from neighbors were frequent.
     In 1985, Gira's Swans bandmate and then-partner Jarboe La
Salle Devereaux (better known simply as Jarboe) moved into the
Bunker. Her initial impressions of the surrounding neighborhood
were severe, to say the least.

*Jarboe: The corner of Ave. B and East 6th Street had a desolate and
abandoned atmosphere. There was graffiti and there were torched cars.
Various storefronts had become DIY art spaces. Drug dealers gathered
at the corner mumbling the names of what they were selling. Random whistles and calls in the form of names alerted amongst themselves approaching buyers and non-buyers. Gutters and sidewalks of
the street had disposed needles.*

Her experiences living in Alphabet City, where she and Gira

---

xii Gira was also known to frequent the nearby Horseshoe Bar at 108 Avenue B
     (it's still there!) where he reportedly wrote many of Swans' lyrics.

remained for nearly a decade, would largely align with those initial impressions. "I would walk in the middle of the street at night
swinging a glass bottle to ward off predators," she recalled. "For-
tunately I was never mugged."

Sonic Youth also used the Bunker as a frequent practice space in
the early and mid-eighties, and wrote much of their 1985 album
Bad Moon Rising in the space. Drummer Bob Bert recalled it as "a
really depressing place. You were really taking your life in your
hands just going over there."

At the time, Swans and Sonic Youth were part of a crop of violently noisy bands—mostly based in or near Alphabet City—who
were influenced by the intensity of hardcore, but also drew on no
wave, post-punk, goth, and/or industrial influences. This loosely
affiliated scene—which also included Pussy Galore, White Zombie, Foetus, Cop Shoot Cop, Unsane, Live Skull, and Rat at Rat
R, among others—never received a name that stuck as firmly as
"no wave" or "hardcore." Some have branded it as an extension of
no wave, and many have identified it as noise rock, but my favorite name by a mile is "pigfuck," first coined in a negative review
of Sonic Youth by critic Robert Christgau.

Both Swans and Sonic Youth played early shows at a short-lived
venue just off Avenue C called SIN Club—"SIN" being short for
"Safety in Numbers," for reasons that are probably obvious. The
unlicensed basement venue, located at 272 East 3rd Street, was only
open for a handful of months before the police shuttered it. But
other spots were popping up nearby as well throughout the mid-
eighties, as the area began to gentrify. On Avenue A, the former A7
had become the gloriously monikered King Tut's Wah Wah Hut,
which hosted occasional performances, including an early iteration
of Blue Man Group. On the other end of the block, the nascent
antifolk scene was setting up camp at the corner of A and East 6th
at both Sophie's Bar and the Chameleon (that scene's remarkable
longevity merits its own chapter, discussed at length in Chapter
Nine). The basement of 118 East 1st Street, just off of Avenue A,
was home to the multidisciplinary DIY venue Darinka, where

They Might Be Giants were practically the house band. Deeper into Alphabet City at 337 East 8th Street was a venue called 8BC (named for its location between Avenues B and C), which hosted shows by John Zorn, Rhys Chatham, Karen Finley, and k.d. lang.

Flanagan: Once the hardcore scene made Avenue A safer for white people, and all those bars started popping up. It was still a dangerous area, but it became a hotspot. You had four bars that were all pretty jumping on the same [block]—A7, Wah Wah Hut, Pyramid, the Park Inn. You also had 24-hour restaurants right there, Odessa and Ray's Candy Store, and you had the park right across the street [for] everybody who was too young to get into the bars, everybody who got kicked out of the bars or were too fucked up to go in, and everybody wanted to hang out outside. It was this perfect little recipe for madness.

Beyond short-lived DIY spaces like SIN Club, the pigfuck bands (who tended to be a little older—meaning, not teenagers) mostly stuck to dive-y bar venues. Pyramid Club was a favorite, as was CBGB. Some, including White Zombie and Pussy Galore, gravitated to a dump called Lismar Lounge (41 1st Avenue), which White Zombie bassist Sean Yseult described as "just a tiny bit cleaner than CBGB's—that is to say, filthy."

White Zombie were formed in 1985 by Parsons students and then-couple Rob Zombie (née Cummings) and Sean Yseult (born Shauna Reynolds). After brief stints living next door to Katz's Deli on the Lower East Side and in Park Slope, Brooklyn, Yseult and Zombie settled into an apartment on East 13th between 1st and 2nd Avenues, paying a combined $300 a month.

Yseult: It was so disgusting, but so cheap. The electricity was free, if you could keep it running! We would have to go in the hallway once or twice a day to steal someone else's fuse when ours popped, which proved dangerous when an infuriated Joe Coleman [a painter and performance artist-ed.] came storming down screaming "Who stole my electricity!" No heat—we almost died a few times from cheap heaters

*catching on fire. No windows of course, and after a year or more, the
drop ceiling collapsed under the weight of leaking pipes and rat shit,
which came cascading down.*

*Did we leave? No, not with $150 rent in the East Village! We
put a big garbage can under the constant leak, and took turns leaving work to trade out the garbage can for another one before it would
overflow. At that point we told our landlords that we would hold out
on rent until they fixed the leak, which they never did, so we lived
for free for another year. Another apartment became available down
in the basement and we told our friend Gerard Cosloy about it, who
[ran] Homestead Records at the time, and he lived down there for a
while with us!*

Though they'd find considerable fame in the '90s as a heavy
metal band, White Zombie's comparatively obscure '80s output
falls squarely in the noise rock/pigfuck category. They shared bills
with the likes of Pussy Galore, Live Skull, and Rat at Rat R, and
played at neighborhood venues like 8BC, Lismar Lounge, and
CBGB. For Yseult, "My favorite place to play was the Pyramid
Club. The vibe was awesome, and having spent my entire life
with bohemian parents and in art schools, I loved the mix of drag
queens, punks, and misfits of all walks. Everyone was welcome
and having a good time."

There was some crossover between early hardcore and pigfuck—for example, Cop Shoot Cop bassist Jack Natz had played
in A7 mainstays the Undead, and Sonic Youth guitarist Thurston Moore briefly joined Jack Rabid in Even Worse. There were
some crossover shows too: most intriguingly, Sonic Youth and
Rat at Rat R joined hardcore bands Nihilistics, False Prophets,
Misguided, and Adrenalin O.D. in a benefit show for the Vancouver Five[xiii] which was staged at, of all places, CHARAS *El
Bohio*'s Assembly Hall.

---

xiii A group of anticapitalist activists who'd been arrested for bombing a chain of
      porn shops that allegedly sold snuff films.

Flier for the Vancouver Five benefit show at CHARAS/El Bohio's Assembly Hall, 8/13/83.

Like many in the hardcore and no wave scenes before them, the pigfuck bands largely came from middle- and upper-class backgrounds. Several of the scene's bands had come out of elite universities and art schools like Brown (Pussy Galore), Sarah Lawrence (Unsane), Rhode Island School of Design (Cop Shoot Cop), and Parsons School of Design (White Zombie).

Though they mostly lived in squalor and many harbored all-too-real drug addictions, in a handful of instances their output verged on poverty tourism, with the very real issues that plagued Alphabet City and the Lower East Side reduced to a mere aesthetic. As Cop Shoot Cop bassist Tod Ashley told writer Carlo McCormick, "We're the only East Village band that's not funded by Grandma's trust fund. To my knowledge, every other band in New York is... They've got trust funds, so they can write songs about not being able to afford their drug habits."[121]

THE TOMPKINS SQUARE PARK RIOTS

Sharp: There was a sweet spot when the East Village was really pretty mellow, around '82–'83. And then starting around '84, it began to get nasty again.

In September 1984, a local paper called the *East Villager* ran a piece by one Johnny Xerox entitled "The Danger Is Here! What Are You Going to Do About It?" Published in both English and Spanish, Xerox's article identified two equally potent threats to the neighborhood: "real estate developers" and "uncaring artists," both of whom are "white middle-class people who do not understand you, and whom you do not understand."[122]

Perhaps it was the changing demographic trends that finally got the city to pay attention to Alphabet City's rampant drug trade. On January 19, 1984, Police Commissioner Ben Ward launched Operation Pressure Point, a campaign to eradicate the drug dealing that had overrun the area. The day the program was launched, over one hundred people were arrested, thirty two of them for felonies. Mayor Ed Koch reportedly watched the proceedings from inside a mirrored undercover van. Two hundred cops were placed in the neighborhood—one on every corner, twenty-four hours a day—and within a month, a whopping 14,285 people were arrested on drug-related charges in the area.

Operation Pressure Point did little to curb actual drug sales: dealers simply relocated further downtown or moved their business indoors. But with the neighborhood's crime now much less visible, rents skyrocketed. Real estate investor Tom Pollak, who came to New York from Aspen specifically to invest in the gentrifying East Village, excitedly told *New York* in 1984 that "ethnic businesses and services will gradually be forced out. Anyone else can be paid to leave... They'll be pushed east to the river and given life preservers."[123]

In an ominous move, developer Samuel Glasser—who had made his fortune by refurbishing East Village tenements and renting units to a primarily white/bohemian tenant base—purchased the long-vacant Christodora Building in 1984 and began transforming it into luxury condominiums. Explaining his motivations, Glasser stated, "I really do believe that an all-poor neighborhood is a bore. The same goes for an all-rich neighborhood. In between is where the fun is...that's what causes creativity and art."[124]

Units in the Christodora became available to the public in 1986, and in an odd twist, Iggy Pop was among the building's early tenants. "I live in a nice [building] and that gets up a lot of people's tree," Pop told filmmaker Bram Van Splunteren in 1993. "But fuck it. What the fuck? I'm not a martyr."[125]

One local who took notice of all the change was Peter Missing (née Colangelo). Missing, a Bronx native, had formed a short-lived industrial band called Missing Foundation in Berlin in 1984; when he relocated to Alphabet City the following year, he assembled a new lineup of the band. Missing Foundation's music was punishing, to say the least: clanging metal percussion was preferred over anything that resembled traditional rock music, while Missing sang anarchist-inflected lyrics through a bullhorn, at least partially so that club owners couldn't cut the PA midset.

Club owners abhorred and frequently banned Missing Foundation, though in all fairness, their penchant for midset arson practically ensured that result. One legendary show at CBGB saw the band set fire to kerosene-soaked trash barrels and throw them into the audience. Still, Missing stressed, "We were not looking for simple destruction... We wanted to bring focus to certain issues and provoke solutions."[126] As club gigs became unavailable, Missing Foundation took to playing unadvertised shows in vacant lots and storefronts, using portable generators. The band also frequently hired Puerto Rican teens from the neighborhood to act as bodyguards at their shows, standing in front of the stage wearing sunglasses and matching Missing Foundation shirts.

The gentrification that was swallowing up Alphabet City became Missing Foundation's raison d'être. Convinced that the country was on the verge of becoming a police state, Missing Foundation began plastering Lower Manhattan with the band's logo, an abstract representation of an overturned martini glass that meant, as they put it, "The party's over."[127]

In Alphabet City, the logo transcended the band to become a catchall signal of pro-squatter, anti-cop, and anti-gentrification sentiment. "I wanted to replace the peace symbol," Missing later explained.[128] Missing Foundation used other street art to push their message, as well: posters they plastered around town declared, "We will not act civilized in this fuckin' city" and "Your house is mine." There were frequent allusions in both their music and graffiti to 1933, the year the Weimar Republic fell and the Nazis took control of Germany. All of it was intended to terrify potential developers and gentrifiers, and it reportedly had some success in slowing that tide—it was alleged that the graffiti had frightened some yuppie interlopers away from setting up house in the neighborhood.

But as parts of Alphabet City were gentrifying, Tompkins Square Park had only gotten more perilous. "Crack had completely taken it over, and a lot of homeless people were living there," Sharp recalled, "which was ironic because there were still a huge number of empty buildings being warehoused in the East Village."

By 1987, the city was home to somewhere between 60,000 and 80,000 homeless people,[129] with the count rising due to lack of social services and infrastructure. Tompkins Square Park itself was home to nearly 150 homeless people,[130] but it had also become a late-night destination for drunken revelers from nearby clubs and bars. Neighborhood organizations expressed varying degrees of dismay over this situation; one, the Avenue A Block Association, demanded a 1:00 a.m. curfew, which the community board approved in July 1988. It's important to note that not all of the calls to impose a curfew in the park had come from new gentrifiers: Several had come from longtime Puerto Rican and Ukrainian residents, who were exasperated by the squatters, junkies, and (yes) rock bands that they felt had wreaked havoc on the neighborhood they called home.

The police began enforcing the curfew within weeks. A small riot on July 31 resulted in four arrests and several injuries, but activists planned another protest for August 6. By 11:00 p.m. that evening, eighty-six police officers on foot and eleven on horse-back were deployed to the park to enforce the curfew. "It's time to bring a little law and order back to the park and restore it to the legitimate members of the community," said Captain Gerald McNamara.[131]

At some point during the protest, a few bottles and bits of debris were thrown at the assembled cops. The police reacted by charging into the crowd en masse and viciously attacking protestors—as well as innocent bystanders caught up in the action. Several cops had their badges covered up, and some reportedly hurled racial and misogynist epithets at their targets.[132]

> *Yseult: I got trapped in the Tompkins Square Riots—I went out that night to get a cup of coffee (yes, at midnight) and as I came out of the bodega, I saw it all happen: The cops in riot gear with their badges taped up; the punks, hippies, and locals facing them, and then sheer melee. I ducked back in to the bodega and could only catch glimpses, out of self-preservation—a cop knocking over a woman and her baby stroller, three cops jumping up and down on top of Dave Insurgent[xiv] across the street like he was a trampoline, just horrific things.*

The violence continued through the night. Around 6:00 a.m., a group of protestors grabbed a police barricade and rammed it through the glass door of the Christodora, where an apartment had recently sold for half a million dollars. They proceeded to ransack the lobby, all the while reportedly chanting, "Die yuppie scum." The riots broke up soon after, and Mayor Koch temporarily rescinded the curfew.

> *Sharp: After the riots, you felt a sea change in what the East Village was going to be. There was more discussion of the development, more and more real estate prices going up, more and more fancy storefronts, more and more boutique-y food places and knickknack places.*

---

xiv   Lead singer of the hardcore band Reagan Youth.

Three months later, CBS Channel 2 aired a three-part investigation by reporter Mike Taibbi entitled "Cult of Rage." Taibbi not only claimed a direct link between Missing Foundation and the riots with the most meager and specious evidence, but concluded that Missing Foundation was no rock band, but rather a Satanic cult.[133]

Gentrification continued apace in Alphabet City after the riots, but the homeless encampment remained in Tompkins Square Park until June 1991, when 350 NYPD officers, some in riot gear, were sent in to evict the two hundred or so residents. Sanitation workers were brought in to throw the homeless population's makeshift tents and personal belongings into dump trucks. To make sure they stayed gone, the park was closed for renovations, which included the demolition of the band shell. Tompkins Square Park's time as a lawless spot that represented everything good and bad about the neighborhood was drawn to a close—just as the neighborhood began to quickly and deeply change.

THE AFTERLIFE OF ALPHABET CITY'S MUSIC HISTORY

As we'll see in Chapter Nine, although the neighborhood was definitively gentrifying in the '90s, quite a bit of oppositional, vibrant subculture remained.

Pyramid Club, for one, continued on as a beacon of underground music and culture. Nirvana made their NYC debut at the club on July 18, 1989, and bands like Deee-Lite, the Flaming Lips, Afghan Whigs, Galaxie 500, Gumball, King Missile, and Babes in Toyland all graced its stage. The club's drag performances decreased as the club's original staffers moved on and the audience began to skew heterosexual, in part because of the havoc that AIDS wreaked upon the LGBTQ+ community.

But there were still flickers of the original Pyramid spirit here and there: From 1993 to 1995, the Blacklips Performance Collective—a queer performance troupe spearheaded by the singer Anohni—presented weekly experimental theater productions on

Monday nights at midnight. Anohni would perform her own songs within the plays, many of which went on to become part of her repertoire when she founded the band Antony and the Johnsons in 1995.

But by the turn of the century, Pyramid Club had largely fallen into self-parody, regularly hosting '80s-themed dance parties. The club's closure was announced in 2020, due to the Covid-19 pandemic, though it briefly reopened in 2021 under new management. In 2022, it was taken over by Nick Bodor, the former owner of Cake Shop (which we'll discuss in Chapter Ten), who has reopened it as a live music venue called Baker Falls.

Throughout the '80s and '90s, CHARAS made several attempts to legally purchase *El Bohio*, all of which were denied. The building's auction was announced in July 1998, and although the proceedings were briefly disrupted when activists let ten thousand crickets loose, it eventually sold to developer Gregg Singer. Singer served CHARAS with an eviction order, although it wasn't enforced until 2001. He reportedly planned to raze the building and erect a college dormitory in its place (presumably for NYU), but his plans were repeatedly denied by the Department of Buildings, and then in 2006 the building was landmarked—meaning it can't be demolished. Mayor Bill DeBlasio attempted to intervene and retrieve the building for CHARAS to no avail; as of this book's writing, the building, still in Singer's possession, has been empty for over two decades.

As the neighborhood gentrified through the '90s, the city evicted many of the squatters in Alphabet City and the Lower East Side. But in 2002, the city transferred ownership of eleven of the twelve remaining squats in the area to the Urban Homesteaders Assistance Board, a nonprofit organization that helped bring the buildings up to code. Once the necessary refurbishments were made, the buildings were officially given to the squatters, with the promise that any future sales would be made to low-income residents.

One such building was the infamous C-Squat (155 Avenue C). The C-Squat remained a magnet for punk bands long after Har-

ley Flanagan and John Joseph moved out, housing members of
such bands as Leftöver Crack, World/Inferno Friendship Society,
Crash Worship, and Missing Foundation. It now legally operates
as a housing cooperative, and in 2012, the building's storefront
became the Museum of Reclaimed Urban Space, devoted to the
history of Alphabet City's squatters.

The former Slugs' Saloon at 242 East 3rd Street is now Rossy's
Bakery, a Dominican cafe.

Since its closure, the former 171A has become a series of restaurants; none have lasted long. When Beastie Boys' Adam Yauch
passed away in 2012, fans assembled a makeshift memorial in front
of the building.

In 1997, former Heart Attack front man Jesse Malin, along with
business partners Johnny Yerington and Laura McCarthy, took
over what had once been A7 (112 Avenue A) and opened a bar and
music venue called Niagara. As of this book's writing, it's still open.

In the decades since Heart Attack broke up, Malin went on to
have a long and successful music career both as front man for the
glam-punk band D Generation and as a Springsteen-esque singer/
songwriter. To his great credit, Malin has invested in several bars
and music venues in the East Village over the years, including
the venerable club Coney Island High (15 St. Marks Place) which
flourished during the '90s.

In a nod to his own past in the building, Malin installed a plaque
in the back room of Niagara celebrating "Pioneers of American
Hardcore and the Birthplace of NYHC." Of course, this totally
disregards all the non-hardcore music that made A7 vibrant, but
that makes sense—it's a reflection of Malin's personal experience.

*Flanagan: Quite honestly, fuck that place. Now all these people are
trying to make a landmark out of something that was a third-rate
club at best. Honestly, A7 was just a fucking hole in the wall. It
was only cool because it let our friends work there and play there. As
far as what it is now, that shit doesn't mean anything to me—the
plaque on the wall and all that bullshit, I don't give a fuck. Jesse's a*

nice guy and everything, but he's just a landowner. He came from a family with money, so he invested in his little location.

Once upon a time, a walk down Avenue A at midnight might have been a terrifying prospect. These days, it's still a terrifying prospect, due to altogether different threats: puking frat boys, shrieking bachelorette parties, and seemingly every single person from the entire tristate area who is turning twenty-one that day.

Rabid: *[Gentrification is] like if you're an artist and you have your palette. You have this one color and you add a dab and it gets a little darker, and then you add another dab and it gets a little darker, and eventually you add so much it becomes this other color. It never happens overnight. Perhaps people like me moving [to the East Village] is what made it more attractive to people who were much more wealthy than me. I was perfectly happy to live on rice and beans; eventually other people came in who were perfectly happy to live on Michelin-starred restaurants.*

Tompkins Square Park's homeless encampments are long gone, replaced by a dog park full of Instagram-famous pets. There's even a wistful Mumford and Sons song named after it. And yet, there's still a little bit of detectable grime. Walking through the park on a recent Sunday afternoon, I was delighted to find a hardcore punk band on a makeshift stage bashing it out for twenty or so mohawked devotees.

Suggested Listening

Sun Ra—*Live at Slugs' Saloon* (rec. 1972)

Bad Brains—*Bad Brains* (1982)

Beastie Boys—*Polly Wog Stew* (1982)

The Stimulators—*Loud Fast Rules!* (1982)

3 Teens Kill 4—*No Motive* (1983)

Cro-Mags—*The Age of Quarrel* (1986)

Swans—*Greed* (1986)

Pussy Galore—*Right Now!* (1987)

Missing Foundation—*1933 Your House Is Mine* (1988)

White Zombie—*It Came from N.Y.C.* (compilation)

8

WORLD CLIQUE:
DANCETERIA AND THE BIRTH
OF THE MIDTOWN MEGACLUB

Justin Strauss: Every club was packed every night of the week—Limelight, Tunnel, Palladium, Area. I don't know where all these people came from.

Michael Holman: You had people from all over the country wanting to come to New York to take advantage of the fun that we were having. The only problem was, those people were the people that we were running away from! Those were the squares and the jocks and the assholes who didn't understand or appreciate creative people. Those assholes that we were running from showed up to New York saying, "Hey, where's the party?" not knowing that they had to create the party like we did—they thought that it would just happen for them.

Up to this point, most of the clubs we've discussed were either small, physically intimate spaces, or—as in the case of the Loft

at 99 Prince Street or Paradise Garage—large spaces that were spiritually intimate by virtue of being private and community oriented.
To some extent, this is my bias as an author—those are the kinds of
clubs I prefer. But those are also the spaces that foster communities
and incubate artists and genres in their infancy. If you're looking
to learn about musical breakthroughs, you're better off looking at
small, labor-of-love venues than a larger spot operating primarily
as a tax write-off for some businessperson.

But even if my focus has been on smaller clubs, larger clubs have
always been part of the fabric of New York City's music culture,
too—from the East Village's Fillmore East, where Jimi Hendrix
and the Allman Brothers performed to thousands of rock fans in
the late '60s and early '70s, to the infamously garish and elitist disco
Studio 54, which opened in 1977. These big clubs never yielded
the same innovations as grassroots scenes, but it would be a lie to
say they didn't have impacts, both positive and negative, that re-
verberated across the city and country's music cultures. Given their
impact on all NYC nightlife, we'd only be telling half the story
if we didn't also talk about big clubs—and, in particular, about a
moment in the '80s when they became the epicenter of the underground.

In the early '80s, as the previous era's live music scenes were
winding down, a new kind of club emerged—a cool, artsy,
Downtown-style club, writ large, thanks to a homeopathic dose
of Uptown-style branding and business sense. These clubs weren't
located in hip neighborhoods; rather, they tackled decidedly uncool areas, assuming that they were offering enough (and that
there were few-enough other nightlife options in the moment)
that the scenesters would follow. And they did—for a time, anyway.

Through a game of one-upmanship among club owners, that
original concept was turned inside out, plastering the city with
soulless megaclubs that made only token gestures of support to a
dying underground. By the time anybody noticed what was taking
place, it was too late—the very concept of a Downtown club culture had already been stretched to the point of abstraction. What

remained was flimsy enough that two preventable tragedies and one malignant public official could deliver a death blow with ease.

That's not to say this is a clear-cut David and Goliath narrative. Rather, this is a story of moral ambiguity and escalating compromise. These megaclubs that gradually diluted the underground also gave a lot of brilliant musicians, deejays, and artists the kind of financial support and professional opportunities that had been previously unavailable to them. The earliest versions of these clubs were well intentioned, and by virtue of their size and scope, they led previously disparate scenes to engage and cross-pollinate in transformative ways. And significantly, they gave an early platform to some of the city's most successful musical exports.

But before we can get to all that, we need to take a step back by just a couple years to the first club to lure "Downtown" away from Downtown: Hurrah.

HURRAH

Jim Fouratt moved to New York from Rhode Island in 1961 to study acting, but after getting arrested at an anti-Vietnam War protest in 1965, he shifted his focus to activism instead. He had a hand in many of the city's best-known activist moments of the late '60s: In 1967, he helped organize the Central Park Be In; also that year, he co-founded the Youth International Party (aka Yippies), a politically radical countercultural group. Fouratt has taken credit for scheming to throw dollar bills on the floor of the New York Stock Exchange, an infamous stunt the Yippies executed on August 24, 1967. After participating in the Stonewall Riots in 1969, Fouratt co-founded the gay activist group Gay Liberation Front. All the while, a day job assisting Clive Davis at Columbia Records kept him aware of music industry trends.

Unlike most hippies, Fouratt transitioned into the punk era seamlessly, frequenting CBGB and Max's Kansas City. In 1978, a friend brought Fouratt to Hurrah (36 West 62nd Street), a small second-story club across the street from Lincoln Center. In its mid-seventies infancy, Hurrah had been a popular disco, hosting the likes of the Village People, but it couldn't compete against behemoth clubs like Studio 54 and Xenon. By the time Fouratt first ventured there, Hurrah had shifted its focus and was billing itself as the first ever "rock disco." Manager Henry Schissler brought in deejays he described to *Billboard* as "former disco people who have learned rock 'n' roll, but who program it as disco,"[134] who spun alongside performances from punk mainstays like Patti Smith, the Ramones, Suicide, the Fast, and the Cramps.

Still, Fouratt saw room for improvement, and said as much to the club's owners. Impressed by Fouratt's proposals, they hired him to help run the club. Fouratt installed video screens above the stage, brought in former Mudd Club deejay Sean Cassette, and began booking punk and post-punk bands like the Misfits, the B-52s, Tuxedomoon, the Stimulators, and the Damned. Fouratt also installed a Mudd Club–style doorman who was instructed to wave in women and gay men but make straight men wait. Fouratt's Hurrah was Downtown in every way—except for its location.

Under Fouratt, Hurrah succeeded, although it was never wholly able to overcome the barriers posed by its commercial disco past or its location: Downtown scenesters had plenty of other venues which were walking distance from their homes and from each other.

Despite reinvigorating the joint, Fouratt didn't last long at Hurrah; he quit when the owners refused to fairly compensate singer Klaus Nomi after a packed show at the club. When Fouratt attempted to reclaim his job the following day, he found he had already been replaced by his former assistant, Ruth Polsky.

Polsky was a New Jersey native who, after graduating from Clark University in Massachusetts, had briefly lived in England. An obsessive anglophile, her sophisticated musical tastes leaned heavily on British post-punk bands, much more so than anything homegrown. Few other bookers in the city paid as much attention to British music at this point (although Hilary Jaeger at Tier 3 came close). With the club now at her disposal, Polsky turned Hurrah into the city's primary hub for visiting British post-punk bands like the Raincoats, the Cure, Gang of Four, Young Marble Giants, Echo and the Bunnymen, and New Order. Over time, she became a one-woman international exchange program, importing UK bands to New York and vice versa. Once British bands were booked at Hurrah, Polsky often went above and beyond to help them get other gigs around town at venues like the Mudd Club and Tier 3, as well as shows in nearby cities.

This work had ripple effects on both sides of the pond. Bush Tetras/Contortions guitarist Pat Place recalled, "After no wave, which was very short-lived, the British bands were all coming in, and they definitely had more of a danceable thing going on. We [Bush Tetras] played with—and loved—Gang of Four, and we were very influenced by what was coming out of England." At the same time, a lot of British bands—New Order, in particular—were influenced by New York's mutant disco music scene; the Bronx-based band ESG were even signed to New Order's label, Factory Records, on the strength of a show they played at Hurrah.

Sadly, Hurrah was not long for this world, closing in 1980. Speaking to the *New York Times* the following year, Polsky laid the blame on larger, less scene-y venues like The Ritz (now Webster Hall) and the Times Square club Bond's International Casino. "As bigger clubs opened up to the music, a price war began and agents started to realize that they could get more money for their bands," Polsky explained. "Once we became one of the smaller clubs we couldn't afford to hire a number of the visiting British and American bands that people wanted to see. And then the smaller clubs started disappearing."[135]

DANCETERIA

After Fouratt parted ways with Hurrah, deejay Sean Cassette introduced him to his soon-to-be business partner Rudolf Piper. Piper's backstory is as wild as Fouratt's: After obtaining a PhD in economics in his native Germany, he moved to Brazil and made a fortune, first as a stockbroker, and then as the owner of Brazil's first chain of American-style laundromats. From there, Piper decided on a whim to relocate to New York and open up a nightclub.

Piper: I knew New York well already, and in those days I felt it was lacking in a lot of bougie comforts. But the energy was there: It was wild, and anything goes—and a place where anything goes, that's a good place! You could not find a decent cappuccino in all of Manhattan in those days, but it had at least twenty S&M clubs.

Seeking out the city's best nightlife, Piper gravitated to the Mudd Club.

Piper: Joey Arias was the doorman at the Mudd Club in those days. I came early—this is a knowledge that I have from Brazilian whorehouses: You should come early, get the girls fresh. I was at the door, and he asked me, "What's the size of your dick?" I assured him that it was big enough for me to come in.

The Mudd Club was nothing, but at the same time, it was a great place. There was no decor: gray walls, shitty Salvation Army furniture, a good sound system, and bands. The ambiance was great, but you looked at the place and that's it. The fact that the Mudd Club was nothing inspired me to do a club that would be like that, but better.

Piper's realization would prove to be massively consequential. The Mudd Club had taken the Max's/CBGB concept of a Downtown punk club and tweaked it by adding the ironic-but-serious disco affectations of deejays, a doorman, and a VIP area. Now Piper would take the Mudd Club's concept and tweak *that* by throwing in another one of Studio 54's defining qualities: spectacle.

Piper used his significant funds to purchase a building at 43 Crosby Street in SoHo. Teaming up with Fouratt and Cassette, the building was transformed into a club called Pravda.

Piper: It was three floors: a basement that was industrial/Bauhaus, a main floor with bands, and a gallery on the top floor. At Pravda, the kind of music that we wanted to play was some edgy new wave that was very mechanical—Kraftwerk, Devo—so I designed this place in a mixture of Bauhaus style and [The Cabinet of] Dr. Caligari.

Pravda opened on November 8, 1979. Hundreds of people showed up for the opening night party, which featured a Betsey Johnson fashion show as its centerpiece. But with the crowd overflowing onto the street, the club's peeved SoHo neighbors—who, you may recall, had already fought a losing battle against the Loft's opening at 99 Prince Street—called the cops and the fire department, who clocked enough code violations to shut the place down. And with that, Pravda closed for good on the same night it had opened.

The fact that Pravda existed for one night made it instantly legendary and granted Piper and Fouratt an extraordinary degree of street cred. But it also created some very real issues. "I'd put all the money that I had into making the club and buying the building and so on," Piper recalled. "Once they closed the club down the day after that party, that party made my career in New York, but I was strapped for cash." Beyond the rent Piper was collecting from tenants in the building's upper floors, a new source of income was needed.[i]

Fouratt found it in the form of a struggling club called Armageddon, located in a converted button factory at 252 West 37th Street, in the unhip Garment District and a stone's throw from seedy Times Square. A band Fouratt was helping out played at Armageddon, but after the gig, the club's management refused to pay them—a point they underscored by pulling out a gun. Fouratt, much as he had at Hurrah, offered to help the owners turn their fortunes around, as long as the band he represented was compensated. The owners agreed, and Fouratt brought Piper in as his partner.

---

i   *Piper: I sold the building some four, five, six years later, when Soho was already "it," for $600,000, which was a fortune in those days. I was laughing because I made a profit; I think I'd paid something around $250,000 for it. Of course, nowadays that building is probably worth $8 million or more.*

The deal the pair struck was that the owners would steer clear of the venue so as not to tarnish it with their "from Long Island" vibe. When asked outright if they were Mafia, Piper smiled and coyly replied, "I mean, to work without a single permit for eight months in Manhattan, you have to have *some* connection." Fouratt, however, has been much more upfront about their background, claiming, "You couldn't do a club at that time that didn't have organized crime involved"[136]—seemingly forgetting that was not the case at CBGB, the Loft, Club 57, or Tier 3, to name just a few.

Fouratt coined the club's new name, Danceteria, taking inspiration from a rug store he'd passed called Carpeteria. Despite Piper and Fouratt's reputations, its success was far from assured—especially given its location.

Piper: The Garment District was really nowhere in those days. I was very concerned that the place would be off the beaten track and the people from downtown were not going to go.

Danceteria officially opened on May 9, 1980, but neither Piper, Fouratt, or the club's actual owners bothered to acquire any liquor or cabaret licensing. They operated Danceteria as an all-night club, open from 8:00 p.m. to 8:00 a.m., working around their lack of a liquor license with a drink ticket system—patrons bought a ticket, and then traded the ticket for a drink at the bar, so no cash was exchanged for booze. Piper attributed part of the club's success to that lack of legality, recalling, "The fact that the club was a complete piracy—in the sense that we had absolutely no permits whatsoever—was sort of an interesting concept."

Equally intriguing was the club's multilevel nature, a riff on what they'd previously attempted at Pravda, which was itself a riff on the Mudd Club. Danceteria's basement had deejays and a dance floor, the ground level had a stage where bands would play, and the second floor had a "video lounge" where patrons could relax. This is Danceteria's most significant contribution to the development of New York nightlife: options. Patrons could venture back and forth between three tonally distinct clubs, all for the price of one.

Pravda deejay Sean Cassette reprised his role at Danceteria, but Fouratt and Piper also brought in Mark Kamins, who'd deejayed at an Uptown disco called Trax (100 West 72nd Street). The two deejays worked in tandem, switching off every two or three songs for twelve hours straight. Though Kamins's disco background and Cassette's punk leanings were a counterintuitive mix, they blended smoothly. "The people that liked punk got into Bohannon and the people that were into my underground black music got into English punk and new wave because the vibe was the same, the feeling was the same," Kamins told writer Tim Lawrence.[137]

On the ground floor, Fouratt resumed booking bands as he had at Hurrah. But Danceteria adopted a broader, genre-bending template that allowed him to spread his wings, introducing an eclectic lineup that gave the Mudd Club a run for its money. Rather than foster a single scene, Danceteria welcomed several, which helped to further break down the genre boundaries the Mudd Club had already chipped away at.

For Pat Ivers, who worked at Danceteria, Fouratt's bookings were indicative of a shift in the city. "There weren't really new bands coming out of New York," she explained. "That energy had peaked." Of course, that's not strictly accurate—there were plenty of new rock bands, particularly in the mutant disco and hardcore scenes.

So while Fouratt booked plenty of local acts at Danceteria, he also drew heavily from a larger touring network of punk-inspired bands from other cities who channeled the genre's more accessible qualities. Ivers recalled, "A lot of bands from Athens, [Georgia,] like Pylon; the Suburbs from Minneapolis. That was actually a great aspect of Danceteria, was that we had so many different American bands."

Even more than stylistic breadth, the most significant aspect of Fouratt's booking was probably his insistence on fair compensation for performers—the very thing that had led to his departure from Hurrah.

Rhys Chatham: Jim is a very politically-conscious person. He thought it was disgusting that these bars were making money hand over fist and paying the musicians a pittance, or just from the door. So Danceteria was the rock club that instituted paying $1,000 for a gig. That was Jim, and once he started doing it, people wouldn't [play for less]. I'll be forever grateful to him for having done that.

Of course, the flipside to that compensation was that Danceteria required bands to not play other local shows too close to their scheduled gig, to ensure maximum turnout. Dany Johnson, a member of the mutant disco band Pulsallama, recalled that "The place we played the most was Danceteria, but we didn't play that many gigs, because when you play at a place like Danceteria you're not supposed to play anywhere else for a month." This policy means that a) local bands become decentralized from the day-to-day life of the scene, and b) the smaller clubs they'd once played regularly now couldn't book them. When clubs like Max's Kansas City, Tier 3, and the Mudd Club folded, Danceteria was at least partly to blame.

According to Piper, much of Danceteria's initial success was due to word of mouth among Downtown scenesters, which he and Fouratt engineered by hiring the most talkative ones.

Piper: We hired the staff not because they were good bartenders— they were not good bartenders, they were terrible bartenders—but they had connections. They were all trendy, and they were all big mouths, so they all were bringing in people. The place was big, so we could give comps away: "Bring all your friends, bring them in for free, and have fun."

A list of the original Danceteria staff now reads like a who's who of '80s artists: visual artists Keith Haring, David Wojnarowicz, Zoe Leonard, David McDermott, Peter McGough, and Chuck Nanney, performance artist Karen Finley, poet Max Blagg, and documentarians Emily Armstrong and Pat Ivers.

Piper and Fouratt could be somewhat controlling of their employees, especially when it came to aesthetics. Mark Kamins was forced to shave off his mustache when Fouratt banned facial hair, and Emily Armstrong recalled Piper telling her, "'You have to dress more sexy.' Hilly [Kristal at CBGB] would have never said, 'You have to dress more sexy.' Someone would have smacked him." It was all part of Danceteria's image of an exaggerated Downtown, in which everybody is hip and stylish and every detail is arranged just so.

To their credit, it worked like a charm. For a few magical months, Danceteria was a resounding success.

> **Piper:** *As the club got more famous, it was impossible to control the press. We didn't even have a press agent, but the articles were coming out, there was no way to stop the press from talking about this. But it was an illegal after-hours club! So suddenly there would be a centerfold in the* Daily News *with photos of Danceteria, and then the record companies started to get wind. They started to book parties at the club, and paid good money, so it was hard to reject.*[ii]

Piper and Fouratt weren't able to totally obfuscate the mob ties that lay beneath the club's DIY veneer.

> **Armstrong:** *We got paid every night in a brown envelope in cash. The leftover money [at the end of the night], they carried out of the club in a shopping bag. It was guys named Tony, you know? It was like every night the books closed. They had no checking accounts, it was a completely cash business.*

With all the attention, Danceteria's mob ties could only keep the cops away for so long. The ticking time bomb exploded on October 4, 1980, when the NYPD raided the club and arrested

---

ii   One major highlight was on June 26, 1980, when the Rolling Stones (minus drummer Charlie Watts) held a press party at the club to promote their new album *Emotional Rescue.*

twenty-one members of its staff. Neither Piper nor Fouratt were present at the time. "It is usual on such occasions for the employees to take the rap," Fouratt later explained, "and we had lawyers at the jail immediately. Everybody was free by 3:30 a.m."[138] Even so, "That left a pretty bad taste in my mouth," said Ivers.

Neither co-founder was charged with a crime, but the extraordinary underground club Piper and Fouratt had built was no more— at least for the time being.

DANCETERIA (REDUX)

After Danceteria closed, Jim Fouratt and Rudolf Piper stayed in business together, taking their skills to a series of other clubs: First, they helped reopen Peppermint Lounge (128 West 45th Street), the club that had introduced the world to the twist and hosted shows by the Beach Boys, the Ronettes, the Isley Brothers, and the Crystals before it closed in 1965. Fouratt and Piper were instrumental in relaunching the club, but fell out of favor with the owners when Fouratt once again insisted on paying performers well. A stint running the once-popular, now-flailing Studio 54 also came to a quick halt as owner Mark Fleischman repeatedly second-guessed their aesthetic, staffing, and booking decisions.

And then in 1982, Piper and Fouratt were approached by John Argento, who ran a Danceteria-inspired, three-story nightclub called Interferon at 30 West 21st Street. The immediate area around Interferon was desolate, although the surrounding neighborhood did have a nightlife history: the club was two blocks southeast from Nicky Siano's original Gallery and not far from the block on 23rd Street between 7th and 8th Avenues which housed the Chelsea Hotel and which had been home to the punk-era club Mothers, the multilevel disco Galaxy 21, and the post-punk venue Squat Theater.

So it was not unreasonable to expect a hip nightclub to flourish in the area, despite its relative isolation. But by the time Interferon opened, most of those clubs were gone and the area was again a no-man's land for nightlife. Bob Blank, who owned a recording studio called Blank Tapes one block south of the club, re-

PHOTO BY THE AUTHOR, 2023.

30 West 21st Street.

called that "After 6:00 p.m., you could lie down in the middle of 20th Street and nothing would hit you." So even though Argento had set Interferon up for the building's owner Alex DiLorenzo, using a similar template to the one Fouratt and Piper had used at Danceteria (ground-level live bands, second-floor deejays, and a third-floor lounge), it had struggled to gain traction.

With Piper and Fouratt on board, Interferon was transformed into a new, fully-licensed and legal iteration of Danceteria. The pair stuck with Argento's setup, but redecorated by bringing in some of Downtown's buzziest visual artists—including Keith Haring, Jean Michel-Basquiat, and Futura 2000—to paint a rotating series of murals on the club's walls.

The new Danceteria officially opened on February 3, 1982,

Print advertisement for Danceteria's reopening, late 1981.

kicking off with a show by a buzzy band from Athens, Georgia, called R.E.M.

Even more so than in its original location, the reopened Danceteria was all about options, options, options. Fouratt resumed booking duties and brought in an eclectic roster of performers that included Bush Tetras, Alan Vega, Half Japanese, Philip Glass, Diamanda Galas, Mission of Burma, Ministry, and Stevie Ray Vaughn. Mark Kamins took over the second-floor deejay booth, solo this time, while other deejays spun between sets on the first floor. Part of the third floor was converted into a video lounge, and part became a restaurant and bar.[iii]

But while it mimicked the original club in its layout and aesthetics, the turn toward full legitimacy meant that yet another step was taken away from the scene's DIY origins.

---

iii   Freddy Bastone remembered the food being "actually pretty decent," and noted that Sex Pistols/Public Image Ltd. front man John Lydon and Clash drummer Topper Headon both ate there regularly.

Jonny Sender: There was an outlaw quality to the first Danceteria, which the second one didn't have. Part of it was architectural; [the second one] was somehow a very nondescript environment. It felt, I don't know if "suburban" is the right word, but it felt office-like, even though it was a club. Even though it still had the community, it was part of the crossover from underground to the broader commercial success and acknowledgment of that scene.

As the second floor's sole deejay, Kamins truly came into his own, reveling in an eclectic, collage-like approach to deejaying that became his calling card. Writing for the *New York Times* in 1985, critic Jon Pareles described a typical set: "Mr. Kamins topped the Liquid Liquid instrumental with bursts from a speech by Swami A.C. Bhaktivedanta, played at 45 r.p.m. for a surreal, rap-like effect; within the hour, he mixed siren sounds, a two-second James Brown scream and vocals by the Egyptian singer Sabah into the dance music."[139]

Kamins's work was appreciated by his bosses, as he was paid a princely $300 a night. He also began moonlighting as an A&R representative for Island Records, where he was instrumental in bringing U2 to America for the first time. Elliott Sharp, who worked for Kamins at Island, regularly hung out in his boss's deejay booth. "The way Mark gauged the crowd was intuitive, just like watching a musician improvise," Sharp said. "It was masterful."

Johnny Dynell had gotten his start deejaying at the Mudd Club and had a brief stint at Pyramid Club before he was brought in to Danceteria (his partner Chi Chi Valenti was also hired as a bartender). In his new gig, Dynell honed the punk/disco fusion he'd first experimented with at the Mudd Club.

Dynell: I used to play Donna Summer's "I Feel Love" at the end of the night, and the Giorgio Moroder mix is like seventeen minutes. The record was 45 rpm, so I would play it at 33 rpm, and then slow the turntable all the way down from there, until it sounded almost

*like Suicide. It was the trippiest thing, and people would go nuts
for it. Larry Levan loved it, he was like, "That is fucking genius."*

Other Danceteria deejays included Dynell's Mudd Club co-
worker Anita Sarko, Bill Bahlman, Richard Sweret, Randa Relich
Milliron, and a barely legal upstart named Freddy Bastone.

*Bastone: When I started playing at clubs in the city, I wasn't even
of age, I was seventeen. I went down [to Danceteria] and gave a cassette to Rudolf, who was walking out of the building. Two or three
months later, I got a phone call from his girlfriend Diane Brill, saying that she would love for me to play at her birthday party, which
was the same day as my eighteenth birthday. She told me, "We never
listen to tapes, but I picked your tape out, put it in, and loved it."*

Just a few months into the new club's existence, Jim Fouratt was
let go. Tensions had been building between him and the unified
front of Piper, Argento, and DiLorenzo. Fouratt has since claimed
that he was again instructed by the club's ownership to pay bands
less money and refused, although Danceteria remained one of the
best-paying clubs in town after he left. Fouratt took his business
partners to court, arguing that they had conspired to rob him of
Danceteria's name (which he'd coined) and concept. Piper said
only that "Jim and I had a problem, he left, and then he sued and
we settled. And so that was that."[iv]

Hilariously, Fouratt was again replaced by his former assistant,
Ruth Polsky. The Anglophilia that Polsky had shown at Hurrah
was in full force when she took over at Danceteria: she booked the
American debuts of the Smiths, the Jesus and Mary Chain, Nick
Cave and the Bad Seeds, and the Teardrop Explodes, as well as

---

iv   Fouratt never worked in nightlife again, although he stayed involved in the
      music business as both a critic for *Spin*, *Billboard*, and *Rolling Stone*, and as
      an executive at Rhino Records and Mercury Records. He also remained
      active politically, and briefly ran for New York's city council in 2009 before
      withdrawing. He also ran for State Assembly in 2016, but lost.

PHOTO BY AND COURTESY OF JOHN A. MOZZER.

Clubgoers at Danceteria during a John Sex and the Bodacious Tatas concert, December 26, 1985.

the Sisters of Mercy, Cocteau Twins, Frankie Goes to Hollywood, Billy Bragg, and the Cult. With access to Danceteria's considerable funds, Polsky's role as a transatlantic musical diplomat only intensified. She had the power to pay British bands enough money to underwrite the rest of their American tours as they slowly built up a stateside fan base.

But more so than she had at Hurrah, Polsky also booked a wide range of local acts at Danceteria, drawing from smaller, nascent, and nonrock scenes: Run-DMC, Joey Arias, Adrenalin O.D., Foetus, Beastie Boys, Live Skull, Liquid Liquid, John Sex, Kool Moe Dee, and John Zorn, alongside left field picks like Sun Ra, Chris Isaak, Bo Diddley, and Tito Puente. Her vision for the club was constantly expanding, and she now had the platform and credibility to pretty much do as she pleased.

Piper: Ruth was better than Jim in the sense that she had a lot of connections with [bands in] London, she was constantly discovering new bands, and she was less antagonistic than Jim. Jim negotiated with the bands in a way that left the other side sour and hurt. Ruth was much smoother, so both sides came out of the negotiation happy.

Polsky's influence on Danceteria's reputation was substantial, but it was equaled by Haoui Montaug, doorman extraordinaire. Montaug had previously worked with Fouratt at Hurrah, and also had stints at Rock Lounge and Peppermint Lounge. Montaug possessed a flawless bullshit detector, and he was playful and generous enough to make the exclusionary concept of a velvet rope seem like it was all in good fun.

Bastone: It would be a goof to watch Haoui pick somebody. He wasn't like Steve Rubell [at Studio 54], who was really kind of obnoxious about it. Haoui had more of a sense of humor, he would ask questions to you in a joking matter.

Montaug would also regularly take Danceteria's stage for *No Entiendes* (Spanish for "You don't understand"), a weekly variety show he co-hosted with Anita Sarko. The show's motto was "If it's good, it's great. If it's bad, it's better." Performers included Madonna, who made her live debut at *No Entiendes*, and the Beastie Boys, who used the platform to explore various side projects including Grandmaster Jew (which found them in full Hasidic garb performing "My Deli," a parody of Run-DMC's "My Adidas").

"[B]eing able to go to this place [as teenagers] felt like a privilege," Beastie Boy Adam Horovitz wrote in 2018's *Beastie Boys Book*. "It felt more like Haoui let us hang out at Danceteria 'cause he knew we'd be safer in there than out writing graffiti or something stupid that dumb kids like us would get into."[140]

Depending on who you ask, some or all of the Beastie Boys were even employed at Danceteria as janitors. As with the original incarnation, the second Danceteria was consciously staffed with Downtown's cool kids to further build its buzz, but where the original location mostly employed soon-to-be art stars, the new one em-

ployed music legends in waiting: LL Cool J was an elevator opera-
tor, Sade Adu was a bartender, and Madonna worked coat check.

Though it initially only occupied three floors, Danceteria
benefited greatly from the fact that the rest of the thirteen-story
building was unoccupied (no noise complaints!), and as the club
flourished, they expanded. The fourth floor became Congo Bill,
a club-within-a-club—Piper referred to it at the time as a "VIP
room but with democratic tendencies, in which if you look great
you are allowed in"[141]—that hosted everything from Soviet-themed
performance art to full-on S&M parties. The rooftop, which they
dubbed "Wuthering Heights," opened up in the warmer months.
The basement was used for parties, including several "BatCave"
parties that Piper and Polsky staged with the entire staff from London's seminal goth club of the same name. Performance artist and
Bongwater vocalist Ann Magnuson staged her "Upwardly Mobile"
cabaret in the elevator; ex-staffer Karen Finley performed in the
unoccupied fifth floor. The otherwise-empty upper floors were
reportedly utilized for all manner of illicit activity.

Even with Danceteria's all-hands-on-deck creativity, impeccable staffing, and multiple owners, Rudolf Piper was the face of
the operation—especially once Jim Fouratt was gone. Piper even
went on a Nickelodeon talk show called *Livewire* in October 1983
to explain Danceteria to a bunch of gawky teens who stared at him
slack-jawed, visually thirsting for the adult freedom and unbridled
creativity Piper represented and described.[v]

THE FUN HOUSE

The Fun House at 526 West 26th Street had a considerable amount
of conceptual overlap with Danceteria: both clubs largely catered
to heterosexual audiences, and both provided those audiences with

---

v   Other *Livewire* guests included Frank Zappa, Afrika Bambaataa, R.E.M.,
     Tom Tom Club, the Ramones, Laurie Anderson, Manowar, Psychedelic Furs,
     Lords of the New Church, and Sugar Hill Gang. Clearly, some arch hipster
     had a day job programming children's television.

multiple entertainment options and sensory experiences. Deejays at both clubs spun a similar mix of post-punk, disco, funk, synth pop, and hip-hop. And yet, despite only being twenty minutes apart on foot, the two clubs might as well have been on different planets. Where the 21st Street Danceteria was a gussied-up take on Downtown's hipster culture, the Fun House was much more spiritually aligned with a lot of other venues we've looked at: all-ages, after hours, unpretentious, a little shabby, but with a lot of heart.

When the Fun House opened in a former print shop in 1979, owner Joe Monk had intended it to be a gay disco. Its initial deejays—which included Bobby "DJ" Guttadaro and Jim Burgess—were nightlife veterans who had already solidified their reputations at clubs like Infinity, Le Jardin, and 12 West. Taking a page from the Loft and Paradise Garage, no alcohol was served at the Fun House, allowing the club to remain open well past last call; its location in an otherwise-quiet industrial area on the far west side meant few neighbors were around to complain. A top-notch sound system by Richard Long, who'd built the Paradise Garage's famous system, was the cherry on top ("If you stood in front of the speakers, it would probably stop your heart," said musician Man Parrish).

But unlike the aforementioned sleek clubs and homey parties, the Fun House's decor was, let's say, high concept: hot dog and ice cream stands, arcade games, and best of all, a deejay booth housed inside a giant clown's head.[vi]

The club failed to draw Monk's intended gay disco audience, but the combination of dancing, a carnival-like atmosphere, and no alcohol all held significant appeal to another demographic: *kids*. Though the club was technically eighteen-plus, that rule was rarely enforced. So where the Danceteria audiences were stylish Downtowners in their twenties and thirties, the Fun House audiences were teenagers from the outer boroughs, mostly Italian and Puerto Rican, clad in cut-off T-shirts and gym shorts.

---

vi   Words cannot convey how bizarre and terrifying this thing was. Put the book down for a quick second and do a Google Image search.

As such, it was a Manhattan club only by the technicality of its location, a convenient midpoint between the Bronx, Brooklyn, and Queens. Whereas many clubs in this book were able to cater to their regulars with the cash brought in by an outer borough bridge-and-tunnel clientele (especially teenagers) of whom they were somewhat dismissive, those *were* the regulars at the Fun House. It was a bridge-and-tunnel club in the most delightful sense; clusters of kids would frequently break out into spontaneous chants of borough pride: "Brooklyn rocks the house!," "The Bronx rocks the house!"

The Fun House's identity coalesced once John "Jellybean" Benitez took up a residency inside the horrifying clown's mouth in 1981. Benitez was a Puerto Rican Bronx native who had come of age attending early hip-hop park jams in his home borough, but was also coming into Manhattan to hang out at underground discos like the Loft, the Sanctuary, the Gallery, and Paradise Garage. Benitez started deejaying as a teenager, first at a club in the Bronx called Charlie's, followed by a series of clubs in Manhattan and Long Island which included Hurrah (when it was still a *disco* disco, not a rock disco), Xenon, Studio 54, and the Electric Circus.

But the Fun House—with its night-long, fourteen-hour shifts, and lack of a coherent preexisting identity—finally gave Benitez the space to spread his wings. With Benitez at the decks, the club's audience ballooned almost instantly, and another spontaneous audience chant was born: "Jellybean rocks the house!"

Benitez's selections cultivated an emerging genre that combined the hard drum machine beats of Bronx hip-hop, the polyrhythmic swing and soulful vocals of classic New York disco, and the cold electronics of Euro disco and British new wave, which came to be known as electro.

Producer Arthur Baker came to prominence through his work on electro's ur-text record, Afrika Bambaataa and the Soulsonic Force's 1982 megahit "Planet Rock." He became the new genre's foremost practitioner.

Baker: The Fun House was very electro[-oriented], so a track like "Confusion" by New Order, or pretty much all my early records worked at the Fun House. Jellybean was my biggest supporter, and more often than not, I was testing my records at the Fun House. Jellybean worked on mixes with me for [Rockers Revenge's] "Walking on Sunshine," [Freeez's] "IOU" and "Confusion," so we'd get the keys to the Fun House to go listen to the record pretty much anytime, with an audience and without. I would bring the tape, throw it on, and sit in the booth and listen.

The process Baker describes is portrayed step-for-step in the music video for New Order's 1983 single "Confusion." As the video begins, the band wraps up a performance at the Paradise Garage while Baker finishes mixing their song (presumably the one we're hearing). Both parties then take cabs to the Fun House, where Baker hands Benitez a reel-to-reel tape of the newly completed mix. The band, producer, and deejay look out from the clown's mouth, taking in the success of their new single among the Fun House's teenage devotees.[vii]

There's something kind of wholesome and endearing about a nightclub full of teenagers playing Pac-Man and dancing to Freeez. Sure, plenty of them were on speed, and okay, a lot of them were having sex, and yes, the club had serious mob connections. But going back through photos and videos from the club, they emanate a gentle, heartwarming dorkiness.

And how's this for adorable: when the Fun House dancers were really feeling a record, they would convey their approval by *barking*.

Man Parrish: Jellybean was playing "Planet Rock" or some Arthur Baker track, and all of a sudden all the kids go, "RUH RUH

---

vii   New Order were hardly New York natives (the band hails from Manchester, England), but throughout the '80s they were ubiquitous at Manhattan clubs of nearly every stripe, from Paradise Garage to Tier 3. Their regular visits to New York clubs like the Fun House, Hurrah, and Danceteria informed the creation of their own Manchester club, the Haçienda, in 1982.

RUH." I said, "Oh my God, what's going on? Is everything OK?"
Jellybean goes, "Everybody's barking at the record, it's their way of
showing that they like it." So I said, "Oh my God, we've got to do
a record where we bark back at the crowd. Wouldn't that be funny?"

The resultant record was "Hip-Hop Be Bop (Don't Stop)." Despite the title, it's a shining example, not of hip-hop, but of electro at its peak.[viii] Parrish—a white, gay man who'd come of age at Max's Kansas City, had his name shorted from Manuel to "Man" by Andy Warhol, soundtracked gay porn films, and collaborated with Klaus Nomi—suddenly found himself performing to rooms full of straight teenagers at clubs like the Fun House, as well as Bronx hip-hop clubs like Disco Fever. "I was a fucking glamorpuss queen," Parrish recalled, "[performing] with Joey Arias, so we'd come in with dry ice and smoke machines and glitter makeup and outfits from Kansai Yamamoto, who used to do clothes for David Bowie. We were the butch version of Grace Jones."

THE ROXY

After Ruza Blue and Michael Holman's hip-hop nights at the East Village reggae club Negril were shut down in early 1982, Blue, sans Holman, briefly moved the party to Danceteria.

Soon after, Afrika Bambaataa and the Soulsonic Force released the Arthur Baker–produced *Planet Rock*—which, as previously noted, is much more of an electro record than a traditional rap record. According to Fab 5 Freddy, the song was inspired by Bambaataa's experiences deejaying at Downtown clubs like Negril and the Mudd Club, because "he felt he had played for this audience and he had a feel for what they would like."[142]

If so, he was right.

---

viii Younger cinephiles will recognize the song from the 2004 film *Shaun of the Dead*, in which the character Ed (Nick Frost) helpfully explains, "It's not hip-hop, it's electro, prick."

Kool Moe Dee: Planet Rock became so universal. It wasn't [just] a big record for hip-hop, it was the biggest record on the planet. Everybody and their mother knew about Planet Rock, regardless of whether they knew about hip-hop at all.

In the summer of 1982, Ruza Blue moved on from Danceteria to a cavernous roller disco called the Roxy, which was located at 515 West 18th Street—eight blocks south of the Fun House. Blue launched her Friday night "Wheels of Steel" parties at the club on June 18, with Afrika Bambaataa, Jazzy Jay, Grand Mixer D.St, and Grand Wizzard Theodore all deejaying, alongside performances by the Rock Steady Crew, the Soulsonic Force, and the Double Dutch Girls, live graffiti by Futura 2000, Fab 5 Freddy hosting, and nary a roller skate in sight. Turnout was encouraging, and within a matter of weeks, Blue was packing the place every Friday with a fairly even mix of Uptown (Black and Latinx kids from Harlem and the Bronx) and Downtown (white punks, artists, club kids, hipsters)—drawing in regulars from both Danceteria and the Fun House.

Holman briefly attempted to resuscitate the Thursday night parties at now-reopened Negril on his own, bringing in Afrika Islam, DJ Kool Herc, and DJ High Priest (aka Nick Taylor, who had played with Holman in the no wave band Gray[ix]). But Holman found it difficult to compete for attention with Blue's large-scale events at the Roxy. He instead turned his attentions to television, first with a series of hip-hop-themed public access shows, and ultimately with 1984's nationally broadcast hip-hop showcase *Graf-*

---

ix　Holman and Taylor weren't the only former members of Gray staking their claim in hip-hop. Their bandmate Vincent Gallo unsuccessfully attempted to rebrand as a rapper called Prince Vince (so named because he lived on Prince Street at the time). And Jean-Michel Basquiat—by now a wildly successful painter—used his newfound wealth and leverage to bankroll and produce a 1983 single called "Beat Bop" by Rammellzee and K-Rob (the former a rapper and artist who was a close friend of Basquiat's, the latter a fifteen-year-old rapper who'd caught Basquiat's eye at Negril).

fiti Rock—the first of its kind, and for many non–New Yorkers, their first exposure to the culture.

One of the Roxy's regulars was an NYU student named Rick Rubin. Rubin, who'd come of age playing in punk bands and checking out shows at CBGB and Max's Kansas City, had become a religious devotee of Holman and Blue's nights at Negril. Rubin's dormitory, Weinstein Hall (5 University Place, room 712), was a short walk from the club, and he began going there with the intention of courting potential rap acts for the nascent record label his parents were bankrolling: Def Jam. When Blue moved to the Roxy, Rubin was one of the couple-hundred people who came to her opening night.

One of Rubin's earliest attempts to merge his beloved punk and hip-hop was a show he dubbed "Uptown Meets Downtown" at the Hotel Diplomat (108 West 43rd Street) on March 26, 1982. Promoted under the "Def Jam Presents" tag, the unlikely bill brought together the rap group Treacherous Three, the post-punk/mutant disco band Liquid Liquid, and the hardcore band Heart Attack. Jack Rabid, who attended the show, recalled it as "a valiant attempt that only partially succeeded. Nobody really tried it again." But as Treacherous Three rapper Kool Moe Dee recalled, there were "way, way more white people there that would be nonexistent at the uptown shows"—a small but decisive step in Rubin's intended direction, foreshadowing his groundbreaking work producing rap-rock crossover hits for Run-DMC and the Beastie Boys later in the decade.

MADGE

Parrish: Jellybean was [in the deejay booth], and there was this girl, we used to call her "the skank" because she stunk. She had black hair and hairy armpits, and she wore a T-shirt that said, "I'm Madonna." Like, he's fucking THAT?? Oh god!

As with Bob Dylan in Chapter One, there's no point in my giving you a detailed biography of Madonna Louise Ciccone—you can find that in any number of places. But like Dylan in the folk scene, one can't tell this story without her.

Madonna moved to New York from Bay City, Michigan, in the summer of 1978. One of her earliest in-print appearances dates from the following year, in the magazine *Addix*: An artfully staged photo of "Madona" [*sic*] in a chic hat and fur coat, with a friend named Latina Latuna, attending Pravda's opening (and closing) night.

Swept up in the post-punk scene, she joined a series of bands: The Breakfast Club, Madonna and the Sky, the Millionaires, and Emmy and the Emmys, with whom she'd regularly gig at Max's Kansas City and CBGB. She was even briefly in a noise band called Spinal Root Gang alongside some early members of Swans.

But though she was *in* New York's underground, she was never truly *of* it. Her eyes were on widespread fame from the outset, which made her a natural fit at the similarly *in*-but-not-truly-*of*-the-underground Danceteria. By 1982, she'd gone solo and was running around town with a demo tape containing rough versions of three songs: "Burning Up," "Ain't No Big Deal," and "Everybody." Though most deejays in the city (including Freddy Bastone) turned her down, Mark Kamins eventually played the "Everybody" demo at Danceteria. "I'm not sayin' the place went mad crazy," he later recalled, "but it worked."[143]

The two began dating, and Kamins helped her secure a deal with Sire Records, with "Everybody" lined up to be her first single. Kamins made his producing debut on the single, which was recorded at Blank Tapes,ˣ a studio located one block south of Dance-

---

x For stylistic breadth and cultural significance, Blank Tapes was arguably Danceteria's equal: the studio's discography includes Television's seminal punk single "Little Johnny Jewel"; disco hits by Musique, Class Action, Crown Heights Affair, and Inner Life; groundbreaking remixes by deejays like Larry Levan, François Kevorkian, and Tee Scott; and no wave/mutant disco albums by the likes of James Chance, Lydia Lunch, Lizzy Mercier Descloux, and DNA. It was the favored studio for genre-bending auteur Arthur Russell, and classic albums by Talking Heads (*Speaking in Tongues*), the Gun Club (*Miami*), Joe Bataan (*Mestizo*), Ashford & Simpson (*Solid*), the B-52s (*Mesopotamia*), Miami Sound Machine (*Eyes of Innocence*), and Sun Ra (*Lanquidity*) were all tracked there.

teria at 37 West 20th Street—so close, the studio's and club's back walls nearly touch. Kamins favored Blank Tapes for his remixing and production work, as much for its convenience as its quality. According to owner Bob Blank, "With all the artists that Mark Kamins brought in, it was very convenient because they would literally go out [to Danceteria], play a mix, and come back at 3:00 in the morning and keep working on it."

A video for "Everybody" was filmed at Paradise Garage, but even so, it was unquestionably a *Danceteria record*, produced by its star deejay and performed by its coat check girl. Madonna made her live solo debut performing "Everybody" as part of Haoui Montaug's *No Entiendes* cabaret on December 16, 1982.[xi] From there, she regularly performed at Danceteria, notably opening for the Smiths' American debut on New Year's Eve 1983.

By that point, Madonna had taken up with Chelsea's other superstar deejay, Jellybean Benitez. The two first collaborated on a remix of Madonna's "Physical Attraction"; Benitez also remixed "Lucky Star" and "Burning Up," and (like Kamins before him) made his debut as a producer with "Holiday."

"It was an anthem of the street before the record even dropped," Benitez later claimed. "Madonna hung out in the [Fun House] DJ booth every night so the crowd knew her and it just exploded."[144]

But as her career took off, Madonna became an increasingly spectral presence in the city. She'd soaked up all of New York's underground music, art, and fashion and converted it into something palatable for suburban tweens across America. And then she moved to LA.

As such, one could view her performance as the titular character in 1985's *Desperately Seeking Susan* as a coda to her early years in the city. One memorable sequence was shot in Danceteria's third floor lounge, in which Madonna (as Susan) dances to "Into the Groove" by Madonna (as herself). She is joined by Gary Glass (Mark Blum), a suburban fish out of water in business attire who

xi   Footage of Madonna's *No Entiendes* performance is viewable on YouTube.

seems to be equally dumbfounded and entranced by the club's hipster denizens. He tries to blend in and dance, but remains visibly uncomfortable. It's a perfect distillation of a shift in the city's nightlife that was already underway—one which Madonna's ascendance underscored and intensified.

CHANGES

At 656-662 6th Avenue, just around the corner from Danceteria and next door to Blank Tapes, sits the Church of the Holy Communion. The Episcopal church, which dates back to the 1800s and

PHOTO BY THE AUTHOR, 2023.

656–662 6th Avenue.

was officially landmarked by the city in 1966, shuttered and became deconsecrated in the mid-seventies.

In 1983, it was purchased by Canadian impresario Peter Gatien, who transformed it into a nightclub called the Limelight. Gatien took full advantage of the church's labyrinthine architecture, transforming the sanctuary into the main dance floor, a small chapel into a bar, and a second-floor library into a VIP room. Though it hadn't been a church for several years, the club's opening was protested by outraged Christians; one sign read, "If you want to get down, get down on your knees."[145]

The Limelight is such a mythical New York club at this point that few people realize it was part of a multinational chain: Gatien opened the first Limelight in Hallandale, Florida, in the late '70s; after its closure, Gatien opened a second Limelight in an Atlanta strip mall, where he created a stir by installing a see-through floor with two live sand sharks swimming around underneath it. The Atlanta club was successful enough for Gatien to open a New York branch in 1983; Chicago and London locations both opened two years later.

When it opened, the New York Limelight took after its neighbor in mixing dance deejays and live rock bands, though less gracefully—bookings were diverse to the degree of incoherence, ranging from Buster Poindexter to Whitney Houston to Suzanne Vega to Mötley Crüe. Gatien seemed to thirst for the same cross-pollination of subcultures that had flocked to Danceteria, but the Limelight was at best a mistranslation of Danceteria's premise by an outsider with little knowledge of the city's actual underground. As Gatien later put it, "The guy in the Armani suit will think the person in the sequins is a total loser, the person in the Mohawk will think the guy in the Armani is a total loser, and they end up entertaining each other."[146]

That same year, riding the success of Madonna's "Holiday," Jellybean Benitez left the Fun House and quit deejaying. He instead pursued a full-time career as a producer and remixer, leading to collaborations with everyone from Paul McCartney to Wang Chung. A young Bronx-raised Puerto Rican and Fun House regular named "Little" Louie Vega took Jellybean's place behind the decks. But without Jellybean's star power to draw teenagers from the outer boroughs, the club closed in 1985. It reopened under a new name, Heartthrob, and ran a few more years with Vega again deejaying. For god knows what reason, the clown head deejay booth stayed put.

By that point, Rudolf Piper could see a shift on the horizon. Though he and John Argento had opened a Hamptons outpost of the club in Water Mill, New York, in 1984, both he and Mark Kamins left their central posts at Danceteria in 1985.

The 21st Street Danceteria closed in 1986. The club briefly reopened (without Piper's involvement) in 1990 in the Martha Washington Hotel (29 East 29th Street). Though veterans like Mark Kamins, Johnny Dynell, and Freddy Bastone were brought in to deejay, it failed to recapture the spark of its previous incarnations. It was put out of its misery in 1993; two years later, the Hamptons outpost also shuttered.

With Danceteria gone, Ruth Polsky poured her energy into starting a company called S.U.S.S. (Solid United States Support), which was designed to help international touring bands navigate the United States. She continued to book shows here and there, too: On September 7, 1986, she set up a record release show for Certain General, a local band she'd been managing, at the Limelight. On the night of the show, Polsky was standing outside the club when a livery car ran a red light on 6th Avenue, hitting a yellow cab which spun out of control. The cab flew onto the sidewalk and into the wall of the Limelight, taking Ruth Polsky with it. She was thirty-one.

TEMPLES OF SHIT

By the mid-eighties, as Downtown's underground music and art scenes were making significant advances into the wider popular consciousness, an antithetical subculture was taking root even further Downtown, on Wall Street. Starting in 1982, the Dow Jones Industrial Average steadily rose, enriching the city's stock traders to a degree previously unseen—so much so that Tom Wolfe dubbed them "Masters of the Universe" in his 1987 novel *The Bonfire of the Vanities*. In that same year's movie *Wall Street*, directed by Oliver Stone, stockbroker Gordon Gekko (Michael Douglas) summarized the pervading mindset: "Greed—for lack of a better word—is good... Greed, in all of its forms—greed for life, for money, for love, knowledge—has marked the upward surge of mankind."[147] That Gekko was objectively the movie's villain seems to have been lost on successive generations of stockbrokers who continue to venerate him as a hero.

And where New York's housing prices declined by 12.4 percent between 1974 and 1980, they rose by a whopping 152 percent between 1980 and 1989. Almost all neighborhoods saw their median prices rise by at least 100 percent, and eighteen neighborhoods saw their median prices increase by 200 percent.[148] No public figure more embodied the growth and excesses of the 1980s real estate boom than Limelight habitué Donald Trump, whose garish 1983 temple to his own greed, Trump Tower, was subsidized by significant tax abatements from the city. This was true of several luxury buildings of the era, costing the city an estimated total of $1.4 billion at a time when public services and municipal jobs were still being cut.

Between March 1977 and March 1984, New York City's economy added over 215,000 white collar jobs while shedding over 100,000 blue collar jobs.[149] Though this was part of a larger national trend away from blue collar industry, the shift was felt acutely in New York, with a growing percentage of the city's low-wage jobs coming from the service industry.

With unimaginable wealth comes unimaginable excess, and these Masters of the Universe were more than happy to indulge. Where New York had long nurtured the romantic image of the cash-poor but experience-rich painter starving in a garret, the 1980s saw Downtown denizens like Jean-Michel Basquiat, Julian Schnabel, and Keith Haring strike gold as their paintings suddenly became big-ticket investment pieces—so much so that Basquiat, who was earning over one million dollars a year by the mid-eighties, began wearing expensive Armani suits while he painted.

Artsy-but-upscale nightclubs like Area and the Limelight helped nurture and solidify the relationships between Downtown's nouveau riche art stars and the city's power brokers; where many artists were enamored with their benefactors' wealth, so too were the benefactors enamored with the creative class's debauched nightlife.

And where the rich go, the not-yet-rich follow. Clubs like Max's Kansas City, Danceteria, the Mudd Club, and Pyramid Club had long attracted a contingent of out-of-towners whose spending was necessary to the clubs' survival. But suddenly there were even more of them coming in, and with Danceteria closing in 1986 and Area closing in '87, they needed somewhere to go. They found it on 14th Street.

Though geographic boundaries in the city have always been a little nebulous, most people would agree that 14th Street marks the boundary between Downtown and Midtown. So it's a bit on the nose that the two clubs that spelled the end of a certain era of Downtown culture both opened blocks apart from each other on 14th Street: the Palladium and Nell's.

The Palladium (126 East 14th Street), formerly known as the Academy of Music, had been hosting concerts since the 1960s, welcoming the likes of the Rolling Stones, the Grateful Dead, Bruce Springsteen, and Kiss. But in 1984, the venue was acquired by Steve Rubell and Ian Schrager, the former owners of Studio 54 who had been jailed for tax evasion and obstruction of justice in 1980. Looking to get back into nightlife, they transformed the concert hall into a monstrous megaclub. With a legal capacity of six thousand people (which was often exceeded), it was the largest nightclub the world had ever seen.

Being the proprietors of a large, glitzy nightclub was nothing new for the former Studio 54 owners, and they understood that their disco-era reputation as starfucking Uptown elitists would need to be obfuscated in order to win over the Downtown scenesters. And so, as Johnny Dynell put it, "Basically everything you could buy that was downtown, they bought." Celebrity artists were brought in to paint murals, well-known deejays were hired (including Larry Levan, Johnny Dynell, Freddy Bastone, and Anita

Sarko), Haoui Montaug was planted at the door, and Rudolf Piper was brought in as the club's director.

Bastone: The Palladium was much more corporate than Danceteria. You could feel the corporation working in the background.

Rubell and Schrager's Palladium could trace its cultural roots in the city back through the Limelight, Area, Danceteria, Paradise Garage, the Mudd Club, and all the way back to the Loft, CBGB, and Max's Kansas City (if not even further back to the Greenwich Village hootenannies and Yoko Ono's loft concerts). But by this point, it was so far removed from those original concepts that the thread was practically unrecognizable—or, in the eyes of Chi Chi Valenti, recognizable in the worst way.

Dynell: Chi Chi and I went to the opening. I had seen it while they were building it, and Steve had given me a tour, but walking into the opening [and seeing it] filled with people and everything, Chi Chi looked around and was just silent. We finally went to the dance floor, and she just went, "This is a temple of shit." I was listening to the sound system, and the lights were incredible, I was just bowled over by everything. [I said,] "Oh, you don't like it?" And she just looked at me and said, "It's all over." And she was absolutely right.

In both design and intention, Palladium came across as a sort of Danceteria on steroids: The main dance floor had a large Keith Haring mural as its centerpiece, flanked by twenty-five rotating video screens. A cathedral-like room upstairs had its walls and vaulted ceiling painted by Francesco Clemente. A basement space featured fluorescent Kenny Scharf murals and surrealist props. The intimate Mike Todd Room, where Anita Sarko deejayed, contained a forty-foot-long Jean-Michel Basquiat mural behind the bar, with lace-covered tables and candelabras that contrasted with its untouched industrial ceiling. A cushioned lounge allowed guests to sit and chat. Performers ran the gamut from Deee-Lite to Neil Young to 2 Live Crew to Einstürzende Neubauten to Liberace.

But by virtue of the club's enormity, the mix of artists, musicians, fashionistas, drag queens, and painfully cool celebrities who once haunted the Danceteria were now joined by the people Haoui Montaug had once turned away: yuppies, models, trust fund kids, and painfully *uncool* celebrities.

> *Piper: I had to make sure that we had at least 5,000 people there every night, six nights a week. Each night had its own personality. Monday night the club was closed for private events. Tuesday night, I put Jerry Rubin[xii] and his Jewish singles night. Wednesday was new wave, live music. Steve Rubell hated that night; he hated bands. He always was high—I don't think I ever saw this guy straight—and he had this thing of interrupting and cutting a show short because people were not drinking during the show. He would say, "After three or four songs, they're off! Close the curtain!" Of course, the bands were not happy with that.*

In 1986, a much smaller club called Nell's opened in a former electronics store at 246 West 14th Street, just a few blocks west of the Palladium. The club was co-owned by restaurateur power couple Keith McNally and Lynn Wagenknecht, as well as actress Laura "Little Nell" Campbell, best known for her role as Columbia in *The Rocky Horror Picture Show.* For Piper, "Nell's brought the spirit of uptown to downtown."

Though it hosted live music and deejays (including Dynell and Jonny Sender), Nell's was primarily designed as a supper club: They served food, and much of the clientele was seated. Beaded chandeliers, Oriental rugs, and low lighting created a swanky but homespun vibe—one exploited in music videos by U2 ("One") and Notorious B.I.G. ("Big Poppa"). The club's 250-person ca-

---

xii　A co-founder of the Yippies alongside Jim Fouratt, Rubin was reborn as an unrepentant capitalist and networker in the late '70s.

pacity led to a door so elitist that even the elites frequently found themselves turned away ("I think that exclusivity was more the reputation than the fact," Campbell protested in 1994).[150]

Nell's was representative of a new trend in the city, one that McNally and Wagenknecht had pioneered: restaurants designed like nightclubs and/or nightclubs designed like restaurants. By 1989, *New York Times* writer Lisa W. Fodedaro recognized that "the people who used to glide past the velvet ropes, leaving the masses outside, are more interested in going to restaurants these days than clubs...dancing has also receded as the raison d'etre for most nightclubs, with the urge to move replaced by the desire to talk and lounge. Food, of course, is a natural accompaniment."[151]

Music played a significant—but not central—role at Nell's. Patrons were entertained by an in-house jazz ensemble, and by the late '80s and '90s, the club's deejays were spinning a compelling mix of house, reggae, disco, and especially hip-hop. "Hip-hop was maturing [in the '90s], making more money, and partying at a place like Nell's meant something," deejay Stretch Armstrong later recalled. "It's like you were entering into a new realm of success and you were in a new social circle[.]"[152]

The introduction of self-consciously "mature" nightclubs like the Palladium and Nell's was well-timed. For the majority of the time frame covered in this book, New York State's legal drinking age was eighteen. Every bar-oriented scene we've discussed, from Gerde's Folk City to CBGB to Tier 3, benefited from this reality, because college-aged kids tend to have the kind of time, energy, and enthusiasm to devote to a nascent music scene that responsibility-burdened adults simply do not.

In December 1982, the minimum age in New York was raised by one year to nineteen, which did not bode well. Things went from bad to worse when studies came out showing that a few other states that had lowered their drinking age from twenty-one to eighteen during the '70s had then seen a documented increase in drunk driving accidents. In 1984, New Jersey senator Frank Lautenberg, with the encouragement of the nonprofit organization Mothers Against Drunk Driving, introduced the National Minimum Legal

Drinking Act. Though states are still technically able to enforce the legal drinking age of their choosing, the act proposed 10 percent cuts to any state's federal highway construction funds if they failed to enforce a minimum age of twenty-one. The act passed and was signed into law in 1984 by President Ronald Reagan; the New York State Legislature in turn raised the legal drinking age to twenty-one, effective December 1985.

Increasingly, eighteen-to-twenty-one-year-olds, the lifeblood of practically every nightlife scene in the city, musical or otherwise, found themselves banned from many of the legal spaces that had been their homes away from home—never mind the fact that, as residents of a geographically condensed, pedestrian-friendly city with extensive public transportation, almost none of them drove. Since they could no longer spend money on alcohol, there was no longer an incentive for bars to let them in. From then on, music venues and nightclubs have had three choices: 1) cater to the tastes and needs of an older, less passionate demographic, 2) not serve alcohol (as had already been the case at the Loft, Paradise Garage, and the Fun House), or 3) break the law and cross their fingers.

There are two things I know to be true about most adults: First, their tastes in art and music calcify as their focus begins to turn elsewhere. Second, they'd much rather sit down than stand up. Both of these realities are poison for any vibrant nightlife scene.

A year and a half after Palladium opened, Rudolf Piper left his position as the club's director and helped open Tunnel, a cavernous eighty-thousand-square-foot building located two blocks northwest from where the Fun House had been. The club's technical address was 220 12th Avenue, but it occupied an entire block between 11th and 12th Avenues and West 27th and 28th Streets. It had previously housed the Terminal Warehouse Company Central Stores Building, and retained train tracks that ran through the center of the building which had once allowed freight trains to load and unload cargo.

Tunnel was owned by two Israelis, developer Boaz Aharoni and Bonjour Jeans tycoon Eli Dayan. Neither had been involved in nightlife prior to the club's opening, so they wisely brought in both Piper and Haoui Montaug.[xiii] According to Piper, he was involved in opening the club "through the end of Danceteria and all through [my time at] the Palladium. The Tunnel took years to get done and it was very expensive."

Like Palladium, Tunnel adopted Danceteria's basic concept of diversity: The main dance floor had the train tracks as its centerpiece; artist Kenny Scharf designed the psychedelic Lava Lounge room; other theme rooms included a Victorian library and an S&M dungeon. Even the gender-neutral bathrooms had a vibe of their own. But this time around, the mix of environments lent itself less to the demographic and generic cross-pollination that Danceteria had fostered, and more to self-segregation. Over the course of the late '80s and '90s, Tunnel nurtured both a mostly white house and techno scene and a mostly Black hip-hop scene that existed side-by-side in the humongous venue, but rarely interacted.

Sender: The big clubs were able to have multiple rooms and multiple deejays, [but] they'd be completely separate parties in different rooms, sometimes with different entrances and different admissions—people would go to one party and stay there all night. They were trying to be all things to all people[, but] it becomes too much, like how if you mix every color together you get gray.

There were also, for the first time, no rock bands—the ties between underground rock and dance culture that had briefly coalesced at the Mudd Club and Danceteria had already started to strain at Palladium, but now they were severed. Anyway, Rudolf Piper had more pressing concerns.

Piper: The place was huge, and it opened just a few weeks after Nell's opened. That was a problem that I suddenly had, which I was

---

xiii Montaug wasn't the only noteworthy person working the door at Tunnel: one of the club's bouncers was a young Mark Sinclair, better known to the world as actor Vin Diesel.

not counting on. Suddenly it was cool to be in a small place, have bottles, models, more sophistication—not rough, underground counterculture. It was the concept of "BoBo": Bourgeois Boheme. You're downtown, but you still want to have a bottle of Johnnie Walker Black at your table. So I had this huge club now that I had to make cool, and that's how the Club Kids started.

The Club Kids—a group of young (mostly white, mostly queer, mostly underage), self-aggrandizing promoters and scenesters with a taste for cartoonish attire and prodigious substance abuse—had their roots at Danceteria, where many went in the club's waning years and where figurehead Michael Alig worked as a busboy in 1984. The Club Kids have very little to do with music (although as a group they tended to gravitate to house and techno), nor were they especially interesting people. They are relevant to the focus of this book only in that their ascendance (and eventual descendance) had severe and long-term negative impacts on the city's nightlife, which in turn endangered the creation and consumption of underground music.

> *Piper: I needed to do something, so I put the Club Kids in the basement and I said, "Everything is free, you'll be [down] here, but you have to go upstairs into the club and entertain—you have to be like a freak show." That's how this formula worked: there were a lot of mainstream people that went to the Tunnel just to see the Club Kids. At the same time, it was a source of worries for me and Eli Dayan, because these people were all underage. There was a problem waiting to happen there.*

In a short time, other clubs like Palladium and the Limelight adopted similar policies, with many even putting Club Kids on their payrolls. The Club Kids were hardly the first professional dilettantes: they were explicitly patterned after Andy Warhol's entourage of "Superstars" who once haunted the back room at Max's Kansas City, only this time around there was no Warhol or Velvet

Underground there to bestow them with lasting significance. Because going to a nightclub and making themselves the center of attention was the totality of their art, the Club Kids weren't threatened by the presence of ogling bridge-and-tunnel types—they were fueled by it. In return, the Club Kids offered these outsiders a nonthreatening, easily understood simulacra of a hedonistic underground that made them feel cool by association.

DJ Mojo: The Club Kids seemed to be kids who came from money but were outsiders in their own communities, so they came to New York and formed their own community, like the Island of Misfit Toys. I understood it, and I'm not saying they're bad people—well, with one exception—but it just wasn't interesting to me.

MARS & SOUND FACTORY

After Tunnel, Rudolf Piper's next venture was also on the far west side of Manhattan, just a bit south of Tunnel: Mars (28-30 10th Avenue, near West 13th Street). The club, which was backed by wealthy Japanese funders, opened on New Year's Eve 1988. It was yet another twist on the Mudd Club/Pravda/Danceteria/Palladium/Tunnel multistory formula, and yet another step removed from that first spark of inspiration. Instead, it embraced a superficial, vaguely "artsy" but largely incoherent wackiness: one area had lava lamps and other psychedelic throwbacks, one had Chinese-style decorations and a repurposed pharmacy sign advertising "Drugs," one had industrial machinery, and one was a throwback to the area's meatpacking past with meat hooks and walk-in freezers. Gone were the commissioned fine art pieces. Still, some of the city's best deejays could be found on different floors, including several Downtown mainstays from the earlier part of the decade (Frankie Knuckles, Dany Johnson, Justin Strauss, Larry Levan, Freddy Bastone) alongside upstarts like Richard Melville Hall, aka Moby, who made his deejaying debut at the club.

Mars, like Limelight, Palladium, and Tunnel before it, translated (or, if you like, watered down) the city's creative underground for the uncreative mainstream, and something became lost with each iteration. Speaking to the *New York Times* in 1989, Piper made his motives for the club clear: "[Clubbing] is no longer only for the elite...[Mars] caters to people who have no interest in the Establishment, but who are not necessarily anti-Establishment."[153] Hal Rubenstein, writing for *New York* that same year, put it bluntly: "'Genius' is how some of [Piper's] nocturnal contemporaries describe him. For others, the word 'sell-out' comes to mind."[154]

That same year, entrepreneur Richard Grant, nightlife impresarios Christina Visca and Phil Smith, and deejay Junior Vasquez opened Sound Factory in a converted warehouse at 530 West 27th Street—one block north of where the Fun House had been, and catty-corner from Tunnel.

Deliberately patterned after the Paradise Garage, where Vasquez had been a regular, Sound Factory served no alcohol, and as such was able to remain open as late as they pleased—which, on a typical Saturday night, meant noon on Sunday. Snacks, juice, and coffee were complimentary, and in a nod to the AIDS crisis looming over the club's largely gay clientele, so were condoms. But running a club that large in a gentrifying area was expensive, and without alcohol sales to depend on, Sound Factory instituted an exorbitant $18 door fee (it was later raised to $20). That said, on at least one occasion they dropped dollar bills from the ceiling, just for the hell of it—which *never* would have happened at the Garage.

With Vasquez spinning the cutting edge of house music, the club attracted a committed post–Paradise Garage audience of gay men.[xiv] The after-hours nature of the club combined with its enor-

---

xiv This included dancers from Harlem's drag ball culture (which is a whole book unto itself), who introduced a dance called vogueing to Downtown denizens at the club; Madonna, a friend of Vasquez's and by then as famous as an entertainer can possibly be, was introduced to the dance there and was inspired by/ripped it off for her 1990 hit "Vogue."

mous dance floor also meant that revelers from Tunnel, Mars, Palladium, Nell's, and the Roxy had somewhere to go after last call.[xv]

And by the early '90s, what had been the cutting-edge of New York dance music was again becoming nationally successful pop, with acts like C&C Music Factory and Deee-Lite following in Madonna's footsteps and deejays like Vasquez, Todd Terry and Danny Tenaglia cranking out remixes that frequently eclipsed the originals (e.g. Terry's remix of Everything but the Girl's "Missing," now considered the song's canonical version).

By 1989, the city's dance club scene was a precarious and ambiguous ecosystem, with megaclubs like Limelight, Palladium, Tunnel, and Mars proliferating alongside elitist sanctums like Nell's, and Paradise Garage descendants like Sound Factory and the Choice. And then, for the first (but not the last) time, a totally avoidable tragedy brought everything to an abrupt stop.

HAPPY LAND

In November 1988, a club called Happy Land Social Club at 1958 Southern Boulevard in the Bronx was ordered to close over several building violations, including a lack of sprinklers, fire alarms or exits; the club was also without a liquor license. There was no official follow-up visit, and the club reopened soon after without addressing any of those issues. The building's owner (though not the club's) at the time was Alex DiLorenzo, former co-owner of the 21st Street Danceteria.

In the early morning hours of March 25, 1990, a man named Julio Gonzalez went to Happy Land to try to reconnect with his ex-girlfriend who worked at the club. After a heated argument, bouncers kicked Gonzalez out. He went to a nearby Amoco sta-

---

xv   In the mid-nineties, Sound Factory opened a smaller offshoot called Sound
     Factory Bar at 12 West 21st Street—the same block that had once housed
     Danceteria. Much more underground than its parent club, it regularly hosted
     deejays like Frankie Knuckles and Little Louie Vega and became a main
     hangout for the city's house deejays and music industry types.

tion and purchased one dollar's worth of gasoline, returned to the club, poured the gasoline around the front door, and set it aflame. The club's other exits had been sealed up to stop people from sneaking in, so with fire spreading across the only working exit, eighty-seven people, mostly from a local Honduran community, died. It was the deadliest fire the city had seen since the Triangle Shirtwaist Company fire, which had occurred seventy-nine years prior on the same date.

The newly elected mayor David Dinkins came to the scene and vowed to crack down on what he claimed were 176 other illegally operating "social clubs." Dinkins expanded the NYPD's night-life task force, which had been formed under his predecessor Ed Koch in response to a lesser nightclub fire in the Bronx. Where Dinkins expected 176 illegal clubs, the task force found 1,391 (a disproportionate amount of which served Latinx and Caribbean communities, as Happy Land had). Building and safety code violations shuttered 505 clubs; 106 of those ignored the vacate orders and were padlocked shut.

Thirteen weeks later, Dinkins was satisfied with the task force's success and cut it down from twenty teams to ten. "We've dried up the majority of clubs," an unidentified officer told the *New York Times*. "We've closed down all the hard-core locations."[155] Still, Inspector Frank Biehler, commander of the NYPD's Public Morals Division, insisted that the reduced task force would continue to surveil existing venues, saying that "The city is playing hardball now."[156]

RUDY AND PETER

By the early '90s, the city's nightlife landscape had undergone such transformation that, despite his having contributed to the results, Rudolf Piper no longer saw a place for himself within it. An attempt to open a Downtown club called Quick in 1990 was unsuccessful, Piper admits, "because things had changed. It just had no identity—it was not hip-hop, it was not Club Kid, it was not disco."

Piper: I didn't want to deal with downtown anymore because it was becoming too problematic. I had gunfights at Mars, which is something that never happened before. The back door was rampantly letting in drug dealers, who were taking spots inside the club—meaning, this corner is my corner and I'm dealing drugs here and nobody touches it. The security didn't want to touch it because the guy had a weapon or was going to seek revenge. I'm also not in favor of calling the police, because if there would be a raid there, they would find drugs, and who's at fault? It's me, and I was not even making [that] money, it was the drug dealer.

His winning streak having ended in a city that no longer enthused him, Piper left to pursue other nightlife opportunities in Aspen, Colorado, and Beverly Hills, California.

Now it was Peter Gatien's time to shine. He had already been nurturing the Club Kids that Piper had discarded at Mars; Michael Alig had been promoting his wildly successful Disco 2000 parties at the Limelight since 1988. Alig later recalled Gatien telling him, "I see something of value in what you're doing, and if you're willing to work with me, then maybe we can make a club that is not solely fabulous and not solely bridge and tunnel."[157]

The outsourcing of nightclubs to independent promoters on different nights was a growing trend, with Alig at its forefront. Where clubs like Danceteria had welcomed multiple genres, allowed them to share a space, and fostered cross-pollination, now clubs just welcomed different genres on different nights and left it at that.

You may have noticed that we haven't talked much about music for a while. Here's why: As the audience for and borders of Downtown nightlife expanded (or, in the case of Nell's, deliberately contracted), music ceased to be the clubs' operating principle. Even flashy '70s' dance clubs like Studio 54 and Xenon foregrounded a specific genre of music: disco. But in the '90s, the decadent nightclub environment itself was the star. One did not need to have particularly good taste, or really *any* taste, in music to go to Limelight and say, "Wow, a club in a church! Who'da thunk?" There was *just* enough music, *just* enough art, and *just* enough outlandish local celebrities to maintain the illusion of an underground. Granted, some club promoters were devoted to underground music—for instance, the Limelight and Mars both became go-to hosts for rave-y techno. But in the context of this book, clubs like Limelight, Tunnel, and Palladium are important for us to talk about not for what they built, but for what they destroyed.

In 1992, Gatien bought the Palladium and Tunnel, both of which had been losing steam following their high-profile openings; he also opened a garish new club near Times Square called Club USA (218 West 47th Street). Alig was brought in to promote parties at those clubs as well. "I think the timing is right," Gatien told the *New York Times*. "In the early 1980s, the big clubs did very well. Then, things were very conservative, with Reagan and all, so you had these sedate little clubs. The '90s remind me more of the late 1970s...[People] are open to having a good time [again]."[158]

Boy, did he miscalculate.

In 1994, New Yorkers elected Republican Rudolph W. Giuliani to be mayor. Giuliani promised to clean up the city, which still retained some of its trademark '70s and '80s grime, to make it more palatable to tourists, co-op owners, and retail chains. Giuliani adopted the "broken windows" theory of policing, in which minor crimes like turnstile jumping, graffiti, and panhandling are prosecuted as though they are major crimes; according to this philosophy, treating small crimes this way will prevent the actual major crimes from occurring (the efficacy of this theory has since been seriously called into question). "Obviously, murder and graffiti are two vastly different crimes," Giuliani insisted. "But they are part of the same continuum, and a climate that tolerates one is more likely to tolerate the other."[159] [xvi]

So yeah, maybe not the best time to be New York's reigning Club King.

---

xvi To be fair, the violent crime rate in the city did decrease by 56 percent during Giuliani's mayoral tenure—although the numbers had already started going down under Dinkins, and the statistics were also decreasing nationally.

If you're a cop on the lookout for low-level, largely victimless crimes, nightclubs are an obvious and easy target. Sensing a turn for the worse, Sound Factory's owners closed up shop in 1995, with Richard Grant explaining, "Contrary to rumor, we did not lose our cabaret license. But we knew that was a danger, so we decided to close."[160] The club reopened that same year as Twilo; a shinier, more moneyed and heterosexual spin on the Sound Factory formula.

The NYPD were desperate to take Gatien down: he was a high-profile nightclub impresario who oversaw multiple dens of iniquity that courted significant Black and queer populations. On top of which, through no fault of his own, Gatien looked the part of a cartoon villain: a childhood hockey accident forced him to wear an eye patch.

On September 30, 1995, the NYPD raided the Limelight, but only three arrests were made, one of which was a club employee who sold pot on the side; someone in the NYPD had tipped them off, and the Limelight's resident ecstasy dealers stayed away that night. But that was enough to further their investigation, and the

Peter Gatien, September 1997.

undercover cops in ridiculous faux–Club Kid outfits and pathetic attempts at drag were regularly finding their way into Gatien's clubs in search of drug-related crimes to pin on him.

By May 15, 1996, they'd found enough, and Gatien was arrested and charged with running the Limelight and Tunnel as what a *New York Times* headline called "drug bazaars."[161] Gatien pleaded not guilty. Though drug dealers had indeed operated out of his clubs, Gatien hadn't explicitly approved or profited off them. He'd simply looked the other way.

And then, in a second instance of a totally avoidable tragedy bringing everything to a complete stop, it turned out that Gatien's highest-profile employee had killed a co-worker.

Angel Melendez, who worked at several clubs including Limelight, famously sold ecstasy. But as his friend, musician and producer Raz Mesinai, explained, "I see a lot of bullshit, like, 'Oh, Angel was a drug dealer.' Everyone was a drug dealer! I was a drug dealer! My mother was a drug dealer! Everyone had drugs! Give me a break. He was the sweetest guy."

In early 1996, Melendez moved in with Michael Alig and his roommate Robert "Freeze" Riggs in their apartment at Riverbank West (560 West 43rd Street). During an argument on March 17, 1996, Riggs and Alig both attacked Melendez with a hammer and smothered him with a pillow, after which they reportedly injected his body with Drano. They left Melendez's dead body in a bathtub full of ice until it began to decompose, at which point they dismembered the corpse and cast it piecemeal into the Hudson River. Melendez's disappearance was noted soon after, and Alig even went around bragging about having done the killing; due to his history of self-mythologizing, few took him seriously.

By that fall, Alig and Riggs still hadn't been caught; in fact, Alig was being courted by the NYPD as a source they could use to take down Gatien. It was only in November 1996, when parts of Melendez's body washed up on Staten Island, that Alig got on the NYPD's radar as a suspect. Once Alig and Riggs were caught, prosecutors were hesitant to charge them with first degree murder—which, in my opinion, is what they'd done—in the hopes that Alig would testify against Gatien for running a drug ring out of his nightclubs. Which, just to be clear, is *way* less bad than killing somebody.

In exchange for testimony, Alig and Riggs accepted a lesser charge of manslaughter and were sentenced to ten-to-twenty years in prison. But the resultant press was like Christmas morning for Giuliani and the NYPD. Here was their proof that broken windows policing was necessary: if Gatien hadn't allowed drugs to be sold in his nightclubs and allowed unsavory characters to populate them, Melendez's death might not have occurred! Or something like that.

> **Mesinai:** *This wasn't something that even went down in a club, this was something that happened in [an apartment]. No one gave a fuck about Angel, but they used it to shut down every club that was open.*

Limelight closed in 1997. In order to pay his exorbitant legal fees, Gatien sold the Palladium to NYU, who demolished it and constructed the sadistically named Palladium Dormitory on the site. Gatien was acquitted of all drug charges in 1998, but in 1999, they finally nailed him for tax evasion. He was allowed to keep Tunnel open until 2001 for the express purpose of making enough money to pay off his $1.88 million tax debt. Once it was paid, Tunnel shuttered, and Gatien was deported to his native Canada.

After the story of Angel Melendez's murder broke in 1997, Giuliani and the NYPD began focusing on the city's Prohibition-era cabaret law, which hadn't been seriously enforced for decades. The law required establishments in residential zones that sold food and drink (even those that didn't serve alcohol) to obtain a special permit for dancing. That license was prohibitively expensive and difficult to obtain, and the majority of otherwise law-abiding clubs hadn't bothered, especially the kinds of clubs we've spent most of this book looking at: smaller spaces that incubate creative communities, but operate with slim financial margins.

When first implemented by Mayor Jimmy Walker in 1926, the cabaret law was used to sniff out speakeasies, but it was disproportionately enforced at jazz clubs, especially those in Harlem. Like Walker before him, Giuliani wielded the cabaret law to target clubs that catered to Black, Latinx, and LGBTQ+ audiences. Giuliani's NYPD also introduced the new M.A.R.C.H. program (Multi-Agency Response to Community Hotspots), in which several municipal agencies would unexpectedly visit targeted clubs (even legal ones) over the course of a single night, citing enough minor infractions to potentially bankrupt them.

Nightclub owners became reasonably paranoid, with many of the larger ones implementing over-the-top security measures and cracking down on underage partiers or individual drug use.

Twilo was shuttered by the city in 2001 after reports of attempts to cover up drug overdoses by putting blacked-out patrons in storage closets or out by the dumpsters, and sending them to the hospital in privately owned ambulances. Richard Grant, Sound Factory's co-owner, attempted to reopen the club at 618 West 46th Street, but like Gatien before him, he was arrested in 2004 and charged with aiding drug sales, only to be cleared of all charges the following year. The legal fees were so steep that the club never reopened.

THE AFTERLIFE OF THE MIDTOWN MEGACLUBS

The original Danceteria at 252 West 37th Street is now GOGI 37, a Korean barbecue restaurant and bar.

The ground floor of the second Danceteria (30 West 21st Street) is currently a showroom for New York Stone, a tile and stone slab distributor. The upper floors have been converted into office spaces.

In 2017, workers at a nearby construction site dug up what appeared to be a WWII-era bomb. That stretch of 21st Street was shut down and evacuated, and the NYPD bomb squad was called in. But as the *New York Post* so perfectly put it, "What they discovered could only cause a disco inferno."[162] Far from a bomb, the phony missile was a time capsule that Danceteria patrons had buried in October 1984, intended to be opened in the year 6984. Its contents included art and written messages, mix tapes, a false eyelash that had reportedly belonged to Diana Ross, Chi Chi Valenti's G-string, and footage of the party the club held in the lead-up to the time capsule's burial.

The Fun House's building at 526 West 26th Street is now part of the West Chelsea Arts Building, a complex of galleries and artists' studios—not a bad fate, as these things go. Interestingly, the Fun House has been commemorated in a mural of its signature clown logo on a wall at East 23rd and Ave. U in Sheepshead Bay, Brooklyn. Given the club's outer-borough audience, it's an appropriate location.

The Roxy (515 West 18th Street) operated on and off in various capacities until 2007, including a long run hosting Roxy Saturdays, one of the city's largest gay dance parties. After its closure, it had a stint as the Hauser & Wirth art gallery, but the building was demolished in 2017. It has been replaced with Lantern House, a bulbous, hideous condo.

After the Limelight (656–662 6th Avenue) closed in 1997, Gatien retained ownership and sporadically attempted to reopen it in the years that followed, even rebranding it as the Avalon in 2003 (after he'd already been deported). But with the police and neighborhood association on his back and legal fees mounting, he closed it permanently in 2007. From 2010 to 2014, it was reborn as the Limelight Marketplace, an unsuccessful mini-mall. In the years since, it has been home to a series of gyms, alongside an outpost of the Brooklyn pizzeria Grimaldi's and a flashy Chinese restaurant called Jue Lan Club.

The Terminal Warehouse building that once housed Tunnel has been converted into a complex of offices and retail spaces, including Uber's New York offices, a health food restaurant called Avocaderia, and an outpost of the La Colombe coffee chain. The atrium space—which was once Tunnel's main ballroom—occasionally hosts events.

Hurrah (36 West 62nd Street), the Palladium (126 East 14th Street), and Mars (28–30 10th Avenue) have all been demolished.

Nell's finally closed in 2004, long past its prime. The space was then acquired by actor Chris Noth (*Sex and the City*'s Mr. Big) and business partner Noel Ashman and turned into a club called NA. That club didn't last long, nor did any of the others that followed it; as of this writing, the most recent tenant, Up and Down, closed in 2021.

The building that housed Sound Factory and Twilo (530 West 27th Street) briefly housed another nightclub called Spirit, as well as a restaurant/night club called B.E.D. where patrons sat on beds for some reason. Since 2011, it has been the McKittrick Hotel, home to the long-running interactive play *Sleep No More*.

As of this book's writing, Rudy Giuliani is tragically still alive. I wish him only the worst.

Suggested Listening

Man Parrish—*Man Parrish* (1982)

Madonna—*Madonna* (1983)

Run-DMC—"Here We Go (Live at the Fun House)" single (1985)

Afrika Bambaataa and the Soulsonic Force—*Planet Rock: The Album* (1986)

Deee-Lite—*World Clique* (1990)

Masters at Work—*The Tenth Anniversary Collection—Part One* (1990–1995) (compilation)

Various—*The Streetwise Records Anthology* (compilation)

9

NYC'S LIKE A GRAVEYARD: THE STORY OF ANTIFOLK

Roger Manning (singer-songwriter): The origin of antifolk is narcissism, in a sense. It's a situation where it's OK to promote yourself, it's OK to think highly of yourself, ego is OK. Over in the West Village it was like, "Oh, we're so humble, we're singer-songwriters and we read a lot of books and we went to college, and we can't be famous or wear sexy clothes or whatever, because we have integrity." Antifolk was like, fuck that. I'm gonna be a rockstar, motherfucker.

By the 1980s, roughly twenty years had passed since Greenwich Village's folk scene exploded, but it seemed nobody had bothered to tell that to the Bob Dylan clones who continued to flock to open mic night at Gerde's Folk City. One of the few remaining 1960s folk clubs in the area, Gerde's wasn't even in its original West 4th Street location anymore—it had moved to 130 West 3rd Street in 1969—and its programming had changed: Music critic and future Yo La Tengo front man Ira Kaplan booked a series at the club

called "Music for Dozens," which welcomed post-punk and indie
bands like Sonic Youth, the Replacements, Meat Puppets, and
Hüsker Dü. But despite these signs of change, the club's Monday
night open mic (aka "hootenanny") kept engaging in 1960s folk
cosplay, even as the audience for such things steadily diminished.

*Cindy Lee Berryhill (singer-songwriter): When I hit New York
City, I really wanted to get downtown into Greenwich Village. That's
kind of what I knew: I'd read the Bob Dylan books, I read the Edie
Sedgwick book, I was a big Warhol fan, that whole thing. I thought,
wouldn't it be cool if there was something going on here? The first
place that I really wanted to hit was Folk City.*

Berryhill, a Los Angeles native, first made her way to Folk City
in 1985 as a stop on a cross-country bus trip. Already an established solo artist in the Los Angeles punk scene, she was put off
by the open mic's traditionalist bent. But scattered throughout the
evening were a handful of performers that Berryhill recognized
as fellow travelers.

*Berryhill: I met these scraggly acoustic guitar players that were funky-
ass musicians like me. A couple of them, the Folk Brothers, handed
me their cassette and it said, "The Folk Brothers—All Fucked Up
With Nowhere to Go." It looked kind of punky. I'm like, "Wow,
you guys are my people. Is there a kind of acoustic punk scene happening here? Because that's what I want." I met other people that
night too: Billy Syndrome, Roger Manning. I just oozed this feeling
of needing to be here.*

The Folk Brothers were singer-songwriters Kirk Kelly and the
mononymous Lach (pronounced "latch," real name unknown).
Lach, who grew up in New York State's Rockland County, had
first made his way to Folk City for much the same reasons as Berryhill. But at the open mics, Lach found his punk-influenced song-
writing less than welcome. "I was playing an acoustic guitar, they

were playing acoustic guitar, they were folk but I'm not folk," he recalled. "Why am I not folk? 'Well, you play too fast and too loud, and you know, you curse and you're obnoxious.'"[163]

Despite his punk influences, Lach viewed folk in a very traditional sense—that is, as music that comes out of a folk tradition. But post-Dylan, the word had long since been dismembered from its origins and slapped onto anybody with an acoustic guitar, "sincere" lyrics, and an earthy image. The Folk Brothers' music was equally informed by punk rock and traditional folk songs, but few at Folk City seemed to catch on to the latter.

Things were only marginally better around the corner at the Speakeasy (107 MacDougal Street)—a newer club, located across the street from where the Gaslight had once been—which hosted its own open mic.

Paleface (singer-songwriter): You'd go in there and it was like a museum. They had all the pictures on the wall of all the folk artists you'd heard about from the '60s, like Joan Baez, Tom Paxton, Phil Ochs, all of them, they were all up on the wall. It was not a happening place, it was basically for tourists.

Manning: You'd get a number at both places [Folk City and Speakeasy], which were around the corner from each other, and then run back and forth between the two and try to make both of your slots happen. And then Minetta Lane, which is a little side street between [the two venues], would be littered with acoustic guitar people just sitting on the stoops and warming up and stuff. You'd make friends with these people who actually had other ideas, and that broadened my outlook on things. I was attracted to Kirk Kelly, who had a traditional Irish music thing going on even in his original songs. Lach would show up with a keyboard (he didn't play guitar yet), and he wasn't very well received, because he was a keyboard player—these people were kind of stuffy. But Kirk and Lach teamed up, and then Cindy Lee Berryhill came to town for a while, and Lach, Kirk, and Cindy were kind of a trio.

Manning, who described himself as being "city-phobic" in his youth, had come to New York by way of New Haven, Connecticut. Finding his way to the Folk City and Speakeasy open mics, he was especially influenced by the trio of Lauren Agnelli, Tom Goodkind, and Bruce Paskow, who called themselves the Washington Squares. All three had come from punk roots—Agnelli had played in the band Nervus Rex and worked as a critic at the *Village Voice*, Paskow had been in the Invaders, and Goodkind had played in the band U.S. Ape and was instrumental in running clubs like Irving Plaza and Peppermint Lounge. You wouldn't have picked up any of that from seeing the Washington Squares, though, who styled themselves as a lovingly parodic take on Peter, Paul and Mary.

Manning: These three characters walked in, intentionally wearing '60s folk singer cliche shit, like berets and striped shirts. They just rolled in and sang some classic Peter, Paul and Mary tune or something from that era, which sounded fucking brilliant. They were punk rockers who decided that the next big thing was folk, and they did it so fucking good. They were totally irreverent, and at the same time, totally respectful. It was so punk, and it was so good.

Though largely forgotten, the Washington Squares were a significant influence on the developing scene that would eventually be dubbed "antifolk," but at that time, folk-punk hybrids were few and far between in the stodgy Greenwich Village scene. The need for a dedicated space that could specifically nurture this community was apparent to performers like Manning, Berryhill, Kelly, and especially Lach.

THE FORT

Berryhill: It was clear that nobody could afford to live in Greenwich Village at this point, and even the East Village was not affordable. Most of the people I knew were living on the Lower East Side.

157 Rivington Street.

At some point in the early '80s, Lach moved into an eight-hundred-square-foot storefront space at 157 Rivington Street. At the time, the Lower East Side,[i] as the East Village had once been, was derelict, crime ridden, and drug infested—which is to say, a home for struggling artists and musicians. "The Daily News did an article on the most dangerous places in New York, and my block was number one," Lach later claimed. "That was a point of pride."[164]

In 1983, Lach began operating an illegal after-hours club out of his home. He dubbed it "The Hidden Fortress" after the 1958 Akira Kurosawa movie, but that was soon reduced to "The Fort."

At the Fort, Lach hosted all-night open mics, known as "anti-hoots," which were as omnivorous as Folk City's were staid. Performers of all stripes cycled through the Fort's open mic (including the anarchist industrial band Missing Foundation, who memora-

---

i Defined as the area east of Bowery and between Houston and Canal Streets.

bly set their drums on fire in the tiny space), but a core group was establishing itself.

> *Manning: I called it the Gang of Four: Lach, Cindy Lee Berry-hill, Kirk Kelly, and me. We were the ones who took up the most space, in a sense.*[ii]

Although the neighborhood was relatively desolate, the Fort wasn't the only venue on its block: across the street at 156 Riving-ton, a squat called ABC No Rio had its own open mic, the Wide Open Cabaret, hosted by artist Matthew Courtney. Fort open mics would always be pretty music heavy, with occasional stand-up comics and spoken word performers to spice things up, but the burgeoning scene's "do whatever weird shit you want, so long as it's honest" spirit was arguably better exemplified at ABC No Rio.

> *Paleface: You met all these crazy characters: There was this guy Dixon, who was an older dude. He was deaf in one ear because when he was a kid, he was in the Pentecostal church where he was killing the chickens and doing the dances and crazy shit, and they yelled in his ear and he went deaf. He was in his fifties, and he did these children's songs that were the greatest children's songs ever. There was George the Communist, who wore a coonskin cap and a suit, and he had "communist" written across his acoustic guitar. There was Redhead, who dressed all in red. At one point, Redhead got a girl-friend named Green Jean, and you would see them walking around the city handcuffed to each other. They were performance artists, and they did this performance at ABC No Rio that was not appreciated by some of the radical female poets there, because it was Redhead spanking Green Jean—that was the act.*

A pivotal moment came in 1985, when Lach hosted a festival at

---

ii   Manning also recalled singer-songwriter Billy Syndrome being a regular presence.

the Fort. It was presented as an alternative to the stodgy New York Folk Festival, just as Downtown's jazz avant-garde had thrown the 1972 New York Musicians' Jazz Festival in response to the Newport Jazz Festival.

Berryhill: For maybe a couple of years, Lach had been putting on a music fest of upbeat acoustic artists at his place on Rivington. In the summer of '85, I said, "Cool, let's meet and talk about that. We'll see if we can pull everyone together into a tightly-knit group to be a part of making this happen and getting the word out."

So Kirk and Lach and I met about this. I think Lach was calling it "The New New York Folk Fest" or something. I said, "You need an edgier name, something that really conveys the vibe." In Los Angeles, I had played a few times at a really cool club called the Anti-Club, so I said, "What about Anti-Folk Fest?" He went with it and put it on the flier.

BREAKING OUT

Most of the musicians hanging around the Fort were exclusively performing at open mics, having been shut out of more professional performance opportunities. "It was almost like playing an open mic *was* the gig," said Berryhill.

Some found an outlet in busking. For Manning, busking became transformative, not just for his own musical practice, but for the city itself.

Manning: My personal abilities and approach evolved from street performing, because you've got to connect with people to make money. I was a subway busker for a good number of years; at various points, I was singing in the subway pretty much full-time. Buskers would get a ticket: The charge was "entertaining passengers," and it was a $10 ticket. It was irritating.

At some point I thought, fuck this. I went to court and I chal-

lenged it. The judge, Diane Lebedeff, kept throwing me hints, like (I'm paraphrasing here), "We're going to put this off until a future date when you can get some legal representation." She couldn't really say it outright, but then the light bulb went off in my head: Wait a minute, this could be a First Amendment case.

She postponed the judgment on this $10 ticket until I got some legal representation. The New York Civil Liberties Union took the case, and they argued that although the MTA is technically privately owned, it's a public thoroughfare and therefore free speech is protected. And [the court] decided, yes, that's true.[165]

So there you have it: every time you see a busker in the New York City subways, you can thank (or blame) Roger Manning.

Berryhill was the first antifolk act to gain any significant traction beyond the Fort/ABC No Rio nexus. Granted, she was already fairly established in Los Angeles, and had even contributed a song to a 1985 compilation called *Radio Tokyo Tapes Vol. 3*,[iii] alongside the likes of Henry Rollins and the Minutemen. Shortly after her arrival in the city, that tape helped her nab a choice gig at the already legendary Pyramid Club. For Berryhill, "It was OK and nice to play the open mics because I met my people, but playing at the Pyramid was transforming."

Manning: Cindy would play at the Pyramid Club, and I'd go, "Wow, really? A solo acoustic player playing in a hip East Village [club]?" It had never occurred to me that you could take a folk guitar into these places. But why shouldn't we?

Toward the end of 1985, the Fort was given the boot from Rivington Street—not terribly surprising, given the illegal nature of the place. The expanding antifolk scene would need to find a new

---

iii   Named for the legendary Venice, CA, recording studio Radio Tokyo, where the Minutemen, Savage Republic, the Bangles, L7, Sonic Youth, Jane's Addiction, the Descendents, and the Rain Parade all recorded.

Cindy Lee Berryhill performing at Pyramid Club.

home. Aside from Berryhill, it had failed to make any significant inroads at Pyramid, which already had plenty of other things going on. But the solution to their problems wasn't too far away—in fact, it was right across the street.

SOPHIE'S & THE CHAMELEON

With the Fort now gone, Lach approached Sophie Polny, a tough-as-nails bar owner who never bestowed a moniker on her establishment at 96 Avenue A ("Sophie's," the name by which it's usually identified, was merely colloquial). Polny allowed Lach to run his open mic on her slowest night. Certainly, the move from an illegal loft venue to a legitimate bar was indicative of the antifolk scene's growing audience and sense of legitimacy—although it also meant a shift away from the pin-drop-quiet open mic audiences to a more traditional bar vibe. But it planted the antifolk flag on the northeast corner of Avenue A and East 6th Street—which it would continue to inhabit in some shape or form, with few interruptions, until 2019.

The Fort's tenure at 96 Avenue A came to a fairly swift and abrupt end when Sophie's was acquired by its next-door neighbor, a newly opened restaurant called Sidewalk Cafe, which was looking to expand its business with a bar. Sophie's reopened at 507 East 5th Street (where it remains to this day), and the Fort relocated alongside it.

Manning: What really helped gel things was a zine called Exposure. *Kristen Johnson and Lynn Robinson, two troublemakers, were hanging around at ABC No Rio and the Fort. [Part of] the concept was that they were going to have a centerfold in it, "Folk Hunk of the Month," and I was the first one. It looks like I'm naked, technically I wasn't naked, but it looks like the guitar's blocking my genitals. Lynn and Kristen were just having a great time, and they would include anything, so Missing Foundation was part of the antifolk scene, and hip-hop was part of the antifolk scene.*

Robinson also became Lach's de facto manager and began working her music industry connections to help advance his career. One of those connections was the very man whose oversized shadow on New York's folk scene helped set this whole thing in motion.

Manning: Lynn Robinson got Bob Dylan to come into Sophie's to see Lach. I was there, I shook his hand. I was singing "Uncle Pen" by Bill Monroe when he walked in. I'd always imagined, "What would I sing if Bob Dylan was there?" and that was not it, but he said he liked it.

Supposedly, a week after Dylan's visit, actor Matt Dillon came by Sophie's. Someone (it's unclear who) was playing a new song they'd written called "The Night Dylan Came" and Dillon mistakenly thought it was about him showing up that evening. It's an amusing anecdote, but it's also illustrative of both the speed with which these songwriters were churning out new material, and the ways in which the tightly knit antifolk scene could at times become

503 East 6th Street.

a feedback loop of inside jokes and references of which outsiders struggled to make sense. This would become problematic for the scene as the years passed.

After a few months at the new Sophie's, the Fort bounced around between a few other bars before the pull of 6th and A drew it back to a bar called the Chameleon (505 East 6th Street). Just around the corner from the original Sophie's space, the space already had an illustrious history: it had previously housed the first iteration of the Nuyorican Poets Cafe from 1975 until 1981.

Though singer-songwriter Ray Brown, a Fort regular, recalls that "the whole scene was like twenty-five people," it was growing. Brenda Kahn and Paleface (like Lach, his real name remains unknown) were both undergraduate students at NYU who were brought into the antifolk fold thanks to Manning's evangelism.

Kahn: I moved to New York to go to NYU in 1985, and I was living in the dorms on 10th Street off of University Place. Roger was always playing in Washington Square Park, and I would walk there

every day, so I saw him a lot. I'd been writing songs since I was 13,
and I really wanted to be one of those cool New York musician people,
but I was just living my student life. I ended up having a conversa-
tion with Roger one day, and he started talking to me about all the
open mics. He showed me the ones in the West Village, and then
he started talking about Lach and Sophie's bar in the East Village.

Roger introduced me to Lach and said, "This is Brenda. She
wants to do a gig here." I was horrified, because I was not ready.
Lach looked me up and down and said, "Are you any good?" Oh
shit. I said, "Yeah, yeah, of course I am," and he just gave me a gig.
That was my first gig in the city. I became a student by day and a
rocker girl by night, and I would huff my way across town with my
black motorcycle boots and my big black overcoat and my too-big-
for-me guitar.

At the Chameleon, the antihoot operated much the same way
as audition night at CBGB—if Lach liked your stuff at the open
mic, the offer of a full gig was inevitable. And once you had a gig
on the horizon, there was no better way to promote it to a receptive audience than by playing a couple tunes at the antihoot.

Kahn: If you showed up to hand out your flier to the people at the
open mic, they would know that you were playing and then they
would come to your show on Saturday. It was kind of like a ma-
chine that fed itself: If you showed up for everybody else, you had a
better chance that they were going to show up when you did a gig,
and vice versa.

The scene at the Chameleon was so vibrant that, like CBGB
before it, much of the real action tended to take place on the sidewalk in front of the club—or, in this particular case, the Sidewalk
a few doors down.[iv]

---

iv   I know, I know. I'm sorry. I couldn't stop myself.

Manning: I wasn't really at Chameleon all that much. I'd go inside there for a minute, and then go hang outside. We'd sit on the sidewalk and play guitars, or go to Tompkins Square Park. And we were hanging out at Sidewalk Cafe, before we had performances there— Chameleon was just a few doors away, so your post-show hangout would be over at Sidewalk.

Since the Chameleon was a bar, and the national drinking age had been raised to twenty-one in 1984, these external spaces were also a valuable way for underage artists to engage with the scene. But few at the time would have predicted that one of the awkward teens loitering outside the Chameleon would become antifolk's biggest breakout success.

BECK

In 1988, a recent high school graduate named Beck Hansen bought a $30 Greyhound bus pass on a whim and decided to leave his native Los Angeles and come see the bright lights of New York City. Though he had never visited before, his NYC roots were significant—his grandfather Al Hansen was a Fluxus artist who'd palled around with Yoko Ono and George Maciunas, and his mother, Bibbe Hansen, had been a teenage Warhol acolyte. In a fun bit of synchronicity, Al and Bibbe had lived at 609 East 6th Street, between Avenue C and Avenue D—a mere two blocks away from what would later become the Chameleon, where Beck—better known by his first name alone—would find his musical identity.

A series of misunderstandings and blunders left Beck homeless soon after his arrival, and he found himself gravitating toward Tompkins Square Park—where, only weeks before, the infamous riots had broken out. Unaware of that fact, Beck took to hanging around (and, at times, sleeping in) the park, which would help fuel his growth as a musician. "[Tompkins Square Park is] where I first started rapping," he later recalled. "There would be like these homeless hip-hop freestyle things happening. We would get up there and do some folk-rap. The seeds of a lot of what I'm doing came out of that time."[166]

For Beck, whose prized possession was the acoustic guitar he toted around, it was inevitable that he would find his way into the antifolk scene that was blossoming just one block south of the park.

Paleface: I met Beck on the street, I just walked right up to him. He was looking in the window of some place, he had an acoustic guitar over his shoulder, and I thought, that dude looks cool. So I went right up to him and I said, "Hey, what's up?" We just started talking. We were friends immediately.

"A lot of us were playing folk music because we couldn't afford all the instruments and, Jesus, it's New York, where are you going to rehearse with a band?," Beck explained, making a solid point about why antifolk in particular might have flourished in that time and place.[167] In previous scenes, musicians could acquire industrial loft spaces in relatively uninhabited areas where they were free to rehearse to their hearts' content. But by 1988, gentrification had filled SoHo and East Village lofts with wealthy yuppies, and cheap space Downtown was increasingly at a premium. Unlike so many of their predecessors, most artists moving to the Lower East Side were living in intentionally residential buildings—which is to say, they all had neighbors. And as any apartment-dweller knows, it's a really dick move to, say, host a five-hour band practice.

Beck began crashing at Paleface's apartment on Noble Street in Greenpoint, Brooklyn, and the pair would frequently busk in subway stations as a duo.[v] At the time, Beck's antihoot performances mostly consisted of traditional folk and blues songs and Woody Guthrie covers. But when Beck asked Lach to book him for a full set, Lach refused—he would only book performers who wrote their own material. Beck later recalled, "I went and got a pen and paper and wrote five songs about stuff like pizza, or wak-

---

v   Thanks, Roger Manning!

ing up after having been chain-sawed in half by a maniac—stuff like that. He finally gave me a Friday night."[168]

In late 1989, Beck was violently mugged on Avenue B. He was miraculously able to hold on to his guitar but was injured badly enough to wind up in the hospital. Shaken by the incident, he moved back to Los Angeles.

In 1989, several of the scene's core performers, including Roger Manning, Paleface, John S. Hall, Cindy Lee Berryhill, Kirk Kelly, Billy Syndrome, and poet Maggie Estep, united for a compilation on 109 Records called *The Broome Closet Anti-folk Sessions*— so named because the performances were all recorded by Roger Manning in his Broome Street apartment. Lach is conspicuously absent (Manning recalled him having some sort of beef with 109 Records owner Steve Gabe), but the compilation is an otherwise extraordinary document of a group of brilliant songwriters and poets, all on the verge of creative and professional breakthroughs.

Still, cracks were showing: Two of antifolk's power couples— Cindy Lee Berryhill and Kirk Kelly, and Roger Manning and Brenda Kahn—had both gone through nasty breakups, creating ruptures in the already small scene (hence Kahn's absence on the compilation). And several musicians from the scene were signing record contracts and shifting their focus from local gigs to touring: Berryhill signed with Rhino Records, Manning and Kelly were both on the punk label SST, and Kahn signed to Columbia. Paleface was discovered at the Chameleon by manager Danny Fields, who had previously managed the Stooges and the Ramones, and who got him signed to PolyGram.

Lach was discovered in 1990 by Danny Goldberg, supermanager to everyone from Sonic Youth to Bonnie Raitt. Goldberg's brand-new Goldcastle label released Lach's debut album, *Contender*— something which, to paraphrase Marlon Brando, Lach very well could have been, had Goldcastle not gone belly-up after the album's release.

While several of his peers were off attaining varying degrees of success, Lach's shot at the big time was DOA. Heartbroken, he quit performing and moved to San Francisco, where he worked construction by day and played music for himself at night. The hoots half-heartedly continued at the Chameleon in his absence (Ray Brown recalled them being run by a group called the Woodpecker Brothers), but not for long. By the end of 1990, the antifolk scene had largely dissipated; the Chameleon closed soon after.

In March 1993, much to everyone's surprise, that awkward teenager who used to hang out outside the Chameleon released a joke-y but undeniable folk-rap song called "Loser." It began gathering steam and within a year, Beck was a full-fledged major-label rock star. Much of the press surrounding his debut album, 1994's *Mellow Gold*, made note of his transformative experiences in New York's underground antifolk scene. Antifolk, a term that few outside Lower Manhattan (or even *in* Lower Manhattan) had ever encountered, was suddenly getting a significant amount of ink.

SIDEWALK

Lach first began to dip his toe back into music in San Francisco, where he began hosting hoots at a coffeehouse called Sacred Grounds. As "Loser" gathered steam in 1993, friends encouraged Lach to seize the moment and start performing again. Though initially reluctant, he eventually booked a European tour for himself, with a short stopover in New York for his mother's sixtieth birthday party.

While in town, he just so happened to swing by Sidewalk Cafe, the restaurant that had taken over the original Sophie's space on Avenue A, where his friend Laura Sativa was bartending. Sativa told Lach that Sidewalk's owners were casting about for something to do with the restaurant's unused back room, and suggested that he resurrect the Fort there. Despite some initial reluctance on his part, Lach later recalled, he "basically made a deal that I would run the back room for like a week or two and get them up and running. I ended up staying there for 15 years."[169]

The offer was too good to pass up: Sidewalk's Israeli-born owners, Pini Milstein and Amnon Kehati, recognizing an opportunity

94 Avenue A.

to drum up some extra business, offered Lach full control over the booking in Sidewalk's back room,[vi] which was already equipped with a PA and a piano. Soon enough, Lach was back living in the city, settling into a nearby apartment on Avenue C. A makeshift "The Fort" sign was installed behind the Sidewalk stage.

In Lach's brief absence, the neighborhood had gone through significant transformations. When Sidewalk Cafe first opened in 1985, the area around Tompkins Square Park was rough, as we saw in Chapter Seven. Clashes between the NYPD and the park's homeless population in 1988 and 1990 led the city to shutter the park from June 3, 1991 to July 25, 1992. Though ostensibly closed for renovations, it also eliminated the park's homeless encampment.

After that, Avenue A gentrified at warp speed—thanks in no small part to Sidewalk's owners. In 1993, the same year Lach restarted the Fort in Sidewalk's back room, Milstein and Kehati

---

vi   The back room was a relatively new addition; Cindy Lee Berryhill recalled that when it was Sophie's, it had been a backyard.

opened a gourmet seafood restaurant called Pisces across the street; it was the first of its kind in the neighborhood. Tellingly, they hired Evil Cirigiliano—formerly one of Tompkins Square Park's homeless residents—to stand outside the restaurant and shoo panhandlers away, for which he was paid $50 a night. "It's kind of a funny moral switch for me, right?" Cirigliano told the *New York Times*. "But I go to school now and I need the money."[170]

The neighborhood's musical identity was changing as well. Sin-é, a cafe located just off Avenue A at 122 St. Marks Place, had opened in 1989. Though it was initially a low-key hangout spot, the cafe's Irish-born owners, Shane Doyle and Karl Geary, started bringing in performers who would play for tips. A Saturday night variety show, the Clumsy Cabaret, welcomed several Fort expats.

Most significantly, singer-songwriter Jeff Buckley came to prominence through his Monday night residency at Sin-é in 1992. Accompanying himself on an electric guitar, the residency gave Buckley the space to experiment, and he would cover songs by everyone from Edith Piaf to Bad Brains. Buckley's reputation grew quickly; his debut EP, *Live at Sin-é*, was released by Columbia the following year. Despite his burgeoning fame, Lach recalled Buckley coming to the antihoots "quite often" around this time.[171]

All of this added up to a neighborhood that would be more hospitable than ever to a folk scene. It didn't take long for new faces to show up, especially after Beck began hyping Lach's open mics in the mainstream music press. And some old faces reappeared, throwing their weight behind Lach's operation and bringing in new fans.

Jonathan Berger (poet; editor, AntiMatters): I first went to Sidewalk fairly soon after it opened as a music venue, in either December '93 or January '94. It was virtually empty. I was there to watch Brenda Khan. I'd heard that she was part of this thing called "antifolk," but I'd only heard the word, I knew nothing about it. Luckily, there were articles on the walls of the Sidewalk describing what antifolk was, so I got this whole history of a scene that I'd never heard of.

This community sounded magical and fascinating to me, and it made me want to come back and be a part of it, just as a witness to what was going on there. And "community" is a strange thing, because the actual show didn't have that many participants. This was a room that could fit maybe 30-40 people at the time, and there were maybe 10 to 25 people there. So it was an intimate space, but it was even more intimate under the circumstances I was seeing. I felt I could connect to people in a space that small. It felt a little like Cheers *to me, where everyone would know your name. I wasn't a performer or anything, I was just a guy that wanted to watch and know people.*

Like Max's Kansas City before it, Sidewalk Cafe was primarily a restaurant. That's where it made its money, allowing Lach to book whomever he liked, without having to worry about the bottom line (it also helped that Milstein and Kehati owned the building outright). Because it wasn't a bar, it could (and frequently did) welcome underage fans and performers without concern. And because it was open twenty-four hours a day, there was no last call to cut the party short—the antihoot could run as long as it needed to allow all interested parties the chance to perform, and people could hang out afterward for as long as they liked.

Like many of the venues discussed in this book, Sidewalk Cafe didn't have a backstage area, which meant that there was little division between the audience and performers (a line that became even blurrier on antihoot nights). However, the back room was right by the stairs to the restaurant's basement, which housed the men's bathroom and, for a time, a pool table. The basement became an unofficial green room for performers at Sidewalk, offering musicians a space to meet, mingle, and collaborate while others were on stage.

Somer Bingham (musician; sound tech and booker, Sidewalk Cafe): The basement was the place to be. You would hear people practicing, bands would form. You'd go up to somebody who you didn't know before and tell them they were awesome. [The community] was really, really facilitated by the way that place was laid out, *because the basement was isolated, and it became sort of like white noise—it didn't interrupt [the show] upstairs.*

Like Hilly Kristal at CBGB, Lach's take-all-comers approach to booking meant that a wide range of sounds passed through Sidewalk Cafe. "Antifolk," already a vague descriptor, became an all but meaningless word at Sidewalk. Sure, there was never a shortage of punky singer-songwriters with acoustic guitars, but antifolk expanded to include every imaginable stripe of performer, from classically trained pianists to beatboxing rappers to straight-up punk bands. By the late '90s, "antifolk" pretty much just meant "anybody who regularly plays at Sidewalk Cafe."

However, not all of the original antifolk artists were on board with the scene's reincarnation at Sidewalk Cafe.

Manning: Part of the West Village thing was those places had drink minimums. I was a person who never spent money on anything, so I hated that drink minimum crap. You go to a jazz show and it costs you a million bucks because you have to buy all those drinks. I'm not saying that's wrong, I understand that they've got to make a living. But when we got to the Fort, we got away from drink minimums, we got away from stodginess, we got away from a lot of shit.

But you become your parents eventually, so at Sidewalk, the antifolk scene became a place of drink minimums and tables and all this shit, instead of a place like ABC No Rio where we'd just sit on the floor, which is what I prefer. I'm not being critical, I'm just saying personally, it's not that kind of place I like to play if I can avoid it.

It's true: although the shows were hypothetically free and performers were paid by passing a tip jar, Sidewalk Cafe did institute a drink minimum. Even performers at the antihoots were required to buy at least two full-priced drinks.[vii]

---

vii   It didn't have to be alcohol, though—soda, tea, and juice were all acceptable, and cheaper.

★ ★ ★

As with many of its predecessors, the scene became codified with the publication of a fanzine, *AntiMatters*. Though he wasn't the publication's founder, Jonathan Berger became involved as a contributor early on, and by 1997, he was single-handedly editing and publishing the zine.

Berger: It was roughly a monthly thing while I was doing it, and it was a publication of 100 copies or so. I was running them off at whatever job I had at the time, or trying to get other people I knew to use their copy services at work as well. I could do it on the cheap, and then I'd get whatever advertising I could from local businesses and acts that had shows that they wanted to promote. Every Monday night I would be offering it to people waiting in line when they were signing up, and then for the rest of the night, I'd just be going around saying, "Hey, buy a copy of AntiMatters."

Several of the people I interviewed for this chapter, without prompting, used a high school analogy to describe their time in the back room of Sidewalk Cafe: They'd come in as freshmen, find their musical voices for a few years, and then "graduate," either by finding greater success in the music industry or moving on to other things. In our conversations, most even identified themselves as part of a specific year's graduating class.

Every "class" of antifolk artists produced significant work and breakout performers, but there was something special about the graduating classes of the early 2000s. To a larger listening public, that particular wave of regulars—which included Jeffrey Lewis, Regina Spektor, Moldy Peaches, Diane Cluck, Langhorne Slim, Trachtenburg Family Slideshow Players, Turner Cody, Ish Marquez, and Dufus—would come to define antifolk just as much as (if not more than) their Chameleon-era predecessors.

Jeffrey Lewis: I graduated from SUNY Purchase in '97. I was broke, and I was spending all my time at Sidewalk and Sin-é. Those were just two places that were free to get in, so being broke and bored and without much of a social scene, I could always just walk in and see whatever was happening. Because I was really trying to make it as an illustrator and a comic book artist primarily, it was a way for me to draw people: I always have my sketchbook, so I would be drawing one performer after another from 8 p.m. until 1:00 a.m. when it ended, because it was good drawing practice. I started to really get into a lot of the stuff that I was seeing.

Going to those places kind of coincided with me starting to make up my own songs, but it took me a while to piece together the idea that I might play there. At one point, I realized that Sidewalk had this open mic night—just randomly, I was there on a Monday night and I realized that it wasn't a normal show night. So I kind of filed that away in the back of my head like, "Oh, I could come here on a Monday night and play my songs some time." I started doing that, and then that really sucked me into the whole world of it.

Diane Cluck: They always had this board out that said "Antihoot Monday Nights." I didn't know what that meant. One night when I was walking home from work, I stopped in.

It had such a buzz that I decided I wanted to somehow be part of that. So I started going and hanging out, but right away, I gave myself a goal that I would write a couple of songs so I could perform. That just became my world for a few years. I started writing two songs a week just to go do this thing.

Westchester native Adam Green had grown up an hour north of the city in Mount Kisco, New York. As a teenager, he began hanging out at a local record store, Exile on Main Street Records, where he met an employee nine years his senior named Kimya Dawson. The two developed a close bond, and Dawson would chaperone Green to indie rock shows in the city. They would occasionally write and record songs together for fun and released an EP in 1996 under the name "The Moldy Peaches." When Dawson moved away to Washington State, Green briefly joined her there. They expanded the Moldy Peaches into a full band and played a

Adam Green, Kimya Dawson, and Paleface at Sidewalk Café, July 29, 2001.

handful of shows before Green returned, moving to Midtown Manhattan with his parents.

> **Green:** *I had a group of songs that I had written, so I just decided to start playing in the subway.*[viii] *I used to play in the West 8th Street N/R train station, I think it was on the uptown side—that was my most common place to play.*
>
> *One time, I was playing and this guy comes up to me and he says, "Are you Jeffrey Lewis?" So I said, "No, who's Jeffrey Lewis?" And he goes, "Oh, I thought you were Jeffrey Lewis. There's this sort of antifolk scene over at the Sidewalk Cafe." He gave me the address and said, "That's where Jeffrey Lewis plays." I'd actually heard of the antihoot before, and I had an awareness that there was at one point some scene in New York that was called antifolk. I knew that Beck had played on that scene, and Beck was the reason why I started to really play folk, but I thought that scene was completely gone.*

From his first antihoot, Green was smitten. He quickly became a regular at the antihoots, which eventually led to the offer of a

---

viii Thanks again, Roger Manning!

full show. Sensing an opportunity, Green invited Dawson and
their Moldy Peaches bandmates to come to New York for the gig.

> *Green: The other people from Moldy Peaches besides Kimya, didn't
> really stay for very long. New York is hard, and they just felt like
> they wanted to go back home. Me and Kimya were just like, fuck it,
> we're going to stay here and try to record an album.*

That album, largely recorded at Green's parents' apartment, features several appearances from other antihoot regulars, a few of
whom would go on to join the live incarnation of the band. Notably, one of those musicians was Chris Barron, who had already
attained international fame in the early '90s as a singer in the band
Spin Doctors, best known for their hits "Two Princes" and "Little
Miss Can't Be Wrong." Barron, who lived close to Sidewalk in
the East Village, had lost his voice in 1999 due to a rare form of
vocal cord paralysis, bringing his career to a halt. When it began
to return in 2000, Barron started showing up at antihoots as a
low-pressure way of gently dipping his toe back into performing.

Barron quickly integrated himself into the community, even
becoming the Moldy Peaches' dedicated lead guitarist for a time
(that's him playing on their best-known song, "Anyone Else But
You"). The idea that a successful rock star would happily take a
supporting role in an amateur, unknown band with songs like
"Downloading Porn With Davo" and "Who's Got the Crack" is,
on its face, ridiculous, but it speaks to just how welcoming and
validating the antifolk scene could be to performers of all stripes.[ix]

BLOWING UP

It would be incorrect to say that none of these artists had larger
audiences in mind. But even though the antihoot welcomed performers regardless of talent or status, the scene that blossomed at

---

ix   Even after returning to his main gig with Spin Doctors, Barron continued to
     regularly hang out and play at Sidewalk.

Sidewalk could at times be guilty of a cliquishness that outsiders and new arrivals found alienating. Several scene-specific inside jokes flew over most listeners' heads—for example, Moldy Peaches' "Downloading Porn With Davo" is a winking tribute to Lach's song "Drinking Beers With Mom," which was itself an attempt to write in the style of Chameleon-era antifolker Tom Clark.

Still, this sense of self-importance within the antifolk scene was a key component of its longevity, as it created a bond between musically disparate artists.

Berger: So much of this scene in particular was making each other think that we were important. Even if we weren't necessarily successful commercially, we can be artistically successful, even if no one is listening to us outside of the bounds of this room.

The tiny scene was soon to be (re)introduced to the world at large—through a series of events that began with Green appearing on a game show in 2000, resulting in a performance that brought antifolk's playful and unselfconscious nature to the MTV airwaves.

Green: One day, I was in a bar and I was singing karaoke, and somebody came up to me and said, "I work for a show on MTV where people sing karaoke [Say What? Karaoke]. Do you want to be on it?" So I said, "Sure." I had a tryout at the MTV building, and I sang the Smash Mouth song "All Star." They said, "Great, you're on the show."

[On the show,] I did the Smash Mouth song, which went over pretty well. Then there was a part where you spin [a wheel] for a song, and I got "Steal My Sunshine" by Len. I kind of like that song, but I decided at that moment to pull this stunt where instead of singing the song, I just sang the Moldy Peaches song "These Burgers," and I got the audience to chant along. For whatever reason, they really went for it. It went on for a long time, this monotonous drone of people chanting, "These burgers are crazy." I lost the game show, but I remember thinking, I'm curious if they'll keep that in when it airs.

A few weeks later, the show came out, and I started to walk down the street in New York and people were stopping me [and saying], "Holy shit, you're that guy from that show." I went to Other Music[x] during this time, and the guy who was working behind the counter was Beans, who was a rapper [in the group Antipop Consortium]. Beans was like, "This dude was just on this show on MTV!" I said, "I have this CD of my music," and he was like, "OK, cool, we're going to take this." Something about what I'd done on TV made the people at Other Music decide that they would carry my CD. I gave them ten copies of my first solo album, which ended up being called Garfield.

Douglas Wolk, who was working for WFMU, ended up purchasing the album, and unbeknownst to me he decided to review it for CMJ, *and he gave it the album of the month. So all of a sudden, through this weird coincidence that I just had my album placed at Other Music because I was on the karaoke show, now I was in* CMJ.

It didn't end there: the *CMJ* review led to a gig at the Mercury Lounge (217 East Houston Street). The club's assistant booker Ryan Gentles took a shine to Green, and in turn introduced him to a band he had just started managing called the Strokes ("He told me they sounded like The Doors"). When the Strokes signed with the British indie label Rough Trade, Gentles recommended that they sign the Moldy Peaches as well.

Green: *The first time that we really had shows that filled up was at the Mercury Lounge. I remember looking out at a pretty full show and thinking, I don't really know a lot of these people. This is what it's like to just be a band that plays shows—as opposed to Sidewalk, where I was performing for my peers that were all songwriters, and they had a number and were waiting for their turn to play a song.*

Sidewalk was the initiation. The currency with which you had respect in that scene is like, do you have the material? Do you have cool songs? But then at the same time it did feel like everyone's relying

---

x   A renowned record store at 15 East 4th Street; it closed in 2016.

on me to go to their shows, and I'm relying on them to come to mine. It's like a cult that you join and you yourselves are each other's fans. So that was when I thought to myself, from now on, when I write a new song, I'm just going to play it at my next show—I don't need to go to the open mic.

Even with their presences at Sidewalk diminished, Green and Dawson took pains to regularly hype their old antifolk pals. The floodgates opened: Rough Trade also signed Jeffrey Lewis, and even released a compilation of Sidewalk regulars called *Antifolk Vol. 1*. A then-unsigned Regina Spektor was brought along to open for the Strokes on their 2003-2004 *Room on Fire* tour.

As it had a decade prior with Beck, antifolk was again gaining mainstream, international attention. European audiences were especially receptive, and spin-off antifolk scenes bloomed in the UK and Germany. The back room at Sidewalk Cafe started getting an awful lot of new visitors.[xi]

Toby Goodshank (singer-songwriter; guitarist, Moldy Peaches): There was a hubbub surrounding Moldy Peaches getting signed to Rough Trade. You'd get people coming in thinking you could get a record deal, that type of vibe. It was the same thing with the emergence of Regina Spektor—suddenly an awful lot of pianists coming through the open mic.

Paleface: At some point Lach had to institute a one-song wonder round [in the antihoot], because there were just too many people.[xii] So you would get one song instead of two. He would do that for two hours, just to move it along.

---

xi   These included future superstars Steffani Germanotta (aka Lady Gaga) and Lizzie Grant (aka Lana Del Rey); Grant briefly became a fixture, but Lach was sufficiently unimpressed with Germanotta's antihoot performance to deny her a show.

xii   A 2006 *New York Times* article puts the average number of antihoot participants around one hundred. (Alan Light, "How Does it Feel, Antifolkies, to Have a Home, Not Be Unknown?" *New York Times*, August 11, 2006.)

By the turn of the century, Alphabet City was well and truly gentrified. Resident Kristina Piorkowska, who spearheaded the Save Avenue A Association, told the *New York Times* in 1998 that the neighborhood had become "an alcoholic Disneyland, a sort of East Village theme park."[172] But Sidewalk remained relatively unaltered, largely thanks to its restaurant business (lord knows an "alcoholic Disneyland" would have considerable demand for all-night restaurants).

And though many from the turn of the century's "graduating classes" had moved on, some old-timers—including Jeffrey Lewis—remained dependable presences in Sidewalk's back room.

Isaac Gillespie (sound tech, Sidewalk Cafe; singer-songwriter): Any time I've ever seen Jeff Lewis playing on a bill, he is in the front row for every other performer on the bill, and he watches their set attentively. He wants to know what people are up to, and I think that that kind of energy trickles down.

POST-LACH

The music industry enthusiasm for the Moldy Peaches, Regina Spektor, Jeffrey Lewis, et al., never translated to much commercial success for Lach, but he did become noticeably more attentive to his own music career around this time: Though his recorded output had been sporadic in the '90s, around the turn of the century, he began releasing albums and touring in the UK with some regularity. In 2008, Lach shockingly announced that after fifteen years, he would be leaving the Sidewalk Cafe, with his final antihoot taking place on June 30. He turned his role as booker and emcee over to singer-songwriter Ben Krieger, who rebranded the antihoot as the less memorable "Monday Night Open Stage."[xiii]

---

xiii In 2011, Lach moved to Edinburgh, Scotland, where he continues to live to this day. In addition to regularly touring the UK, he also began a new Monday night antihoot in Edinburgh.

In 2011, the first signs of trouble began to appear at Sidewalk Cafe when the owners decided to renovate the restaurant. But even in Sidewalk's temporary absence, the antifolk scene continued to thrive as several other open mics popped up to fill the void. Sidewalk Cafe *was* antifolk, but antifolk was no longer *just* Sidewalk. When it finally reopened, the restaurant introduced "The Krieger Burger," an off-menu burger only available to back room regulars for $5, as a way of thanking them for sticking around.

Krieger left his post at Sidewalk Cafe in 2014, passing the torch to Somer Bingham, who became Sidewalk's third and final booker.

Bingham: As that area changed and the clientele changed in that neighborhood, the front was accommodating that [new] crowd, and then the back was still a relic of what the past was. A lot of people got priced out, not just of the neighborhood, but of the city. I was booking a lot of going away parties, because someone was moving to California or Portland or Charlottesville or wherever. It felt like sand through the hourglass—not in an ambiguous way, but, what can we do to slow it down?

Berger: The East Village was becoming more expensive and therefore less available, but it was also becoming less interesting and desirable for the kinds of people that would be going to open mics. Performers, even if they were trust fund kids, would be less attuned to those kinds of wealthier neighborhoods.

CLOSURE

Lewis: Sidewalk was not a money-making concern for the guy who owned it. That's why Sidewalk was able to exist for so long, because if they had to survive based on making a profit, they would have gone away a long time ago. The fact that it didn't have to compete financially allowed it to become a petri dish in a way that other places don't have the opportunity to: In other places, if a band books a gig and they don't bring in X number of people through the door or sell X number of drinks, there's pressure to not have it be that way.

Sidewalk just didn't have any of that pressure, they did not care if there was nobody there, or there were two people there, or there were 10 people. It allowed for stuff to happen in a looser way that no place else has really replicated.

There were any number of good reasons for Sidewalk Cafe's 2019 closure. But the primary cause seemed to have little to do with the gentrification that had otherwise ransacked Alphabet City: Pini Milstein—the restaurant's (and building's) primary owner, whose goodwill allowed the antifolk scene to flourish without ever becoming profitable—retired.[xiv]

Bingham: I think Pini particularly loved having a venue. On nights when that place was full and it was a party, he would just kind of wander back and I would see him smile and [look] excited. There was something about that vibe that I think he really, really enjoyed being part of.

Sidewalk Cafe's final day was February 23, 2019. One last open mic was held at 3:00 p.m., hosted by Bingham with "special guest" Jonathan Berger. From 6:30 p.m. to midnight, Sidewalk hosted its last show. It was a star-studded affair: Regina Spektor, Adam Green, Diane Cluck, and Jeffrey Lewis were among the performers; Lach even "returned" to read a poem over FaceTime from his current home in Scotland.

Antifolk—with its inclinations toward plainspokenness, humor, and vulnerability—never quite made it into the corpus of painfully hip New York music to the degree that, say, punk or no wave did (though, ironically, antifolk's take-all-comers philosophy makes it one of the punkest scenes to ever exist in the city).

But in a place where most venues are lucky to have ten good years, the back room at Sidewalk Cafe stayed vibrant for twenty-

xiv Milstein's co-owner Amnon Kehati passed away in 2015.

six. Though a lot of factors played a role, it's impossible to under-estimate how important it was that the scene never really turned a profit. With the entire scene oriented around an open mic night, there was little financial pressure around who got to play, how many people wanted to see them, or whether the music they played was seen as commercial or fashionable. No bad blood developed over end-of-the-night payouts, since nothing was ever promised and cash would simply be divided from whatever was collected in the tip jar. By avoiding many of the overt trappings associated with commercial success, antifolk was able to cultivate a vibrant underground scene that lasted a quarter of a century.

Even though most accounts of New York music history glaze over it, or only bring it up as a footnote to stars like Beck and Regina Spektor, I would argue that antifolk and Sidewalk Cafe are every bit as significant—and as quintessentially New York—as any other scene or genre mentioned in this book.

Green: It's very underrated. There were so many great songs writ-ten in this particular scene. A lot of these people, like Jeffrey Lewis, Turner Cody, Diane Cluck, Kimya, Regina, Dufus, Ish Marquez— these were some of the best in New York City at that time. But it was so underground that it never really took off, and I don't think it gets a fair shake. There could be compilations upon compilations of recordings from those years of all those different artists, like [the '60s garage rock compilation series] Pebbles or Nuggets or one of those compilations. There could be a five-album set of just awesome Side-walk Cafe songs that no one's ever heard of before.[xv]

THE AFTERLIFE OF THE ANTIFOLK SCENE

In March 2019, the investment firm Penn South Capital paid $9.6 million for the former Sidewalk Cafe building at 94-96 Avenue A. At the time, Penn South's founder, Parag Sahawney, said, "We have a new restaurant tenant that will keep the open mic tradi-

---

xv   Somebody, for the love of god, please do this.

tion alive. We love the East Village and believe in preserving what make [sic] it so special. We had a very peaceful transition from the previous landlord who also owned and managed Sidewalk. That owner has now retired from business and had no interest in staying on as our tenant."[173]

That October, the space became a restaurant called August Laura. At the time, owners Laura Saniuk-Heinig and Alyssa Sartor claimed that they intended to keep the music scene involved in some form or another, but those assurances never really amounted to anything. But then, neither did August Laura: it closed in December 2021.

The fate of the former Chameleon Club at 505 East 6th Street is cooler: It's now home to Club Cumming, a queer-focused bar co-owned by actor Alan Cumming, which regularly hosts burlesque, cabaret, and drag shows, and dance parties. It's one of the last cool things in the area (presumably, Cumming does well enough at his main gig that he doesn't need it to turn a profit).

Sophie's, at 507 East 5th Street, remains open. As East Village bars go, it's fine.

Folk City's second incarnation at 130 West 3rd Street is now home to the Fat Black Pussycat, a bar and comedy club. The former Speakeasy at 107 MacDougal Street is now the Grisly Pear, which is *also* a bar and comedy club.

The antifolk scene itself has become more diffuse, without a central base of operations. This was exacerbated by the arrival of the Covid-19 pandemic in March 2020, just over a year after Sidewalk's closure. And yet, antifolk refuses to die. Other open mics, run by Sidewalk regulars, continue to pop up around the city; there were even virtual open mics at the height of the pandemic. Against all odds, the grand tradition of folk music hootenannies in New York City—which stretches back to the Almanac Singers in the early 1940s—survives.

Suggested Listening

Cindy Lee Berryhill—*Who's Gonna Save the World?* (1987)

Roger Manning—*Roger Manning* (1988)

Various—*Broome Closet Anti-Folk Sessions* (1989)

Lach—*Contender* (1990)

Paleface—*Paleface* (1991)

Brenda Kahn—*Epiphany in Brooklyn* (1992)

Various—*Lach's Antihoot: Live From the Fort at the Sidewalk Cafe* (1996)

The Moldy Peaches—*The Moldy Peaches* (2001)

Jeffrey Lewis—*The Last Time I Did Acid I Went Insane* (2001)

Various—*Antifolk Vol. 1* (2002)

10

WHAT WOULD THE COMMUNITY THINK: DOWNTOWN MUSIC, THE LOWER EAST SIDE, AND THE CULTURAL DEATH OF MANHATTAN

James Marshall: The arts are what brought New York back, and they'll never get credit for it in that sense. In my mind, Johnny Thunders did a lot more for New York than Rudy Giuliani or Mike Bloomberg ever did. The city was built by junkies and gangsters and fuckups. That's who made this town, and that's why people wanted to come here. Then greed steps in, and all of a sudden these buildings that were falling down are worth a fortune.

Ask a Baby Boomer and a Millennial to define the geographic boundaries of the Lower East Side and there's a decent chance they'll give you vastly different answers—and they'll both be right. For much of its existence, the term "Lower East Side" referred to everything east of Broadway between East 14th and Canal Streets, which was largely a slum full of poor immigrant families. Starting in the mid-sixties, some people—both in the counterculture and the real estate industry—began referring to everything between East 14th and Houston as the "East Village" in order to rebrand it, associating it with the touristy, gentrified Greenwich Village. The name stuck, but it took a while to catch on—many who were living in the East Village during the '70s and early '80s still refer to it as the Lower East Side.

In fact, throughout the '70s and '80s, renaming portions of the Lower East Side were considered an essential element of gentrification by real estate types: There's "Nolita" for the area *no*rth of *Little Ita*ly and south of Houston. And for those who still found the sanitized East Village too déclassé, the portion west of Bowery and south of Astor Place became "NoHo" (*no*rth of *Ho*uston), piggybacking on SoHo's elite reputation.

By the late '80s, a new demarcation of the "Lower East Side" had become more or less canon: the area south of Houston, north of Canal, and east of Bowery. Alongside Alphabet City/Loisaida, which was already on the path to gentrification, it was the last part of the Lower East Side to retain any trace of the poverty and neglect, or the bohemian subculture, that had once defined it.

As portions of what had once been the Lower East Side were peeled off, rechristened, and made palatable to moneyed interests, they inevitably became less hospitable to experimental music and art. By the turn of the millennium, the entirety of Manhattan's cutting-edge music culture was located in a handful of venues, most within a few blocks of the Lower East Side.

During this time period, a number of overlapping scenes entered into tenuous but successful unions, in an attempt to outrun the forces of greed and conservatism that sought to squash them. Club bookings became eclectic, unexpected scenes cross-pollinated, and new sounds emerged. But it's key to remember that it didn't all happen by choice—almost every musical underground in Manhattan united into a single musical underground, just to survive.

And it worked. Until it didn't.

★ ★ ★

After the stock market boom in the '80s, NYC went into an economic recession from 1989 to 1993. Rents fell as they had in the '70s, and the *New York Times* noted in 1991 that, according to unnamed experts, "gentrification may be remembered, along with junk bonds, stretch limousines and television evangelism, as just another grand excess of the 1980s."[174] In the same article, the *Times* quoted Elliott Sclar, a professor of urban planning at Columbia, as saying, "Rich people are simply not going to live next to public housing."[175] But just four years later, the *Times* quoted Peter Salins, a professor of urban planning at Hunter College, who predicted, "Eventually, practically all of Manhattan, south of the northern edge of Central Park, will be gentrified, all the way down to the Battery, and that includes the Lower East Side."[176]

Absurd as that may have sounded at the time, there were signs that Salins was onto something—that gentrification was continuing, even in what had been considered the most ungentrifiable of neighborhoods. There were a smattering of venues and performance spaces on the Lower East Side during the '80s: notably, ABC No Rio, which opened at 156 Rivington Street in 1980, hosted antifolk open mics and hardcore punk shows. Across the street, Lach began his Fort open mics in his apartment at 157 Rivington. No Se No, a former Puerto Rican social club at 42 Rivington, became an art gallery that doubled as an after-hours rock club.

In 1989, artist Ulli Rimkus opened a bar called Max Fish at 176 Ludlow Street, formerly home to a Judaica shop named for its proprietor, Max Fisch. It attracted a community of musicians and artists who had all been living in the area, but who'd previously needed to cross Houston Street to find a hangout spot within their subcultural milieu.

THE KNITTING FACTORY

When we last checked in with loft jazz at the end of Chapter Two, the community was shrinking. By the late '70s, loft venues across Downtown were shuttering as fatigued artists cracked under the burdens of maintaining a DIY scene, and/or moved on to greater fame in Europe.

Pianist Matthew Shipp came of age in Delaware listening to much of the cutting-edge jazz New York produced during its '70s heyday, and when he moved to the city in 1983, he "expected to get off the train and the whole jazz intelligentsia would be waiting for me." What he found was less encouraging.

Shipp: The first day I was in New York, I ran into [violinist] Billy Bang on the street, so I stopped and I said, "Oh, Mr. Bang, I just moved to town. I'm a really big fan of yours." And he goes, "Oh, you are? Can I borrow $10?" I was scratching my head like, What the fuck am I getting myself into? And then I met [saxophonist] Frank Lowe. These are people that I grew up listening to. I said, "Mr. Lowe, I just moved to town," and we shook hands, and then he turned around and threw up, because he was really high. All that was my introduction.

As the mostly Black loft jazz scene struggled to keep afloat, a younger, mostly white scene of younger musicians was also coalescing in the area which combined free jazz, minimalism, and no wave/post-punk influences—a new genre that came to be called "Downtown music." This scene—which included John Zorn, Elliott Sharp, Robin Holcomb, Mark Miller, Wayne Horvitz, Eugene Chadborne, and former DNA members Arto Lindsay and Ikue Mori—would occasionally perform at venues like the Kitchen, Pyramid Club, and CBGB. But they lacked a dedicated, aboveground venue of their own. So, like their loft jazz predecessors, they primarily played in unlicensed, community-oriented DIY spaces.

One such space was Studio Henry (1 Morton Street, at Bleecker). A practice-space-slash-venue, it was located in the basement of a Greenwich Village pet store called Exotic Animals from 1976 to 1984.

Sharp: You never knew what kind of creatures you might find walking on the floor. One time, we were going to play a gig and Mark

Miller pulled down his bass drum case to pack, and when he opened the top, hundreds of water bugs came pouring out—it was a scene right out of a Cronenberg film. But one great thing about Studio Henry was when people began to play, the crickets began to sing. When you had a loud gig, there'd be a lot of crickets, because they would escape from the pet store where they were food for the lizards.

Saxophonist and composer John Zorn also briefly ran a club of his own called the Saint in the storefront of his Alphabet City apartment building at 204 East 7th Street. There is little documentation of the venue (or Studio Henry, for that matter), but it's important to note as the first of several venues in the area in which Zorn became involved.

As we've seen, DIY venues like Studio Henry and the Saint tend to be fleeting, and by 1987, the Downtown music scene and the avant-garde jazz scene were both in need of a more permanent home base. Together, they found an unexpected savior in a new, vaguely Middle Eastern–themed cafe called the Knitting Factory (47 East Houston Street), owned by a recent Wisconsin transplant named Michael Dorf.

When he moved to the city in 1986, Dorf was managing a Madison-based band called Swamp Thing and running a label called Flaming Pie Records. Neither were doing well, and his attempts to establish himself in the city's music industry were gaining little traction. Dorf later recalled, "I was very close to moving back to Wisconsin when I stumbled on a [former] Avon Products office at 47 East Houston Street."[177] Recognizing the space's potential, Dorf convinced his friend Louis Spitzer to team up with him on a combination café/art gallery. Dorf dubbed it the Knitting Factory, taking inspiration from a discarded Swamp Thing album title, *Mr. Bludstein's Knitting Factory.*

Sharp: It was just a herbal tea coffeehouse where [Dorf] was booking folk acts. He knew zero about New York music. Wayne Horvitz approached him about doing a series, Wayne promoted it on its

PHOTO BY THE AUTHOR, 2023.

47 East Houston Street.

own, and people came. So Dorf smelled money, and it began to be more and more downtown music, to the point where Dorf began to say that he invented the downtown scene.

By 1988, the Knitting Factory had established itself as the major hub for Downtown music, free jazz, and other avant-garde sounds.

Greg Tate: The booking of those seven or eight loft [venues] that had been going strong from '75 to '82 just became concentrated at the Knitting Factory. Michael Dorf and all those guys, they saw a void and really filled it.

Unlike the loft/DIY venues that preceded it, the Knitting Factory was a fully licensed and functioning bar and restaurant. Though the venue was ostensibly open to any and all experimental music, its bustling environment meant that some artists felt more comfortable in the space than others. As *Village Voice* critic Kyle Gann noted, music at the Knitting Factory "has to be aggressive enough to compete with the serving of drinks…[What] you were going to hear was loud improvisation—not that that was the only game in town, but the spaces were no longer set up for anything else."[178]

Still, by virtue of its enviable position as the commercial home of the Downtown avant-garde, the Knitting Factory became a go-to hangout spot for experimental artists of all stripes.

Shipp: If I was in town, I stopped by the Knitting Factory every night, even if I was only there for ten or fifteen minutes, because it was really close to where I live. I maybe heard a set, but mostly it was just to be around and make business contacts and stuff.

Like so many clubs we've seen, the Knitting Factory's central location also played a role in its success. It wasn't in an out-of-the-way industrial neighborhood, or desolate area, the way many earlier loft jazz or Downtown music spaces had been. Instead, it was in the exact center of Houston Street, a major thoroughfare and transit hub where all but the most uptight suburbanite would feel comfortable.

Sharp: It was halfway between SoHo, the East Village, and the West Village. You could walk to it, it was easy to get to from subways, so it was a place where people didn't feel threatened to go. It was safe for tourists, so most of the scene was tourists. There began to be more and more tourists, and then the booking policy began to be more geared towards bands that would bring in more tourists. But it's always that way—the gentrification of the music scene follows the same rules as the gentrification of real estate.

Given Dorf's background as the manager of a rock band, and given Downtown music's overlap with the wilder corners of post-punk and no wave, it was inevitable that the Knitting Factory would also welcome underground rock bands alongside jazz and Downtown performers. With those rock artists now sharing space with experimental music, cross-pollination was almost inevitable.

Sonic Youth, in particular, became a bridge between the mainstream rock world and the less accessible corners of free jazz and Downtown music. By the early '90s, the band had transcended their no wave and pigfuck roots to become a major label act who palled around with superstars like Nirvana and Neil Young. Even so, all four members of Sonic Youth—Thurston Moore, Lee Ranaldo, Kim Gordon, and Steve Shelley—delved into a plethora of side projects and one-off collaborations with free jazz and Downtown artists, bringing sounds that most listeners would find inaccessible and perplexing to a major international audience.

William Hooker (drummer): [The new scene] wasn't about free jazz, it was about rockers and noise, and people actually being open to me and what I was doing. When I met Thurston and Lee, these guys already had the keys to the kingdom. They had booking agents, so I didn't have to do the legwork. All of a sudden you're not playing for ten or fifteen hardcore jazz listeners, you're playing for people that have never heard anything like this in their lives.

Though Sonic Youth found widespread acceptance, for the most part, New York's post-punk rock bands in the late '80s and early '90s weren't much better off than free jazz or Downtown artists in terms of venues. There was Wetlands Preserve (161 Hudson Street), the hippie-rock launch pad for the careers of both the Spin Doctors and Blues Traveler, which also welcomed the occasional punk band or hip-hop act. Brownies, which opened in 1989 at 169 Avenue A, leaned heavily on out-of-town touring bands, running the gamut from Neutral Milk Hotel to Sugar Ray. Maxwell's (1039 Washington Street) in Hoboken, New Jersey, became a hub. And there was the reliable but increasingly lame CBGB. Local artsy, post-punk bands like Railroad Jerk or Blonde Redhead, whose music was starting to be identified as "indie rock," had few venues within city limits to call home.

The scene was so discouraging that the indie band Kicking Giant, which formed in New York in 1990, relocated to Olympia, Washington, two years later because they found the scene there to be much more vibrant. Singer/guitarist Tae Won Yu later recalled that "coming from New York, where people are just standing around, and there seemed to be no purpose to play music except to say that you just did...the eye-opening experience of playing in Olympia was that it was kids and they really loved it."[179]

This state of affairs led indie rock to be absorbed into the Knitting Factory mix, with shows by Yo La Tengo, Galaxie 500, Jeff Buckley, Beck, Smog, and They Might Be Giants. Though avant-garde and jazz artists had performed at rock venues like CBGB, Mudd Club, A7, and Danceteria, and rock artists occasionally played at avant-garde institutions like the Kitchen, the Knitting Factory was arguably the first venue where all of these communities met as equals (in terms of their respective bookings, at least), which led to some interesting results...and to Soul Coughing.

Knitting Factory doorman Mike Doughty, who had developed a reputation for delivering comedic freestyle raps on the job, recruited regulars Mark Degli Antoni, Sebastian Steinberg, and Yuval Gabay to form the band Soul Coughing in 1992. The band's alternative rock/jazz/hip-hop/spoken word fusion would find a considerable audience beyond Downtown with their 1994 major label release *Ruby Vroom*.

Soul Coughing are an especially glossy example of the cross-pollination taking place at the club. While most bands tend to gig with and spend time around similar-sounding bands, at the Knitting Factory, an indie rock band might forge close bonds with an electronica deejay or a loft jazz mainstay twice their age. This is why there's no cohesive "New York City sound" when it comes to '90s NYC rock bands: the diversity *is* the sound.

★ ★ ★

By the late '80s, the Knitting Factory's success had inspired Michael Dorf to expand its reach well beyond the confines of 47 East Houston Street. He spun off a record label (Knitting Factory Records), released multiple *Live at the Knitting Factory* compilations, curated a festival of New York improvisers in Holland, staged a "Knitting Factory Goes Uptown" show at Lincoln Center's Alice Tully Hall in 1988, and in 1990, began promoting an annual two-week-long, multivenue festival called the What Is Jazz? Festival. The club itself was also growing, with the Knitting Factory buying out Estella's, a basement-level Peruvian restaurant in their building, and transforming into a two-story venue in 1989.

That expansion set the stage for an even larger one: In 1994, the Knitting Factory left 47 East Houston Street for a larger three-story space at 74 Leonard Street in Tribeca. A main floor ballroom predominantly featured indie rock, electronica, and hip-hop, while two smaller basement and sub-basement rooms continued to host experimental music. In some ways, the Leonard Street Knitting Factory resembled a less flashy version of the 21st Street Danceteria, with its musical options spread across multiple floors (although the Knitting Factory's shows were individually ticketed, so patrons couldn't go back and forth between them).

Not everyone was on board with the club's reinvention—especially some of the experimental musicians that had given the original Knitting Factory its reputation. "It became less friendly," said Arto Lindsay. "It was more in tune with Dorf's ambitions in the way it was run." But for a younger crop of experimental artists, the Leonard Street Knitting Factory was as welcoming and delightful an environment as the city had to offer.

DJ Spooky (turntablist; writer): The Knitting Factory had no rules—it was like, whatever goes. There were a lot of different rooms and every room had a different flavor. You'd go in there and there's one band playing Indian music, there's another band playing hip-hop, you go downstairs and someone's doing death metal. There was one gig where me and Aphex Twin played, and he came out and played sandpaper on a turntable and it was crazy noise.

DJ Spooky (born Paul D. Miller) is a perfect example of the kind of cross-pollination the Knitting Factory fostered: As a deejay and producer working with sampled and scratched vinyl, he superficially scans as hip-hop, but his music also encompasses dub, ambient, jazz, Downtown music, musique concrète, no wave, drum and bass, contemporary classical, and techno influences. Spooky first came to prominence via parties he threw at the Gas Station (194 East 2nd Street), the Alphabet City squat and DIY art space where he lived in the early '90s. He eventually found himself part of an East Village–based scene that became known as "illbient" (Spooky and his sometime collaborator DJ Olive both claim to have coined the term).

As a scene that was initially oriented around all-night multimedia parties and improvisational sample-based music, illbient would likely have remained an obscure "you had to be there" phe-

DJ Spooky at a Soundlab party, 1997.

© ALICE ARNOLD.

nomenon were it not for the culture of genre-bending and cross-pollination that the Knitting Factory fostered. Indeed, by 2000, Spooky was improvising in a trio with Yoko Ono and Thurston Moore at the Knitting Factory Jazzfest.

THE COOLER

The Knitting Factory got its first viable competitor in 1993, with the opening of the Cooler at 416 West 14th Street, in the Meat-packing District. As the name might suggest, the neighborhood had been home to numerous slaughterhouses and meatpacking plants in the earlier part of the twentieth century; the Cooler was named in tribute to the space's past as a basement-level meat freezer.

"When I first opened the Cooler, everybody was telling me, 'You're going to close in six months,'" the club's mononymous owner Jedi recalled. The Meatpacking District was hardly an intuitive location for a music venue at the time. Up to that point, the area was best known as the home of legendary '70s and '80s gay sex clubs like the Anvil, the Mineshaft, the Hellfire Club, and the Toilet, rather than any more traditional forms of entertainment. Though those clubs were mostly closed or closing in the '90s, and some other alternative nightlife, like the Johnny Dynell/Chi-Chi Valenti-helmed club night Jackie 60 had popped up, the neighborhood remained primarily known as a hub for sex work. On the other hand, it was bordered by two bourgeois enclaves: the West Village and Chelsea.

Where the Knitting Factory welcomed jazz, Downtown music, indie rock, experimental electronica, and the occasional hip-hop show, the Cooler had even broader boundaries, hosting every imaginable genre and subgenre of music that Jedi could get his hands on, with a calendar that DJ Spooky called "freewheeling and hyper-eclectic." Performances ranged from Punjabi *bhangra* to dub reggae to psychedelic folk to free jazz to Moroccan *gnawa*.

But the Cooler was less the Knitting Factory's competitor than its successor. With its move to Tribeca, the Knitting Factory had made a play for the big time; the Cooler took its place as the new home for scenes that didn't have a home.

Don Fleming (singer/guitarist, Velvet Monkeys, B.A.L.L., Gumball; producer): If I was doing a side project with some weirdo, whatever, the Cooler would just book us. It had the right audience for that kind of thing: People would go there expecting something a little abnormal.

These days, the Cooler is best remembered for indie rock, and not unreasonably so—Beck, Elliott Smith, Cibo Matto, the Strokes, Unwound, Lunachicks, Cat Power, the Dirty Three, Yeah Yeah Yeahs, the Make-Up, Smog, and innumerable Sonic Youth side projects all played there. But the Cooler also served as a major venue for hip-hop in the city at a time where many clubs that welcomed the genre were being targeted by the NYPD.

Jedi: Busta Rhymes played there, Pharoahe Monch, Xzibit. Black Eyed Peas played the Cooler twice, Eminem played twice, the Fugees played twice. All those [deejays] were hanging out there—Red Alert, Stretch Armstrong. There are so many people who came to see indie shows there who never knew the Fugees or Eminem played there, nor did they care.

Although Jedi opened the Cooler during the waning days of David Dinkins's mayorship, the club's existence largely coincided with the Giuliani administration. As we saw in Chapter Eight, Giuliani was using cabaret license laws to target nightclubs for harassment—especially smaller spaces like the Cooler. And while the Meatpacking District was desolate when the club opened, it didn't stay that way for long, as high-end boutiques, restaurants, and flashy nightclubs swooped in. Giuliani and the NYPD were keen to help speed that process along.

For Jedi, the sustained police harassment became too much to bear, and in June 2001, he shuttered the club and left nightlife behind.

Jedi: I was getting burned out with that whole Giuliani situation, and my landlords were getting more obnoxious. I wasn't really having fun anymore, I was being squashed by problems with the cabaret laws, and I didn't feel like there was a reason to go on any further. The run of my club was about six and a half years, and that was long enough. I would rather be [an] intelligent performance space for six years than be a fucking milquetoast piece of shit for twenty five years.

VISION FESTIVAL

While Downtown's free jazz scene was experiencing an expansion of opportunities and audiences at clubs like the Knitting Factory and the Cooler, those were pretty much white clubs, with white owners, largely white audiences, and a calendar that leaned heavily on white performers—something that every Black performer that I spoke to about this era was quick to point out.

This doesn't, however, mean that the Black free jazz community was being wholly subsumed by the white Downtown music world.

Bassist William Parker and his wife, the poet and dancer Patricia Nicholson Parker, had been organizing occasional festivals and concerts around the East Village and Lower East Side for years, including the celebrated Sound Unity Festivals in 1984 and 1988. In 1996, Nicholson Parker staged the first Vision Festival—a five-day free jazz festival—at the Learning Alliance (324 Lafayette Street), with performances by some of the genre's foremost practitioners including Rashied Ali, Matthew Shipp, Milford Graves, Joseph Jarman, Amiri Baraka, and Daniel Carter. In a nod to the crossover that had begun at the Knitting Factory, John Zorn and Thurston Moore also performed.

Through Nicholson Parker's nonprofit organization Arts for Art, the Vision Festival has continued annually, and has been staged at various venues across Downtown Manhattan and Brooklyn, including the Clemente Soto Velez Cultural Center, the Knitting Factory, CBGB, the Angel Orensanz Center, Roulette Intermedium, and Judson Memorial Church.

Shipp: That's the scene here now. When you think of Black jazz on the Lower East Side, Arts for Art is the scene. They don't have a venue per se, even though [Nicholson Parker] does a lot of performances in their office space, but that is the scene. They have their whole history in this neighborhood; they pursued the music for years and years despite being completely shat upon and [ignored], but they just kept at it. That is an instrumental part of looking at this neighborhood from the '70s to now and what exists for "the Black music scene," looked upon as separate from the white improv scene.

Though it can feel a bit depressing to say that the Vision Festival is exactly as much avant-garde jazz as Manhattan can handle these days—about a week or so worth each year, as well as occasional smaller shows at the Arts for Art offices—there is something instructive in how they've outlasted every venue that tried to merge the experimental with the commercial, by prioritizing staying true to their vision instead of making compromises to hold on to a specific, brick-and-mortar space.

Cooper-Moore: In my world, the two of them, the Parkers, they're the center of what we do. They're the idealists. Early on, they saw what it was about: doing it for yourself, doing your whole organization, putting out your own recordings, the home concerts. They understand that it's not just playing the music, it's also staying alive and being in community. And I do think I can say honestly that the Art for Arts/Vision Festival community is a community.

TONIC

The World Wide Web—which would do as much to radically reinvent the city and its music scenes as any geographic, demographic, economic, or political changes—reached the public in 1991 but hit critical mass in 1995 with the debut of the Netscape Navigator and Internet Explorer browsers. That same year, Nick Bodor, John Scott, and Melissa Caruso-Scott opened one of the city's first internet cafes, alt.coffee (137 Avenue A)—a hip but unassuming coffee shop that birthed two of Manhattan's last great music venues: Tonic and Cake Shop.

For Bodor, alt.coffee was never "a cyber cafe or an online coffeehouse—I looked at it as a real beatnik coffeehouse, but in the '90s." That innate tension between the past and future was on full display in the changing Alphabet City area, which Bodor described as "better [than it had been], but it was still basically where every junkie in the tristate area would come to cop heroin."

Ted Reichman (accordionist): Many aspects of the neighborhood were represented at alt.coffee. The Moldy Peaches were in there all the time before they got famous. You'd see famous people in there, and then you'd see people passing out.

Reichman, a friend of the Scotts', had been hanging around alt. coffee from the outset, even lending a helping hand during some of the initial construction. When the possibility of hosting live music in the shop came up, Reichman was an obvious choice.

Reichman kicked off a Monday night residency for his trio with drummer John Hollenbeck and bassist Reuben Radding, but settled into a curatorial role for the weekly series. "It was always stuff from the jazz and improvised music worlds," he acknowledged. "I wasn't rigidly against booking other kinds of stuff, but there were so many other rock 'n' roll venues around that it never even occurred to me to book a rock band."

The Scotts only stuck around alt.coffee for a couple years. In 1997, another opportunity presented itself just a few blocks south, at 107 Norfolk Street in the Lower East Side.

Melissa Caruso-Scott: We had read about the available space in the Times. It had formerly been the home of Kedem Kosher Winery, and there was a photo of the huge, old wine casks that really caught our attention. We initially thought it would make for a perfect wine bar. In the fall of 1997, we brought Ted Reichman with us to see

PHOTO BY THE AUTHOR, 2023.

107 Norfolk Street.

the space, survey the acoustics, and discuss the possibility of extending our alt.coffee weekly music series there.

In 1997, one could no longer open an avant-garde, "Downtown music"–type venue in the middle of Houston Street—as the folks at the Cooler would surely attest, you could barely run one in the Meatpacking District anymore. The only place where one might find rent low enough, and the police disinterested enough, to operate an experimental music space was on the Lower East Side—which, as the *Times* had predicted years before, was in the midst of becoming the last Manhattan neighborhood below Central Park North to gentrify.

The opening of Mercury Lounge (217 East Houston Street) in 1993 was a major turning point. In those heady, post-Nirvana days, rock music was back on America's cultural radar, and opening a rock venue in one of the city's final remaining hip enclaves made sense. "I thought it was going to be more of a local music club," co-owner Michael Swier told the *Times* in 1997, "but it hasn't turned out that way."[180] That's not terribly surprising—little of the alternative rock that was gaining commercial traction was coming out of the city. Mercury Lounge primarily became a hub for buzzy touring bands, an inclination which was only exaggerated when the club's owners opened the larger Bowery Ballroom at 6 Delancey Street in 1998.

Other clubs followed Mercury's lead: In 1995, Luna Lounge opened at 171 Ludlow Street and Arlene's Grocery opened around the corner at 95 Stanton Street. Though Arlene's saw some controversy over their policy of never paying performers, both clubs did help to incubate a new homegrown indie rock scene that emerged in the late '90s and early '00s, with bands like Jonathan Fire*eater, the Strokes, Yeah Yeah Yeahs, Interpol, and the Mooney Suzuki. As early as 1997, *Times* writer Jon Pareles postulated that between the new clubs and all the musicians living in the area, "at certain hours, say about 11:30 on a Friday night, it seems more guitars are being carried along Ludlow Street, between Houston and Stanton Streets, than on any other block in New York City."[181]

So while the Scotts were certainly taking a risk on quiet Norfolk Street, it wasn't entirely without precedent. The area was *just* hip enough to suggest that an experimental venue could survive on its fringes. Amusingly, the pair teamed up with another John-and-Melissa couple, John Sarefield and Melissa Soon, to transform the winery into Tonic, a combination venue (run by the Scotts) and hair salon (run by Sarefield and Soon) which opened for business in 1998.

Reichman: When Tonic first opened, it was not exclusively a music venue—they were going to have comedy, they were going to have a swing dance night, there was going to be all this other stuff. I was going to do a one-night-a-week thing, which I saw as a way to bring in [musicians] who want to do something a little less casual than a free improv night at alt.coffee. But I didn't have super grandiose ambitions for it, because it was one night a week and it wasn't going to really be a music venue. They didn't even have a sound system at that time.

But on the strength of Reichman's bookings, Tonic began to gather a reputation as a quality venue for experimental music—and one that was sorely needed. Although the Cooler booked plenty of out-there stuff, the sheer breadth of Jedi's vision meant that no one scene could be fully incubated there, and with the Knitting Factory's expansion on Leonard Street, the avant-garde was taking a back seat. The tipping point—for both Tonic and the Knitting Factory—came from one of the latter venue's signature artists, and was precipitated by Michael Dorf's experiments with the Knitting Factory brand on the nascent World Wide Web.

Alan Licht (guitarist): The Knitting Factory had done an internet broadcast of a rehearsal [John Zorn] was doing there before a show, without his permission. So Zorn went ballistic when he found out, and then he was like, "I'm never playing Knitting Factory again."

Having washed his hands of the Knitting Factory, Zorn approached Tonic's owners about presenting a two-month festival at their venue. That festival, which ran from June 24 to August 16, 1998, marked the point at which Tonic transitioned from a cafe with music to a full-fledged music venue. After the festival, Reichman briefly resumed booking, but Zorn encouraged the Scotts to adopt a rotating curatorship.

Caruso-Scott: Zorn's series introduced us to key players in the scene, but we ourselves only knew a handful of musicians when we opened. It made sense for us to continue to invite established players, who had their own community of players to draw upon, to curate. This curatorial process offered musicians a chance to book a month of music as they saw fit (and for most this was their first time doing something like that) and it served as an educational opportunity for us.

Tonic's rotating curatorship became a who's-who of the Downtown avant-garde, with Thurston Moore, Elliott Sharp, Arto Lindsay, Living Colour guitarist Vernon Reid, percussionist Susie Ibarra, and harpist Zeena Parkins all taking on the role. "Curators had free admission in perpetuity," Caruso-Scott explained. "We started to become a place for musicians to hang and to also be introduced to players they hadn't heard before. New connections were being made regularly."

Beyond the rotating curatorship, clarinetist David Krakauer began booking a Sunday afternoon klezmer brunch series, while Sunday nights hosted an indie singer-songwriter series with the likes of Will Oldham (aka Bonnie "Prince" Billy), Fountains of Wayne, American Music Club's Mark Eitzel, and Magnetic Fields' Stephin Merritt.

To their great credit, Tonic's owners sought musicians' input not just for booking, but for any and all ways they could make their venue as artist-friendly as possible. "We relied on musicians to help us develop policies that would be in effect for the next nine years," said Caruso-Scott. "We didn't enforce drink minimums, we tried to make shows affordable, and our payment structure was favorable to the artist."

© RAHAV SEGEV/ZUMAPRESS.COM/ALAMY.

Saxophonist John Zorn, drummer Hamid Drake, and singer Mike Patton performing at Tonic on September 5, 2003.

Licht: I really did like it right away. I thought the decor was really great, with that exposed brick and the wooden ceiling. It sounded really good in there, and I liked the fact that it wasn't just the bar, it had a cafe feel. It wasn't like other venues, which were always dives— especially in New York. I instantly preferred it to the Cooler and the Knitting Factory.

As integral as the rotating curatorship was to Tonic's reputation and vibe, the realities of keeping a business afloat meant that it couldn't last without some interference.

Caruso-Scott: Musicians are not always thinking about the business end of things. They might think it would be great to give an unknown artist a Friday night or even a whole week. They might not see the disadvantages of booking a whole month of artists who they wish to support but who don't have a large enough following.

Tonic's rotating curatorship was short-lived, although they continued to rely on musicians' expertise and connections. For a short time, drummer Chris Corsano worked with Caruso-Scott on booking the venue, but when Corsano left in 2000, Alan Licht saw an opportunity and proposed himself as Corsano's replacement.

Under Licht's tenure, Tonic's tone changed subtly but decisively. Licht has long had a foot in both the indie rock and avant-garde worlds: his bands Love Child and Run On were signed, respectively, to the seminal indie labels Homestead and Matador, and he's collaborated extensively with both indie rock types (Royal Trux, the Boredoms, Television's Tom Verlaine, and multiple Sonic Youth side projects) as well as jazz and minimalist performers (including drummer William Hooker and experimental guitarists Loren Mazzacane Connors, Keiji Haino, and Oren Ambarchi). With Licht at the helm, Tonic's bookings delved into the midpoint between indie rock and the avant-garde.

Matthew Mottel (keyboardist, Talibam!): The way the Cooler booked shows, you'd have Blonde Redhead and William Hooker on

THIS MUST BE THE PLACE

a three-band bill. Tonic, especially under Alan, moves to: set one at 8:00, set two at 10:00, and set three at midnight. Three different shows, three different ticket prices. So in that moment, you lose that open forum—the people that want to see William Hooker don't get to interact with the people that want to see Blonde Redhead.

The reality of the situation was that buzzy indie rock shows in gentrifying Manhattan simply drew better than outré jazz. Licht's bookings kept Tonic on the cutting edge, it was just an ever-so-slightly different edge: Licht fondly recalled booking early shows by then-unknowns Animal Collective and the National; other highlights during his tenure included Daniel Johnston, Cibo Matto, Vincent Gallo, Regina Spektor, Tony Conrad, Peaches, Rashied Ali, Norah Jones, Matana Roberts, Xiu Xiu, Peter Brotzmann, William Parker, Akron-Family, and Faith No More/Mr. Bungle vocalist Mike Patton.

Beyond live performances in the main space, Tonic's basement—dubbed SubTonic—hosted several popular recurring deejay nights, including the Friday night techno party the Bunker, DJ Olive and Toshio Kajiwara's experimental night Phenomena, and the garage rock party New York Night Train. As Greg Tate noted, "Tonic realized that there was a younger audience that would come out for experimental music, especially if it was connected to drum and bass, hip-hop, trip hop, techno, and the whole illbient thing that was happening."

By 2001, Tonic's musical offerings had diversified to the point where they assumed the Cooler's role as a hub for any and all underground sounds, just as that club had effectively picked up the baton from the original Knitting Factory. That's not to say that the Cooler's loss wasn't acutely felt; it's always better to have more than one venue around to host every single underground scene all at once.

But I suspect Tonic flourished where the Cooler faltered for two reasons: First, Tonic wasn't really putting on a lot of major hip-hop shows the way the Cooler did, which had the unfortunate side effect of attracting police attention. And second, where the Meatpacking District was being transformed into a chichi shopping and nightlife district, the Lower East Side was still in the early stages of the gentrification cycle. "The neighborhood was mostly Hispanic," Licht explained. "They're playing salsa out of their car, they're not playing [experimental guitarist] Marc Ribot."

Dana Wachs (sound tech, Tonic; musician, Vorhees): The neighborhood felt like the stories that you used to read about New York back when the Mudd Club still existed—a bit ramshackle, but also completely populated by beautiful families from so many different cultures. There was a big Hispanic and big Chinese immigrant crossover, and it felt nice to me, like this romanticized idea of New York in the sense that it was very multicultural. I didn't have a real sense of gentrification—ironically, being somebody who was gentrifying without realizing it. I was too young to recognize the step I was taking [moving into the neighborhood]. But I also couldn't afford to live anywhere else.

9/11

You don't need me to tell you what happened in New York City on September 11, 2001. If you were alive and conscious at the time, the moment you found out about it is probably seared into your brain forever.

9/11's impact on the city is a book unto itself, and much of it is beyond the scope of this one. But there were a few key aspects of the fallout that had both immediate and long-term impacts on the city's music scenes.

Most significantly, the city—*especially* Downtown—took a massive financial hit: a Chamber of Commerce report from November 2001 estimated an $83 billion gross loss for the city as a direct result of the attacks, especially in the fields of tourism and retail. Polling showed that "some potential visitors feel the need for permission to enjoy themselves again in a place where tragedy has occurred...[so the city's] marketing campaigns should take advantage of the fact that New York City continues to be perceived as an exciting and vibrant place, rather than appeal to the sympathy of potential visitors."[182] According to Lower Manhattan Development Corporation co-founder Matt Higgins, "It was important to send out a global call to come to New York as a patriotic act."[183]

Much of rural and suburban America had viewed the city skeptically for decades (as Woody Allen famously declared in 1977's *Annie Hall*, "The country looks upon New York like we're left-wing, communist, Jewish, homosexual pornographers"[184]), but suddenly Americans of all stripes adored the city, and they all had brand-new "I ♥ NY" shirts to prove it. People from around the country *did* begin to see New York tourism as a patriotic act—as the writer and performer Reverend Jen summed it up in her 2003 book *Reverend Jen's Really Cool Neighborhood*, "Suddenly, the tank top–sporting, macho metropolis was a pity fuck for fat Oregonians."[185]

This isn't to say that, prior to this, New York was somehow 100 percent free of tourist traps—we're talking about a city that, in the late '90s, had a Planet Hollywood, a Hard Rock Cafe, a Motown Cafe and a Harley-Davidson Cafe, all within a three-block radius.[186] But after 9/11, it felt like the spots that catered to tourists were no longer cordoned off in Midtown. They were spreading into the part of New York where people actually lived—even those with edgier lifestyles.

Emily Armstrong: Around our block [on Orchard Street], we have four or five 20-story hotels, and they all got their approvals right after 9/11. They gave out a gazillion liquor licenses, all in an effort to save Lower Manhattan. And now we're living with the vestiges of what happened.

After a decade of widespread disinterest in the city's rock scenes, the period after 9/11 saw a renewed passion for New York rock 'n' roll—or at least, a nostalgic, heavily sanitized version of it. The Strokes, a buzzy new band of Upper East Side rich kids, had been building a local reputation since their formation in 1998, with many of their early gigs taking place at clubs like Arlene's Grocery and Mercury Lounge. Their self-consciously retro "punk" look and Velvet Underground–meets-Television sound scanned as "Classic NYC" to European music journalists. Having already released their 2001 debut album *Is This It* abroad, the band were set to release the domestic vinyl edition on 9/11, with CDs soon to follow.

Is This It featured an ostensibly anti-cop song called "New York City Cops." The lyrics have very little to do with cops, instead mostly recounting a debauched night out in the city (as many of the songs on *Is This It* did). But when the subject of the NYPD does arise, singer Julian Casablancas laments, "They ain't too smart." After 9/11, that sensibility was no longer in vogue—the NYPD, who'd been insufferable under Giuliani (if not long before), were now (rightfully, in that moment!) being hailed as heroes for their response to the attacks.

Domestic copies of *Is This It* were recalled, "New York City Cops" was cut from the track list, and another song, "When It Started," was rushed out to replace it on the CD. Still, the resultant press about the song's removal helped vault the band to national stardom. Here was another "New York" thing that outsiders could understand, and therefore ♥. At long last, the Lower East Side indie scene had produced some genuine, honest-to-god rock stars.[i]

MIKE

9/11 occurred in the waning days of Giuliani's final term as mayor. Prior to the event, polls had indicated a leftward shift in the city's political future, a natural pendulum swing away from two terms under a Republican in a Democratic city. But the panic and xenophobia that swept the country after 9/11 changed that course: Michael Bloomberg, a billionaire CEO and lifelong Democrat who ran as a Republican with Giuliani's endorsement, was elected mayor.

---

i   Just to be clear, *Is This It* is a phenomenal album—easily one of the century's best. That can still be true, even if it was made by a bunch of trust fund kids in predistressed jeans, and even if a bunch of normy bozos liked it.

Crackdowns on nightlife, already flourishing under Giuliani, went into overdrive as Bloomberg strove to rebuild the city in an image that would appeal to tourists, especially wealthy ones.

Much like his predecessor Giuliani, Bloomberg's tactics overwhelmingly targeted lower-income Black and Latinx communities. As he said in 2015, defending his "stop and frisk" policy, "We put all the cops in minority neighborhoods... [b]ecause that's where all the crime is. And the way you get guns out of the kids' hands is to throw them up against the wall and frisk them."[187]

On March 9, 2003, the Bloomberg administration launched the 311 hotline. Ostensibly a number you could call for information about or access to nonemergency city services, it's just a way to call the cops on people and businesses that bothered you even though they haven't committed any crime—a nonemergency spin-off of 911.

And a lot of people—especially the new, moneyed residents Bloomberg was wooing—don't like loud bars. James Marshall, who owned the Alphabet City bar Lakeside Lounge (162 Avenue B), recalled the absurd lengths the authorities would go to when responding to 311 noise complaints.

> *Marshall: The quality of life patrol would just come in to the bar and write tickets for every fucking thing possible. When they would show up for the noise complaints, they would stand outside with the decimal reader and wait for the bus to show up, and then when the bus showed up, they would turn the meter on. It was guaranteed to go over 60 decibels, because the bus itself is like 85 decibels when it revs up. You can't fight a noise ticket, you're automatically guilty. I remember the first noise ticket we got was $2,500, and the next one was going to be $5,000, and the next one after that is $10,000— each time it doubles.*

Less than a month after 311 debuted, the Bloomberg administration banned smoking in the city's bars, restaurants, childcare/youth centers, schools, hospitals/healthcare facilities, commercial establishments, places of employment, indoor arenas, bingo facilities, and zoos. But of course, there's only one place on that list where patrons regularly expected to puff away in comfort. I doubt anybody's waxing nostalgic about the halcyon days of New York's dark, seedy, smoke-filled zoos.

I hate it when people smoke indoors. It makes my eyes water and my clothes smell. But as promoter Todd Patrick pointed out, "The smoking ban did a lot more than ban smoking." Random targeted enforcement meant that bar owners had to constantly be on watch: staying open after-hours, welcoming underage patrons, and hosting music without a cabaret license were all greater risks, now that the NYPD was going around looking for smoky bars to slap with a $400 fine.

Of course, if smokers can't smoke indoors, that means they have to smoke outdoors. Which means that they're going to be having (probably inebriated) conversations outside of the bars, where anyone and everyone can hear them. Which means more 311 noise complaints.

TONIC'S END

The success of bands like the Strokes, Yeah Yeah Yeahs, and Interpol (all veterans of Mercury Lounge and Luna Lounge) created international interest in the Lower East Side as a chic, gritty party destination. Tourists flocked to the neighborhood for a taste of authentic "hipster" nightlife. Older, artsier businesses were pushed out and replaced with bars that sold $6 Budweisers to people in American Apparel hoodies. In 2003, a cupcake bakery opened on Rivington Street (they're really good cupcakes, but still). By 2006, Lindsay Lohan and Kate Moss were writing scandalous graffiti in the bathroom of Darkroom (165 Ludlow Street), an infamous Lower East Side bar/coke den.

At first, none of this seemed a threat to Tonic. Even after the introduction of 311, they weren't getting noise complaints, as the former Kedem winery was only a single floor and basement, meaning there were no upstairs neighbors, and the building was flanked with empty lots on either side. And location-wise, they seemed far enough off from the mania of Ludlow Street for any developer to want to grab the space and flip it into another cupcake joint.

That finally changed in 2006 when developers broke ground in the neighboring lot at 105 Norfolk Street. Over the course of a year, they constructed a sixteen-story condo building covered in reflective, blue-tinted glass, imaginatively dubbed the Blue Condominium.

The Blue Condominium opened for business in 2007, with one-bedroom apartments going for $850,000. It *was* a perfect visual manifestation of the gentrification under Bloomberg. But according to Licht, "Because that [Blue Condominium] building went up, the common perception is that it was gentrification that squeezed out Tonic. But that's not really totally accurate.

"Tonic was like a nonprofit music venue that was functioning as a for-profit music venue, and that's just not sustainable in the long term," Licht explained. "Technically the reason Tonic closed was that they were way behind on their rent." Though Tonic had long been renting the building from the owner of the winery, that landlord eventually sold the building to a larger real estate company, who raised the rent as soon as they were able to do so. Necessary renovations due to fire safety concerns also expanded the club's maximum capacity, which wasn't as positive as it sounds.

Licht: The capacity went from 180 to 220, which is not that big of an increase. But if you can pack a show of 220 people, you're talking about an act that has a booking agent, and if they're selling out Tonic for 220 people, the next time around, he's going to be calling Mercury Lounge where the capacity is 290,[ii] or the Knitting Factory which is 300. They're not going to be coming back to Tonic over and over again.

With the enlarged space, some of the more left field artists who had helped give Tonic its initial reputation felt that they were once

---

ii   It's actually 250, but Licht's point stands.

more demoted, as they had been at the Knitting Factory after its move to Leonard Street. "There was more stuff that was designed to fill the space than it was [about] a certain aesthetic," said Elliott Sharp. "Those of us who kind of made the place happen for the first few years were then relegated to less important nights of the week."[iii]

On top of it all, structural issues rendered Tonic's plumbing temporarily inoperable. As Caruso-Scott put it, "We were in deep water (literally too)." Dana Wachs recalled the installation of a porta-potty in the club's lobby as an especially low point.

The club came very close to shutting in 2005, but benefit concerts by the likes of Devendra Banhart, Yoko Ono, Yo La Tengo, Medeski Martin & Wood, and John Zorn kept it afloat for another two years. Still, as they approached the end of their second five-year lease in 2007, Tonic's finances were simply stretched too thin to survive, and the club's $10,000-a-month rent went unpaid for months. In Licht's memory, Tonic's owners were also burnedout. "Marc Ribot sat down with John, Melissa and I, and laid out how Tonic could keep going as a nonprofit, but John and Melissa were just not interested."

Tonic's final night was April 13, 2007. Zorn, who had first put Tonic on the map, led two sets of improvised music, while the Bunker staged its final dance party in SubTonic. The following day, Ribot and musician Rebecca Moore led a protest in which musicians improvised inside the club from 11:00 a.m. until 5:00 p.m. as workers cleared the space out. When the club was finally emptied,

---

iii   Many of those artists had also moved on to a new favorite club: The Stone, opened in 2005 by John Zorn in a former Chinese restaurant at 16 Avenue C. A throwback to the days of Studio Henry, the hundred-seat venue proudly sold no drinks or merchandise, and 100 percent of the door went to performers. Zorn underwrote the club with profits from his own Tzadik Records label, as well as private donations and occasional benefit shows. The Stone adopted the rotating curator model that Zorn had first introduced at Tonic, but which it had long since shed. In 2018, the Stone relocated to nicer digs within the New School's Arnhold Hall at 55 West 13th Street, where it is going strong to this day.

police officers arrived and informed the musicians that they were trespassing and would be arrested if they didn't vacate the premises. Ribot and Moore both refused and were led out of the club in handcuffs as supporters cheered them on from across the street.

With Tonic gone, the avant-garde scene has continued to survive, largely inhabiting nonprofit and privately funded venues like the Stone in Manhattan, or Issue Project Room and Roulette Intermedium, both located in Downtown Brooklyn. Arts for Art continues to present the Vision Festival annually, as well as periodic programming throughout the year. From a certain angle, these venues are preferable: there are no rowdy bars to distract the artists or fans, and because of their operating models they don't need to be as concerned about turnout.

But on the other hand, few if any of those venues are ever going to book the contemporary equivalents of what Cat Power or Animal Collective were early in their careers. Granted, those kinds of indie rock artists aren't at a loss for places to play. But without the regular cross-pollination of disparate scenes in a comfortable, informal setting where artists regularly hang out, something is lost. Scenes become more insular, more stratified, and less adventurous. Everybody just ends up hanging out around other people who like all the same stuff they do. Where's the fun in that?

CAKE SHOP

In 2005, as Tonic was already on the verge of closure, John Scott and Melissa Caruso-Scott's old alt.coffee business partner Nick Bodor, his brother (and alt.coffee barista) Andy Bodor, and partner Greg Curley opened Cake Shop at 152 Ludlow Street in 2005, taking the club's name from the Swell Maps' song "Cake Shop Girl."

Cake Shop resembled CBGB in the '80s and '90s, after it opened their Record Canteen and Pizzeria in adjacent storefronts: the club's ground level was an actual, honest-to-god cake shop, selling coffee, drinks, and baked goods, with a small record store tucked into the back, while the 120-capacity basement hosted nightly shows for 21+ audiences, booked by Andy Bodor. For him, "The dichot-

152 Ludlow Street.

omy of the upstairs being quiet and the downstairs being insane was part of [the concept]."

> **Nick Bodor:** *A lot of venues have a clubhouse feel, and I hate that. It's exclusive, you're not part of this—this would happen a lot in Brooklyn. I'm like, fuck, dude, I've got money in my pocket, I just want a beer and a shot—it's a shitty feeling. So we were always really aware that at Cake Shop everybody [was welcome]: If it's a Wall Street bro, take his money. If it's an art school kid, get him a muffin at the end of the night.*

Thanks to its location, Cake Shop was able to fit both brothers' visions, serving as a home base for the city's indie underground *and* a welcoming entry point to the scene for curious outsiders—much as clubs like Gerde's Folk City and Tier 3 had been.

Much of the club's appeal came from its top-notch booking. While Nick Bodor and Greg Curley took care of the business end, Andy Bodor was given carte blanche to book as he saw fit. His tastes were finely honed, which Cake Shop's calendar reflected: Mostly indie rock, especially of the lo-fi, twee, and psychedelic varieties. He even sought out obscure older artists he loved (including Miracle Legion, Small Factory, Hüsker Dü's Grant Hart, and Oh-OK) and enticed them to come play, at times to minuscule crowds. "My favorite shows were the smaller shows, where I was maybe one of 20 people just loving it," he said.

Still, Cake Shop's impeccable booking and homespun environment made it a club that many found worth going out of their way to attend. Practically every major Brooklyn-based indie act that emerged during Cake Shop's existence played there, including Vampire Weekend, Dirty Projectors, Titus Andronicus, Real Estate, Woods, the Pains of Being Pure at Heart, and Sharon Van Etten. The gregarious Bodor brothers were there practically every night, with Andy running the door and Nick behind the bar, which added to the feeling of community.

Jeffrey Lewis: Cake Shop was almost definitive of the next phase of the Lower East Side. It was so close to the J train, which was one stop across the Williamsburg Bridge from Williamsburg, so it was very convenient. It was a literal bridge, if you will, between the Lower East Side and Williamsburg. It was very well-placed for that era where a lot of people were living in Williamsburg [but were still] coming to the Lower East Side, even though nobody could afford to live on the Lower East Side anymore.

The DIY indie sensibility that Cake Shop fostered meant that it stood out on the Lower East Side in the late '00s and early '10s, where it was surrounded by mediocre rock clubs like Pianos and Arlene's Grocery, and an endless string of fratty bars whose over-served patrons went so far as to stage vomiting contests in the middle of the street.[iv]

---

iv   An actual documented thing that happened ("Hipsters Finally Kill the LES," Gawker.com, June 28, 2006: https://www.gawker.com/183960/hipsters-finally-kill-the-les, accessed June 3, 2022).

The fundamental issue of Cake Shop's location was revealed to me over and over when interviewing Brooklyn-based indie musicians from this era. When asked if there was anywhere in Manhattan where they liked playing or hanging out, they'd often say no—their scene was, as USAISAMONSTER guitarist Colin Langenus said, "full Brooklyn." When I mentioned Cake Shop, their responses almost always went something like, "Oh yeah, I forgot all about that place! I loved it so much. We played there all the time." It was a wonderful club, but as a Brooklyn outpost in an unwelcoming Manhattan, it never fit comfortably into either category.[v]

It's also a sign of how quickly and thoroughly the Lower East Side was changing that Cake Shop's calendar full of cult-y indie rock bands—the kind that just a few years prior would have alienated Tonic's experimental musicians but drawn audiences that helped to keep that club afloat—was now a risky financial proposition in and of itself.

Cake Shop's finances were eternally precarious. On top of which, according to Andy Bodor, "We got pummeled by underage drinking. A 20-year-old rookie cop came in and got served twice by the same bartender in a week's span. We got an insanely high fine, and it crushed us. We were trying to pay off that debt forever."

Cake Shop, which *Spin* rightly recognized as "Manhattan's last great rock club,"[188] had its final night on New Year's Eve 2016. Its closure was the final blow in Manhattan's decades-long run as the center of musical innovation.

Nick Bodor: People really, really loved that place. I don't go around saying, "I'm Nick from Cake Shop," but when it comes up, people are really sweet. Greg [Curley, Cake Shop's co-owner] and I would

---

v   In 2009, the Bodors opened a second club in Williamsburg, Brooklyn, called Bruar Falls (245 Grand Street). It closed in 2011, partly due to creative differences with one of the club's investors, but also due to the fact that they had simply gotten there too late: Williamsburg was already full of great venues by that point.

get this all the time in Brooklyn when we were open: We'd meet someone and they'd say "Oh, I love Cake Shop," and we'd ask, "When's the last time you were there?"

"Five years ago."

"You should have come in more often." It was rare that we actually said that, but it was very true. Everybody loved it, but people ultimately just didn't spend enough money there.

THE AFTERLIFE OF THE DOWNTOWN SCENE AND THE LOWER EAST SIDE

The top floor of the original Knitting Factory (47 East Houston Street) is now Estela, an acclaimed bistro—much like the original Knitting Factory, their menu seems vaguely Mediterranean. The lower level is now Botanica Bar.

As far as I can tell, the old Cooler in the basement of 416 West 14th Street hasn't been much of anything for some time. The ground level is a retail space; I suspect the basement is used for storage.

With Tonic (107 Norfolk Street) long gone, it continues to shock me that no developers have bothered to demolish the single-story building. But lo and behold, it's still there. After Tonic closed, the space remained empty until 2012, when it became the Lisa Cooley Gallery. That gallery closed in 2016, and as of this book's writing, the space is again vacant.

Thanks to a 2008 rezoning, the Lower East Side saw a stark rise in average rents and on-premises liquor licenses. Between 2000 and 2018, the number of liquor licenses more than tripled, with the Lower East Side zip code 10002 going from 41 licenses to 175. Of those, the highest concentration is within the section of the neighborhood contained between Houston, Allen, Essex, and Delancey Streets. Among residents, that area has become known as "Hell Square," New York's very own Bourbon Street.

A 2017 study by Hunter College graduate students tracked the ways the neighborhood's quality of life has decreased since that rezoning: In addition to the rise in noise pollution, rents, and idiots, the Lower East Side also saw a rise in rapes and felony assaults at a time when the numbers were receding elsewhere in the city.[189]

In the center of Hell Square, the former Cake Shop is now a cocktail bar called Kind Regards, of which Nick Bodor is part owner. On his personal website, co-owner Thatcher Schultz describes the club as "a DJ-centric venue celebrating the Lower East Side's historic roots in music. The unique bi-level layout transports you downstairs to a Miami nightclub in the '80's, and upstairs to a seasonally decorated cocktail bar."[190] It is a better fit on modern-day Ludlow Street than Cake Shop was when it closed.

But even with the condos, hotels, and puking contests that have transformed the area, some aspects of the Lower East Side remain intact. As Greg Tate pointed out, "If you go over to Houston Street, the pizza places are still there, the falafel places are still there, Katz's Deli is still there. The non-creative aspect of the neighborhood is still very present."

Suggested Listening

Elliott Sharp—*Fractal* (1986)

John Zorn—*John Zorn's Cobra: Live at the Knitting Factory* (rec. 1992)

Cat Power—*What Would the Community Think* (1996)

DJ Spooky—*Riddim Warfare* (1998)

Matthew Shipp Trio—*The Multiplication Table* (1998)

Medeski Martin & Wood—*Tonic* (2000)

Masada—*Live at Tonic 2001* (2001)

The Strokes—*Is This It* (2001)

Alan Licht—*A New York Minute* (2003)

11

THEY THREW US ALL IN A TRENCH AND STUCK A MONUMENT ON TOP: DIY IN WILLIAMSBURG AND BEYOND

Charlemagne Palestine: When I was a kid, you didn't even say you were from Brooklyn. It was like a favela, like you'd come from the garbage. Now wherever I go, I say I'm from Brooklyn and the look in everybody's eyes is like I said that my father is the King of Sweden. Who would have ever imagined that our shitty Brooklyn would become the art capital of the world?

Kevin Morby (singer-songwriter; bassist, Woods; singer/guitarist, The Babies): It felt like we were the kids in Peter Pan *or something. Everybody rode bicycles, nobody had a car, no one had a real job. It was just this endless party that never stopped—until, eventually, it did.*

Long before it became the home of an internationally recognized music scene or a worldwide buzzword for youth-oriented branding,

Williamsburg, Brooklyn, was just an unspectacular place where people lived. Connected to Manhattan by the Williamsburg Bridge (constructed in 1903), turn-of-the-twentieth-century Williamsburg was an enclave for upwardly mobile immigrant communities who had left the Lower East Side in search of calmer, more spacious digs. It was also an industrial center, home to a number of factories that mostly produced foodstuffs—beer, mustard, spices, and most prominently, sugar. It was the most densely populated neighborhood in the most densely populated city in the country.

But much like SoHo and Tribeca before it, Williamsburg's industries dried up in the mid-twentieth century, which led to an increase in both street and organized crime activity, alongside an exodus of longtime residents to the suburbs or other parts of the city. By the late twentieth century, three significant communities remained in the area: Hasidic Jews from the Satmar sect, Italians, and a Latinx community mostly from Puerto Rico and the Dominican Republic. All three were self-contained, personally and geographically, and rarely mixed. Williamsburg's industrial areas were near-abandoned for decades.

But as Downtown Manhattan became inhospitable to all but the wealthiest residents around the turn of the century, the more impoverished artists and musicians who would have previously gravitated there were forced to look elsewhere. They discovered, to their pleasant surprise, that Williamsburg was full of the kind of dirt cheap, formerly industrial buildings that had fueled the scenes around SoHo and Tribeca—and it was a single subway stop away from the East Village (on the L train) or the Lower East Side (on the J/M/Z).

From the 1990s to the 2010s, Williamsburg took up Downtown's mantle, playing host to a range of sounds and scenes that all got grouped together under the increasingly meaningless "indie rock" tag. But as the cost of living rose citywide, Williamsburg's ascent marked the moment when living an artistic life anywhere in New York became logistically difficult and nearly financially impossible. This time around, everyone had to work to make rent, to put on shows, to keep the artists and venues involved afloat. It represented a turning point at which bohemian life in New York required an intense level of focus, business sense, and work ethic, merely to keep existing.

ARCADIA

Composer William Basinski and his partner, painter James Elaine, moved to New York from San Francisco on April Fool's Day 1980. Both native Texans, the couple had spent the previous few years living together in San Francisco before heading east. Through his first decade in the city, Basinski struggled to make headway.

> *Basinski: I was so insecure that it never occurred to me, unfortunately, to go to the Kitchen and ask if I could sweep the floor or lick envelopes or something just to get my foot in the door. I was working as a cashier at Times Square gay strip clubs or the night shift at X-rated movie houses, shit like that. Eventually, I started to meet other musicians and play in lots of different bands, but my private, personal work was still not really happening, and nobody really got it outside of the art world.*

Initially, Basinski and Elaine lived in a large loft space at 351 Jay Street in Downtown Brooklyn, and Basinski would stage occasional concerts there over the course of the decade. When the building's tenants were evicted by the city in 1989 to make way for an urban renewal project, Basinski and Elaine took a buyout and began looking for another space in which they could continue to stage events. They found it at 118 North 11th Street in Williamsburg, in what had once been the Hecla Iron Works factory, built in 1896.

> *Basinski: We found it abandoned and full of pigeons. At that time, the north side of Williamsburg was all empty factories, but these Realtors just bought up everything when it was dirt, dirt, dirt cheap and*

started bringing in artists, because they knew the drill. We got a fairly cheap rent: $1,500 for this 4,000 square foot ruin on the third floor.

Basinski and Elaine dubbed their renovated loft "Arcadia." Though it was not Williamsburg's first-ever DIY space, it was the first significant one, and arguably the first SoHo-style loft venue in the area: Both Basinski and Elaine were aware of their Manhattan predecessors, and took inspiration from those that remained—especially La Monte Young and Marian Zazeela's Dream House, which Basinski described as a "major, major, major" influence. Arcadia was also the first Williamsburg venue to be a regular destination for audiences from outside the neighborhood, many of whom had never ventured into Brooklyn.

Like the Dream House, Arcadia was visually stunning, awash in colored lights, lavish fabrics, and rococo ornamentation.[i] Even more so than their Jay Street space, Basinski and Elaine ran Arcadia as a formal venue, which they subsidized in part by running a side business renovating and selling classic cars.

Basinski: We did three seasons—spring, summer and fall—for maybe four or five years. We would have four shows [per season], something like that, and they would be once a week or maybe once every two weeks. We were featuring young people in the neighborhood that we had heard about and went to see, and we would nurture unknown artists like [Anohni].[ii]

We were all like a company. Somebody would work the door and somebody would do coat check or whatever when they weren't on the bill. Everyone helped out and everybody got paid but me. We always lost money, but what are you gonna do? We could have fun

---

i   The decor can be seen in the cover photos for Jeff Buckley's 1994 album, *Grace*, which were shot at Arcadia by photographer Merri Cyr.

ii   Singer Anohni Hegarty, who has previously fronted the band Antony and the Johnsons, came out as transgender in 2015 and uses she/her pronouns.

William Basinski at Arcadia, 1990.

© JAMES ELAINE, COURTESY OF WILLIAM BASINSKI.

The ballroom at Arcadia, 1990.

© JAMES ELAINE, COURTESY OF WILLIAM BASINSKI.

and do what we wanted. That's what the whole point of being in a loft was about.

IMMERSIONISM

As Arcadia was gathering steam in the early '90s, other DIY venues began to open in Williamsburg. Basinski emphasized that it was a small community where everyone went to each other's spaces, but there was extraordinary stylistic range.

They Might Be Giants—the indie pop duo of John Linnell and John Flansburgh—had already been making a name for themselves around the city when they both moved to Williamsburg in the late '80s.[iii] Around that time, Linnell and his roommate Brian Dewan ran a small DIY venue called Quiet Life out of a disused funeral parlor on the ground floor of their building at 18 Havemeyer Street, hosting low-key shows by their band alongside up-and-comers like Lucinda Williams and Laura Cantrell.

The East Village–based antifolk scene was also dipping its toe into Williamsburg, with singer-songwriters like Billy Syndrome and Paleface both performing at the Lizard's Tail at 99 South 6th Street. The club, which opened in 1988, was run by a pair of European expats—Terry Dineen from Ireland and Jean-François Pottiez from Belgium—who lived upstairs.

The Lizard's Tail made enough waves to be featured in the *New York Times* in 1990, where writer Peter Watrous describes it as "pure bohemia, reminiscent of the Lower East Side in the early 1980's," noting that Williamsburg "is on the verge of staking a claim for itself as an art scene."[191] Unfortunately, that write-up came out the same weekend as the pivotal Happy Land fire that kick-started a crackdown on nightlife spaces; the Lizard's Tail shuttered soon after.

After the Lizard's Tail closed, Pottiez and Dineen began organizing parties they dubbed "Cat's Head." The parties, which fea-

---

iii   Their 1986 music video for "Put Your Hand Inside the Puppet Head" shows the band performing by the otherwise desolate Williamsburg waterfront.

tured elaborate installations and performance art alongside bands like King Missile and Cop Shoot Cop, were staged twice in 1990—once on July 14 in a former mustard factory on North 1st Street, and again, on October 6, in a warehouse at North 10th Street and Kent Ave.

> *DJ Olive (turntablist, artist): Cat's Head was kind of a free-for-all—everybody joins in and somehow makes something. There were lots of people there, maybe four hundred. And then the police come, and they're just walking around trying to figure out what to do. [Dineen and Pottiez] were talking to the main cop. They get on the phone, some phone calls are made, all the while the party was on pause for like forty-five minutes. Then a couple giant limos pull up. [Dineen, Pottiez, and the cops] all jump in a limo, drive around for half an hour, and come back—party's back on!*
>
> *That was the beginning of gentrification in Williamsburg. That's where it was decided that, from 1990 to 1995, just leave this shit alone, because it's going to raise the [property] value. There's this grace period where it's just a free-for-all.*

After Cat's Head, other immersive parties sprang up around Williamsburg, a microscene that has since been dubbed "immersionism." This scene included a series of elaborate parties thrown by a collective called the Lalalandia Entertainment Research Corporation, many of which took place in a converted warehouse at 141-155 South 5th Street that they dubbed El Sensorium. Collective co-founder DJ Olive (born Gregor Asch) fondly recalled a monthly party called "The Omni-Sensorial Sweep Out," where large-scale art and sound installations created "a science fiction, futuristic effect." Though most Lalalandia parties eschewed traditional deejays or bands in favor of interactive sound sculptures, they did host the occasional live act, notably including Deee-Lite.

By 1993, Lalalandia had moved out of El Sensorium and passed the space along to members of four bands—Fly Ashtray, Uncle Wiggly, Smack Dab, and The Gamma Rays. The new tenants rechristened it Rubulad, named for the letters that corresponded to their phone number. Rubulad was initially concieved to be a practice space, recording studio, and ad-hoc venue that could serve as a homey alternative to alienating Manhattan bars. But like Lalalandia before them, they soon began throwing elaborate themed parties (promoted solely by word of mouth) with all manner of decor, costumes, and performances.

By the mid-nineties, the initial wave of DIY venues in Williamsburg was receding. Lalalandia disbanded in 1995. Basinski and Elaine still lived at Arcadia, but gradually stopped hosting events. And outsiders were catching on: in 1997, *Utne Reader* dubbed Williamsburg the Third-Hippest Neighborhood in America, bested only by New Orleans' Lower Garden District and San Francisco's Inner Mission.[192]

DJ Olive: By '95, rents in Williamsburg had tripled. It was no longer viable at that point: As soon as you're paying a third of your income on your rent, you've got to work. So most of the cool people moved, a lot of them went to Berlin or Budapest or Prague, and that was [the end of] the initial scene. By 2000, it was done. What came after was very trendy, like eggs Benedict on every fucking corner. It just depressed me. It felt unstoppable, and to tell you the truth I felt…not responsible, but definitely like a cog in making it happen with all the parties that we did. There's a kind of regret, but at the same time, those were the best times of my life.

THE FIRST WAVE OF BROOKLYN INDIE ROCK

While immersive party spaces and speakeasy-like venues flourished in Williamsburg throughout the '90s, indie rock was still largely confined to Downtown Manhattan venues like the Cooler, the Knitting Factory, and Brownies, as well as Maxwell's in nearby Hoboken, NJ.

Todd Patrick (aka Todd P; concert promoter): It was very expensive in New York, but at the same time, nobody would live in Brook-

lyn. Brooklyn was both dangerous and boring: It was where you could be mugged, but it was also where your grandma lived.

Jeffrey Lewis: There was no inkling in '99, even in '00, of shows in Brooklyn. I remember hearing about some guy I knew who was struggling—he was so beyond the pale of hopelessness, he lived on Bedford Ave and North 5th in Williamsburg. Like, my god, this guy's life is so fucked up and shitty, he lives in Williamsburg.

By the mid-nineties, the days of a band living and rehearsing in a cheap, spacious SoHo or Tribeca loft were long gone—all of Manhattan's once-industrial areas had become bourgeois. The few affordable apartments that remained around the Lower East Side and Alphabet City were in residential buildings, much too cramped and with too many neighbors for a band to rehearse. Cheap spaces for bands to practice in, located in isolated-enough places where no one would complain, were practically nonexistent in Manhattan. But that kind of space was still available in Brooklyn, and not just in Williamsburg.

Drummer Kid Millions (born John Colpitts) moved to New York in 1996 after graduating from Middlebury College in Vermont, alongside his pseudonymous friends Hanoi Jane and Bobby Matador, with the express purpose of forming the band that became Oneida.

Millions: Bobby's only priority was, where are we going to play? He walked into a Realtor that was at Fulton and Vanderbilt [in Clinton Hill] and said, "I've got a band, I'm looking for a place to play." And the Realtor said, "There's an upstairs [above the Realtor's office]. It's full of stuff now, but you could move the stuff out and play up there." It was an old club, it had a stage and a bar and everything, and it was just sitting unused. So that's where we lived. It must have cost us $200 [a month], maybe. We played in that place at all hours, at full volume, and we never, ever, ever had one visitor.

Black Dice formed in 1997 in Providence, RI, by Rhode Island School of Design classmates Hisham Bharoocha, Sebastian
Blanck, and Bjorn Copeland, alongside Copeland's high school–
aged brother Eric Copeland. They relocated to Williamsburg in
1998.

*Bharoocha: Our friends who had moved here the year before had a
"loft," which was just a converted cinder block garage on Graham
Avenue, right off Meeker. Bjorn and I lived there with some other
people—I think there were five people or more living in this garage.
The rent was like $300 or $400, divided by five. We were able to
practice there, which was awesome—but terrible for the neighbors;
we were totally inconsiderate. We did shows there, too. I think we
did !!!'s first New York show in that loft.*

Nebraska native Pat Noecker moved to New York on New
Year's Eve 1997, and recruited fellow Nebraskan Ron Albertson
to join him with the purpose of forming a band.

*Noecker: I found a sign that [Liars'] Angus [Andrew] and Aaron
[Hemphill] had put up on Bedford Avenue. People posted a lot of
flyers on Bedford Avenue, but there really wasn't shit in Williamsburg at that time.*

*I was living in this house at 314 23rd Street in South Park Slope,
right by the cemetery. There were four people living there, our rent
was $525 each, we had the whole house to ourselves, and we could
practice in the basement. It really defied the socioeconomic challenge
other musicians in New York face: we had a free practice space where
we could set up. Angus and Aaron would come over, and we'd rehearse three times a week. That's where Liars wrote that first record
[2001's They Threw Us All in a Trench and Stuck a Monument On Top].*

*There were some [other] bands starting to form here with that
[DIY] sensibility—let's get in the basement, let's buy a van, let's*

Poster for a Liars show celebrating the release of They Threw Us All in A Trench and Stuck a Monument On Top, *with Yeah Yeah Yeahs and The Apes, on October 5, 2001. The show was promoted by the Twisted Ones at a short-lived DIY venue called BPM (237 Kent Avenue).*

practice and hit the road. I started meeting Oberlin kids like [Yeah Yeah Yeahs members] Brian Chase and Karen O and Nick Zinner[iv] - art school people who got into punk rock. We all had crappy jobs; no-body had any money besides the Yeah Yeah Yeahs. Before you knew it, there were maybe twenty really cool bands in New York City that came out of DIY culture, fostered by Fitz and the Twisted Ones.

"Fitz" is John Fitzgerald, one quarter of the party/show promoting team the Twisted Ones with Arthur Arbit, Etain Fitzpatrick, and Erik Zajaceskowski. Although the Twisted Ones threw parties in multiple spaces, their primary venue was Zajaceskowski's loft at 401 Wythe Avenue, aka Mighty Robot.

---

iv   Chase and O went to Oberlin; Zinner attended Bard College.

Zajaceskowski: We started throwing parties with bands—just the bands that were around at the time, none of them were big yet. Everyone's just in a band, and friends, and they all worked at coffee shops and [used clothing store] Beacon's Closet.

Millions: Those early Twisted Ones shows had a certain S&M component. Fitz's girlfriend and other women would be wearing hoods and standing on pedestals with swords in the middle of the show. And they would have interstitial S&M psychodrama events, where they would have a guy with a collar led out on all fours, the woman [leading him] would be hooded and have a sword, and they would play [the Velvet Underground's] "Venus in Furs" over that.

A SCENE COALESCES

Millions: There was no scene. When the articles came out [in the early '00s], they were manufacturing this scene. Like the issue of Time Out with Liars on the cover, which had a bunch of Brooklyn bands in it—we had never met any of them. But I have to give the credit to the press in a weird way, because they were seeing this thing [that we didn't].

By the time the 1990s gave way to the 2000s, indie rock in Williamsburg was *a thing*, if not yet *the* thing. The new millennium saw new bands begin to call the area home. Several of them convened in a complex of practice spaces in the basement of 75 North 4th Street, located underneath a warehouse for the clothing company Triple 5 Soul (where members of Yeah Yeah Yeahs and TV on the Radio were employed) and the offices of a new underground magazine called *Vice*.

Bharoocha: We [Black Dice] were the first people to move in. We stayed in that space for a long time, and it became the practice space building of that era. Interpol and Battles were practicing there before they were big, TV on the Radio was in that basement. We shared our practice space with Animal Collective, Gang Gang Dance, and White Magic.

Enough of a scene was coalescing in Williamsburg by 2001 that the neighborhood spawned its first fully licensed, 100 percent legal rock club, Northsix (66 North 6th Street). That same year, entrepreneur and designer Eben Luxx (née Burr) opened a bar called Luxx at 256 Grand Street. Prior to his club, Luxx recalled, "There was nothing [in Williamsburg before Luxx that was] geared toward upper middle class hipsters."[193]

Luxx hosted early performances by Yeah Yeah Yeahs, the National, and Deerhoof, but it was best known for its Saturday night dance party, Berliniamsburg, hosted by deejay Larry Tee. A NYC nightlife mainstay since the '80s who'd first made his name at Palladium and the Roxy, Tee reinvented himself at Berliniamsburg, pioneering what he dubbed "electroclash"—a punk-tinged, Eurotrash-y, aggressively sexual subgenre of electronica epitomized by Berliniamsburg performers like Fischerspooner, Miss Kittin, Avenue D, and Scissor Sisters. It was so successful that Tee added a second party at Luxx, Mutants, on Friday nights. "Larry was responsible for many people's first foray into Williamsburg," noted promoter Todd Patrick. "Larry was getting huge crowds, 500 people in a room that could only hold 100."

Back in 1996, the median rent for a one-bedroom apartment in Williamsburg had been $800, compared to $1,600 in the East Village. But by 2003, the average one-bedroom in Williamsburg was $1,600 and rising, while the average East Village rent was $2,000. A 2003 *New York Times* article officially declared Williamsburg "over," claiming that hipster types were abandoning the neighborhood and returning to Lower Manhattan. A real estate agent quoted in the article identifies the neighborhood's new residents as "not artists, but artistic types—graphic designers and literary agents." One Williamsburg resident, *BlackBook* editor Jess Holl, is quoted as saying, "Everyone is trying so hard to be different, but in the end, they end up looking the same. It's not the same artsy community I first saw back in 1999."[194]

And yet, the New York indie rock scene was still decidedly centered there, with new bands continuing to stream into affordable lofts in Williamsburg and adjacent neighborhoods like Greenpoint, Bushwick, and Bed-Stuy.

Guitarist Colin Langenus and drummer Thom Hohman had formed the USA Is a Monster (typically stylized USAISAMONSTER) in Boston, before relocating to Brooklyn in 2003.

Langenus: We had a loft space in Bed-Stuy at 880R DeKalb Ave. Thom and I built it out, and we lived, practiced six days a week, and recorded there. Economically, we were not having to work too much—the rent was $375 a month, [split] between Thom and his girlfriend, me living in the practice space, and a fourth room that we would rent off and on. Before we moved to town, our buddy told us to check out the dumpster outside Perelandra [Natural Food Center, 175 Remsen Street] in Downtown Brooklyn. It literally was free food: They'd throw away cold soy milk and eggs and produce. So our rent was $375 and food was, I'm not exaggerating, borderline free. Whenever I think of that time, [I see it as] really luxurious, but if you look at it from a different angle, I was living in a practice space and eating out of dumpsters.

For Langenus, the emerging Brooklyn scene differed from its predecessors in one crucial way: while Manhattan is small but dense, Brooklyn is much more spread out, so musicians living in adjoining neighborhoods could still be geographically distanced. "Brooklyn bands couldn't just walk to a bar and see the whole scene," said Langenus.

TODD P.

Though the scene around Williamsburg was already building by 2001, its role as the city's new musical epicenter is largely due to the work of one Todd Patrick, aka Todd P.

Originally from Texas, Patrick moved to Portland, Oregon, in the '90s, where he ran a beloved all-ages venue called 17 Nautical Miles. After an attempt to open a larger venue floundered, he hooked up with a band called A John Henry Memorial, agreeing to book a national tour for them in early 2001 on the condition that they allow him to join as their keyboardist. When the tour ended in New York, Patrick decided to stay and moved in with a bandmate's ex-girlfriend in Long Island City, Queens.

He felt socially and creatively adrift in the city until that October, when a friend asked him to help book a show for a touring band called the Lowdown. With another friend's help, he found a Greenpoint loft in which to stage the show, owned by musician Dan Seward from the psych/noise band Bunnybrains. "It was very successful," Patrick recalled. "There were over 100 people in this tiny loft, I'd be surprised if it was 500 sq ft."

His timing was impeccable: The Twisted Ones' Fitz had recently relocated to Berlin. Erik Zajaceskowski was still running Mighty Robot, but with Fitz gone, there was a clear void begging to be filled. Patrick began booking shows in bars and loft spaces around Brooklyn (and a few in Manhattan), which were promoted via his barebones website (toddpnyc.com) and an expanding email list.

The timing likely worked in Todd's favor for another reason too, and not a good one: His first show was one month after 9/11. With the literal and figurative stench of death permeating Lower Manhattan for months after the attack, venturing downtown was a difficult thing for many to do; Williamsburg likely offered a less emotionally fraught environment in which to try and have fun.

Patrick: It was an economic boom time. A temp agency had placed me at Bank of America Securities as an executive assistant, so I was making $75,000 a year (in 2001 money) without a college degree. That's what facilitated my ability to [book shows]. I was going in, usually hung over as hell, and using their T1 internet connection and free long distance, both of which were hard to come by if you weren't in a corporate setting. I could do my actual job in half an hour each week and spend the rest of the time [booking shows].

Before 2003, most of my shows had been in underground spaces or improvised spaces that I'd created out of the second floor or back room of a bar. I'd done a couple successful shows at Luxx, so Eben Luxx asked me if I wanted to do Sunday nights there. It was the night after Berliniamsburg, so I started coming in early on Sundays and cleaning, because the place would be fucked up [from the night before]. Eben noticed I was doing this, and he offered me a job as the manager. I said, "I don't want to be the manager, I want to book the place. That I could do well." He didn't want me for that, so I became the manager, and I wasn't very good at it.

It was just as well: by the time Patrick started working there, Luxx's star was already fading. It closed in October 2003.

MONSTER ISLAND

At the same time Luxx was closing, Mighty Robot was dealing with noise complaints. It was time to move on, and Zajaceskowski and his partner Rachel Nelson began to conceive of something that went beyond just a "music venue," more akin to the immersionist spaces of the early '90s. To that end, Zajaceskowski found a fifteen-thousand-square-foot, two-story former spice factory at 210 Kent Avenue. Since 1994, the building had been home to a visual arts collective called Flux Factory, which had been priced out of the space in 2002.[v]

The newly acquired building was dubbed Monster Island.

Zajaceskowski: It was too expensive and big for me to just do, so I had to bring in other people. I decided to get the people that seemed the most hungry in the neighborhood. At first it was me and Karl LaRocca from Kayrock Screenprinting [who operated a print shop in the complex]—just the two of us signed the lease. Then we recruited Vashti Windish, who opened Live With Animals Gallery, and we

---

v   Flux Factory relocated to Long Island City, Queens, where they remain to this day.

recruited Todd P., who was doing a lot of shows at the time. It was a huge giant building, so we decided, let's each take a different area, and you just run it how you want to and do your own thing.

After Luxx's closure, Patrick had gone back to working a nine-to-five day job, all the while promoting shows in a variety of spaces. But the prospect of once again operating his own venue, as he had in Portland, was too good to turn down; he quit his job and took over the basement at Monster Island, transforming it into a venue he called Llano Estacado,[vi] named for a region in his native Texas.

In addition to Llano Estacado, Patrick turned a portion of Monster Island into rehearsal spaces that he rented out to bands. As Patrick made little-to-no money from shows, those rehearsal studios became his only source of income for years. Secret Project Robot similarly made the bulk of its income from turning a portion of its space into rentable art studios.

One room in Patrick's practice space quadrant was too small for bands to rehearse in, so he leased out the room free of charge to a rotating series of caretakers, most of whom were musicians or were otherwise involved in the scene. Their sole responsibility was to fix whatever problems would arise.

Patrick: The first [caretaker] was Dave Longstreth from Dirty Projectors. Dave had just graduated from Yale and didn't know what he was gonna do, so it gave him a chance to live here without having a job. He wrote the [2007] Rise Above *record in that space.*

Llano Estacado kicked off on February 4, 2005, with performances by Animal Collective and the Icelandic instrumental folk band Storsveit Nix Noltes, but it was not long for this world.

The problem began in early 2004, around the same time that Monster Island was getting going, when a flashy club called Vol-

---

vi   Though the actual Spanish pronunciation would phonetically be "Yano Estacado," the venue's name was explicitly pronounced with a hard *L* sound.

ume opened in a warehouse at 99 North 13th Street. It hosted a handful of performances by the likes of Franz Ferdinand and Dizzee Rascal, until some shady practices attracted the attention of the local police department. "Volume was doing every trick in the book to piss off the police, so finally the police and the fire department teamed up and busted it," Zajaceskowski explained. "It was so successful for them that they started going after everything in Williamsburg."

The issue wasn't just a club or two skirting safety codes. As the 2000s rolled on, Williamsburg's real estate was considered desirable to folks who wanted to live in a neighborhood famous for its DIY arts scene, but still demanded bourgeois comforts. While venues had evaded police attention for the prior decade—recall DJ Olive's comment that they were viewed as a force *for* gentrification by landlords in the '90s—by the mid-2000s, they had outlived their usefulness to the people who were trying to make bank selling Williamsburg.

At the time, the city was finalizing a plan to rezone 175 previously industrial blocks of Williamsburg and Greenpoint waterfront, allowing developers to raze these empty factories and replace them with forty-story condo towers and a public waterfront park. The city included an incentive that allowed developers to build larger-than-regulation buildings if they set aside a portion of the apartments as low-income housing (most developers declined to take the city up on it). For the first time in years, Williamsburg's venues—and Monster Island in particular, which was in the footprint of the proposed condo towers—were subject to police scrutiny.

The 94th Precinct Police Department raided Monster Island on March 4, 2005. They picked a perfect night to do it: there was a building-wide party, with bands playing in both Llano Estacado and Live With Animals and an underground film festival in Secret Project Robot, all for a mere $8 cover. According to Zajaceskowski, "They came in with the fire chief and the police chief, kicked in every door, and arrested people. And then for two months, they would come back every day, even when there was nothing going on."

The police didn't shut Monster Island down, but they did cite the building for numerous code violations. Patrick opted to temporarily shutter Llano Estacado and bring it up to code, but his plans were stymied when a decision was made to put the kibosh on all live music in the building. Without income from shows to cover the rent, Todd was evicted, although he was able to keep his rehearsal spaces.

Rachel Nelson: It was about a year [after the police raids] before we started having music again. I thought, we're all going about this the wrong way, we need to heal this relationship. I went and met with the police and said, "This is what we do: We're artists, we're running an art space. Sometimes we have events, sometimes the events are crowded, sometimes people bring their beer. It's not a rave, we're a bunch of rock 'n' roll people, artists, and weirdos." And I swear, there was sort of a quiet agreement: "You [the police] can give tickets to people with open containers outside—there's going to be lots of them—and that'll be your payment. Just never come in." And they never, ever came in again after that.

It was pretty peaceful for the remaining five years there. There were no licenses, we were 100% illegal. It was just this thing of being weirdly, brutally honest—that was my personal strategy, and we kept using it with other precincts when we moved. Instead of being found out, we just told them about us, which is why we ended up always having decent relationships with the police.

A portion of what had been Llano Estacado became Oneida's rehearsal space and recording studio. After lifting the moratorium on live music, the remainder became Monster Island Basement, a performance space that was available to all the building's tenants- including Todd P.

Patrick: They let me do one show a week. Erik and Rachel resented me. They didn't like that I was getting all this attention, and they had a very low opinion of me for a long time because I had a dark, ugly period of years where I was drunk off my ass. They thought I was this degenerate drunk; I was a drunk, and I was a degenerate too I suppose, but I was also doing good work. I didn't stop putting on shows after that, I just started doing them all over the place.

GLASSLANDS & PARIS LONDON NEW YORK WEST NILE

Monster Island was the first indie rock megacomplex on the Williamsburg waterfront, but it would soon become eclipsed by a massive building that occupied an entire block of Kent Ave. between South 1st and South 2nd and contained multiple addresses along all three streets. The building, which had once served as storage and offices for the nearby Domino Sugar factory, housed several venues simultaneously, which at various points included Glass House, Glasslands, Paris London New York West Nile, Death By Audio, and 285 Kent. We've already seen a few instances in which several of a scene's key venues have operated side by side, but this was possibly the most extreme example of venue proximity the city's ever seen.

The building belonged to Joe Markowitz, a Hasidic entrepreneur whose electronics business, CTA Digital, operated out of an office along the South 2nd side of the building. The first venue to show up was Glass House Gallery, opened in 2004 at 38 South 1st Street by multimedia artists Brooke Baxter Bailey and Leviticus. The pair paid roughly $2,000 a month for the space, where they also lived (unbeknownst to Markowitz).

Despite its name, Glass House was less of a traditional "gallery" and more of an anything-goes multipurpose art space, much like El Sensorium and Secret Project Robot before it.

Baxter Bailey: My intention was never for it to be an underground music venue. We'd throw a lot of parties in order to promote collaborative art, where we'd set up canvases for people to paint, and we'd have musical instruments or typewriters out. It was this utopian thing: Everybody is an artist, everybody is creative, nobody is better than

The Kent Avenue complex that housed Glass House, Glasslands, Paris London New York West Nile, Death By Audio, and 285 Kent.

anyone else. I was very, very passionate about going against the elit-
ist idea that you need to have your work up in a gallery to be an art-
ist, or you need to have a gig at Mercury Lounge to be a musician.

Not long into their tenure, Baxter Bailey's friend Derek Stanton, a member of the band Awesome Color, pointed out that Glass House's future was likely unsustainable on just beverage sales at their parties. He suggested that they start booking bands. In short time, acts like TV on the Radio, Grizzly Bear, and the Moldy Peaches were playing intimate shows there.

Glass House closed in 2006 when Baxter Bailey and musician Rolyn Hu (a member of the band True Primes) negotiated a deal with Markowitz to take over a different space in the building around the corner at 289 Kent. Both the size and rent were roughly double that of Glass House.

The new space was dubbed Glasslands. Like Todd P. and Secret Project Robot, Baxter Bailey and Hu helped subsidize their venue by partitioning off portions of the space to rent out as art studios and practice spaces. Glasslands, like Glass House before it, was adorned with a rotating series of art installations,[vii] but it was a slicker operation: within months of opening, Glasslands became a fully licensed bar and venue.

For the first six or so months, Todd P. handled a significant amount of the booking at Glasslands—a lifeline for him post–Llano Estacado—until they insisted he stop booking all-ages shows. "We were moving towards becoming legitimate, and I didn't want to do anything to get us shut down," Baxter Bailey explained.

A year after Glasslands opened, a second venue called Paris London New York West Nile (henceforth PLNYWN) opened next door at 285 Kent, all thanks (in a roundabout way) to Lou Reed.

Multidisciplinary artist Zeljko McMullen moved to New York in 2005 after graduating from Oberlin. Broke and desperate for work, he responded to a Craigslist ad looking for an assistant to the assistant of "a New York–based musician/photographer." McMullen interviewed for and got the gig, only to learn that said musician/photographer was the legendary Velvet Underground front man. "I wasn't even ever supposed to meet him," McMullen said. "I was just going through his Velvet Underground archives, reorganizing his office, and running to Bed Bath and Beyond to get a space heater." But soon after, Reed's assistant quit; McMullen assumed the job and also became a member of Reed's touring band, using a modular effects rig to process the sound of Reed's guitar in real time.

McMullen first began looking at Williamsburg spaces while searching for a storage space for Reed's gear.

McMullen: [I found the building] on Craigslist. I was standing outside it on Kent Avenue, and in my mind I thought, this is what I want. I decided to accept it before even seeing it.

---

vii Glasslands' defining aesthetic feature was arguably a massive cloud installation that hovered over the stage, which was made by Vashti Windish, proprietor of the Live With Animals gallery in Monster Island.

Lou and I were at an airport getting ready to go play this show in Telluride, and I was signing the lease on the space—I found some donut shop at JFK that had a fax machine, and as I was faxing in the lease, Lou said, "Well, [my manager] says that moving my office to Brooklyn is going to look bad in the music scene. If you need help with it, I can help you get it or whatever, but I'm not going to move the whole operation over there." I decided to just do it myself.

He boarded the plane before me, and before I even got back to the plane, he texted me complaining that he didn't have the window seat. I just snapped. I grabbed a taxi from the airport, went to the office in SoHo, packed [my things] up, and went over to the space. From the cab, I just started calling different artists and musicians and saying, "Hey, remember that space I was telling you about? Do you want to move in?" I found five other people and we moved in in September 2006.

From the outset, PLNYWN was both a performance space and a residence. The two-thousand-square-foot space housed anywhere between four and eight people at any given time, with the total rent costing roughly $3,000.[viii]

McMullen: We were very different from most of the other spaces in Williamsburg at the time. We never actually charged for our shows (we were always donation-based), and we never sold alcohol, we let people bring their own drinks. I wanted more people to have access to it. Most of the people that came to our shows were artists that were interested in weird, cutting-edge stuff, who were able to come without spending $50 on going out and having drinks and paying for tickets.

Like Glasslands, PLNYWN also had community events, like vegetarian brunches with installation art. They even left the door

---

viii Some tenants opted to rent rooms as nonresidential studio spaces, including none other than Tony Conrad, the avant-garde musician who had collaborated with John Cale in La Monte Young's Theater of Eternal Music, and was briefly in a nascent version of the Velvet Underground alongside Cale and Reed.

open on nights when there were no events planned, so people waiting to attend shows at nearby venues could stop in.

TODD TAKES OVER

The closure of the Llano Estacado could have been catastrophic
for Todd P., but it was arguably one of the best things that happened to him. After Llano Estacado (and even more so after he
parted ways with Glasslands), he was no longer married to any one
venue. And the range of venues he found was stupefying: there
were still shows at bars in Brooklyn and Manhattan (though those
numbers dwindled), but there were also art spaces, churches, community centers, ethnic restaurants, and even a makeshift canvas
tent on the construction site of a sewage treatment plant in industrial Greenpoint.[ix]

With a seemingly infinite number of spaces in play, he became
a booking juggernaut. "Todd was sort of like a drug cartel at one
point," Nelson said. "There wasn't a thing that went through New
York City that didn't go through Todd."

Patrick's prominence was the result of several factors. The first,
and probably the most obvious, is branding. A visitor to the Mudd
Club may or may not have been aware of owner Steve Mass's name,
but they'd certainly have heard of the venue. At a Todd P. show,
it was the opposite: you went to a Todd P. show, wherever it was,
because it was a Todd P. show, which you'd likely learned about
from *his* email list or website.

Patrick's early embrace of the internet as a medium to get the
word out about his shows meant that you didn't have to encounter
a flyer or check the *Village Voice* each week to find out about his
shows—instead, information about these very underground shows
was available in one centralized place that anyone could access at
any time. Though Patrick wasn't the first person to set up a web-

---

ix   The tent was called Uncle Paulie's, and it became one of Todd P.'s regular
      venues for a while. I can tell you from my own experience that it was exactly
      as weird as you're imagining.

site or email list devoted to upcoming shows, he was tireless in updating and promoting them, which *was* unusual. The email list allowed him to reach people who had no previous knowledge of the Brooklyn indie rock scene—meaning that for many people, Patrick *was* the scene.

Having already booked shows in Oregon and Texas, Patrick's network extended beyond the bounds of the city to lesser-known touring acts, but he also kept his ear to the ground locally. Unknown local bands were booked to open high-profile shows—in fact, acclaimed pop-punk duo Matt & Kim are so named because Todd booked them before they'd gotten around to choosing one; he simply billed them as "Matthew and Kimberly." Plus, as Woods front man and Woodsist Records owner Jeremy Earl noted, "If you were on a Todd show, you didn't even have to worry about promoting it, because his email list was so huge, there would always be people there."

The second significant factor in Patrick's ascension was financial transparency. Bands played for a percentage of the door, but they were always shown a detailed accounting of the night's finances. Bands who tour on a small-scale, DIY level are subject to all kinds of shady business practices, fudged numbers, and broken promises, so this was a stark contrast. Not everyone approved of the way he divided the money, but you could always depend on him to be honest about it.

Bharoocha: To this day, he is super upfront about money stuff. At the end of the show, there's the cash, and on the envelope with the cash he'd write the breakdown: The bar got this, security got this, venue got this. And then he'd say "What do you think about this breakdown?" and you'd say, "Yeah, that's great" or "Let's give the touring band a little more." Just super honest and clean.

The third and arguably most significant factor was that Patrick was one of the few promoters letting underage people into small indie rock shows, and the only one aggressively publicizing that fact. Though plenty of teenagers had flocked to clubs like CBGB and Max's Kansas City at their peaks, the flow of young people diminished when the national drinking age was raised to twenty-one in 1984. Plenty of bars continued admitting teens in on the sly, but that practice decreased after the one-two punch of the Happy Land fire and the Club Kid murders, as mayors Dinkins, Giuliani, and Bloomberg all systematically targeted music venues and dance clubs in nightlife crackdowns. The 2003 smoking ban and the introduction of the 311 hotline made it even harder for teens to slip into 21+ shows, as the NYPD became even more of a presence at clubs.

At the same time, NYU began expanding in the mid-eighties, swallowing up the West and East Villages and flooding them with students. This meant that by the early '00s, the city had an ever-increasing number of eighteen- and nineteen-year-old kids moving to town, who, because they were attending an expensive, elite college, likely had disposable cash and free time. And yet, there was a decreasing number of places for them to go hear music. Larger clubs like Bowery Ballroom, Irving Plaza, and the Knitting Factory were all booking established bands with significant followings; for kids who wanted something genuinely underground, it often seemed as if there was only Todd.

Patrick's shows had always been all-ages, even when at dive bars, but it was often unspoken—plenty of the small, out-of-the-way bars just didn't card. As Todd recalled, "I would do shows in bars and I would say, 'We're going to be all ages tonight, all right?' and they'd just say, 'You have enough people to drink though, right?'" But with bars now less open to the idea of all-ages shows, Patrick simply diversified his venues and became more explicit about the fact that the shows were all-ages.

Starting in 2004, he also began hiring (mostly college-aged) interns to help book and staff shows.

Patrick: I started getting a lot of press and the interest level got higher, and I decided to put together a crew of around 10 people. I never had them just work as interns, I always had them also working as door people or bartenders at the shows so they could make money. My [philosophy] was that if they were doing a job where money changes hands, they should make money. If they're doing work where I don't make money, which is the office [organizational work], then nobody did.

With all these kids getting the same education from Patrick, it was inevitable that as some began promoting their own shows, his operational template—with all his idiosyncrasies and tastes—became canonical.

Two of Patrick's interns, Joe Ahearn and Ric Leichtung, would go on to become major bookers in their own right. Ahearn was a New York native with an impeccable Downtown pedigree—his father, Charlie Ahearn, directed the seminal hip-hop movie *Wild Style*, and his mother Jane Dickson is an acclaimed painter. As a teenager in the city, he'd organized impromptu shows in his parents' Tribeca basement because, with 21+ clubs out of reach, "there was nothing else to do. Which of course is ridiculous in New York City, but it did feel like that." Attending his first Todd P. show, "I was like, this is exactly what I've been looking for. I started answering emails for him the next week."

Leichtung, an NYU student from San Francisco, was similarly inspired.

Leichtung: I was a very, very square kid that didn't really drink or have any reason to have a fake ID, so when I came here I could only go to all-ages shows, and the only person that was doing that kind of stuff consistently was Todd P. I was obsessed with these baby bands who would probably draw 50 or 100 people in New York City, and Todd was the only [promoter] that saw value in these people.

Ahearn: Most of the day would be spent at Todd's apartment in Long Island City, working on answering emails, listening to bands, writing copy for promoting shows, things like that. We would all be logged into the same email account at the same time, all five of us in the room, and we would take turns playing music from different bands. We'd usually listen to at least two songs, and then everybody would give their feedback.

Leichtung: I did anything and everything. I would be working at the door, working "security," so to speak (a 20-year-old child, not intimidating at all). I would be cleaning toilets, pouring bleach all over the floor and mopping it, setting up the PA, moving a bunch of items, going to the store to buy a bottle of aspirin so that you could use the top of it as the [hand] stamp for the evening. At that time, nobody was paid. Bartenders maybe got tips, or sometimes everybody would split all of the tips equally. The perk was really just being a part of it.

Todd got so busy that he needed people to start answering his emails. After booking a bunch of shows as Todd on his email, I realized that the planning part of booking and making events happen was more intuitive and easier than I had previously thought. I booked my first show in either 2008 or 2009: Thee Oh Sees, Ty Segall, the Skeletons, and Zs at Death by Audio. I got lucky and it sold out. From there, I was like, I should just be doing this.

As both Ahearn and Leichtung began booking higher-profile shows in many of the same venues where Todd was already active, they became seen by bands as an accessible, credible alternative (and potential pipeline) to the perennially swamped Todd P. As Real Estate bassist Alex Bleeker noted, "Everyone knew that these guys had been trained by Todd P., and if you couldn't get Todd to write back to you, Joe still might write back to you."

By 2007, Todd P. was the highest-profile all-ages promoter in New York City, but he was far from the only one. Because of his influence, as well as the influence of predecessors like Secret Project Robot, DIY bookers and all-ages venues were popping up around Brooklyn with increasing regularity. Most of them were short-lived, or only hosted shows occasionally, but new bands and underage listeners found themselves with no shortage of options. These ranged from lovably scrappy dumps (Goodbye Blue Monday, a Bushwick art space and coffee shop overflowing with bric-a-brac) to terrifying death traps (the Bodega, which was temporarily forced to close when their toilet fell through the floor midshow).

The options were becoming substantial enough to necessitate a streamlining of all that information. *Showpaper*, a biweekly print publication, launched in 2007; according to Patrick, "It was expressly created to give [paying] jobs to all these kids who wanted to be involved." Printed on a single sheet of newsprint and distributed free around the city, one side contained a listing of every all-ages show in the greater New York City area (suburbs included), while the other contained a unique piece of poster-sized artwork, suitable for framing.[x]

DEATH BY AUDIO

In 2005, Oliver Ackermann—guitarist in A Place to Bury Strangers and owner of the Death By Audio effects pedal company[xi]—moved into a warehouse space at 49 South 2nd Street in Williamsburg, in the same complex that already housed Glasslands and PLNYWN.

Ackermann: The landlords were probably surprised that we even wanted to rent the space. Williamsburg wasn't that cool at the time. I think at first they were thankful that we could take this space that probably should have been condemned. The [initial] rent was $2,700, divided among six of us, plus utilities and stuff like that.

The space was by no means perfect—it was full of dirt, debris, water, and mold—but it gave Ackermann and his roommates plenty

---

x   Contributors included Psychic TV/Throbbing Gristle singer Genesis Breyer P-Orridge, actor/painter/musician John Lurie, conceptual artist Cory Arcangel, cartoonist Ron Rege Jr., Lungfish front man Daniel Higgs, and the celebrated punk artist Raymond Pettibon.

xi Famous fans of Ackermann's pedals have included Lou Reed, U2's The Edge, My Bloody Valentine's Kevin Shields, Lady Gaga, Lauryn Hill, Nine Inch Nails' Trent Reznor, and members of the Foo Fighters.

A Place to Bury Strangers rehearsing at Death By Audio.

of space in which to live, make music, paint, build pedals, and do whatever else their hearts desired.

Two of Ackermann's pedal-building interns, Matt Conboy and Jason Amos, had been looking to move into a space of their own, and Conboy was clear from the outset that he "wanted to live in a warehouse and put on shows." When a second space adjacent to the one Ackermann and his roommates were in opened up in 2007, Conboy and Amos jumped on the opportunity. The space that Conboy and Amos moved into was less warehouse-y and more office-like, with checkered floors and white walls. "I think maybe it was the typing pool for the Domino Sugar factory," Conboy said. The pair quickly transformed it into a venue, which they named after Ackermann's effects pedal company.

According to Conboy, "At the very beginning, I was kind of in charge of booking, and a lot of our shows were just coming from Todd." But within a year, Edan Wilber, one of Patrick's go-to sound engineers, began booking shows at Death By Audio, too. Wilber's enthusiasm for the shows and the venue was so apparent that after a few months, Conboy and Amos decided to just hand the booking over to him entirely.

Wilber: Matt and Jason said, "You love this more than us, you're doing a better job. Why don't you just handle the calendar, and if we have stuff, we'll bring it to you." Todd was kinda hands-off, which was a sweet thing for him to do. I know it was one of the places that he loved to book at, but he was supporting me.

Wilber's presence transformed Death By Audio into something extraordinary, even among the now-crowded field of Brooklyn DIY venues. He upgraded the sound system, brought artists in to paint a rotating series of murals on the walls, and booked an impeccable roster of bands. His tastes skewed toward punk, noise, and garage rock, which became Death By Audio's niche—regularly hosting bands like Titus Andronicus, Screaming Females, Ty Segall, and the Oh Sees (those boundaries occasionally stretched to include the likes of rappers Das Racist, no wave legend Arto Lindsay, and comedian Eric Andre). Though there was some overlap with the booking at nearby venues like Glasslands, Death By Audio's all-ages status, lower overhead due to lack of licensing, good sound, the specificity of Wilber's taste, and his and Conboy's approachability as peers all combined to put their venue at the top of the heap for a subset of young, DIY-minded artists and fans.

Morby: It was super cheap, I could drink underage, and everyone was smoking cigarettes indoors. The bar was a plastic table where they were selling warm beers from the night before. It just felt like that scene in the first Ninja Turtles movie where they're all sitting around smoking cigarettes and playing video games.

Jordan Michael Iannucci (booker, JMC Aggregate, The Silent Barn): Edan would gleefully tell booking agents and managers to go fuck themselves all the time, because he knew that people wanted to

play there enough that they would have to deal with him anyway.
He was getting the shows from the artists, not the agents.

"BROOKLYN"

At the exact time that the DIY scene was blooming in Williamsburg, the neighborhood's larger music culture was becoming commodified. The international buzz generated by acts like the Yeah Yeah Yeahs and TV on the Radio in the early '00s had gotten Williamsburg tagged as an epicenter of cutting-edge music. Whenever that happens, major corporate money and influence is usually not very far behind.

In the summer of 2006, promoting team Jelly NYC began booking free all-ages Sunday concerts in the then-empty swimming pool in Williamsburg's McCarren Park, welcoming established acts like Les Savy Fav, Of Montreal, MGMT, and Beirut; by the following summer, megapromoter Live Nation was also staging paid shows in the pool. In 2007, Northsix, the neighborhood's first rock club, was acquired by the company Bowery Presents, who enlarged the club and changed its name to Music Hall of Williamsburg. Manhattan clubs like Luna Lounge (2007), the Knitting Factory (2008), and the Living Room (2014) relocated to Williamsburg in search of hipness transfusions. In 2010, sneaker company Vans opened the House of Vans, a free concert venue in a converted warehouse along the Greenpoint waterfront. Not to be outdone, sneaker company Converse opened Converse Rubber Tracks, a state-of-the-art recording studio in Williamsburg which gave free studio time to buzzy indie bands.

Things were booming so much that the very word "Brooklyn" became shorthand for an exaggerated, commodified tweeness: beards, ukuleles, tote bags, Pabst Blue Ribbon, farm-to-table food, ironic tattoos, library science degrees, blah blah blah. It got so bad that by 2010, a Brooklyn-themed bar called the Brooklyneer opened...in Greenwich Village.[xii]

---

xii   Their menu includes multiple foods named after seemingly random Brooklyn neighborhoods, like "Cobble Hill French Dip."

Rents and condo buildings were both going up, and Williamsburg's new arrivals were wealthier (or at least more comfortable flaunting their wealth) than their predecessors.

> *Basinski: The rent just kept going up and up and up and up [at Arcadia] and finally in 2008, we just had to get out. By then, I was living in California with Jamie [Elaine]. I had five tenants in [Williamsburg], and I would just come back a couple times a year to scare everybody and clean. But it had gotten to the point where, once you start getting people that could pay more money, you start getting assholes.*

This real estate feeding frenzy had a lopsided effect on Williamsburg's native communities. The Hasidic and Italian communities continue to have formidable presences in portions of the area, as does the longstanding Polish community in neighboring Greenpoint. Only Williamsburg's Puerto Rican and Dominican communities—which is to say, the non-white ones—have been significantly reduced, pushed out of their homes by landlords who wanted to make room for more moneyed tenants. As Dr. Frances Lucerna, founder of the community activist organization El Puente de Williamsburg, put it in 2019, "The displacement has been massive. I would almost say violent…[people] talk about it as a ground zero for what you do not want to have happen in your community."[195]

In addition to real estate racism, this was also the era in which Williamsburg became a hotspot for the unfortunate trend of "hipster racism"—the notion that, within an ostensibly progressive community, overtly racist behavior is acceptable when presented as an ironic joke, and to say otherwise is just overblown political correctness. Hipster racism was hardly a new concept (try giving Lou Reed's 1978 song "I Wanna Be Black" a spin), but its early and mid-2000s renaissance proved especially loathsome.

The most significant promoter of hipster racism (as well as equally insidious hipster misogyny and hipster homophobia) was

Williamsburg's own *Vice* magazine, which had maintained offices in the neighborhood since 2000. To wit: one 2004 edition of their notorious "Do's & Don'ts" street fashion column includes the context-less quip, "What is it with Puerto Ricans where they're perpetually 10 years old? Oh yeah, they don't have a dad."[196] An (ironic?) interview that same year with Al Qaeda–supporting Saudi dissident Mohammed Al-Massari by writer Tom Dunon, entitled (what else?) "Kill Whitey," opens with the hard-hitting question, "Wassup? We heard that Osama Bin Laden was your boyeee?" and is riddled with n-bombs.[197]

> **Baxter Bailey:** Vice *came to me and wanted to do a young Republicans convention at Glasslands. I'm like, "Are you out of your fucking minds? No way, and fuck you for hosting it! Why do you even want to do it at Glasslands? Go to the Marriott."*

In retrospect, it's unsurprising that co-founder Gavin McInnes (who parted ways with *Vice* in 2008) went on to start the neo-fascist terrorist group Proud Boys in 2016.[xiii] But at the time, enough people ate that shit up that *Vice*, in many people's minds, became synonymous with Williamsburg culture. The fact that a publication that trafficked so heavily in grotesque racism was thriving in a neighborhood where longtime residents of color were in the process of being run out revealed an ugly side of Williamsburg's bohemian culture—one that had perhaps always existed but was becoming more pronounced.

SILENT BARN & MARKET HOTEL

As Williamsburg became less and less accessible, young artists sought out the nearest cheap area in which they could set up camp. For many, the answer was one neighborhood over in Bushwick.

---

xiii Their first meeting in 2016 was held at Tommy's Tavern in Greenpoint, where Todd P. had booked shows a decade prior.

Ironically, Bushwick's quintessential DIY venue was technically located in Ridgewood, Queens: the border between the two boroughs runs along a street called Wyckoff Avenue, and the Silent Barn, at 915 Wyckoff, was located on the Queens side. But few venues would come close to epitomizing Bushwick's rise, or its decline.

The Silent Barn was founded by a band called the Skeletons, who moved into the space in 2005. The Skeletons hosted a few shows in the space, but they didn't stay long. The building's fate was sealed, though—a series of artists and musicians began cycling through.

Joe Ahearn, who had already made a name for himself booking shows at various venues around Brooklyn, moved into the Silent Barn in 2008 and began booking shows there. Though Todd P. didn't move in, he paid a fifth of the $3,000 rent for the privilege of booking there as well—granting him his first somewhat-permanent venue since Llano Estacado's closure.

915 Wyckoff Avenue.

Ahearn: The sort of default policy on basically everything at the Silent Barn was: Yes. Everybody would get a yes as long as everybody understood that everybody else also probably got a yes, so there were always lots of things that were happening at the same time. It was hard to even be aware of anything else that was going on because there was just so much exciting stuff coming through the space.

Even more than other live/work venues in New York, the Silent Barn's residential status was inescapable: The first things you saw when you entered were the residents' bedrooms. There was no stage in the show space; bands simply set up in the kitchen, with the sink and refrigerator serving as their backdrop. Residents frequently went about making dinner and showering as shows took place; as Ahearn explained, "The idea was that there being a show and people performing were not an alternative to what one does with their time, but a constant that could be folded into it."[xiv]

Though Patrick and his followers had already been booking shows throughout Bushwick, the Silent Barn was arguably the first venue to establish its own clear identity and following. Though it was geographically distanced from the Williamsburg waterfront's DIY hub, the Silent Barn became a satellite for the same community.

Bleeker: Two of our [Real Estate] band members were living off the Halsey stop in Bushwick, which just felt like the middle of nowhere. But the Silent Barn was there, so at some point, one of my bandmates asked Todd if we could practice there, and he said yes. Maybe we paid him money, but if we did I don't think we really paid much. Because we were practicing there, we got asked to play a couple shows. That opened a door, not to Todd directly, but to peo-

---

xiv A basement served as an alternate venue for smaller-scale shows, which allowed the Silent Barn to host multiple shows in a night, or stage dual-floor megashows—as resident G. Lucas Crane put it, "that's like some Knitting Factory shit."

ple like G. Lucas Crane [a Silent Barn resident and member of the band Woods—ed.] and Joe Ahearn.

In 2008, Patrick, with the help of the punk band So So Glos, found a disused second-floor nightclub at 1140 Myrtle Avenue in Bushwick. Throughout the '60s, '70s, and early '80s, it had been a series of clubs that featured everything from salsa to house music, but it was shuttered after the Happy Land fire and had remained empty ever since, though it was briefly used as a set in the 1990 film *Ghost*. It left much to be desired—there was no heat or ventilation, barely functional electricity and plumbing, and a *Blues Brothers*-esque proximity to the above-ground J/M/Z tracks. But it was larger than any of the regular DIY venues in Brooklyn, enough to be a formidable competitor to Manhattan institutions like Bowery Ballroom.[xv] They called it the Market Hotel.

Todd ran the Market Hotel as a wholly unlicensed venue, and much like the Silent Barn, it was residential. The So So Glos lived there when not on tour, as did a rotating cast of tenants that included Leichtung.

Leichtung: The Market Hotel was ideal for somebody like me who was just still learning about how to book shows, because a lot of the burden that comes with owning and operating a brick-and-mortar legal venue—the permitting, the liquor licenses, all those financial and logistical hurdles that make it so difficult to conduct business specifically in New York City—were simply not there.

THE SECOND WAVE OF BROOKLYN INDIE ROCK

The Silent Barn and Market Hotel were both indicative of a larger trend, with musicians and artists moving to Bushwick rather than Williamsburg. The band Meneguar had been at the forefront of

---

xv   The legal capacity is 450, compared to Bowery's 575—but of course, Market Hotel paid little attention to their *legal* capacity.

that shift when they moved into a house at 229 Bushwick Avenue around 2004–2005.

Jeremy Earl: At the beginning, there were five people living there, and we were each paying $250 a month. The neighborhood wasn't gentrified at all; there was a pizza place on the corner, a Mexican bakery right next door, and that was it. It was a rear house, so you had to walk through another apartment building to get to it, and because we had that buffer and weren't directly on the street, we didn't get many noise complaints—which is crazy, because we would be playing all day, all night. Having that freedom to practice in your home was really good for us, and a big part of what allowed us to be in the city.

While at the house, Earl started a new band called Woods, which came to include his Meneguar bandmate Jarvis Taveniere, Kevin Morby, and G. Lucas Crane. All but Crane lived there, and Taveniere ran a makeshift studio out of the house, recording the likes of Vivian Girls and Real Estate—both of whom released early records on Earl's label Woodsist Records.

Vivian Girls—the trio of Cassie "Ramone" Grzymkowski, Katy "Kickball Katy" Goodman, and Frankie Rose—formed in 2007.

Ramone: I started hanging out a lot at this spot in Greenpoint called the Orphanage [97 Green Street] that was like my home away from home. They had shows there maybe twice a year. Frankie Rose lived there, and we weren't very close at first, to put it mildly. I would sleep on their couch a lot, and we'd all get brunch the next day. One time, Frankie was sitting next to me and she just turned to me and said, "Hey, do you want to jam?" I thought, ok, that's weird, you haven't been the nicest to me, but sure, I'll give it a go. I invited Katy [Goodman], who I'd known since I was fifteen, because we needed a bass player. We rented a shitty-ass, tiny rehearsal space below the Roebling Tea Room [143 Roebling Street] for $80 a month. It was so small, it smelled terrible, but it was perfect.

The first Vivian Girls show was at this house, 131 Tompkins in Bed-Stuy. It was a house that had shows pretty regularly.

Morby: There were eight people there. And then a couple months later, they were selling out Death By Audio.

Vivian Girls were a revelation: a lo-fi, all-female punk trio with an aggressively DIY work ethic and short, catchy songs that were equally vulnerable and tough. Ramone's nom-de-plume, bestowed upon her in high school, was appropriate and earned— like the Ramones before them, Vivian Girls' sound was rooted in '60s garage rock and girl group pop, but synthesized in a fresh way that was distinctly of their era. Brooklyn's network of DIY venues was quick to recognize their significance; as Cake Shop co-owner Andy Bodor put it, they "inspired pretty much all of Brooklyn."

Morby: Vivian Girls are like the Velvet Underground of my lifetime. Bands like Best Coast or Dum Dum Girls, I have no doubt in my mind that they wouldn't exist without the Vivian Girls. Woods were really influenced by them, Crystal Stilts, Blank Dogs. The guys in Real Estate seeing Vivian Girls, who they knew from high school in Ridgewood, NJ.—that gave them the confidence to go for it.

The first time Vivian Girls sold out Death By Audio, the New York Times *came to write about it. That just felt huge, and it was crazy to see people getting turned away. Vivian Girls were becoming the biggest thing in the whole scene, and it was really exciting to watch. It felt like Vivian Girls, in theory, could become as big as the White Stripes.*

Vivian Girls were the first major act to emerge from a new wave of younger indie bands that had been reared on Todd P. shows and music blogs. These bands had the good fortune of forming at a time when DIY venues were multiplying across Williamsburg, Greenpoint, Bushwick, and Ridgewood. They were aided by social media platforms like Myspace that allowed both bands and bookers to network, as well as a cadre of local music blogs (nota-bly *Brooklyn Vegan*, *Stereogum*, and *Oh My Rockness*), and a music press that looked to said bloggers for the next big thing.

But like so many of the scenes that preceded them, the most sig-nificant factor in the scene's growth was arguably economic: The 2008 stock market crash and collapse of the housing and job mar-kets occurred as many of these musicians were freshly out of col-lege. This meant that a) many musicians and their peers couldn't get nine-to-five jobs even if they'd wanted to, leading them to pursue alternative lifestyles and cheap or free nightlife options, and b) the transformation of Williamsburg and Bushwick into luxury enclaves, already well underway, was temporarily paused, with sev-eral half-built waterfront condos remaining unoccupied for years.[xvi] In 2012, Hurricane Sandy ravaged the Williamsburg waterfront, causing additional delays and buying the scene even more time.

By 2012, Real Estate were a major band who could have played any number of "next-level" venues. Instead, they chose to do a big January 28 homecoming show with Todd P., who booked them at K&K Super Buffet—an all-you-can-eat Chinese restaurant at 341 St. Nicholas Avenue in Ridgewood, Queens—alongside Black Dice, Dog Leather, and the Babies.

Morby: I showed up early, and it was a gross buffet with all these people eating, and no stage. There were going to be a thousand people coming to this, it was going to be the biggest Todd P. show I'd ever been to, so I was really wondering where the stage was. And then an hour before the show, Todd came in with one kid who must have been an intern, they had wood and a drill gun, and they just put to-gether a stage. Maybe I'm making this up, but I remember there being a moment where Todd was duct-taping the stage together. An hour after the stage was built, a thousand people started to trickle in. And

---

xvi Legally, anyway—the abandoned Williamsburg waterfront developments became popular squatting sites.

then after the show, Todd broke the stage down, and we all partied in this Chinese restaurant until 4:30 in the morning.

285 KENT

After significant rent increases, PLNYWN closed in 2010. With the space vacant, John Barclay, an electronic music promoter, came in. Barclay officially used it as a photography studio, but threw raves in the space, which he renamed Bohemian Grove. But after one of his raves was raided by the NYPD vice squad in December 2010, Barclay passed the lease along to Todd P., who gave it a third and final name—285 Kent—and brought in his one-time intern Ric Leichtung to share booking duties.

Though 285 Kent had the precarious illegality of a DIY space, because of its size and the music industry tier at which it operated, it couldn't be an incubator for new artists in the same way that Death By Audio was or PLNYWN had been. For Alex Bleeker, 285 Kent "was sort of the beginning of the scene-y element starting to overshadow the music. You started seeing people who were part of that bro-y club culture taking cabs over from Manhattan to hang out there." But it is important to note that 285 Kent took great pains to expand the boundaries of what kind of community could be fostered in a north Brooklyn DIY venue, and made more of a conscious effort to regularly book performers of color than their predecessors had.

Soon after 285 Kent opened, Brooke Baxter Bailey and Rolyn Hu sold Glasslands to promoters Jake Rosenthal and Rami Haykal, who had already been booking shows there under the moniker Popgun Presents. Whatever DIY cred Glasslands had held on to from the Glass House days disappeared, with Rosenthal and Haykal running it even more explicitly like the legal, commercial venture it had always been.

Still, for the majority of bands and showgoers, all the venues along the three-block stretch of Kent Ave.—including the 285 Kent/Glasslands/Death By Audio complex and Monster Island—were part of the same scene.

Ramone: Even if I wasn't going to a specific show, I would go to that strip of Kent just to hang out on the street, because I knew I would see friends. It was like a party on the street, every night, and I knew everybody.

VENUES CLOSE

By the end of 2010, the housing market was bouncing back from the 2008 collapse, and the pause on Williamsburg waterfront's construction ended. But the first dominos to fall on the DIY scene weren't in Williamsburg: the Market Hotel was raided and shuttered by the NYPD on April 4, 2010, in the middle of a show by the band Smith Westerns. Given its precarious combination of size and illegality, it was perhaps inevitable—as *Gothamist*'s Jen Carlson wrote at the time, "Rickety stairs, shaking floors, bathroom doors that never shut, impossible to avoid smoking rooms, sound delays, *teenagers*, getting screamed at for being within 50 feet of the front door...there have been plenty of times we secretly wished Market Hotel...would get raided when we were inside."[198]

In an email to his email list soon after, Todd acknowledged that "the space may end up able to do shows again in its current situation, but realistically we need to be more legal to really survive. To pull this off we need to raise something like $100,000. This is a high number but not an impossible one."[199] In the meantime, people kept (illegally) living there.

Then, in July 2011, the Silent Barn was shuttered and its tenants evicted as part of a M.A.R.C.H. raid (*M*ulti-*A*gency *R*esponse to *C*ommunity *H*otspots), in which several municipal agencies including the NYPD, FDNY, Department of Health, State Liquor Authority, and Department of Buildings come into a venue and slam it with enough fines and citations to put it out of business.

G. Lucas Crane (resident, Silent Barn; tape manipulator, Woods): [The raid that closed the Silent Barn] was so funny, because it was during a poetry reading. Everyone was sitting on the floor, there's one person reading poetry, and then twenty cops came in. They stuck that [vacate order] on the door and everybody got really freaked out and left. [The residents] all went around the corner to sleep at the sound guy's house.

The police had padlocked the door so that we couldn't get in there, but it was pretty easy to sneak in, so the next day Joe Ahearn snuck in the back. The entire fucking place was just completely destroyed: doors kicked in, someone's mattress thrown into the middle of the room and peed on, everything smashed, completely defiled, and all of our things were stolen.

We didn't have any [security] cameras or anything like that, but the high point of our Encyclopedia Brown–esque investigation was that there was a wedding store across the street—they had a security camera, and we knew that their camera angle could see our front door. On the security footage was a team of big men and a rented white van with hand trucks that came in hours after the cops shut everything down. And you know, you can just look at some guys and know, those are fucking cops.

The Silent Barn's residents planned to reopen in some capacity and used the online crowdfunding website Kickstarter to raise money toward that end.

Crane: The Kickstarter made like $40,000 in twelve hours or something. Of course, Kickstarter is very public, you have to publicize it to make crowdfunding work, so the landlord [saw that we'd] raised that much money that fast. That brought us into a new hell world, with that fucking slumlord saying, "You can have a new lease, but it's going to cost $40,000"—the exact amount of money that we'd raised. Weird.

Patrick: When the landlord suddenly had a building with a vacate order on it and they stopped paying rent, he got mad. They jerked him around for a little bit—he was very involved, and said, "What if I pay for you guys to get your shit cleaned up and you run a legit space?" They said yes, but eventually they got an architect who said,

"I can make this legal, but you can't live here." It's against the law to live in a commercial business. So they [bailed,] and the landlord was mad as hell.

Once it became clear that reopening as a residential venue at 915 Wyckoff wouldn't be an option, the Silent Barn's residents began looking elsewhere. Instead, at the landlord's suggestion, Patrick partnered with musician Sam Hillmer of the band Zs to transform 915 Wyckoff into a new, fully legal venue called Trans Pecos.[xvii] It opened in December 2013.

Patrick: I started to see shit online after that, where all these young, idealistic kids have this idea that I'm a scumbag. They'd been told that I was somehow in cahoots with the landlord, and all these conspiracy theories. A lot of the really earnest support dried up, because of the fact that [Trans Pecos and Market Hotel] had to be overtly commercial projects.

In Williamsburg, Monster Island closed down in September 2011, under less fraught circumstances.

Nelson: There had been full transparency: The landlord said, "You can have it for seven years, you're never going to have it for longer." They weren't bad guys. And it was a really good deal, it was less than fifty cents a square foot. Everybody tries to make these endings of things have a villain. There wasn't really a villain.

The Kent Avenue complex that housed Death By Audio, Glasslands, and 285 Kent seemed safe for the time being,[xviii] even though

---

xvii Like Llano Estacado before it, the name comes from a region in Todd's native Texas.

xviii Other tenants at the time included the indieScreen movie theater, Ran Tea House, the offices of Genius Media, the acrobatic/trapeze school the Muse Brooklyn, and the film and TV production studio Windmill Studios.

the surrounding area was sprouting new restaurants, bars, boutiques, and daycare centers. But by 2013, it was clear to the building's tenants that their good fortune was on the verge of being
reversed.

*McMullen: Joe Markowitz started getting older. His sons [Leo and
Sol] were not so utopian-minded, they were a little bit more busi-
nesslike with their approach. In 2013, I think Joe might have had a
stroke or something,[xix] and then they took full control of the building.
The Housing Authority Commission came over and locked us out
and then gave us twenty four hours to get everything out.*

285 Kent was the first to close. Their four final "farewell"
shows, on January 11, 17, 18, and 19, 2014, included some bigger names like Dan Deacon, Fucked Up, DIIV, and Wolf Eyes, as
well as artists with deep ties to the space, like former PLNYWN
resident MV Carbon and Bohemian Grove promoter John Barclay's band DUST.

*Emilie Friedlander (journalist; co-founder, Ad Hoc): The closing
of 285 Kent felt emblematic for me. 285 had always been flirting
with the above-ground, and there was almost this sense that as it got
better and better and [the venue] got more and more hyped, that coincided with it no longer being sustainable. It had entered this space
of being recognized as this cultural thing, but it wasn't big enough
and mainstream enough to survive, either.*

Shortly after 285 Kent closed, rumors began circulating that
Vice, who had built their trendy hipster racism into a multimedia
empire, were eyeing the Kent Avenue building for their new headquarters. *Vice* had developed from a hateful little print magazine to
a slightly less hateful media empire that included internet videos,

---

xix According to Matt Conboy, he had brain surgery.

an HBO show, a decent record label, a credible journalism department, and an in-house ad agency—and it was looking to expand.

> *Conboy: When we first heard that* Vice *were coming in, it was implied that they were just going to take the Kent Avenue part of the building. I honestly thought, you know what, that might be great for us because maybe we could coexist. Thank God it's them and not J. Crew or somebody who's going to be mad that there's punk shows happening here. So yeah, joke's on me.*

Vice's relocation was no doubt aided by the $6.5 million tax break it received from the state as a reward for keeping their offices in Williamsburg. In advance of 285 Kent's closure, before *Vice*'s takeover of the building was announced, their music-oriented vertical *Noisey*[xx] published an article entitled, "Why the Closing of 285 Kent Doesn't Matter." Writer Gary Suarez argued that "the neighborhood is hardly the hipster utopia it once was purported to be a decade ago," and anyway, other DIY venues would spring up to take its place.[200] A month later, *Noisey* gave away a season pass to Glasslands as a contest prize, claiming that "nothing pleases us more than getting sweaty and dancing around at Glasslands."[201]

Death By Audio staged a mammoth, seventy-five-day closing party from September 10 to November 22. Wilber booked several big-name bands, many of whom had played at Death By Audio in their infancy. In the hallway and residential portions of Death By Audio, they staged an art exhibit called Death By Art, curated by Joe Ahearn, who had moved in there after the Silent Barn closed. Conboy filmed it all, releasing the footage in his 2016 documentary *Goodnight Brooklyn—The Story of Death By Audio.*

It should have been a frictionless send-off, but of course, it wasn't. *Vice* began construction on the space well before Death By Audio closed, creating several health and safety risks.

---

xx   Full disclosure: this book's author has written for *Noisey* in the past.

© EBRU YILDIZ.

Edan Wilber and Matt Conboy at Death By Audio, 2014.

Wilber: *Joe Ahearn found a brick in his bed that had just fallen from the upper floor through a hole in the ceiling, which would have hit him if he had been in bed. It was psychological warfare, for sure.*

Pettily, they also sent in painters to paint over a mural in the Death By Art show that read "Fuck You Shane," referring to *Vice* co-founder Shane Smith.

At the final show on November 22—which featured Lightning Bolt, A Place to Bury Strangers, JEFF the Brotherhood, and Grooms—copies of *Vice* were distributed to the crowd and ripped to shreds. "Those were my and Matt's personal copies of *Vice* that we had collected since 2000," Wilber explained. "I found 14-year-old magazines that I had kept in my periodicals collection, and I honestly didn't plan on getting rid of them."

Glasslands, the oldest venue in the building, was also the last to leave. Its closing night was New Year's Eve 2014, with performances by DIIV, Sky Ferreira, Smith Westerns, and Beverly. Fewer tears and less ink was spilled over its demise than that of its neighbors, likely because its legal, licensed status and 21+ door policy meant that nobody could wax nostalgic about transcendent, formative experiences they had there as teens.

Vice took over the building in 2015. Within the scene, the back-to-back closures of so many beloved DIY venues initiated a good deal of public soul-searching about what had happened, both *to* them and *because of* them, to a degree that few of their predecessors had demonstrated.

> *Noecker: It's like in* Star Trek: The Next Generation, *when the Borg comes through and just wipes out everything in its path—that's what the property market did to the music scene. A culture of automatons coming through to erase individuality and creativity, because resistance is futile. The real estate industry just destroys culture, while pretending to be the harbingers of it. Can we start a successful creative place without fearing it being taken away by some trillionaire? Not really.*

> *Bleeker: I think it's silly to not look at ourselves as a gentrifying force. I'm not laying blame on anyone, but when people were screaming about those* Vice *offices opening, it rubbed me the wrong way to have all these predominantly white kids who were hanging out and choosing to be artists, who were then screaming about gentrification.*

BUSHWICK

> *McMullen: After Williamsburg ended, nobody moved to a central neighborhood anymore. People moved all over, to Ridgewood, Bed-Stuy, Long Island City, Middle Village, Gowanus, Sunset Park. A lot of people did start some sort of micro hub in their different areas, but it was never the same.*

Of course, an awful lot of them kept going to Bushwick—or, as a portion of it became known, "East Williamsburg."[xxi]

---

xxi Recall the transformation of the Lower East Side into the "East Village."

The conversations around the scene in Bushwick are racially, economically, and culturally complex in a way they never were along the largely abandoned Williamsburg waterfront. It's hard to do a full assessment of the situation, in part because it's still ongoing at the time of this book's writing, but it's been clear for years that the spread of largely white DIY art and music spaces (and the legit spaces and moneyed tenants that follow) into an economically distressed and Latinx and Black neighborhood[xxii] is, let's say, fraught.

While Williamsburg's scene largely took place in disused industrial spaces, Bushwick is largely residential. This meant that artistic gentrifiers were not only taking apartments away from long-time residents, but building venues that abutted residential spaces. Loud, drunk show attendees who ducked outside to smoke and chat were now doing so under the apartment windows of families that had to get up the next morning for work and school. And because the Black and Latinx communities who called Bushwick home were by and large not landowners, they didn't receive any benefit from the arts spaces popping up and making property in the area more valuable. For most of the preexistent Bushwick community, it was a lose-lose proposition.

Though *Vice*-style "hipster racism" had fallen out of fashion by the '10s, it was replaced with a flippant, Pollyanna-ish Obama-era "post-racial" attitude, summed up perfectly by Ilana Wexler on Comedy Central's *Broad City*: "Statistically, we're headed towards an age where everybody's going to be, like, caramel and queer."[202] That attitude helped the growing influx of moneyed Bushwick residents to be at best unaware of, or at worst apathetic to, the larger socio-economic repercussions of their behavior.

In 2012, with the money they'd raised on Kickstarter, the Silent Barn reopened in a new building at 603 Bushwick Avenue in Bushwick. Because it was a three-story residential building, with ground-level storefronts and apartments above it, they were now

xxii According to the 2010 US census, Bushwick was 65.4 percent Latinx and 20 percent Black.

legally able to operate with a show space, multiple artists' studios, residences, a recording studio, an organic garden, and even a combination record store/barber shop called Deep Cuts. Commendably, efforts were made to reach out to the preexisting Bushwick community, which included bringing in the group Educated Little Monsters, "a music and arts group serving Bushwick youth whose communities are severely impacted by gentrification."[203]

The Silent Barn lasted six years in the new space, with those involved admirably attempting to run it as a nonhierarchical collective. But from the outset, it was burdened with financial difficulties, and it shuttered in 2018.

Leichtung: I think a lot of people at the Silent Barn viewed the balance sheet as an option. This is the way that DIY venues and community spaces should be run, but they cannot be run that way in gentrified New York City. It was a painful lesson that the community had to learn.

When the second Silent Barn closed, the plan was to turn the building over to Educated Little Monsters, but that plan fell through. At the time of this book's writing, the storefronts at 603 Bushwick Avenue appear to be empty and available for rent.

After Monster Island closed, Secret Project Robot relocated to 389 Melrose Street in Bushwick, which they ran in much the same DIY, lovingly ramshackle way they always had. In 2016, facing a 50 percent rent increase, Secret Project Robot again moved, reopening in 2017 as a fully licensed bar and venue at 1186 Broadway, along the Bushwick/Bed-Stuy border.

Nelson: It was the worst mistake we ever made. It totally ruined it for us, because it became too official.

Secret Project Robot's Myrtle Avenue location shuttered in April 2019, just shy of its two-year anniversary.

★ ★ ★

Wilber: We came [to the Williamsburg waterfront] because there was no one there. But there's no place we can go now that's not going to drive up rent prices for the family that's been living there forever. I lived in New York long enough to see that those tragedies happen all over, and some of them really hit me hard.

I saw a woman that used to run a restaurant in Greenpoint collecting cans; she saw me and got embarrassed and ran away. It was the saddest thing, I fucking broke down. The last thing I want to do is make an art space that makes an area desirable and causes this for anyone else. That's why I've always been afraid of opening a new place.

Beyond the thorny issue of gentrification, ethical concerns about DIY spaces were also amplified after thirty-six showgoers died in a fire at the Oakland, California, DIY venue Ghost Ship on December 2, 2016.

Leichtung: During Todd's heyday, you thought about safety to the degree of just making sure you didn't get sued or shut down. Moments like Ghost Ship really open your eyes to see that the way the 285 Kent was run was not ethical, not safe, and could never happen again for that reason.

Conboy: I am fearful that what we did is not possible anymore, in New York City or anywhere, after the Ghost Ship fire. I certainly don't want anybody to be injured or die just for art. The cruelty of the whole situation is that these underground spaces exist because they're necessary, but they exist in a way that is unsafe because our society does not value them.

THE AFTERLIFE OF THE BROOKLYN SCENE

Numerous other scenes in this book fell apart quickly due to burnout, bad business decisions, rising rents, or trends moving on. But the Brooklyn indie scene survived as long as it did because it was run, by and large, by organized, problem-solving people who were dedicated to keeping things going, even when it low-key ruined their lives. It's a sign of how creative life in New York City has changed—it's a struggle for artists to even live here now, let alone maintain a fertile creative scene. But it's also a testament to what people can create with drive, vision, and an email list.

While performing at 285 Kent's third-to-last show, musician Dan Deacon likened Todd P. to "all of the Batman villains and Spiderman heroes in one person,"[204] which is a pretty accurate summary of where the guy stands these days.

As we've seen, there have been complaints (some more valid than others) of reckless endangerment, exploitation of free/cheap young labor, and taking credit for others' work. Regardless, New York City's twenty-first-century musical landscape would have looked very different—and much, much worse—without his single-minded cultivation of an all-ages, anti-corporate, economically sustainable scene for over two decades. As Jordan Michael Iannucci put it, "Todd used to get too much credit for a lot of things, and now I think he doesn't get *enough* credit for things."

In 2013, the last of the Market Hotel's remaining residents left the space. Along with a group of about thirty-five volunteers, Todd created a nonprofit organization called the Market Hotel Project, and as their current website (markethotel.org) put it, they were able to raise funds through "small investments and loans from not-wealthy people...in hopes to provide an example that even ambitious projects can be accomplished by regular people of middle-class means."[205] Despite an abundance of obstacles, they were able to bring the space up to code.

In December 2015, Market Hotel began putting on shows again, using their nonprofit status to gain temporary event permits and single-day beer and wine licenses obtained for every individual show, and then putting whatever money was made into further renovations. They became a fully licensed, legal, all-ages venue in the summer of 2018. But that's only the half of it: as a nonprofit community space, the Market Hotel has also hosted everything from after-school programs to yoga classes to municipal public hearings.

The building at 118 North 11th Street that once housed Arcadia sat empty for years. It has recently reopened as Hecla Iron Works, "The only historic landmark zoned for office space in Williamsburg."[206] Looking at their photos of the current interior, one can still make out the groin-vaulted ceilings that gave Arcadia its signature palatial look.

Thankfully, at least one of these stories has a happy ending. In 2019, Rachel Nelson and Erik Zajaceskowski were walking by the Williamsburg Bridge with their son and got the idea to go see what had become of the original Mighty Robot space. In doing so, Nelson recalled, "We just happened to run into the landlord, and of course, the landlord remembered Erik."

Zajaceskowski: I had heard it was empty when I ran into him, and that it was trashed, so I said, "Show me the space," because I wanted to take some photos of it. It took me forever to convince him, but I finally got him to show me around. I have never seen a place so trashed—and we've seen a lot of trashed places! After showing me around he said, "You want to rent it?"

Nelson: We signed a lease on March 1st, 2020—seventeen days before we went into lockdown. We have a much smaller space for shows because we ended up building bigger art studios, but we have a really cute fifty-person venue, and we've had a few shows. We only want to do things with our friends now—people who know the deal and want to hang out.

As of 2022, Secret Project Robot continues to operate out of the original Mighty Robot space. When you compare it to everything else that happened to the original Williamsburg scene, it's not that much of a win. But it is definitely *a* win. And in a place as brutal as present-day New York City, you've gotta count every win.

PHOTO BY THE AUTHOR, 2023.

401 Wythe Avenue.

Suggested Listening

Oneida—*Enemy Hogs* (1999)

Liars—*They Threw Us All in a Trench and Stuck a Monument on Top* (2001)

Black Dice—*Beaches & Canyons* (2002)

William Basinski—*The Disintegration Loops* (2002-2003)

TV on the Radio—*Young Liars* (2003)

Vivian Girls—*Vivian Girls* (2008)

A Place to Bury Strangers—*Exploding Head* (2009)

Real Estate—*Real Estate* (2009)

Woods—*Songs of Shame* (2009)

Various—*Start Your Own Fucking Show Space* (rec. 2014)

CONCLUSION

NYC GHOSTS AND FLOWERS

Paul Zone: In New York, there's always one building going up, one coming down. But I never subscribe to all that "I couldn't live in New York, it's really changed" stuff. "Oh, wasn't there a building here?" "Wasn't there a club that used to be there?" Blah blah blah blah blah. It was like that in the '70s too: All of those hippies in the '70s were wishing it was the '60s again. No big difference.

I'm a relentless New York City culture booster, but I have to admit that music venues (especially those of the illegal or semilegal variety) have become discernibly harder to operate in recent years. There are a number of reasons—the rising costs of living; increased visibility to law enforcement and landlords via social media; increased attention to safety concerns. And of course, there are only so many empty buildings in NYC—as those numbers dwindle, the opportunities get fewer and fewer.

Erik Zajaceskowski: Not that long ago, it felt like there were the most underground spaces I had ever seen. They were everywhere! And now it's down to the least I've ever known of.

These are all real problems, and we can't ignore them. But we also don't do ourselves any favors by insisting that there are no options, no solutions, no ways out. If we want to fight for the future of New York City music, there are still tools we can use. To that end, there are a few recurring factors that pop up again and again in the various scenes we've looked at, and they're worth articulating.

First and foremost, the majority of these venues kept their overhead low. They opened in unspectacular spaces that were relatively cheap due to their undesirable locations and/or derelict conditions, and for the most part, there was little remodeling done. The Gaslight, CBGB, the Mudd Club, 171A, the Silent Barn—these were seriously janky spaces, but it didn't matter in terms of their ability to draw an enthusiastic crowd or serve as a home base for their communities. Costs were minimized through any number of methods, with a lax approach to licensing being an especially popular one. In rapidly gentrifying New York City, this is admittedly becoming harder and harder to do, but it is not impossible.

Despite their slim financial margins, many of these venues and promoters didn't skimp on treating their performers and regulars with overt respect. This could manifest in any number of ways— regular free admission, fair compensation, exceptional sound, booking nascent acts who have yet to find their audience—but the end result is that the performers leave feeling valued and eager to return. The Folklore Center, the Mudd Club, and Sidewalk Cafe all took it one further by hanging photos of beloved regulars on the wall in an ever-evolving "who's who."

Elliott Sharp: When you're a musician coming to New York and not having any gigs or having any money, you need to be known by the doormen [so that] you'd get in for free. So you might play to a packed room, but half the people were on the house. But that also made it feel great, because it felt like a community. These are your people, even if you didn't know them.

A lot of these venues were also open very, very late. The Gaslight, the Loft, Paradise Garage, A7, the original Danceteria, and

Sidewalk Cafe all kept the party going well past last call, through the morning. Some of them didn't even really get going before midnight! Come 5:00 a.m., the curious outsiders who've come to gawk, the disinterested friends of friends of the bands, and the skeezy horndogs have all gone home, and you're left with people who are genuinely engaged in whatever it is you're building. All-night hours also allow these venues to serve as safe spaces for people who would prefer not to spend the night at home.

Many of these scenes also embraced (and were in some cases driven by) teenagers. I know, I know—they're really obnoxious. But they're also often the most passionate and devoted fans, they are desperate for community, and they have the kind of expendable time and energy that are rarely available to adults. Indeed, several people I spoke to cited the 1985 raising of the national drinking age to twenty-one as a major factor in their scenes' deterioration. Most of the scenes that successfully weathered that storm were ones that didn't depend entirely on alcohol sales for their bottom line.

There have always been other ways for venues to make money: cover charges, memberships, food sales, renting out space for band rehearsals or art studios. And as we've seen, there is something to be gained by removing booze from the equation—both legally and spiritually.

Kenny Carpenter: When we first went out to these places like the Gallery and the Loft and the Paradise Garage, none of them had alcohol. That's one of the things that made those clubs so special. Because once you introduce alcohol, then everything changes. The owners and the promoters have a different motive for doing the party: They have their eyes on how much they're going to make at the bar, as opposed to, let's do the best party possible.

Similarly, there is a lot to be gained by offering free or cheap food. Max's Kansas City, Studio Rivbea, the Loft, Club 82, and Paradise Garage all provided free grub to their attendees, while CBGB, Sidewalk Cafe, and Cake Shop made it available at artist-friendly prices. This can make all the difference for a venue that is cultivating a young, struggling scene—which then attracts paying outsiders. On the other hand, Max's, Sidewalk, Ali's Alley, and Studio We all successfully relied on food sales for their income, which granted them a flexibility in booking that many other venues lacked. Food also gives patrons another reason to stay put, since they won't have to go to elsewhere to satisfy their midshow munchies.

Finally, scenes benefit from having accessible, welcoming entry points for outsiders, like Folk City's hootenannies, CBGB's audition nights, Lach's open mics, or Todd P.'s email list. It also helps to have publications that double as road maps to their scenes, such as *Sing Out!*, *Rock Scene*, *The Big Takeover*, *AntiMatters*, or *Stereogum*. Of course, today, we're dealing with some issues that earlier scenes never had to contend with, like smartphones and the way that most of our lives are lived at least partially on the internet.

DJ Spooky: Maybe there's a different kind of real estate now, which is real estate of how people think about digital space. What [this book is] focusing on is the legacy of physical space and how certain conditions generate certain kinds of music, but now most of that has pivoted to a digital context.

Brenda Kahn: You weren't plugged in 24/7, so if you wanted to see people and hang out, you had to show up. I think it's a little harder now because people aren't being forced to be uncomfortable, and they're not being forced to be face-to-face.

These days, a new band can instantly connect with one hundred other bands worldwide who sound exactly like them, rather than make do with the handful of bands in their neighborhood who might be doing something different that could eventually lead to cross-pollination. And with every step of the way often documented and posted online (whether the artists want it or not), there's little opportunity to develop gradually outside of the public eye. Some clubs in New York—notably, the influential dance club Nowadays—have banned the use of phones on the dance floor, which is an imperfect but effective buffer.

I don't know what the solution is, but I know that it exists. The more we become removed from our immediate surroundings and engulfed by the noise of the internet, the more we cede control of our environment and culture to the forces of homogenization and conformity. But there is also that much more to be gained by investing our time, energy, creativity, and resources into safe, nurturing, independently owned, community-oriented venues—as Todd Patrick put it, "The whole idea of an IRL space is massive" in our current era. It can, and should, be done everywhere, all the time.

William Parker: They used to say, "Come to New York, there's enough rats and roaches for everybody!" Well, they don't say that anymore. New York has changed a lot, but I think people are resourceful. It's harder to survive, but you can do it.

Jeffrey Lewis: Even if New York City is completely dead, even if New York City is completely finished, there's still enough people showing up in New York City who are too stupid to know it's finished, and the fact that they think it's happening makes it happen. No matter how much the people living here know that it's dead, there's always a million new people showing up that haven't heard that news yet.

It's easy to bemoan the loss of "old NYC," the collapse of the music industry, or the effects of social media and cell phones, and call it a day. But as we've seen, the best scenes are born out of a mixture of dissatisfaction with the present circumstances, and the ability to notice and seize the opportunities that they provide. There is always something of value to be said, some new way of saying it, and somewhere to do so. And remember, *just because you don't know about it, doesn't mean it isn't happening.*

So if you want to complain about the state of music in New York City (or anywhere), I'd suggest that you first start going out most nights of the week, every week, for at least a couple years. Do your due diligence and find the smallest, most out-of-the-way clubs and DIY spaces you can. Show up early and stay for the whole night so that you can watch every performer on every bill, and make sure you buy merch from all of the ones who even slightly impress you. If at the end of all that, you still want to whine about the dearth of quality music and nightlife, go ahead—*then* you'll actually have a leg to stand on.

Justin Strauss, who as Milk 'n' Cookies' front man was hanging out at Max's Kansas City and CBGB, and who has been an active participant in the city's underground nightlife ever since, *does* have that leg to stand on. He's worked steadily as a deejay since his Mudd Club debut, and he has an enviable backlog of experiences to weigh the current options against. Even so, his assessment of New York's current nightlife landscape was wholeheartedly enthusiastic.

> *Strauss: There is a very healthy club scene in New York now. Good Room is incredible, I love playing there. Bossa Nova Civic Club is just this hole in the wall that all these kids started going to, and it's so fun to deejay there—everyone's so amped and excited. There's Elsewhere, Jupiter Disco, [the list is] endless. There's a lot of great clubs, and they're all packed right now, which is awesome.*

I am not going to give you a laundry list of all the cool clubs and parties in New York City, because by the time you're reading this, half of them will have closed or ceased to be cool—plus, that would take away all the fun of finding them yourself. But I will say that from what I've seen, there's still plenty of vibrant, diverse, underground music and nightlife in New York City. Dance music in particular seems to be in the midst of an incredible renaissance right now.[i] You might have to trek out to Ridgewood, Queens,

---

i   Uncoincidentally, Secret Project Robot's Rachel Nelson noted that "When people go to see rock shows, the bar makes like 25 percent of what they'd make at a deejay [night]," since the audience at the latter doesn't have to be as focused on the performer.

to experience it, but so what? These kinds of experiences *should* be effortful.[ii]

And in some ways, nightlife is a less risky proposition in New York than it's been in decades. In 2017, thanks to the efforts of city councilman Rafael Espinal and several grassroots activists, the city repealed the ninety-one-year-old Cabaret Law that the NYPD had aggressively used to shutter venues since the Giuliani administration. That same year, the city council also passed an Espinal-sponsored bill to create an Office of Nightlife, with the goal of acting as an empathetic and proactive liaison between nightlife businesses, their neighbors, and law enforcement. The following year, Ariel Palitz was appointed that office's first senior executive director.

Palitz had previously owned Sutra Lounge, a hip-hop club at 16 1st Avenue, from 2004 to 2014. She became politicized when, in the club's first year of existence, she "had a chronic neighbor who made me the number one most complained-about bar in New York for almost ten years." In her view, "When people complain about nightlife, to me, they're complaining about the lack of coordination of services to address the unique impacts of life at night."

To that end, Palitz has spearheaded several campaigns, including the creation of the Lower East Side Quality of Life Improvement Plan, designed to reorganize the implementation of city resources (e.g. parking, sanitation, policing) to better mesh with the realities of the notoriously late-night "Hell Square" neighborhood (Palitz prefers to call it "Social Circle"). She has also proposed the creation of twenty-four-hour nightlife districts in less residential neighborhoods, so that "all those people that still want to keep going could just go there, [which would] draw people out of those residential neighborhoods."

Arto Lindsay: People have been lamenting so loudly: "The changes in New York, the gentrification, it's not what it used to be, young

---

ii   I recommend checking out Barbie Bertisch and Paul Raffaele's zine *Love Injection*, which does a phenomenal job of documenting and promoting NYC's contemporary dance music culture, as well as the dance music cultures of yore.

people can't move here anymore if they want to be artists, blah blah blah." People have been bitching about this for a long time, and there's a lot of truth there, but people also tend to forget that even when all these white kids could move to the Lower East Side, there were people living down there that had little kids, that couldn't [afford to] live anywhere else. It wasn't so romantic for them, you know?

G. Lucas Crane: *What's the end game of gentrification? There's only three people living in the city and everything's clean?*

The history of New York City itself begins with a prototype for every wave of gentrification that followed, when Dutch traders forcefully displaced the Lenape tribe in order to take over the area they called home. This original sin gets reenacted over and over, and though today's gentrifying real estate developers are every bit as blatant as the Dutch East India Company, they now frequently conscript well-meaning artists to do some of their dirty work.

Are artists inherently a gentrifying force? Not necessarily; they can embed themselves in their chosen community seamlessly and conscientiously. But the construction of music scenes—sonically, interpersonally, demographically, and spatially—is inextricable from acts of destruction: in order to make room for new ideas and new communities, something else has to be removed.

It's hard to look at the present-day Lower Manhattan and North Brooklyn landscape, and the playpen for the 1 percent it's all become, and say that it was worth it. But it's also hard to listen to *Marquee Moon* or *Return to Cookie Mountain* and say that the artistic communities that took root in those places were a mistake. I don't know what the answer is, just that we need to keep asking the question.

★ ★ ★ ★ ★

ACKNOWLEDGEMENTS

I am profoundly indebted to so many people that generously took the time to speak with me over the phone, Zoom, or in person, or corresponded with me via email. Although not everybody ended up being directly quoted, each and every one of them helped inform the text: Sal Abbatiello, Ahmed Abdullah, Oliver Ackermann, Alison Aguiar, Joe Ahearn, Beau Alessi, Emily Armstrong, Arthur Baker, William Basinski, Freddy Bastone, Brooke Baxter Bailey, Drew Beck, Jonathan Berger, Cindy Lee Berryhill, Bob Bert, Hisham Bharoocha, Somer Bingham, Bob Blank, Alex Bleeker, Richard Boch, Andy Bodor, Nick Bodor, Bill Bragin, Alan Braufman, Ray Brown, Kenny Carpenter, Melissa Caruso-Scott, Rhys Chatham, Diane Cluck, Sesu Coleman, Judy Collins, Matt Conboy, Cooper-Moore, Jayne County, G. Lucas Crane, Peter Crowley, Robin Crutchfield, Debe Dalton, Brooke Delarco, DJ Mojo, DJ Olive, DJ Spooky, Sharon D'Lugoff Blythe, Alix Dobkin, Johnny Dynell, Jeremy Earl, Peter Feigenbaum, Harley Flanagan, Don Fleming, Joshua Fried, Emilie Friedlander, Isaac Gillespie, Toby Goodshank, Peter Gordon, Claude "Paradise" Gray, Adam Green, Seaton "Raven" Hancock, Carolyn Hester, Michael Holman, William Hooker, Jordan Michael Iannucci, Pat Ivers, Hilary Jaeger, Jarboe, Jedi, Dany Johnson, Brenda Kahn, Joe "Truck" Kasher, Joey Kelly, Kid Millions, Kool Moe Dee, Jimi LaLumia, Colin Langenus, Ric Leichtung, Jeffrey Lewis, Alan Licht, Arto Lindsay, Miriam Linna, Joey Llanos, Josh Lozano, Michael Macioce, Roger Manning, Nick Marden, James Marshall, Michael McMahon, Zeljko McMullen, Legs McNeil, Denise Mercedes, Raz Mesinai, Kevin Morby, Matthew Mottel, Colleen "Cosmo" Murphy, Rachel Nelson, Pat Noecker, Antonio Ocasio, Chandra Oppenheim, Paleface, Charlemagne Palestine, Ariel Palitz, William Parker, Man Parrish, Todd Patrick, Tom Paxton, Rudolf Piper, Pat Place, Jack Rabid, Cassie Ramone, Genya Ravan, Ted Reichman, Martin Rev, Ruby Lynn Reyner, Amy Rigby, Victor Rosado, Alex Rosner, Paul Rutner, Buffy Sainte-Marie, Adam Schatz, Rebecca Seatle, Jonny Sender, Ben Seretan, Yvonne Sewall, Elliott Sharp, Jeremy Shatan, Douglas Sherman, Matthew Shipp, Peter K. Siegel, Cynthia Sley, Noel Paul Stookey, Justin Strauss, Greg Tate, Happy Traum, Richard Vasquez, Lee Ving, Dana Wachs, Edan Wilber, Brooke Young-Russell, Sean Yseult, Erik Zajaceskowski, Tony Zanetta, and Paul Zone. Thank you all for entrusting me with your memories; I hope I have done them justice. (This seems as good a place as any to mention that some quotes have been lightly edited and condensed for brevity and clarity.)

Extra thanks to Beau Alessi, Alex Bleeker, Nick Bodor, Brooke Delarco, DJ Spooky, Denise Mercedes, and Matthew Mottel, who all went above and beyond to introduce and vouch for me to several of their contacts. Thanks are also due to Michael Berlin, Lori Eastside, Arthur Magida, Sam Monaco, Spencer Scanlon, Wendy Serkin, Tom Tierney, and Anna Wood for making valuable introductions.

Extra gratitude goes out to Sal Abbatiello, Claude "Paradise" Gray, and Kool Moe Dee, whose incredible stories formed the backbone of a chapter about hip-hop's early years in the Bronx and Harlem that was ultimately cut. It was a mind-blowing honor and delight to speak with all three of you; please know that these cuts were agonizing to make.

Two of the people I interviewed, Alix Dobkin and Greg Tate,

tragically passed before this book's release. Both were giants within their respective communities, and I consider myself incredibly lucky to have spoken with them. May their memories be a blessing.

Thanks to Alice Arnold, William Basinski, Jonathan Berger, Cindy Lee Berryhill, Sesu Coleman, Matt Conboy, Peter Crowley, James Elaine, Harley Flanagan, Laura Lee Flanagan, Hilary Jaeger, Tom Marcello, Denise Mercedes, John A. Mozzer, Clinton Navkral, Pat Noecker, Victor Rosado, and Ebru Yildiz for generously donating extraordinary photos and memorabilia from their personal archives.

This book would not exist without the guidance, faith, and enthusiasm of my editor, Peter Joseph. Thank you, Peter, for approaching me back in 2019 with the initial idea for this project; for giving the green light to what was supposed to be a compact 80,000-word book (ha!); for not freaking out when I delivered something considerably lengthier; and for transforming that unwieldy tome into something coherent and navigable.

Thanks as well to Eden Railsback, Elliott Smith, Tracy Wilson, Shirley Komosa, Grace Towery, and everyone else at Hanover Square Press who helped make this book as good as it could be.

I'm grateful to every single person that's come on one of my walking tours over the past five years, for giving me the opportunity to hone my narrative skills, test out my theories, and deepen my expertise. Thank you for spending your free time and hard-earned cash to listen to me talk about the music and the city that I love.

Thanks to Anna Lomax Chiaratikis Wood for taking me seriously and treating me as a scholar before I even thought of myself that way. Being able to work alongside you and learn from you has been one of the great honors of my life.

And what kind of New Yorker would I be if I didn't thank my therapist? Bridgit, you're a lifesaver.

My parents, Ira Rifkin and Ruth Berlin, have always believed in me more than I've ever believed in myself, and I would be nowhere without their love and support. My father—a brilliant and accomplished writer and editor—was also one of the first people to read an early draft of this book, and his perspective, guidance, and sharp editorial eye were invaluable.

Two of my oldest and dearest friends, Joey Lawton and Taylor Pavlik, were also early readers, and their critiques and suggestions were indispensable. Many other wonderful friends supported me through this process in a variety of ways, which I will thank them for in person.

And of course, I couldn't have done any of this without Gabrielle Moss, the love of my life. Her unwavering support, encouragement, guidance, and input have sustained me throughout this process. Thank you, Gaby, for all of it.

Soon after I began working on this book, my older brother Brady passed away. He lived and breathed music and was far more knowledgeable about it than I'll ever be. Truthfully, I got into all this stuff as a kid primarily because I wanted to connect with and impress him, and it breaks my heart that I can't share this book with him. This is for you, Brady. I love you and I miss you.

APPENDIX

TIMELINE OF SIGNIFICANT EVENTS

In the interest of narrative, the events in this book are organized by subject rather than a streamlined chronology. With that in mind, here's the chronological sequence of all the major events discussed, to help you understand these stories within that context.

1957:
- Izzy Young opens the Folklore Center on MacDougal Street
- Rick Allmen opens the Cafe Bizarre on West 3rd Street

1958:
- The Gaslight opens

1960:
- Yoko Ono and La Monte Young stage a concert series at Ono's Chambers Street loft
- Gerde's Folk City opens

1961:
- The Bitter End opens

- Folk singers riot in Washington Square Park
- Bob Dylan moves to New York
- Peter, Paul and Mary form

1964:
- Slugs' Saloon opens

1965:
- Mickey Ruskin opens Max's Kansas City
- Ed Sanders opens the Peace Eye Bookstore

1966:
- The Sun Ra Arkestra begin their monthly residency at Slugs' Saloon

1967:
- George Maciunas opens the first Fluxhouse Cooperative

1968:
- Ornette Coleman moves to 131 Prince Street

1969:
- The Stonewall Riots give birth to the city's gay rights movement

1970:
- David Mancuso throws his first Loft party at 645–647 Broadway
- Studio We opens
- Alan Vega and Martin Rev play their first shows as Suicide

1971:
- Hilly Kristal opens Hilly's on the Bowery
- A SoHo zoning resolution allows artists to reside in their work spaces
- The New York Dolls form and the Magic Tramps relocate to New York from California, effectively kicking off the glam rock era in New York

1972:

- Lee Morgan is killed at Slugs' Saloon, after which the venue closes
- Philip Glass moves to 10 Bleecker Street
- The Gallery and Studio Rivbea open
- The New York Musicians' Jazz Festival is organized in response to the Newport Jazz Festival relocating to the city

1973:

- The Mercer Arts Center collapses
- The Kitchen relocates to Broome Street
- Ali's Alley and 501 Canal open
- Hilly Kristal rebrands Hilly's on the Bowery as CBGB & OMFUG, Television play there for the first time

1974:

- David Mancuso is evicted from 645-647 Broadway, temporarily pausing the Loft parties
- Ornette Coleman leaves 131 Prince Street
- Max's Kansas City closes for the first time
- The Gallery closes at its 22nd Street location and relocates to 172 Mercer Street

1975:

- "Ford to City: Drop Dead"
- The Loft reopens at 99 Prince Street
- Environ opens
- Tommy Dean Mills reopens Max's Kansas City
- Charlemagne Palestine moves to 64 North Moore Street

1976:

- Studio Henry opens

1977:

- Paradise Garage opens
- The Gallery closes

1978:
- Mudd Club and the Roxy open
- Studio Rivbea closes
- Rudolf Piper moves to New York
- A five-night no wave festival is staged at Artists' Space, which leads to the recording and release of the *No New York* compilation later that year

1979:
- Pyramid Club, Fun House, and Tier 3 open
- Danceteria opens at its first location, 252 West 37th Street
- Ali's Alley closes

1980:
- ABC No Rio opens
- Tier 3 closes
- Danceteria closes for the first time

1981:
- A7 opens
- Max's Kansas City closes for the second and final time
- Michael Holman and Ruza Blue start promoting hip-hop nights at Negril
- AIDS first emerges in New York
- Beastie Boys and Sonic Youth form; Thurston Moore and Ann DeMarinis organize Noise Fest at White Columns

1982:
- Passage of the 1982 Loft Law, protecting residents of formerly commercial properties from unreasonable living conditions, evictions, and unfair rent increases

1983:
- Danceteria reopens at 30 West 21st Street
- Area and Limelight open
- Mudd Club closes
- Lach organizes his first hoots at the Fort

1984:
- Congress passes the National Minimum Drinking Age Act, raising the legal drinking age from eighteen to twenty-one
- David Mancuso is evicted from 99 Prince Street and relocates the Loft to East 3rd Street
- A7 closes

1985:
- The first New York Antifolk Festival is staged at the Fort
- Sidewalk Cafe and the Palladium open
- The Fun House closes

1986:
- Danceteria closes for the second time
- Nell's and Tunnel open

1987:
- The Knitting Factory opens in its first location at 48 East Houston Street
- Paradise Garage closes, owner Michael Brody dies of AIDS shortly after
- Area closes

1988:
- The Tompkins Square Park Riot

1989:
- Arcadia and Sound Factory open

1990:
- Eighty-seven people die in a fire at the Happy Land club in the Bronx

1991:
- The first Lalalandia parties are thrown in Williamsburg
- Tompkins Square Park closes for repairs, evicting the homeless population

1992:

- Larry Levan dies

1993:

- Lach begins holding hoots in the back room at Sidewalk Cafe
- Bottle service is first introduced to New York nightlife at Tunnel

1994:

- David Mancuso is evicted from East 3rd Street, after which the Loft struggles to find a permanent location for several years
- The Knitting Factory relocates to 74 Leonard Street
- The Cooler opens

1995:

- alt.coffee opens
- Sound Factory closes

1996:

- "Club Kid" Michael Alig kills Angel Melendez, leading to a crackdown on nightclubs
- The first Vision Festival is staged at the Learning Alliance

1998:

- Tonic opens

1999:

- Mighty Robot opens

2000:

- The Cooler closes

2001:

- Todd Patrick moves to NYC and begins organizing DIY shows
- Tunnel closes

- The Strokes release *Is This It*, bringing renewed attention to the city's rock scene
- The World Trade Center is attacked on 9/11

2003:
- Mayor Michael Bloomberg's administration unveils the 311 hotline and bans smoking indoors

2004:
- Monster Island and Glass House open along the Williamsburg waterfront

2005:
- Cake Shop opens
- The Williamsburg waterfront is rezoned from industrial to residential

2006:
- CBGB & OMFUG closes
- Paris London New York West Nile, Glasslands, and Silent Barn open

2007:
- Death By Audio opens
- Tonic, alt.coffee, and the Roxy close
- Hilly Kristal dies

2008:
- Lach leaves Sidewalk Cafe
- Market Hotel opens

2010:
- Paris London New York West Nile becomes 285 Kent
- Market Hotel is shut down

2011:
- Monster Island closes
- The Silent Barn is shuttered and vandalized

2012:
- The Silent Barn reopens in Bushwick

2014:
- Death By Audio, Glasslands, and 285 Kent are all forced to close after their building is leased to Vice Media

2015:
- Market Hotel reopens

2016:
- David Mancuso dies
- Cake Shop closes

2017:
- The city creates the Office of Nightlife

2018:
- The Silent Barn closes for the second and final time

2019:
- Sidewalk Cafe closes

2020:
- City nightlife shuts down due to Covid-19

ENDNOTES

1   Jeremiah Moss, "Find A New City," Jeremiah's Vanishing New York, May 3, 2010, http://vanishingnewyork.blogspot.com/2010/05/find-new-city.html, accessed June 3, 2022.

2   Brian Eno in conversation with Richard Evans, Luminous Festival, Sydney Opera House, Sydney, AU. Text at http://www.moredarkthanshark.org/feature_luminous2.html, accessed June 3, 2022.

3   Alan Lomax, *Selected Writings 1934-1997* (New York: Routledge, 2003), p. 333.

4   Ralph Lee Smith and Madeline McNeil, *Greenwich Village: The Happy Folk Singing Days—1950s and 1960s* (Mel Bay, 2008), p. 17.

5   Cafe Bizarre menu, viewed at https://www.worthpoint.com/worthopedia/york-city-rick-allmens-bizarre-coffee-1782561786, accessed June 3, 2022.

6   Dave Van Ronk with Elijah Wald, *The Mayor of MacDougal Street* (Philadelphia: Da Capo Press, 2006), p. 95.

7   David Hajdu, *Positively 4th Street: The Lives and Times of Joan Baez, Bob Dylan, Mimi Baez Fariña, and Richard Fariña* (New York: Farrar, Straus and Giroux, 2001), p. 48.

8   Carroll Newsom, Letter to Newbold Morris, April 21, 1961. Cited in Stephen Petrus and Ronald D. Cohen, *Folk City* (New York: Oxford University Press, 2015), p. 132.

9   Mary Perot Nichols, "Morris Ban on Singers in Sq. Divides Villagers," *Village Voice*, April 27, 1961, p. 16.

10   Memorandum by Newbold Morris, March 13, 1961. Cited in Petrus and Cohen, *Folk City*, p. 122.

11   "Folk-Singing Ban Upset on Appeal," *New York Times*, July 7, 1961, p. 52.

12   Bob Dylan, Chronicles Volume One (New York: Simon & Schuster, 2004), p. 258.

13   "'Village' Cafes Defy Zoning Violations," *New York Times*, March 26, 1964, p. 39.

14   *Broadside #1*, February 1962, p. 1.

15   Richie Havens with Steve Davidowitz, they can't hide us anymore (New York: Spike, 1999), p. 47.

16   Van Ronk, p. 149.

17   Alan Lomax, "The 'Folkniks'—and the Songs They Sing," in *Selected Writings 1934-1997*, p. 195-196.

18   J.R. Goddard, "The MacDougal Scene: II. Modern Version of a Bosch Painting," Village Voice, June 20, 1963, p. 6.

19   Alix Dobkin, My Red Blood (New York: Alyson Books, 2009), p. 171.

20   Izzy Young, "Frets and Frails," in *Sing Out!*, Vol. 14, No. 6, January 1964, p. 77.

21   Ellen Sander, *Trips: Rock Life in the Sixties—Augmented Edition* (Mineola: Dover Publications, 2019), p. 64.

22   Kyle Gann, "The Part That Doesn't Fit Is Me: Yoko Ono, The Inventor of Downtown," *Music Downtown* (Berkeley: University of California Press, 2006), p. 24.

23   Michael Kolomatsky, "New York City's Most Expensive Neighborhoods," *New York Times*, October 28, 1921, https://www.nytimes.com/2021/10/28/realestate/new-york-citys-most-expensive-neighborhoods.html, accessed June 3, 2022.

24   Interview with LaMonte Young and Marian Zazeela by Gabrielle Zuckerman, American Public Media, July 2002 (https://soundcloud.com/innovadotmu/la-monte-young-and-marian-zazeela, accessed June 3, 2022).

25   "The Fluxus Cooperatives of Soho," fluxusfoundation.com, http://fluxusfoundation.com/fluxus-as-architecture/essays/the-fluxhouse-cooperatives-of-soho, accessed June 3, 2022.

26   Christopher Gray, "Streetscapes: 80 Wooster Street; the Irascible 'Father' of Soho," *New York Times*, March 15, 1992, Section 10, p. 7.

27   Steven Thrasher, "Philip Glass's Life as an East Village Voice," *Village Voice*, February 1, 2012, https://www.villagevoice.com/2012/02/01/philip-glasss-life-as-an-east-village-voice, accessed June 3, 2022.

28   Stanley Crouch, "Jazz Lofts: A Walk Through the Wild Sounds," *New York Times*, April 17, 1977, Section SM, p. 111.

29   Val Wilmer, *As Serious As Your Life: Black Music and the Free Jazz Revolution, 1957-1977* (London: Serpent's Tail—repress, 2018), p. 92.

30   John S. Wilson, "Newport in New York—Harmony in Black and White," *New York Times*, June 24, 1973, p. 17.

31   Crouch, "Jazz Lofts."

32   Michael C. Heller, Loft Jazz (Oakland: University of California Press, 2017), p. 84.

33   Crouch, "Jazz Lofts."

34   Yvonne Sewall Ruskin, *High on Rebellion: Inside the Underground at Max's Kansas City* (Thunders Mouth Press, 1998), p. 21.

35   Sewall Ruskin, p. 24.

36   Sewall Ruskin, p. 84.

37   Sewall Ruskin, p. xii.

38   Quoted in Steve Dollar, "The Club Everyone Wanted to Be In," *The Wall Street Journal*, September 15, 2010.

39   David Mancuso interview, *Mick Music Page*, http://www.mickmusicpage.net/data/theloft.html, accessed June 3, 2022.

40   Sara Oliver Gordus, "Walt Whitman's Watering Hole: Pfaff's Cellar, NYC," *The Rumpus*, June 2, 2010, https://therumpus.net/2010/07/02/walt-whitman%e2%80%99s-watering-hole-pfaff%e2%80%99s-cellar-nyc, accessed June 3, 2022.

41   Vince Aletti, "Soho vs Disco," *Village Voice*, June 16, 1975.

42   Ibid.

43   Interview with David Mancuso, Discomusic.com.

44   Mel Cheren, *My Life and the Paradise Garage: Keep on Dancin'* (New York: 24 Hours 4 Life, 2003), p. 105-106.

45   Bill Brewster and Frank Broughton, "Interview: David Mancuso," Red Bull Music Academy, November 15, 2016, https://daily.redbullmusicacademy.com/2016/11/david-mancuso-dj-history-interview, accessed June 3, 2022.

46   Frank Owen, "Paradise Lost," *Vibe*, November 1993, https://fxowen.

wordpress.com/golden-oldies/larry-levan-paradise-lost-vibe-november-1993, accessed January 15, 2023.

47   Interview with Manny Lehman for *Vinylmania* magazine, undated.

48   Frankie Knuckles email to Global-House Internet Mailing List, May 18, 1997.

49   Will Coldwell, "'The 1970s Club Scene in New York Was Special': Nicky Siano," *The Guardian*, April 7, 2017.

50   Jeff "Chairman" Mao interview with Nicky Siano, Red Bull Music Academy 2016 (https://www.redbullmusicacademy.com/lectures/nicky-siano, accessed June 3, 2022).

51   Cheren, p. 111.

52   DJ Tim Spins interview with Larry Levan, https://www.djtimspins.com/larry-levan-interview, accessed June 3, 2022.

53   Kris Needs, *Dream Baby Dream: Suicide—A New York Story* (Omnibus Press, 2017), p. 235.

54   Vince Aletti, "Soho vs. Disco: The Story of the Loft," *Village Voice*, June 16, 1975.

55   Ibid.

56   Ibid.

57   Brewster and Broughton, 2016.

58   Lisa Robinson, "Boogie Nights," *Vanity Fair*, January 6, 2010, https://www.vanityfair.com/culture/2010/02/oral-history-of-disco-201002, accessed June 3, 2022.

59   Cheren, p. 199.

60   Owen, "Paradise Lost."

61   Patricia Morrisroe, "Soho: Under the Gun," *New York*, June 4, 1984, p. 38.

62   Ibid.

63   Sarah Schulman, *The Gentrification of the Mind: Witness to a Lost Imagination* (Berkeley and Los Angeles: University of California Press, 2013), p. 26.

64   Mao, 2016.

65   Anthony Depalma, "About Real Estate; Why the Saatchi Agency Will Move to Hudson St.," *New York Times*, July 10, 1985, Section B, p. 9.

66   Cheren, p. 383-384.

67   http://www.mercerhotel.com, accessed June 3, 2022.

68   Review by Charles Shaar Murray, *New Musical Express*, March 1, 1975.

69   Ibid.

70   David Byrne, *How Music Works* (San Francisco: McSweeney's, 2012), p. 253.

71   Roman Kozak, *This Ain't No Disco: The Story of CBGB* (Faber and Faber, 1988), p. 15.

72   Byrne, p. 255.

73   Kozak, p. 3.

74   Kozak, p. 103.

75   "New Prosperity Brings Discord to the East Village," *New York Times*, December 19, 1983, Section B, p. 3.

76   Lucy Sante, "Beastie Revolution," in Michael Diamond and Adam Horovitz, *Beastie Boys Book* (New York: Spiegel & Grau, 2018), p. 15.

77   "History 101," Bloodhoundgang.com, via Wayback Machine, https://web.archive.org/web/20020211005135/http://www.bloodhoundgang.com/history101/history101fn.html, accessed June 3, 2022.

78   Bruce Lambert, "Neighborhood Report: NOHO; When a Hotel Stops Looking Like the Palace," *New York Times*, December 12, 1993, Section 13, p. 6.

79   Ibid.

80   Sarah Ferguson, "Bowery Bummer," *Village Voice*, March 1, 2005.

81   Ibid.

82   Keith Gessen, "Between Punk Rock and a Hard Place," *New York*, June 10, 2005.

83   "Clubbed," Ira Robbins, *Spin*, August 2005, p. 81.

84   Gessen, "Between Punk Rock and a Hard Place."

85   Ferguson, "Bowery Bummer."

86   Thomas J. Lueck, "Bloomberg Offers City's Help as Deadline Nears for CBGB," *New York Times*, August 31, 2005, Section B, p. 2.

87   Jennifer Steinhauer, "City Cracks Down on Nightclubs and May Revise Its Policies," *New York Times*, November 10, 2002, Section 1, p. 41.

88   Robbins, "Clubbed."

89   Alyssa Rashbaum, "CBGB Landlord Declines Lease Renewal Despite

NYC Rally," Spin.com, 9/1/05, https://www.spin.com/2005/09/cbgb-landlord-declines-lease-renewal-despite-nyc-rally, accessed June 3, 2022.

90 Kristal, "History by Hilly."

91 Michael Clancy, "CBGB Made Hilly Kristal a Millionaire—His Ex Got Nothing," *Village Voice*, September 11, 2007.

92 Roy Edroso, "Hilly Kristal Ex Says He Hid $ From Her," *Village Voice*, December 4, 2008.

93 Axl Rosenberg, "John Varvatos Isn't Just an Asshole—He's a *Lying* Ass-hole," Metalsucks.net November 6, 2007, https://www.metalsucks.net/2007/11/06/john-varvatos-isnt-just-an-asshole-hes-a-lying-asshole, accessed June 3, 2022.

94 Zach Baron, "Meet Extra Place, the Semi-Secret, 'Never Open to the Public' Performance Space Underneath the Old CBGB," *Village Voice*, November 5, 2010.

95 Jeremiah Moss, "Targeting the East Village," *Jeremiah's Vanishing New York*, https://vanishingnewyork.blogspot.com/2018/07/targeting-east-village.html, accessed June 3, 2022.

96 https://rentevgb.com, accessed January 13, 2023.

97 NYPD, *Welcome to Fear City: A Survival Guide for Visitors to the City of New York*, 1975, https://researchdestroy.com/welcome-to-fear-city.pdf, accessed June 3, 2022.

98 Ibid.

99 Kevin Baker, "'Welcome to Fear City'—the inside story of New York's civil war, 40 years on," *The Guardian*, May 18, 2015.

100 Andrew Sarris, "Ocean Tide," *Film Comment*, November-December 2010.

101 Kenton, "Here's Mudd in Your Sleaze."

102 Reynolds, p. 266.

103 Reynolds, p. 268-271.

104 Dr. Michael E. Mann interview with Debbie Harry and Chris Stein, "Sing For Science," Season 2, Episode 4: "Blondie: Rapture," January 31, 2022.

105 Jeff Chang, *Can't Stop Won't Stop: A History of the Hip-Hop Generation* (New York: St. Martin's Press, 2005), p. 150.

106 Michael Holman, "An Interview With the DJ Africa Bambaata of the Zulu Nation," *East Village Eye*, January 1982, p. 22.

107 David Browne, *Goodbye 20th Century: A Biography of Sonic Youth* (Philadelphia: Da Capo Press, 2008), p. 53.

108   Jon Pareles, "Dance and Music Clubs Thriving in Era of Change," *New York Times*, November 12, 1982, Section C, p. 1.

109   Michael Musto Facebook post, October 23, 2015, https://www.facebook.com/michael.musto.96/posts/904991292871035, accessed June 3, 2022.

110   Howard W. French, Michael Wines, Todd S. Purdum, "Melee in Tompkins Square Park: Violence and Its Provocation," *New York Times*, August 14, 1988, Section 1, p. 1.

111   Royal Young, "Ed Sanders' New York Fugging City," *Interview*, December 14, 2011.

112   Pete Hamill, *Downtown: My Manhattan* (New York: Back Bay Books, 2005), p. 210.

113   Unidentified author, "Youth: The Hippies," *Time*, July 7, 1967.

114   Don McNeill, "The Youthquake and the Shook-Up Park," *Village Voice*, June 8, 1967.

115   Interview with Carlos Garcia by Lisa Zapol, Greenwich Village Society for Historic Preservation—East Village Oral History Project, https://media.villagepreservation.org/wp-content/uploads/2020/05/15035105/Garcia_CarlosTranscriptFinalforWebsite-1.pdf, accessed June 3, 2022.

116   Interview with Carlos "Chino" Garcia by Leyla Vural, The New York Preservation Archive Project, https://www.nypap.org/oral-history/carlos-chino-garcia, accessed June 3, 2022.

117   Kestutis Nakas and Brian Butterick, "We Started a Nightclub: Building the Pyramid," *PAJ: A Journal of Performance and Art*, Vol. 37, No. 3 (111) (September 2015), p. 22-45.

118   Pareles, "Dance and Music Clubs Thriving in Era of Change"

119   Kestutis Nakas and Brian Butterick, "We Started a Nightclub: Building the Pyramid."

120   Nick Soulsby, *Swans: Sacrifice and Transcendence—The Oral History* (London: Jawbone Press, 2018), p. 52.

121   Carlo McCormick interview with Tod Ashley in *Seconds #21*, 1993.

122   Johnny Xerox, "The Danger is Here! What Are You Going to Do About It?" *East Villager*, September 15-30, 1984; quoted in Ada Calhoun's *Saint Marks is Dead* (New York: W.W. Norton & Co, 2015).

123   Craig Unger, "The Lower East Side: There Goes the Neighborhood," *New York*, May 28, 1984, p. 40-41.

124   Christopher Mele, *Selling the Lower East Side: Culture, Real Estate, and Resistance in New York City* (University of Minnesota Press, 2000), p. 243.

125   Jeremiah Budin, "Let Iggy Pop Show You Around the East Village in 1993," Curbed, June 17, 2013, https://ny.curbed.com/2013/6/17/10232250/let-iggy-pop-show-you-around-the-east-village-in-1993, accessed June 3, 2022.

126   Colin Moynihan, "A Stirring Icon That Shook Things Up Turns 20," *New York Times*, April 29, 2002, Section B, p. 3.

127   http://www.petermissing.de/MF.html, accessed June 3, 2022.

128   Lincoln Anderson, "Artist Who Was Once the Center is Now On the Fringe," *The Villager*, Vol. 75, No. 12, August 10, 2005, https://patterson.no-art.info/gallery/2004-09-12_missing.html, accessed June 3, 2022.

129   Philip Lentz, "Koch's Plan for Disturbed Homeless Under Fire," *Chicago Tribune*, November 22, 1987.

130   French, Wines, Purdum, "Melee in Tompkins Square Park."

131   Ibid.

132   Ibid.

133   "Cult of Rage," aired on NY CBS Channel 2, November 28-30, 1988.

134   Roman Kozak, "NY Hurrah Reborn," *Billboard*, February 12, 1979.

135   Robert Palmer, "Pop Jazz; The Bloom Has Faded at Small Rock Clubs," *New York Times*, May 29, 1981, Section C, p. 23.

136   Michael Musto, "Nightlife Legend Jim Fouratt Talks What Really Happened at Stonewall and Birthing Danceteria," *Paper*, April 7, 2017.

137   Tim Lawrence interview with Mark Kamins, 2008, https://www.tim-lawrence.info/mark-kamins-interview, accessed June 3, 2022.

138   Iman Lababedi, "Average Normal: Jim Fouratt," *East Village Eye,* January 1982, p. 21.

139   Jon Pareles, "Dance Clubs Put Spin on New Disks," *New York Times*, January 29, 1985, Section C, p. 13.

140   Diamond and Horovitz, p. 133.

141   "Rudolf Piper—Danceteria—1983 Nickelodeon Interview," https://www.youtube.com/watch?v=haHXisfvoeI, accessed June 3, 2022.

142   Frank Broughton, "Fab Five Freddy on New York Hip-Hop and the Birth of a Global Phenomenon," DJHistory.com, 1998, https://daily.redbullmusicacademy.com/2019/01/fab-5-freddy-interview, accessed June 3, 2022.

143   Lucy O'Brien, *Madonna: Like An Icon* (New York: Reprint, It Books, 2008), p. 57.

144   Andy Thomas, "Nightclubbing: The Fun House," Red Bull Music Acad-

emy, October 18, 2013, https://daily.redbullmusicacademy.com/2013/10/nightclubbing-the-funhouse, accessed June 3, 2022.

145 Amy Virshup, "The Club Beat," *New York Magazine*, July 2, 1984.

146 Justin Monroe, "Interview: Notorious Club Owner Peter Gatien Talks About the 'Limelight' Documentary & Hip Hop's Best Party Ever," *Complex*, September 19, 2011, https://www.complex.com/pop-culture/2011/09/interview-peter-gatien-limelight, accessed June 3, 2022.

147 *Wall Street*, dir. Oliver Stone.

148 The Furman Center for Real Estate & Urban Policy, "Trends in NYC Housing Price Appreciation," 2008, https://furmancenter.org/files/Trends_in_NYC_Housing_Price_Appreciation.pdf, accessed June 3, 2022.

149 Rosalyn Deutsche and Cara Gendel Ryan, "The Fine Art of Gentrification," *The Portable Lower East Side*, Vol. 4, No. 1, Spring 1987.

150 John Marchese, "The Mighty Nell's," *New York Times*, February 27, 1994, Section 9, p. 1.

151 Lisa W. Fodedaro, "Disco-Dining the Night Away," *New York Times*, December 1, 1989, Section C, p. 1.

152 Vikki Tobak, "Nightclubbing: Nell's," Red Bull Music Academy, April 15, 2019, https://daily.redbullmusicacademy.com/2019/04/nightclubbing-nells-nyc, accessed June 3, 2022.

153 Fodedaro, "Disco-Dining the Night Away."

154 Hal Rubenstein, "The Man From Mars: Behind the Velvet Rope Club Impresario Rudolf," *New York*, April 17, 1989, p. 50.

155 James C. McKinley Jr, "Dinkins Reduces Task Force On Safety of Social Clubs," *New York Times*, June 30, 1990, Section 1, p. 27.

156 Ibid.

157 Christopher Bollen, "In a rare interview with Interview magazine, King of the Club Kids Michael Alig discusses the history of the Club Kids at length, his experiences in behind bars, his plans of life post-jail and why he thinks Lady Gaga would have been the perfect Club Kid," Oh No They Didn't!, https://ohnotheydidnt.livejournal.com/46042881.html, accessed June 3, 2022.

158 Peter Stevenson, "Is Nightlife Dead?" *New York Times*, September 27, 1992, Section 9, p. 1.

159 David R. Francis, "What Reduced Crime in New York City," National Bureau of Economic Research, The Digest: No. 1, January 2003.

160 Steve Weinstein, "RIP Richard Grant—Founder of NYC After-Hours Institution Sound Factory," *Vice*, January 22, 2015, https://www.vice.com/amp/en/article/jp. 3gx/rip-richard-grantfounder-of-nyc-after-hours-institution-sound-factory, accessed June 3, 2022.

161 Elisabeth Bumiller, "U.S. Claims 2 Nightclubs Are Drug Bazaars," *New York Times*, May 16, 1996, Section B, p. 1.

162 Daniel Prendergast and Mara Siegler, "Time capsule triggers bomb scare in NYC," *New York Post*, July 5, 2017.

163 Mike Evans, *Waking Up in New York City: A Musical Tour of the Big Apple* (London: Sanctuary Publishing, 2004), p. 108.

164 Filthy Pedro, "Lach talks antifolk history & boozing with parents," Antifolk.com, August 29, 2014, http://www.antifolk.com/lach-interview, accessed June 3, 2022.

165 *People v. Manning Docket No. 5N038025V (Criminal Ct. N.Y. Cty. 1985).*

166 Eric Gladstone, "Beck: a Midnight Cowboy and the Rhythms of the Universe," *CMJ New Music Monthly*, July 1996, p. 26.

167 David Cavanagh, "The Devil Inside," Q, July 1997, p. 92-99.

168 Mark Kent, "Loser or Legend?" *Option*, March 1994.

169 Jake Offenhartz, "'So Weird But Amazing': An Oral History Of Sidewalk Cafe & Antifolk," Gothamist, February 27, 2019, https://gothamist.com/arts-entertainment/so-weird-but-amazing-an-oral-history-of-sidewalk-cafe-antifolk, accessed June 3, 2022.

170 Randy Kennedy, "NEIGHBORHOOD REPORT: EAST VILLAGE; Beyond Bohemian: Superdeluxe on Avenue A," *New York Times*, September 25, 1994, Section 13, p. 6.

171 Offenhartz, "'So Weird But Amazing': An Oral History Of Sidewalk Cafe & Antifolk."

172 Andrew Jacobs, "A New Spell for Alphabet City; Gentrification Led to the Unrest at Tompkins Square 10 Years Ago. Did the Protestors Win That Battle But Lose the War?" *New York Times*, August 9, 1998, Section 14, p. 1.

173 Sydney Pereira, "Penn South Capital Buys Sidewalk Cafe Building For $9.6M," Patch.com, April 4, 2019, https://patch.com/new-york/east-village/penn-south-capital-buys-sidewalk-cafe-building-9-6m, accessed June 3, 2022.

174 Thomas J. Lueck, "Prices Decline as Gentrification Ebbs," *New York Times*, September 29, 1991, Section 10, p. 1.

175 Ibid.

176   Nick Ravo, "After A Retreat, Gentrification is Marching To the Fringes," *New York Times*, October 29, 1995, Section 9, p. 1.

177   Shaun Brady, "Remembering the Original Knitting Factory," *Jazz Times*, May 11, 2020.

178   Gann, *Music Downtown*, p. 117.

179   Gail O'Hara, "An Interview With Tae Won Yu," *Chickfactor* 17, Autumn 2012.

180   Jon Pareles, "The New Bohemia: It's East of SoHo and Still Unspoiled," *New York Times*, September 26, 1997, Section E, p. 1.

181   Ibid.

182   New York City Partnership and Chamber of Commerce, "Working Together to Accelerate New York's Recovery: Economic Impact Analysis of the September 11th Attack on New York City," November 2001, https://www.pfnyc.org/reports/2001_11_ImpactStudy.pdf, accessed June 3, 2022.

183   Nicole Lyn Pesce, "Number of tourists to New York reached record level last year after lows following 9/11," *New York Daily News*, September 8, 2011.

184   *Annie Hall*, dir. Woody Allen. 1977.

185   Reverend Jen, *Reverend Jen's Really Cool Neighborhood/Les Misrahi* (New York: Printed Matter Inc., 2003), p. 15-16.

186   Mervyn Rothstein, "57th St. Site in Demand By Theme Restaurants," *New York Times*, April 2, 1997, Section B, p. 5.

187   German Lopez, "Mike Bloomberg's stop-and-frisk problem, explained," Vox.com, February 25, 2020, https://www.vox.com/policy-and-politics/2020/2/21/21144559/mike-bloomberg-stop-and-frisk-criminal-justice-record, accessed June 3, 2022.

188   Andy Cush, "Cake Shop, Manhattan's Last Great Rock Club, Will Close After New Year's Eve," Spin.com, December 26, 2016, https://www.spin.com/2016/12/cake-shop-manhattans-last-great-rock-club-will-close-after-new-years-eve, accessed June 3, 2022.

189   Gretchen Bank, Melissa Giroux, and Francisco Sandoval, "Hell Square: Contested Space and Proliferation of Liquor Licenses for On-Site Consumption on the Lower East Side," URBG 790 Urban Development Workshop, Professor Sigmund Shipp, May 2017.

190   https://www.thatcherindustries.com/kindregards, accessed June 3, 2022.

191   Peter Watrous, "Pop/Jazz; Tomorrow's Stars Today in Brooklyn's Small Clubs," *New York Times*, March 23, 1990, Section C, p. 26.

192 Denny Lee, "Has Billburg Lost Its Cool?" *New York Times*, July 27, 2003.

193 Lisa Selin Davis, "'Grand' Plans," *Brooklyn Paper*, October 12, 2003.

194 Lee, "Has Billburg Lost Its Cool?"

195 Alex Williamson, "Rezoning Retrospective: Activists Look Back on the Battle for the North Brooklyn Waterfront," BrooklynEagle.com, November 21, 2019, https://brooklyneagle.com/articles/2019/11/21/rezoning-retrospective-activists-look-back-on-the-battle-for-the-north-brooklyn-waterfront, accessed June 3, 2022.

196 Vice Staff, "Dos and Don'ts," *Vice*, Vol. 11, No. 5—"The Party Issue," 2004.

197 Tom Dunon, "Kill Whitey," *Vice*, Vol. 11, No. 10—"The Hate Issue," 2004.

198 Jen Carlson, "Market Hotel Goes Dark After Police Raid," Gothamist.com, April 5, 2010, https://gothamist.com/arts-entertainment/market-hotel-goes-dark-after-police-raid, accessed June 3, 2022.

199 Ibid.

200 Gary Suarez, "Why the Closing of 285 Kent Doesn't Matter," *Vice*, January 10, 2014, https://www.vice.com/en/article/rjkjb6/285-kent-shutting-down-why, accessed June 3, 2022.

201 A. Wolfe, "Win! Win! Win! A Glasslands Spring Season Pass," *Vice*, February 7, 2014, https://www.vice.com/en/article/rnk8k6/win-win-win, accessed June 3, 2022.

202 *Broad City*, Season 1, Episode 4: "The Lockout."

203 "Silent Barn closes, Educated Little Monsters not taking over the space," Brooklyn Vegan, April 30, 2018.

204 *RIP 285 Kent* (Pitchfork, 2014), https://pitchfork.com/tv, accessed June 3, 2022.

205 https://www.markethotel.org/about, accessed June 3, 2022.

206 https://www.heclaironworks.com, accessed June 3, 2022.

INDEX